"A rare blend of experience, insight and urgency, this book is a must read for every Australian who wants to really make a difference"

MICHAEL KLIM OAM

Discover your Cause
Take Action
Make an Impact
Find your Purpose

PAUL BIRD

First Published in Australia in 2026
By Morpheus Publishing
Geelong Victoria 3216
www.morpheuspublishing.com.au

Paperback ISBN: 978-1-923650-25-1
Ebook ISBN: 978-1-923650-26-8
Ingram ISBN: 978-1-923650-27-5
Author: Paul Bird
Editor: Hannah Remminga
Cover Graphics: Mylan Carascal
Typesetting: Oseyi Okoeguale

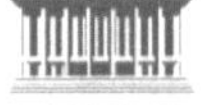

A catalogue record for this book is available from the National Library of Australia.

DISCLAIMER

The information contained in this book is for general informational purposes only. The author and publisher are not offering any medical, legal or professional advice. While every effort has been made to ensure the accuracy and completeness of the information provided, the author and publisher assume no responsibility for errors or omissions or any outcomes or consequences resulting from using this book's content.

COPYRIGHT

DISTRIBUTION

This book is distributed by Morpheus Publishing and is available through authorised distributors, booksellers, Morpheus Publishing website.

COPYRIGHT PERMISSIONS

For copyright permissions or any other inquiries, please contact:

PUBLISHER: Morpheus Publishing
www.morpheuspublishing.com.au ||
hello@morpheuspublishing.com.au || +61403 564 942

AUTHOR: Paul Bird
https://www.morpheuspublishing.com.au/authors/paul-bird

Be the change you want
to see in the world

ATTRIBUTED TO
MAHATMA GANDHI

For more go to
www.bethechange.com.au

CONTENTS

INTRODUCTION

You cannot get through a single day without having an impact on the world around you. What you do makes a difference, and you have to decide what kind of difference you want to make

"DR JANE GOODALL"

"What do you do for a living?"
"I work for a charity."

After a hesitation, 1 of 2 reactions then ensues.

1. I embark with quickening speech and rising animation to relate the desperate need and life-changing impact of my charity, expecting an immediate epiphany from the recipient who will fall to their knees and devote their life to the cause. Instead, they become glassy-eyed and try to avert my gaze, before exclaiming "that must be so rewarding" and finding an excuse to go and find safety; or

2. "I've been looking to donate to [*charity*]. Do you think they're any good?" As I contemplate the myriad of permutations of possible responses to this question, it is I who becomes glassy-eyed as I try to avert their gaze and find an exit.

We all want to 'do the right thing' and support a 'good cause'. Indeed, as a social species, it is hard-wired in us, with nearly two-thirds of the planet's population donating money to charity each year[1]. Two-thirds of donors cited the reason as 'I care about the cause / to make a difference'[2].

But Australia is in a perfect storm with a steady decline in giving when it is needed more than ever, our giving responding to crises and rarely to the underlying cause, and our governments missing in action with the reform of the policy, systems and services that only perpetuate the issues. As a result, our social and environmental crises are only getting worse whilst billions of taxpayer dollars are spent without ever knowing the efficacy, outcomes, value for money, or impact.

Given the over 60,000 registered Australian charities, the lack of published 'what works' evidence or outcomes achieved, the constant barrage of heartfelt appeals, the daily news of social and environmental crises, and the occasional scandal, it is no wonder that Australians are increasingly confused and disengaging from charities. Today, we are only 68th in the world in the average percentage of income donated, behind Canada, New Zealand, the United States and the UK[3].

Australians increasingly believe that their 'drop' can't make a real difference in an ocean of need, are untrusting of charities, and are unable to navigate the charity labyrinth. Unsurprisingly, we are ever more sceptical, disillusioned and apathetic that charities can actually make the difference advertised.

Are our charities the latest examples of Macquarie Dictionary's 2024 word of the year - *enshittification* - where their programs and services do not live up to their marketing hype, whilst the social and environmental crises we face continue to fester?

The result is a merry-go-round of the same needs and issues that simmer away, periodically rising to the surface to get short-term attention by the media, governments and supporters as a national crisis. The resultant promise of action is invariably seen as a good start, but it is insufficient, lacking long-term and consistent investment in prevention and early intervention, effective evidence-based responses, and the necessary governmental policy and system changes.

Due to constant budget pressures and the need to be seen to respond in the 24/7 media cycle, politicians rebadge existing programs as new funding or herald reallocated spending in a knee-jerk response. In the meantime, less than 2 per

---

[1]Introduction
Charities Aid Foundation (2025) *World Giving Report 2025*, p.8
[2] Ibid p.18
[3] Ibid p.36

cent of government funding is spent on prevention measures, despite knowing that each dollar saved today saves 6 in the future, and the social and environmental crises in this country, outlined in the Themes in this book, only continue to worsen.

To make matters worse, our social services labyrinth is funded and delivered by government departments and providers in service-based silos – education, employment, training, homelessness, mental health, family violence, child protection, disability - without the coordination with other services, even though, as we will see in this book, the issues are always interrelated and co-dependent. The revolving door of Commonwealth and State/Territory governments, short-term output-based service contracts, lack of evaluation, and the omission of recipients in service design and implementation, mean that billions of dollars are spent responding to the day-to-day urgent needs as our services struggle to cope. Little attention is paid to prevention, early intervention or reforming the policy and systems that allow the crises to fester and grow.

We are no nearer to breaking the cycle of intergenerational disadvantage than when Tony Vinson identified 'postcode poverty' decades ago. He found that just 1.7 per cent of postcodes across Australia accounted for more than seven times their share of the major factors that cause intergenerational poverty[4]. Today, a child in Fyshwick, Broadmeadows, Playford, Aurukun or Claymore is highly likely to follow in the footsteps of previous generations and be unskilled or unemployed, a victim of family violence, suffer from drug and alcohol dependence, have mental health issues, and be incarcerated[5].

We like to think of ourselves as the land of the 'fair go'[6], but with growing income inequality, the highest 20 per cent of us live in a household with 5 times as much income as the lowest twenty per cent[7]. As a result, 760,000 children live in poverty, and 2 million households skip meals or whole days of eating. The housing and cost of living crises are only exacerbating the inequity with more Australians seeking help from charities just to put food on the table, fuel in their car or pay the utility bills.

---

[4] Vinson T (2007) *Dropping Off the Edge: the distribution of disadvantage in Australia,* Jesuit Social Services and Catholic Social Services Australia

[5] Vinson T & Rawsthorne M (2015) *Dropping Off the Edge 2015: Persistent communal disadvantage in Australia,* Jesuit Social Services and Catholic Social Services Australia

[6] Horne D (1964) *The Lucky Country,* p.20

[7] Australian Council of Social Service and University of New South Wales (2018) *Inequality in Australia 2018,* NSW

Homelessness continues to increase. A record 280,000 Australians were assisted by homelessness services in 2023-24, not counting the over 70,000 requests for emergency accommodation turned away, with one in six an unaccompanied young person. Our service system is not coping with those experiencing persistent homelessness, having risen by 28 per cent over the last 5 years to 37,800, and the decades-long lack of government procurement of public housing means that Australia needs an additional 640,000 homes for people experiencing homelessness and extreme housing stress.

Now the leading cause of homelessness, the prevalence of family and domestic violence (FDV) is endemic. Over 1 in 4, or 2.7 million, women have experienced FDV since the age of 15. FDV-related sexual assault victimisation rates have increased by 78 per cent between 2014 and 2023 with more than 1 in 2, or 120,000 police-recorded assaults related to FDV nationally (excluding Victoria) in 2023[8] - although it is estimated that this only represents 40 per cent of actual levels due to under reporting[9] given that fewer than 1 in 10 women who experience sexual assault in Australia contact police. Even then, the New South Wales justice department revealed in 2024 that just 7 per cent of sexual assaults reported to police resulted in criminal conviction[10].

With over half of these women having children in their care, 2.2 million Australians have witnessed partner violence against their mothers when they were children[11]. The impact on these children includes emotional and social issues, anxiety and depression, poor educational and employment outcomes, suicide ideation, contact with youth justice and homelessness[12].

Tragically, 1 woman is killed every 11 days on average by an intimate partner and 1 in 6 homicides relates to intimate partner violence, with 9 in 10 of those victims being women[13]. Over 2 million women and 693,000 men have

---

[8] Australian Government Australian Institute of Health and Welfare (2024) *Family, domestic and sexual violence. FDV reported to police* at https://www.aihw.gov.au/family-domestic-and-sexual-violence/responses-and-outcomes/police/fdv-reported-to-police

[9] Equity Economics (2021) *Nowhere to Go. The Benefits Of Providing Long-Term Social Housing To Women That Have Experienced Domestic And Family Violence*, Everybody's Home. p.7

[10] https://www.theguardian.com/australia-news/ng-interactive/2025/feb/07/without-punishment-can-a-different-kind-of-justice-offer-something-more-to-sexual-assault-survivors-ntwnfb?CMP=Share_iOSApp_Other

[11] Australian Government Australian Institute of Health and Welfare (2023) *Family and Domestic Violence* at https://www.aihw.gov.au/family-domestic-and-sexual-violence/types-of-violence/family-domestic-violence

[12] Equity Economics (2021) *Nowhere to Go. The Benefits Of Providing Long-Term Social Housing To Women That Have Experienced Domestic And Family Violence*, Everybody's Home. p.13

[13] Australian Government Australian Institute of Health and Welfare (2024) *Domestic homicide* at https://www.aihw.gov.au/family-domestic-and-sexual-violence/responses-and-

experienced physical and/or sexual violence from an intimate partner since the age of 15.

Child abuse is widespread in Australia. 1 in 7, or an estimated 2.7 million Australians aged 18 years and over, have experienced childhood physical and/or sexual abuse before the age of 15 perpetrated by an adult, with 1.7 million being women. 9 in 10 have known their abuser[14].

As our ongoing national shame for the oldest continuous living culture on the planet, the intractable disadvantage of our First Nations peoples shows little sign of improvement, with the 2025 Closing the Gap report showing only four of the 19 targets on track[15]. On every social issue, Indigenous people suffer many times more than other Australians – 9 times the homeless rate, 6 times the rate of domestic homicides, 10 times the rate of children in out-of-home care, 10 times the rate of racism, and 20 times the rate of young people in youth justice.

As a reportedly successful multicultural country where we are all migrants or descendants of migrants in our post-European history, we should also be ashamed that racism and discrimination are rife in Australia across education, business, media, government, online and the community, denying hundreds of thousands of migrants and refugees the opportunity for better lives in their new home.

And as a compassionate nation that 'punches above its weight' in international human rights, is it justice that we lock up traumatised children, as victims of child abuse and family violence, from the age of 10, setting them on a criminal career path?

The prevalence of people living with mental illness is at a record high, with the determinants of mental health either not improving or getting worse. The latest National Report Card from the government's Mental Health Commission notes that 'overall, the data continues to paint a concerning picture of the state of

---

outcomes/domestic-homicide#:~:text=One%20woman%20was%20killed%20every,(ADFVDRN%20and%20ANROWS%202022).

[14] Australian Bureau of Statistics (2023) *2021-22 Personal Safety Survey* at https://www.abs.gov.au/statistics/people/crime-and-justice/personal-safety-australia/latest-release

[15] Productivity Commission (2025) *Closing the Gap Annual Data Compilation Report*, July 2025, Canberra

mental health and wellbeing in Australia. We are also not seeing improvements in the system's effectiveness in meeting demand or preventing distress[16].

Meanwhile, the progress towards gender equality and disability inclusion is excruciatingly slow, whilst the social cohesion that binds our communities together and makes life worth living is unravelling under the pressure of these crises.

Then there is the very survival of our species. With the last 3 years the hottest years on record, our planet is now 1.5°C above pre-industrial temperatures, already at the target set in the Paris Agreement. Australia has now warmed 1.51°C and we can't fail to see the effects of climate change around us as droughts, floods, fires, cyclones and heatwaves become more frequent and intense. Even if nations make good on their net zero promises, there is a 90 per cent chance that we are still on track for 2.4°C of global warming which will lock in centuries of irreversible changes to the climate system. We will see life-threatening levels of heat on the east coast with temperatures regularly exceeding 50°C in summer, combined with longer and more intense bushfires and droughts[17] which will accelerate the loss of productive farmland and threaten our food security. Storms and flooding will have violently reshaped our coastlines, and unique ecosystems have been damaged beyond recognition – including the Great Barrier Reef, which no longer exists[18]. The Australian government also warns that health and social support services may not keep up with more frequent, severe and longer events.

With the 'collective attention span of a lightning bolt'[19], we know that politicians and their governments, with their reactive short-termism, cannot be relied upon to enact good, long-term policy. In fact, there is an 'unspoken belief that good policy is bad politics'[20].

Now for the good news. We all have the power to make change. Indeed, focused, collective action is the only thing that has done so. This engagement

---

[16] National Mental Health Commission (2024) *National Report Card 2023*, Sydney at https://www.mentalhealthcommission.gov.au/sites/default/files/2024-07/national-report-card-2023_0_0.pdf

[17] Gergis J (2024) *Highway to Hell. Climate Change and Australia's Future*, Quarterly Essay, Issue 94, p.19 & 24

[18] Australian Academy of Science (2021) *The risks to Australia of a 3°C warmer world* at https://www.science.org.au/supporting-science/science-policy-and-analysis/reports-and-publications/risks-australia-three-degrees-c-warmer-world

[19] Macklin J & Deane J (2025) *Making Progress. How Good Policy Happens*, Melbourne University Press, Carlton, Victoria, p.viii

[20] Ibid p.58

Giving is good for you

nurtures and sustains us and gives us the all-important sense of purpose and belonging that is so fundamental to our existence.

The former Lord Mayor of Melbourne and Chairman of Channel 7, Ivan Deveson AO, talks about the stone in your shoe. It niggles at you, touches a nerve and grates on your conscience. It is those injustices that prick your conscience and make you feel uncomfortable, even outraged, and generate the energy, passion and commitment to act.

As you'll see in this book, it may come from personal experience, listening to a news bulletin, listening to a friend, watching a video on social media, or this book.

We all have the opportunity to harness our humanitarian instincts to end the suffering of our fellow Australians and enable fundamental basic human rights in this affluent country - education, food, shelter, livelihood, safety, health and dignity. This won't happen overnight. Real change can take generations, but we stand on the shoulders of the millions of Australians who have cared before us.

At the same time, by giving of ourselves and our resources, we can receive fulfilment, passion, purpose, joy and meaning in our lives.

Having worked with charities over the last 30 years in housing and homelessness; education, training and employment; alcohol and other drugs; mental health; children and families; young people; social enterprise; impact investing; disability; environment; and international development, this book is your invitation to explore your cause, find your passion, take action and create real and lasting change so, together, we can build a future where millions of Australians can thrive — and where you, too, can discover the purpose and pleasure that comes from living for something larger than yourself.

GIVING IS GOOD FOR YOU

'Making a difference in people's lives-and seeing it with your own eyes is perhaps the most satisfying thing you'll ever do. If you want to fully enjoy life - give'

MICHAEL BLOOMBERG 21

In the dictator game, each subject is assigned a role as either a dictator or a recipient. Each dictator then makes a single decision, allocating a fixed amount between themself and an anonymous other. Dictators are paid for the amount they decide to keep for themselves. Recipients are paid for the amount the dictators decide to pass on.

Standard dictator games have been conducted across a variety of cultures and populations. Average transfers typically range from 25-40 per cent of the endowment. Participants also have a strong preference for equality, with a large share of equal division decisions.

The experiment shows that if we were purely self-interested and rational, we would take the entire endowment, leaving nothing for the recipient. Instead, our natural capacity for kindness, compassion and empathy creates *altruism* – the desire to help someone else without reward for ourselves – which is hard-wired in all of us.

Our biology confirms this. When we see or hear about suffering, our amygdalae, a part of the brain's threat-detection system, light up. We feel the stress of it first and then empathise with it. During a moment of empathy, the part of the brain connected to pleasure also activates, triggered by the hormone

[21] Santi J (2016) The Giving Way to Happiness. Stories and Science Behind the Life-Changing Power of Giving, New York, p.237

dopamine. This means we also receive a reward to calm the stress response and slow the heart rate, priming us to approach the person suffering rather than respond to the original fight-or-flight signal. Our pituitary gland then releases oxytocin — the love hormone — to help prompt our caregiving behaviours and enable us to respond with kindness.

Research shows that this ‘helper’s high’ boosts self-esteem, elevates happiness and combats feelings of depression.

So, it turns out, money - by giving it – *can* buy you happiness!

In the words of leading social commentator, Hugh Mackay ‘no one can promise you that a life lived for others will bring you a deep sense of satisfaction, but it's certain that nothing else will’[22].

But wait, there’s more. Giving can give you what money can’t buy - a higher purpose. Remember Maslow and his hierarchy of needs? The pinnacle of the pyramid is self-actualisation where ‘people are, without one single exception, involved in a cause outside their own skin, in something outside of themselves’[23].

In the words of the indefatigable Greta Thunberg, ‘before I started school striking I had no energy, no friends, and I didn’t want to speak to anyone. I just sat alone at home with an eating disorder. All of that is gone now, since I have found meaning in a world that sometimes seems shallow and meaningless to people’[24].

Giving your time will also improve your health.

20 years ago, Allan Luks conducted a study of over 3,000 male and female volunteers, which concluded that regular helpers are 10 times more likely to be in good health than people who don’t volunteer due to the ‘helper’s high’ of the endorphins released that reduces the body's stress[25]. Giving time and skills through volunteering can be very meaningful and rewarding, improving your mental health and wellbeing by giving you a sense of achievement and purpose; feeling part of a community and valued; enhancing self-esteem and confidence;

---

[22] Mackay H (2024) *The Way We Are. Lessons from a lifetime of listening*, Allen & Unwin, NSW, p.269

[23] Maslow A (1971) *The Farther Reaches of Human Nature*

[24] https://x.com/GretaThunberg/status/1167916944520908800

[25] https://allanluks.com/helpers_high

building new skills and relationships; and combating stress, loneliness, social isolation and depression[26].

Giving is also good for business. Staff volunteers are less likely to want to seek jobs elsewhere and are more likely to believe that the company is a great place to work. When employees feel they are a part of something bigger, they develop a stronger connection to their workplace[27].

However, we need to be mindful that when the giving is not seen to lead to a reduction in the needs, the ongoing activation of this suffering-empathy-reward-kindness loop can cause compassion fatigue, resulting in a decline in the ability to feel sympathy and empathy, and accordingly, act from a place of compassion. This can lead to detachment and negative emotions, including anger, annoyance, intolerance, irritability, scepticism, cynicism, embitterment, and resentfulness[28].

Unfortunately, with the barrage of charity appeals that spotlight the urgent needs, the 24/7 media headlines on our social and environmental crises, and the lack of good news of the progress made, compassion fatigue is real here, leading to a decline in the number of Australians donating.

This book is the antidote. It shows that we all have the opportunity to change the underlying causes of our national crises to create a new future for millions of Australians and be proud of the country we care so much about.

---

[26] https://www.healthdirect.gov.au/benefits-of-volunteering

[27] Khan M & Tran K (2025) *The science behind giving back: how volunteering can make you happier at work* at https://www-atlassian-com.cdn.ampproject.org/c/s/www.atlassian.com/blog/strategy/employee-volunteering-guide/amp

[28] Stoewen D (2020) *Moving from compassion fatigue to compassion resilience Part 4: Signs and consequences of compassion fatigue*. Can Vet J. 2020 Nov;61(11):1207-1209. PMID: 33149360; PMCID: PMC7560777

RIGHTS NOT WELFARE

'Where, after all, do universal human rights begin? In small places, close to home – so close and so small that they cannot be seen on any maps of the world. Yet they are the world of the individual person; the neighbourhood he lives in; the school or college he attends; the factory, farm or office where he works. Such are the places where every man, woman and child seeks equal justice, equal opportunity, equal dignity without discrimination. Unless these rights have meaning there, they have little meaning anywhere. Without concerned citizen action to uphold them close to home, we shall look in vain for progress in the larger world'

ELEANOR ROOSEVELT[29]

Eleanor Roosevelt is up there as one of the world's greatest human rights activists. When her husband was then Governor of New York, they took a small boat used by state officials to do inspections in order to visit the state's institutions - prisons, asylums, hospitals for crippled children. He would discuss what new buildings were needed and, as he had trouble walking due to infantile paralysis, she would go inside to see how it was run and ensure the inmates were getting proper food, medical care and sleeping arrangements.

---

[29]Rights not welfare
Roosevelt F (1958) *Where do universal human rights begin?*, statement on 27 March 1958 at the presentation of the book "In your hands: a guide for community action" to the UN Commission on Human Rights; sometimes called "The Great Question" speech

From him, she learned to observe. In their many train journeys, Franklin would watch crops, how people dressed, how many and the condition of the cars, and even the washing on the clothes lines.

As the First Lady, and despite the protocol that 'the President's wife does not go out informally except on rare occasions to old friends', Eleanor visited World War I veterans who had been evicted from their encampment by the army. As she refused to have a Secret Service agent to accompany her everywhere, she was given her own revolver.

With the Quakers, she went to see the appalling conditions of the coal miners in the company houses in the mining towns in West Virginia. She was told that, after deductions for rent and oil for their lamps, only a dollar was left for the week. With 6 children in the family, they only had scraps that 'you or I might give to a dog'.

Eleanor liked the Quaker's model of men and women working on homesteads and other projects to use their abilities and develop new skills, mirroring her past experience with her handmade furniture social enterprise to provide an occupation for young men who would otherwise leave the farms for lack of income.

Her passion for young people, regardless of their background or colour, to have a voice led to the establishment of the National Youth Administration. This followed her advocacy for coloured people to have full civil rights, which prompted complaints from southern Senators. Her strong support for women led to trips around the world to talk to and inspire women's groups, and even to setting up her own press conference just for women journalists who were not getting any work.

After her husband's death, she was asked to be a United States delegate to the new United Nations General Assembly from her work with the American Association for the United Nations. She believed the United Nations to be the one hope for a peaceful world. She was the only woman on the delegation and feared that, if she failed, all women had failed, which meant little chance of women serving in the future.

At the UN, she considered, as its first chairman the year after the end of World War II, her work on the Human Rights Commission to be her most important task. The Commission had been tasked with writing the United Nations Declaration of Human Rights and the Covenants. She set a gruelling schedule, finishing at 11 each night, and got it done by Christmas 1947 despite the 'vast social and economic differences between the various countries'. The

Declaration was proclaimed by the United Nations General Assembly in Paris a year later.

And all this whilst writing a daily newspaper column 6 days a week for the past 12 years.

The *United Nations Declaration of Human Rights*[30] set out for the first time the fundamental universal rights and freedoms for all, no matter nationality, place of residence, gender, national or ethnic origin, colour, religion, language, or any other status. Across all member nations, it sets out human, civil, economic, and social rights, asserting these rights are part of the 'foundation of freedom, justice and peace in the world'.

Australia played an important role as 1 of the 8 nations involved in drafting the Universal Declaration, due largely to the influential leadership of Dr Herbert Vere Evatt, the head of Australia's delegation to the UN. In 1948, Dr Evatt became President of the UN General Assembly, the year of the Declaration's ratification.

The 30 Articles stipulate our global aspiration to fundamental human rights, including the right to education and a decent standard of living, including food, clothing, housing, medical care and social services[31].

Since then, the Declaration has led to over 70 legally binding international human rights treaties.

Interestingly, Australia is the only Western democracy without some kind of national Human Rights Act or Bill of Rights. Our Constitution only provides for the right to vote, protection against acquisition of property on unjust terms, the right to a trial by jury, freedom of religion and prohibition of discrimination based on State of residency. Does the latter mean our interstate rivalry - banana benders, cockroaches, sandgropers, crow-eaters – is illegal? Or is it just 'the vibe'?

This global consensus on universal fundamental human rights saw the growth of charities that focused on protecting the rights of the poorest and most marginalised, as opposed to coming to the aid of the needy as prescribed by religious doctrine.

Most charities began as small groups of people who recognised an abuse of human or environmental rights and saw insufficient responses to address the needs, driven by the unwavering belief that these rights and needs could and

[30] https://www.un.org/en/about-us/universal-declaration-of-human-rights

[31] https://www.amnesty.org/en/what-we-do/universal-declaration-of-human-rights/

should be addressed. This could be the right to adequate income, health, shelter, justice, education, food, livelihood, dignity, safety or care.

What are the rights that you are willing to stand up for?

CHOOSING A CHARITY

'The best way to find yourself is to lose
yourself in the service of others'

MAHATMA GANDHI

As the oldest continuous living culture in the world, we know that Aboriginal and Torres Strait Islander people's strong connection to family, land and culture forms the foundation for their social, economic, and individual wellbeing.

Historically, charity is most commonly associated with religion. Judaism first emphasised *tzedakah,* or almsgiving, as the obligation of the wealthy to give to the poor, but also the right of the poor to receive these gifts, whilst the English word 'charity' appeared in the fourth Century when Saint Jerome translated the Bible from Greek into Latin.

In medieval Europe, the Church bore the responsibility for organising and promoting poor relief. It was not until the sixteenth century that the state began to take over this role.

In England, following the Reformation movement's dismantling of the Catholic Church, the largest institution addressing the growing needs of poor people in age-old traditions of almsgiving and charity, the *Elizabethan Statute of 1601* provided the first definition of 'charity' as a way to provide greater guidance and incentives for the private sector to bring their resources to bear on the growing problem of poverty.

In Australia, in the 19th century, Christian charities were the main institutional assistance protecting poor people from starvation and homelessness, starting with the NSW Society for Promoting Christian Knowledge and Benevolence (now the Benevolent Society) in 1813. Following a request from Bishop

Polding, in 1815, Irish nun, Mary Aikenhead, founded the Sisters of Charity to serve those living in poverty.

Today, the Charities Act stipulates that to be recognised as a charity, an organisation must be not-for-profit (an organisation that does not operate for the profit, personal gain or other benefit of particular people); have only charitable purposes that are for the public benefit (to the general public or to a 'sufficient section of the general public' and can have purposes that are 'incidental or ancillary to'); not have a disqualifying purpose; and not be an individual, a political party or a government entity[32].

Today, the Australian charitable sector is large and opaque.

There are over 60,000 charities registered by the government's Australian Charities and Not-for-profits Commission (ACNC) - a confusing name given it only regulates the charitable institutions that it registers - and an estimated 300,000-600,000 not-for-profit organisations.

Contrary to public perception, the number of registered charities has remained relatively stable for the last decade with revoked charities often exceeding newly registered charities. Most are small. Nearly a third of registered charities have an income of less than $50,000 and nearly half are volunteer-run and have no paid employees.

For those thinking we have too many charities, we have one charity per 439 people in Australia, compared to 447 for Canada, 395 for the UK, 257 for the USA, and 183 for New Zealand. My view is that the number of charities is healthy and represents both the ongoing unmet need and the compassionate society that we are fortunate to live in.

The issue is not too many charities, but the competition and the lack of cooperation and collaboration between them, which creates duplication, gaps and fragmentation of services, as well as regularly reinventing the wheel, leading to sub-optimal outcomes and one reason why our social issues are not improving.

Although declining, religious charities remain the largest type at 1 in 5, followed by social welfare and education. Environmental charities have increased over the years, but still only account for one in thirty.

The latest report from the ACNC shows assets of charities total $489 billion and total revenue of $222 billion, comprising $14 billion, or six per cent, in

[32]Choosing a charity https://www.acnc.gov.au/for-charities/start-charity/public-benefit

donations; a third in goods and services; and half in government funding. The top 0.05 per cent of charities receive 20 per cent of all the donations.

As well as harnessing 3.7 million volunteers, charities employed 1.54 million people, or over 1 in 10 of all Australians.

Whilst on average only a small proportion of total income for the sector comes from donations, the smaller the charity, the more reliance on donations (for instance, 39 per cent for small and very small charities) and less use of government funding (only 12 per cent for small and very small charities)[33].

As legal entities, charities are either charitable trusts, incorporated associations under State/Territory legislation, or companies limited by guarantee (instead of shares) under the Corporations Act. To be a registered charity, the constitution needs to include: the charitable purpose; that it is established to operate on a not-for-profit basis (that is, any profits must be directed back into achieving the purpose of the charity, and the company cannot operate for the profit, personal gain or other benefit of certain people, such as its members, directors, employees or their friends or relatives); and prevent any of the company's surplus assets to be distributed to any current or former members of the company if the company is wound up.

Charities can apply for 1 or more tax concessions from the Australian Tax Office (ATO). All should be endorsed as a *Tax Concession Charity (TCC)* so they are exempt from income tax on any net profit. Then, being endorsed by the ATO as a *Deductible Gift Recipient (DGR)* entitles charities to receive gifts which are deductible from the donor's taxable income.

Evolving haphazardly over the last century, the DGR system is outdated, confusing and no longer fit for purpose. As a result, half of registered charities currently miss out. There are 52 DGR endorsement categories, each with specific criteria, grouped as: health; education; research; welfare and rights; defence; environment; the family; international affairs; sports and recreation; cultural organisations; fire and emergency services; and ancillary funds.

As part of its strategy to double philanthropic giving in Australia by 2030, the Australian Government in 2024 created two new general DGR categories for community charity trusts and community charity corporations, allowing community foundations to attract more philanthropic funding, including from private ancillary funds.

---

[33] Australian Charities and Not-for-profits Commission (2023) *Australian Charities Report 11th edition* at https://www.acnc.gov.au/tools/reports/australian-charities-report-11th-edition

Additionally, charities can gain the status of a *Public Benevolent Institution (PBI),* entitling their employees to be exempt from Fringe Benefits Tax (FBT) up to $30,000 a year (grossed up) – a cap that has not changed since I asked Treasurer Peter Costello in 2000, whilst on the Charities Consultative Committee, what the amount represented. He answered 'the value of a car and a bit more'. This means that PBI charity employees can package otherwise FBT-able expenses and not pay income tax or FBT on about $16,000 of their pay. This was designed to bridge the gap between what charities can pay compared to the government and the private sector, but the ATO was not happy with the loss of tax revenue and the amount has not been indexed since.

The definition of 'benevolent' goes back to a 1931 legal case, *Perpetual Trustee Co Ltd v Federal Commissioner of Taxation,* where the High Court stated that a benevolent organisation is required to be 'organised, conducted or promoted for the relief of poverty, sickness, destitution, helplessness, suffering, misfortune, disability, or distress'. Further advice from the ACNC Commissioner states that 'activities must be directed towards relieving the needs of its beneficiaries'.

This unhelpful and archaic definition bars charities that work in prevention, early intervention and to change societal views, policies and systems, as well as animal welfare and environmental charities, from becoming PBIs.

Following their 2024 inquiry into philanthropy in Australia, the Deputy Chair of the Productivity Commission noted that 'the system that determines which charities can receive tax-deductible donations has grown in an ad hoc way over decades and has no coherent policy rationale. The complexity and inconsistency of the system sees many charities that create clear community benefits miss out'[34].

The report proposed an overhaul of the DGR system that would make it simpler and fairer. It focused on activities that are likely to generate the greatest net benefits for the community. The Productivity Commission estimated that the recommended changes would increase the number of charities that can receive tax deductible donations from about 25,000 charities to around 30,000 to 40,000 charities[35].

---

[34] https://www.pc.gov.au/inquiries/completed/philanthropy/report#media-release

[35] Commonwealth of Australia (2024) *Future foundations for giving Inquiry report,* Report no. 104, Productivity Commission, Canberra at https://www.pc.gov.au/inquiries/completed/philanthropy/report/philanthropy.pdf

Charities may also be registered as a *Health Promotion Charity* if their principal activity is to 'promote the prevention or control of disease in human beings' and be entitled to apply for DGR status.

Registered charities are entitled to show the symbol below and, unless classified as small with annual revenue under $500,000, must submit an Annual Information Statement and annual financial reports. You can view these and other information - ABN, contact details, size, profile, status, responsible persons and governing documents - on the ACNC website (www.acnc.gov.au), with a link to the Australian Business Register to show the charity's tax status.

Whilst it is tempting (and easier) to rely on the information posted on the ACNC, or use a service which does so, this data does not enable an adequate assessment of the effectiveness of the charity in achieving its purpose or the impact of its work. I explain why below.

My checklist for choosing a charity (in order of consideration) is as follows.

1. Belief and purpose

Charities begin as a small group of people recognising that the needs of a specific cohort or community are not being met, and they believe these needs can and should be addressed.

This belief in the right to human dignity in the form of safety, education, health, justice, shelter, food and livelihood is the basis for a 'rights-based approach' employed by most charities as the basis of their work.

For instance, many Australian charities believe in the right to shelter with the purpose of ending homelessness, including Launch Housing and The Salvation Army.

The right to safety with the purpose of ending family and domestic violence motivates Our Watch, ANROWS, and many other charities working in this sector.

The right to education drives Teach for Australia and The Smith Family, whose purpose is to 'overcome educational inequality caused by poverty'.

The right to enough food has led to the growth of charities such as Foodbank, Second Bite, OzHarvest, and FareShare.

However, in the quest to be more like businesses with professional managers, many charities now have a corporate-inspired vision and mission.

Whenever I join an organisation, I ask everyone what the vision and mission is. The record so far is three consecutive words. Nicely displayed in the reception and illustrated with smiling faces, the vision and mission are usually devised by the management team in planning workshops. A painful process with endless word smithing, the end result, albeit well-meaning, is akin to world peace and inevitably fails to capture a succinct and compelling case for the future, as well as the heritage, belief, and the purpose of the organisation.

As *Good to Great* author, Jim Collins, notes, 'we must reject the idea – well intentioned, but dead wrong – that the primary path to greatness in the social sectors is to become 'more like a business''[36].

So, my advice is to get to the heart of the charity's *raison d'etre*. With over two-thirds of Australians saying they would give more to charity if they knew more about the results and impact that a charity has[37], next, can the charity clearly show its progress to achieve its purpose?

2. Demonstrated outcomes

In amongst the inspiring stories and smiling recipients, pie charts and infographics, the annual reports of charities look impressive but rarely outline the outcomes or impact that demonstrate the longitudinal progress to their purpose (or their purpose at all).

The most generally accepted methodology for connecting processes to purpose and to be able to articulate and measure each stage is a *theory of change* or *program logic*, which can be carried out on an organisational, program or project level.

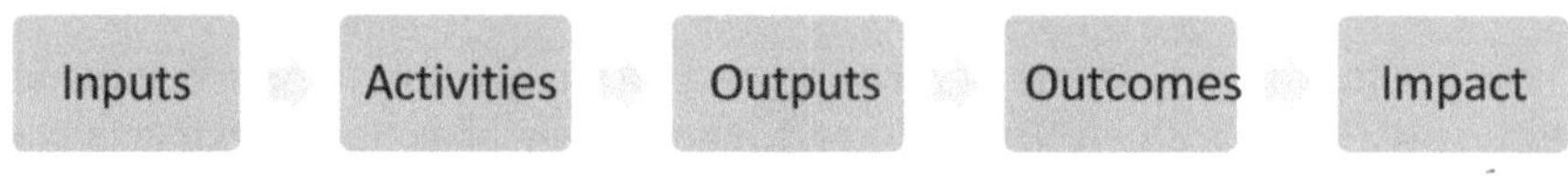

[36] Collins J (2006) *Good to Great and the Social Sectors. A monograph to Accompany Good to Great*, UK

[37] Charities Aid Foundation & Workplace Giving Australia (2025) *Giving in Australia 2025*, p.19

In this model:

- *Inputs* are the resources needed for the activities to occur, including people, money, assets, say the trainers, room hire, and course materials for a charity that educates children who have dropped out of school
- *Activities* are the specific interventions that will take place, for instance, the number of classes by subject
- *Outputs* are the results of the activities, such as the number of participants trained
- *Outcomes* can be divided into short, medium and long term. They represent the result of the outputs and their effect, such as the measured educational attainment or skills acquired, as well as getting into work or tertiary education. Then there is the evidence gathered to demonstrate to governments a change in education policy, system and resources that would prevent the cohort from dropping out of school or intervene earlier to get them back to school
- *Impact* is the holy grail as the closest measure to fulfilling the charity's purpose as the social or environmental change envisioned, such as the financial and wellbeing benefits of the trainees, their families and communities, together with a change in the mainstream education system to intervene in non-attendance early, for instance, a policy that places the responsibility of truancy with the school

This model needs to be developed from right to left, starting with the impact desired to further or achieve the charity's belief and purpose, respectively. In this example, the charity's belief in the right to education for all can only be achieved in the long term by an inclusive, skilled and resourced government education system (impact). The short-term 'band-aid' teaching intervention by the charity (outputs) must be accompanied by evidence of the longer-term economic and social benefits of the outcomes it achieves, alongside the government policy, service system and resource changes needed.

The UK's National Philanthropy Centre has two excellent free Starting Guides - *Theory of Change in Ten Steps*[38] and *Understanding Impact*[39].

Given that the biggest impact any charity can make is improving government policies and service systems that address the underlying causes of our social

---

[38] https://www.thinknpc.org/resource-hub/ten-steps/

[39] https://www.thinknpc.org/resource-hub/understanding-impact/

and environmental issues, the next step is for the charity to gather and harness their evidence of better outcomes to advocate for change.

3. Advocacy for change

Our charities and the service systems are increasingly failing to cope with the urgent daily needs. We have to try and get 'ahead of the curve' by changing the government policy, systems, services and resources that underpin the issue, approach and service provision, which, as shown in the Themes, including to prevent or intervene earlier.

In order of increasing importance, the levels of change can be categorised as:

Individual - immediate

As this book illustrates, most of our services respond to the immediate suffering of those in urgent need, whether it is a family getting grocery donations to be able to put food on the table, a homeless mother fleeing domestic violence needing emergency accommodation for the night, a child being abused taken into out of home care for their safety, a tradie with suicide ideation needing ongoing therapy, or a young person leaving incarceration and needing work.

Whilst these interventions can alleviate the crisis, they do little to address its underlying causes and reduce the ongoing need.

Individual - transformative

Given that the current trajectory of the family and/or individual's life has led to their crisis - whether it is offending, abuse of a child or suicide ideation – the challenge is to enable them to envisage and change their behaviour to a more positive life course. This typically involves forming new relationships (including with a significant other in the person's life), acquiring new skills and capacities (such as emotional regulation or qualifications), educational attainment to be able to enter the workforce, rehabilitation from drug dependence, ongoing mental health treatment, or simply having hope and being able to see a new future.

As outlined in this book, the challenge is that charities, as service providers, are typically funded to provide one of these services and not necessarily required to coordinate with others.

Sector wide

Taking the Themes in this book, sector-wide change involves the government's reform of a service system and policy change. For instance, the pressure on the governments from the continued rise in deaths of women from intimate partners and rates of Family and Domestic Violence (FDV), voiced as a 'national crisis', meant governments acted to create a target - the *National Plan to End Violence against Women and Children by 2032* to enable a coordinated governmental response and resourcing for prevention, early intervention, response, recovery and healing.

Another policy change was achieved by the *Home Stretch* coalition of charities, supported by philanthropy. Government policies required the child protection system to begin preparing a young person to leave care as early as 15 years, while most would leave their care placement during their 16th or 17th year. In comparison, children residing at home in the wider community with one or both parents are remaining at home longer, with 85 per cent of young people still in the family home.

The CREATE Foundation found that over a third were homeless in the first year of leaving care; nearly half of the boys were involved in the juvenile justice system; and almost a third were unemployed. The international evidence showed that extending care by 3 more years to 21 would halve youth homeless rates, double education engagement, reduce the youth arrest rate by 40 per cent, and hospitalisation rates would decline by a third. For every dollar spent on extending care, government would save itself $2[40].

After 7 years of relentless campaigning focusing on 1 single unwavering issue - to extend the leaving care age for young people in out-of-home care from 18 to 21 years in all Australian jurisdictions - as of 2024, this is now the policy of every State and Territory[41].

In March 2024, a coalition of almost 100 homelessness services from across Australia launched the *Home Time* campaign to highlight the nearly 40,000 young people (15-24 years) who came to homelessness services alone in 2022/23. After seeing a homelessness service, 44 per cent of them were still homeless. The campaign calls for a new approach for government system change to develop and maintain a national pool of 15,000 dedicated youth tenancies; provide linked support services to enable young people to pursue their individual goals and transition to full independence; and address the rental gap to ensure viability for housing providers and landlords offering tenancies to young people who have been homeless.

---

[40] McDonald P (2024) *How we achieved "the most significant Australian child welfare reform in a generation"*, Australian Journal of Social Issues. 1 August 2024 DOI: 10.1002/ajs4.361 at https://thehomestretch.org.au/news/how-we-achieved-the-most-significant-australianchild-welfare-reform-in-a-generation/

[41] https://thehomestretch.org.au/

As detailed in the homelessness Theme, a new government policy to enact zero functional homelessness (when all experiences of homelessness in a community are rare, brief and non-recurring; and this is sustained over time) based on the evidence gained from the growing 'advance to zero' programs in our cities, would ensure the resourcing and coordination of government funded services needed to achieve this goal.

In view of the lack of progress in disability inclusion and gender equality, another policy change could be to legislate targets for female company Board directors, or a proportion of those employed with a disability.

A change in state and local government planning policies to provide sufficient spaces and resources for leisure and social community engagement (or even just enough road width to allow a bus service) would build social cohesion, including seeding community groups.

In each Theme, you'll see how policy and system change are desperately needed and how much impact it would make.

Societal

This is where societal attitudes positively change over time, albeit slowly, and with periods of little change. For instance, the disability inclusion Theme outlines the pervasiveness of ableism in our society. The gender equality Theme articulates the ongoing male power imbalance and the Theme on racism and discrimination cites the ubiquitous mistreatment of minorities.

In my lifetime, there has been progress with gender equality, the awareness and treatment of mental health and wellbeing, the exposure of FDV, the celebration of people with a disability through sport, and the widespread acceptance of the LGBTQI+ community, including marriage equality.

However, frustratingly, societal behaviour change can be glacial or stuck and at times, I feel that, in the immortal words of Blackadder, 'we've advanced no further than an asthmatic ant carrying some heavy shopping'.

Government can play a role in changing attitudes through public education campaigns, such as the recent *Consent Can't Wait*, to encourage adults to positively influence the attitudes of young people around consent and healthy, respectful relationships to reduce the unacceptably high rates of sexual violence in our community.

Based on 'you can't be what you can't see', role models play an important catalyst in our society, whether from community, sporting, business or arts backgrounds.

In summary, these aspects of change can be shown as:

Importance →

Individual - immediate	**Individual - transformative**	**Sector-wide**	**Societal**
Assists an individual's immediate needs	*Changes an individual's trajectory*	*Policy and system changes*	*Changes in attitudes and culture*
Examples: • Soup kitchen • Foodbank • Emergency accommodatio n • Legal aid • Mental health treatment	Examples: • Education, training eg in a youth foyer or social enterprise • Employment • Transitional, social or affordable housing	Examples: • Ending FDV by 2032 • Payment by outcomes for social enterprises	Examples: • Role models • Government education campaigns • Community campaigns

Head of the Paul Ramsay Foundation, Professor Kirsty Muir, distils the levers for change into 3 categories:

Technical work: changes to polices, programs, practices, legislation and regulation, including research to understand what works and what does not, and for whom, and to test alternative models;

Where the resources go: changes to where funding flows, who makes the decisions, how resources get used (time, talent and treasure) and how the work gets done (individually, in coordination with others, or through genuine collaboration); and

Hearts and minds: understanding, galvanising and changing attitudes, beliefs, values and fears, who has something to gain, who has something to fear and who has something to lose[42].

---

42 https://www.paulramsayfoundation.org.au/news-resources/is-systems-change-possible-how-do-we-put-it-into-action

Leadbeater & Winhall add that 'systems are often hard to change because power, relationships, and resource flows are locked together in a reinforcing pattern to serve the system's current purpose. Systems start to change fundamentally when this pattern is disrupted and opened up. Then a new configuration can emerge, serving a new purpose'[43].

To achieve this change, charities need to be the catalysts through the evidence-based demonstration of the effectiveness of their current or new practices, together with the government policy and service system changes required.

4. Evidence-based, participatory practice

Unfortunately, the white saviour complex is alive and well in Australia. Too often, projects and programs are designed on office whiteboards without a clear understanding of the problem's complexity, the challenges involved, or the engagement and consultation required with the cohort or community, as well as the interests of the funder. Rarely do the funder's timeframes allow for proper research, development and co-design, let alone implementation.

Furthermore, this approach ignores the inherent capabilities of the recipient community, including their knowledge, networks, resources and skills.

The principle 'nothing about us, without us' stems from the premise that policies, procedures, rules, projects, programs, and services should never be created for any population without explicit input from the very population that is impacted.

Recipients should be seen and valued as co-producers and citizens, rather than being viewed only as clients, consumers or customers. If so, the intervention produced is more lasting and effective when the beneficiaries care about and support what they create.

The engagement and input from the users of the program or service are crucial to assess and improve its efficacy. To do so, charities should maintain service user groups to provide this feedback. This involvement can go beyond consultation to being active in decision making and governance, including representation on the board.

---

[43] Leadbeater C & Winhall J (2021) *System Innovation On Purpose,* The Rockpool Foundation at https://rockwoolfonden.s3.eu-central-1.amazonaws.com/wp-content/uploads/2022/10/SII_SystemInnovationOnPurpose_2021.pdf?download=true

For instance, Vision Australia has a Client Reference Group to gain advice and feedback on specific matters relating to the experience of our clients and direction of the organisation that regularly meets with the Board[44].

At the youth drug and alcohol agency, YSAS, we followed Hart's Ladder of Participation, which escalates from 'young people are consulted and informed' to 'adult-initiated shared decisions with young people' to 'young people lead and initiate action' to 'youth-initiated, shared decisions with adults'[45].

An evidence-informed approach to practice requires the integration of this ongoing input, as well as the evaluation of programs and services, research into good practice in the sector and practitioner development and expertise.

Otherwise, how does the charity, supporters and community know 'what works' for the people they serve? How can they show that their programs and services are effective in responding to the needs and achieve lasting impact? How can value for money be determined?

As government contractors and service providers, charities tend to do things 'to' and 'for' a cohort, so please look for evidence of user groups, community consultation, practice development and external evaluations.

In order to deliver their services, maintain confidence of their stakeholders, maintain their supporter base and preserve their social licence to operate, charities need to demonstrate organisational accountability.

5. Accountability

I keep in my office a framed poster advertising the headline from *The Age* on 23 May 2003. It reads 'Red Cross says sorry to Bali victims'. The horrific bombings in the Kuta nightclub district on the night of 12 October 2002 killed 202 people, 88 of whom were Australians. A further 153 Australians were injured.

The Australian Red Cross launched an appeal promising that 90 cents in every dollar collected would go "directly to the victims" of the bombings[46]. 6 months later the press reported that 'only about $4 million of the $14.3 million collected

---

[44] https://visionaustralia.org/about-us/governance/client-reference-group

[45] For instance, see https://ymhac.rnao.ca/sites/default/files/2016-10/Harts%20Laddar.pdf

[46] https://www.smh.com.au/national/how-the-red-cross-got-it-wrong-20030524-gdgtc6.html

had so far reached victims, and that 3 ambulances it said had been delivered to Bali had not arrived'[47].

The outrage was led by the victims who wanted to know why so much of the money was being diverted into Red Cross projects, such as spray-on skin, a tuberculosis program and upgrading of the blood bank in Bali. Federal Ministers and former staff joined in, one saying that 'part of the problem facing the organisation is the hopelessly out-of-date governance and management structure'[48].

They were asked why they hadn't learned the lessons from the resignation of the head of the American Red Cross over revelations that more than $30 million in charitable donations intended for the families of the September 11 victims had been set aside for programs unrelated to the disaster.

In the end, the Red Cross demonstrated that 70 per cent of the money fundraised was spent on the needs of victims, but the damage was already done.

17 years later, in the face of the worst bushfires in Australia's modern history, another generation of Australian Red Cross leadership had to defend the same accusations of the retention of donations on administration and slow spending in response to the emergency[49].

To operate, all organisations need a social licence, or the 'informal acceptance granted to an individual or organisation by a local community'[50]. I keep this poster to remind me that, despite a reputation built over many decades, charities can't take their heritage for granted and can very easily lose the trust and respect of the public by poor decision making, communication and governance.

However, there is 1 area in which charities have a justified reluctance to be transparent.

The vast majority of donors that I have encountered over the years have only 1 criterion for their charitable giving - how much of my donation is swallowed up by overheads. The perception is that the higher the admin cost, the lower the

---

[47] https://www.theage.com.au/national/red-cross-sorry-for-misleading-fund-raising-20030523-gdvr3j.html

[48] https://www.smh.com.au/national/how-the-red-cross-got-it-wrong-20030524-gdgtc6.html

[49] https://www.theguardian.com/australia-news/2020/jan/24/australian-red-cross-defends-spending-10-of-bushfire-donations-on-office-costs#:~:text=The per cent20Australian per cent20Red per cent20Cross per cent20has,raised per cent20directly per cent20to per cent20a per cent20cause.

[50] https://ethics.org.au/ethics-explainer-social-license-to-operate/

money spent directly on services and so less 'good' the charity is doing for my contribution.

This perception is perpetuated by regular media headlines - 'Charitable Christmas giving: How much of your donation goes to those who need it?', 'Millions in charity donations 'wasted' on administration costs, red tape', and 'Millions in donations blown on administration costs'.

The reality is that all organisations, be they for-profit or not-for-profit, need to spend on office rent, human resources, training, accountants, information technology and administration to manage their compliance with laws and regulations, governance requirements, information technology systems, cyber security, risk management, staff and financial management. After all, you want your charity to be well-managed, financially accountable, cyber-safe, and legally compliant.

Although a national standard chart of accounts has been developed by the sector and the ACNC, there is no requirement to use it, no accepted accounting definition of what constitutes administration costs, and no external audit sign-off to verify their accuracy. As charities include different costs in administration, no direct comparison is therefore possible.

The administration cost ratio is even more variable due to the revenue amounts chosen for the calculation. For instance, if the ratio is calculated to total revenue from the financial statements, including non-fundraising income such as government grants, the ratio reported bears little relation to how much the donor's contribution was spent on beneficiaries.

As the ACNC notes 'assessing and comparing charity administration costs is difficult and it can be misleading'[51].

The recent Blueprint Expert Group considered an action to update National Standard Chart of Accounts and embed it in accounting software, but the improvement did not make it into the final *2024 Not-for-profit Sector Development Blueprint*[52].

Given the fierce competition for the dollar, charities face pressure not to include the full cost, including overheads, as this could lead to being outbid on costs, turning away funders, and undervaluing their ask. The pressure by donors and funders on charities to incur low administration costs is called the *nonprofit*

---

[51] https://www.acnc.gov.au/for-public/understanding-charities/charities-and-administration-costs

[52] Blueprint Expert Reference Group (2024) *Not-for-profit Sector Development Blueprint*, p.78, action 73

starvation cycle[53] - a vicious cycle that fuels the persistent underfunding of the capacity of charities.

The recent *Paying What It Takes* report by Social Ventures Australia and the Centre for Social Impact confirmed that charities are underinvesting in critical capabilities due to a pervasive belief that funders are reluctant to provide the full financial support needed to create impact. The report also found that charities that spend less on indirect costs are not necessarily more efficient nor more effective than those that do not. Indeed, there is clear evidence that spending insufficient resources on indirect costs can potentially reduce overall effectiveness[54].

The report found that 'the average indirect costs of the not-for-profits analysed were 33 per cent of the total costs, with significant variation between 26 per cent and 47 per cent. This is comparable to the minimum of 29 per cent indirect cost funding found in a US study of 130,000 charities. By contrast, funding agreements often only included indirect costs of between 10-20 per cent of overall costs. A significant proportion of not-for-profits stated that they underreported their indirect costs to funders due to a pervasive belief that funders are unwilling to fund more than 20 per cent of indirect costs[55].

To compound the issue, a 2025 study has found that 'current Australian governments do not provide adequate funding for services procurement; nor do they provide adequate indexation for ongoing contracts and service delivery or adequate capital inputs to meet policy and regulatory change'[56].

In registering with the ACNC, charities must comply with reporting requirements on their activities (Annual Information Statement), a list of Board members, and upload their annual audited financials (optional for small charities). You can see this information on the ACNC website, including whether it is late in being submitted.

The experience of the Board Chair, Board members, and CEO is important in guiding the organisation, and their biographies can usually be found on the

---

[53] Goggins Gregory A & Howard D (2009), *The Nonprofit Starvation Cycle*, Stanford Social Innovation Review, Fall 2009

[54] Social Ventures Australia and the Centre for Social Impact (2022) *Paying what it takes: funding indirect cost to create long-term impact*, Social Ventures Australia at https://www.socialventures.org.au/wp-content/uploads/2024/07/Paying-what-it-takes.pdf

[55] Ibid p.3

[56] Gilchrist D.J., & Perks B (2025) *Real Costs, Real Impacts: A Path to Social Services Sustainability*, Centre for Public Value, UWA Business School, Catholic Social Services (Australia) Ltd, Canberra at https://www.uwa.edu.au/schools/-/media/centre-for-public-value/resources/250315-real-costs-real-impacts-final.pdf

charity's website. The CEO's messages in the newsletters, blogs and social media can be a good gauge of their understanding of the cause, not just their charity, and their insights into change.

Although not required by law, a charity's annual report is key in demonstrating its progress to its purpose through the outcomes and impact achieved over time. In reality, though, annual reports are more like promotional brochures filled with smiling pictures, activity infographics, heartfelt stories, and financial pie charts.

For fear of losing the confidence of its stakeholders, annual reports rarely include an admission and analysis of 'lessons learnt' from programs and services that didn't achieve their expectations. This lack of questioning perpetuates the defence that every charity is doing 'good work' and so deserves support.

The combined reserves of Australian charities amount to nearly $300 billion[57]. Before COVID, it was a general rule to have 3 months' worth of service expenditure in reserves. As reserves only exist from unspent donations and surpluses from government funding, they should be spent on furthering the charity's purpose, not hoarded. Whilst reserves and JobKeeper saved thousands of charities from liquidation during COVID, prospective donors increasingly assess the level of reserves in their giving decision, as well as whether the investment policy of the charity includes ethical investments and impact investments, especially related to the cause.

Next, charities cannot operate alone if they are to achieve the outcomes that their service recipients desperately need.

6. Collaboration

With all governments viewing the private sector as more efficient, alongside the need to limit the rising cost of public services in the face of idling government revenue, the open tendering out of government services from the early 1990s has transformed how charities operate.

Established immediately after World War II, the Commonwealth Employment Service was privatised by the Howard government in 1998. The resultant Job Network encouraged independent providers from the private and community

---

[57] Australian Charities and Not-for-profits Commission (2024) *Australian Charities Report. 10th Edition* p.39

sectors to compete to find jobs for the unemployed. The same government opened up aged care to market competition.

In 2012, Australia's vocational education and training sector was restructured by governments with the introduction of market-based funding and a voucher system, effectively privatising the sector and impacting TAFE (Technical and Further Education) institutions. State governments reduced barriers to entry, granting hundreds of new players a licence to establish themselves as colleges, market to students, and teach them. Course design was left up to these new colleges so they could provide education when and where students needed it.

As we will discuss in the Disability Inclusion Theme, government disability services were privatised under the NDIS (National Disability Insurance Scheme) in 2016.

Unsurprisingly, as subsequent government inquiries have found, private providers are adept at maximising revenue and profit from the new service systems and, at times, at the expense of those they serve.

Typically, governments design a mainstream service system that caters for the majority of people that need the services (or initially have some specialist services) with scheduled fees for outputs, such as a putting someone in a job for 26 weeks, completion of a certified training course, a level 4 aged care resident for a day, or an hour of physiotherapy for a disabled child.

Over time, the government seeks to reduce the number of providers and squeeze costs by reducing fees (or not increasing fees with inflation) and issuing tenders with larger geographic areas or range of services to drive economies of scale.

This means that charities that managed to win a service contract are gradually forced out by larger commercial providers, resulting in an exodus of not-for-profit managed community services, including child care and aged care. Now with the NDIS, with a median loss of 4 per cent and 12 per cent over the last 5 years, not-for-profit disability services that support some of the most vulnerable Australians are being forced to close[58].

With studies showing high staffing ratios and better safety records in not-for-profit providers, accusations of profit before people have been regularly levelled at the government's approach[59].

---

[58] https://www.theguardian.com/australia-news/2025/nov/24/not-for-profit-disability-services-closing-ndis-price-caps

[59] https://www.communitydirectors.com.au/articles/the-real-cost-of-profit-how-human-services-became-a-commodity-and-children-paid-the-price

Mission Australia had this challenge when the new employment services tender came up. With 700 staff employed, the larger contract with payment in arrears required millions of dollars more in cash flow they didn't have. So, they formed a new joint venture company with Providence USA, which tendered and won a number of Job Active services, retaining about 2/3rds of what Mission Australia had previously, with staff now working for the new company. This was still painful, with many staff made redundant, especially in Queensland, where no services were won.

However, there was a crucial change in the new service. Instead of Centrelink staff enforcing the rules on job seekers, the responsibility was transferred to the Job Active case managers. This meant Mission Australia staff having to breach the jobseeker for not following the requirements, such as job interviews, leading to the withdrawal of their benefits, whilst Mission Australia's community services responded to the effects of the resultant poverty, homelessness, drug and alcohol misuse and mental illness.

The position was clearly untenable, and to its credit, Mission Australia divested its stake in the joint company and left Job Active to focus on its leading homelessness, housing, family, children, and youth community services.

Whilst the tendering out of government services over the last 30 years has seen the growth in government revenue to over $100 billion, or over half of all charity income, the competition for government service contracts has resulted in charities becoming increasingly protective of their brand and what they see as their intellectual property. Consequently and understandably, charities are reluctant to disclose their 'what works' evaluation information or cooperate with others in the sector.

Unfortunately, the result is the lack of demonstrated good practice or outcomes, service improvement, integrated client-centred services or coordinated collaboration for policy, systems and funding change. As a result, these charities may be complicit in maintaining the very policy and service systems that fail to enable the outcomes that their recipients need and deserve.

But place-based, shared goal alliances are possible, as outlined in the *I Have a Dream* chapter, such as the *Go Goldfields* alliance.

So, it is important to look for the collaborations, alliances, networks and sector bodies that the charity actively participates in, especially across service sectors and with research institutions.

Then, with the growing need, charities need to 'push the envelope' to challenge the status quo and innovate to improve outcomes.

7. Innovation

It was a proud day when the head of the government department that funded us came in to get his daily coffee from the young barista. The first time could have been a 'pity purchase' driven by the altruistic wish to patronise the charity café to support the cause. But the quality of the coffee and service made the café his regular stop off before work.

I was heading up the largest youth alcohol and other drug service in the country. The drug and alcohol dependency, chronic mental health issues and anti-social behaviour typically resulted from violence, abuse, sexual assault and parental alcohol and drug taking at home from an early age. It is no wonder that this became normalised behaviour and repeated in the next generation who tended to make the same choices in life.

The drug taking represents self-medication to alleviate the pain of the trauma. In an accepting, non-judgmental and evidence-based approach, the objective of the rehabilitation is to develop their coping, social, and life skills and relationships, often with a 'significant other' in their life, so the drug taking becomes an increasingly smaller part of their lives.

Our belief was that these young people deserved, as a basic human right, to live the lives we take for granted – of dignity, respect, supportive relationships, good health, a safe home, education and training, work and financial independence.

However, without a different environment to go home to after leaving rehabilitation, they could lapse back into abusive relationships, prostitution, homelessness and reoffending. For many, it was a revolving door to return to prison or our services. Or ending their lives.

Their future as welfare recipients, like generations before them, involved a merry-go-round of justice, mental health, alcohol and other drug, domestic violence, homelessness, unemployment and emergency health services.

With sustainable employment the best intervention we can make for young people, and just 11.7 per cent of jobseekers ending up with jobs lasting at least 26 weeks through the government employment services[60], social enterprises are commercial businesses that provide training and work experience to a cohort that would not otherwise be employable in a real work environment with professional staff as role models, as a transition to mainstream employment.

[60] https://www.theguardian.com/business/2025/nov/03/majority-jobseekers-unable-to-get-long-term-work-despite-private-agencies

From day one, and for the first time in their lives, young people are treated as workers, and not welfare recipients on another program that they have to attend.

Leaving a government meeting one day, I walked past a café in the lane behind the office block. With the rise of Melbourne's hipster café scene, the shop appeared out of place with specials scrawled on the window, a hunk of dehydrating roast meat on the counter and a handful of pies ageing in the warmer. Over the next 2 months, I walked the same way to and from the meetings without seeing a customer.

With the government putting in place a social procurement policy, I knew that a social enterprise café could be a preferred catering supplier to the 2,000 public servants next door, and a refit and rebranding could attract coffee and lunch customers from nearby office blocks.

Legendary chef Andrew McConnell, who had helped me with the Charcoal Lane social enterprise restaurant, asked his designers to lend a hand. Looking through Paul Kelly song titles, *Ways and Means* was chosen (I was outvoted on *Leaps and Bounds*).

Young people in the last stages of recovery came into work, making their own way on public transport, to give them work experience and the start of a CV. Treating them as a valued worker gave them affirmation and a completely different perspective. They came back excited to want to work and plan for their future study or apply for a job.

In view of the now proven ability of social enterprises to transition unemployed Australians with significant personal and vocational barriers to mainstream employment, the Australian government is developing the sector's capacity over the next 2 years to be able to claim job outcome funding from the government's employment services system. This policy change will be a game changer for the sector, enabling the scalability of thousands of social enterprises and encouraging the establishment of thousands more.

In my experience, charities have an inherent culture of innovation as they endeavour to stretch budgets further to address the rising and complexity of needs, as well as having to respond to the ongoing political change and the ebbs and flows of fundraising income.

In striving to attain their purpose, charities need to invest in pilot programs and services that utilise their evaluation to design and test different ways to achieve better outcomes and provide the evidence needed to advocate for policy, system and program change with government.

Sadly, I've seen hundreds of trials funded by donors come and go. All achieved new or better outcomes, but none attracted ongoing funding to enable sustainability. So, it is vital that charities collaborate with a range of partners, including research institutions, governments, peers in the sector and philanthropy, and have a plan to become sustainable upfront.

CHALLENGES TO CHANGE

'It is not the strongest of the species that survive, nor the most intelligent, but the one most responsive to change'

ATTRIBUTED TO CHARLES DARWIN

Those of us working in the health, social and environmental sectors want the same thing - to be able to make a lasting difference to the lives of the people we support or the ecology of our habitats. In reality, we spend our days in the emergency wards of poverty and disadvantage, homelessness, family and domestic violence, mental illness, youth justice, racism and discrimination, gender inequality, disability inclusion, climate change and fractured communities trying to cope with the relentless tide of the daily needs.

The tide is rising. Not because people don't care, but because our systems are built to reward activity, not improvement. We reinvent solutions, govern in short cycles, manage to contractual outputs instead of outcomes, set few meaningful targets, work in disconnected service silos, and seriously underinvest in prevention and early intervention.

If we want different results, we must change how we design, measure and collaborate.

Reinventing the wheel

The interest and energy rose in the Board meeting as the time came to discuss the new initiatives that the foundation was going to fund. The manager excitedly summarised an innovative proposal from a leading charity. The project would go into low-income households and help them reduce their energy usage through draught proofing, insulation, and education. The philanthropically funded trial would be evaluated in the hope that the government would fund a scale-up.

As I rolled my eyes, I explained that I had delivered the same program 15 years before, but with the added outcomes of employing jobless public housing tenants who knew the neighbourhood in a social enterprise that enabled the skill development needed for them to gain jobs.

The Federal and State/Territory political cycles every 3-4 years mean that, at any point in time, we are in either in the midst of a promised policy change, system reform or introduction of new programs, or are due to have this change following a change of government. This means it is very difficult to take a long-term, consistent approach to social and environmental challenges that need to be addressed over many years, even generations.

It is no wonder then that over 8 in 10 Australians agree that politicians generally think too short term when making decisions[61]. The Climate Change Theme of this book gives a great example of the effect of changing political ideologies on the government's policy on committing, or not committing, Australia to a reduction in greenhouse gas emissions and the flawed basis of our reductions.

The result is that we have a patchwork of thousands of projects, programs and services that are incomprehensible, even to those in the sector, let alone to the Australians that need help. Each has different contact periods, funding levels, eligibility criteria, geographical area coverage, service models, contracted outputs and reporting requirements. Notwithstanding that frontline service workers do an amazing job of trying to make sense of this labyrinth to link in other needed local services for the people they support, there is service duplication and gaps.

Each Theme in this book illustrates the government policy and system changes made, for good or bad, and those changes that are desperately needed.

Public servants reduced to contract administrators

Over the years, I've known many skilled, passionate and committed people in the public service. All, over varying periods of time, have become frustrated and disillusioned with the lack of change they are able to achieve, the short political cycles, regular departmental restructuring, long working hours and the lack of recognition. They have left to pursue more fulfilling and successful roles

---

[61]Challenges to change
Susan Harris Rimmer S, Stephenson E and Hawkins T (2024) *Fair Go for All: Intergenerational Justice Policy Survey*, Everygen, Griffith University, Australian National University at https://www.everygen.online/2024/06/11/a-fair-go-for-all/

in academia, think tanks, business and charities, having previously felt that their efforts were going into managing risk and drafting daily briefings for their Ministers.

The result is that few public servants now have any knowledge of the sector they work in and the charities they contract. They are reduced to being administrators who annually monitor contracted activities and outputs. Expert consultants have to be brought in to (re)design programs and services, who could be their former colleagues, which then get competitively (re)tendered out in accordance with the government's procurement policy.

As explained in this book, the social crises our nation faces are interrelated and feed off each other in vicious circles. For instance, poverty fuels family and domestic violence (FDV), which leads to child abuse, mental health issues and homelessness, which, in turn, worsens poverty, and so on.

Whilst the issues are intertwined, the services delivered by charities are not. Because they are funded by service sector-specific government departments – such as education, employment, training, homelessness, child protection, mental health or FDV – charities, as contractors, provide services in their sectors, often with limited or no knowledge of other providers and their services in the same sector, or those in other sectors. As a result, the charities funded by these departments are also operating in these service sector silos.

It doesn't help that the government departments must internally compete for resources and so tend not to collaborate, let alone know what's going on in other departments.

Consequently, the result is short-term contracts with specified outputs in the service silo, such as the number of participants and activities provided. The contractor, understandably, focuses on meeting these targets in order to get paid, uncertain whether the contract will continue and what other programs or services exist in their sector or local area, irrespective of the outcome on the lives of the people receiving the service.

In my experience, when charities realise they can achieve better outcomes by delivering different activities or outputs beyond those stipulated in their contract, the public service discourages any contract alterations due to the additional workload and required approvals.

Because contract services are delivered in isolation from other services and outcomes are not considered in the contract, measured, or evaluated, billions of taxpayer dollars are spent without knowing the ongoing change in the lives of recipients or communities.

As a result, our social and environmental challenges are not improving, despite the periodic government attention and injection of additional funding.

Lack of measures and targets

I was on the Board of a homelessness agency when the incoming Prime Minister, Kevin Rudd, declared homelessness a 'national obscenity' and committed to halve the number of homeless in Australia and accommodate all those sleeping rough by 2020.

Within a week of coming to power, the charity was approached by the Victoria-based cabinet Ministers for a visit to understand the issues. For the first time, we felt that homelessness was getting the high-level political attention it deserved and were excited to see a change.

The subsequent white paper, *The Road Home*, was, and remains, the only national comprehensive plan to tackle homelessness. It pledged $1.2 billion over 4 years to build new housing and increase services for the homeless.

In response, the Leader of the Opposition, Tony Abbott, refused to commit, saying it was unrealistic and couldn't be met. Unfortunately, it turns out that he was right.

15 years later, the National Cabinet agreed to an ambitious new national target to build 1.2 million new well-located homes over five years from July 2024 under the new National Housing Accord[62].

State governments, in turn, have provided targets for local governments to meet their targets focused on higher density in activity areas with public transport to mitigate the high cost of new infrastructure. Under the NSW government's goal of 377,000 new homes under the Accord, councils that meet and beat new housing targets will be given extra cash for sporting facilities, parks, footpaths and road maintenance. A new council league table will compare planning performance between areas[63].

However, analysis by KPMG reported that developers have yet to begin work on almost 40,000 new homes across Australia despite being granted building approvals, due to the higher cost of materials and finance, making it harder for

---

[62] https://treasury.gov.au/policy-topics/housing/accord#:~:text=On%2016%20August%202023%2C%20National,states%20and%20territories%20last%20year.

[63] https://www.theguardian.com/australia-news/article/2024/may/29/nsw-government-housing-targets-councils-extra-funding-grant-program

developers to build larger projects profitably. In contrast, increases in interest rates have limited buyers' purchasing power[64].

Furthermore, the construction industry already faces a shortfall of 80,000 workers[65].

In 2023, the Victorian government released a housing statement that included plans to speed up development approval times, rebuild the ageing social housing towers and unlock land in established suburbs in an effort to build 800,000 new homes over the next decade.

A year later, with the Australian Bureau of Statistics reporting that the number of new home constructions in Victoria had slumped to a decade low, only 55,653 homes were completed in the past twelve months in Victoria, nearly 3,000 less than the previous year[66].

Since Prime Minister Bob Hawke's promise in 1987 that no Australian child would live in poverty, I can understand why governments are reluctant to set measures and targets. They can provide ample ammunition for the opposition and disillusion the electorate. I'm sure the annual Closing the Gap report press conference is not a pleasant experience for the Prime Minister of the day, given the ongoing under-realisation of the goals.

But targets enable political will, transparency, consistency and accountability. And progress.

In 2022, Treasurer Jim Chambers recognised that 'by failing to put values at the forefront of how our economies work, we also leave behind reams of wasted talent, a degraded environment and social dislocation'[67]. Following New Zealand and Canada, his *Measuring what Matters* represents Australia's first national wellbeing agenda by tracking a range of outcomes broader than traditional economic measures under five wellbeing themes:

- *Healthy:* A society in which people feel well and are in good physical and mental health, can access services when they need, and have the information they require to take action to improve their health.

[64] https://kpmg.com/au/en/home/media/press-releases/2024/05/housing-crisis-deepens-as-new-homes-struggle-to-get-out-of-the-g.html

[65] https://www.theguardian.com/australia-news/2025/apr/15/australia-does-not-have-enough-tradies-to-fulfill-labors-housing-promise-experts-say

[66] https://www.abs.gov.au/media-centre/media-releases/dwelling-approvals-decline-june

[67] https://ministers.treasury.gov.au/ministers/jim-chalmers-2022/articles/capitalism-after-crises

- *Secure:* A society where people live peacefully, feel safe, have financial security and access to housing.
- *Sustainable:* A society that sustainably uses natural and financial resources, protects and repairs the environment and builds resilience to combat challenges.
- *Cohesive:* A society that supports connections with family, friends and the community, values diversity, and promotes belonging and culture.
- *Prosperous:* A society that has a dynamic, strong economy, invests in people's skills and education, and provides broad opportunities for employment and well-paid, secure jobs[68].

A list of currently reported measures accompanies these themes. Whilst not perfect, it provides the start of a nationwide focus on societal wellbeing. In 2025, the NSW Government committed to a *Performance and Wellbeing Framework* to monitor its delivery of services and track the overall quality of life of the people of NSW[69].

Inter-connectedness and siloed services

In the chilly hall of the local community centre, I stood in front of representatives from over forty charities and government departments providing services across the gamut of health and social services - primary and allied health, mental health, drug and alcohol, housing, homelessness, family and children, domestic violence and out-of-home care.

A former McKinsey consultant, CEO of Foundation for Young Australians, and chair of Commonwealth Advisory Committee on Homelessness, the new Minister for Mental Health, Women's Affairs and Community Services, Mary Wooldridge, knew much about the State's complex and siloed array of health and human services. She wasted no time in issuing a *Case for Change*[70] to address the complex and interrelated nature of individual and family problems and entrenched disadvantage and established the *Service Sector Reform* project.

---

[68] Australian Government (2023) *Measuring What Matters. Australia's First Wellbeing Framework* at https://treasury.gov.au/sites/default/files/2023-07/measuring-what-matters-statement020230721_0.pdf

[69] NSW Treasury (2025) *NSW Government Response to the Parliamentary Inquiry into Performance and Wellbeing* at https://www.parliament.nsw.gov.au/ladocs/inquiries/3045/NSW%20Government%20Response%20to%20the%20Parliamentary%20Inquiry%20into%20Performance%20and%20Wellbeing.pdf

[70] State of Victoria, Department of Human Services (2011) *Human Services: The Case for Change*, Melbourne

There was much excitement and anticipation in the room packed full of charity CEOs for the first consultation. Like a football supporter at the first game of the season, anticipation, passion and hope overrode the disappointment of past experiences. Called courageous, brave and ambitious, for the first time the government spoke of co-designing a system that would genuinely place people at the centre of a coordinated, sustainable and quality service system.

We were told that, with individual health and human services being provided by contracted agencies to each family member, often without any knowledge of the other, a family could easily accumulate over 50 interventions a week. The resultant revolving door of case workers was costly and confusing, and achieved little sustained change. The growing complexity and interrelatedness of their needs meant that this siloed approach was not working.

For better outcomes for the people we supported, we all wanted to see 'placed-based, people-centred, integrated services'. Indeed, this has been a lifelong aspiration for all sector CEOs that goes to the heart of the right of people to receive appropriate, coordinated and timely services that address their needs.

What gave us hope was that Mary Wooldridge realised that the government, which created the service system, had to fundamentally change and that it needed the cooperation and support of the sector. No Minister had attempted this reform.

Important projects need good branding, and the workshop started with the presentation of the new Services Connect logo and its dramatic change from the traditional conservative blue theme of departmental documents. Now, a more vibrant and urgent bright orange would lead the way. With new Services Connect lanyards and pens at the ready, we eagerly enlisted.

In that community centre, for the first time, we discussed and compared our service offerings. Their various service locations, eligible cohort, entitlement criteria, assessment methods, reporting requirements and referral points. It was a revelation.

In another example of the disruption of political change, Mary's party lost the next election and the project petered out. No attempt to coordinate services with charities and government across health and social services has been made since.

But, a decade later, there is a growing movement of community-based and owned, locally coordinated services to enable specific outcomes, such as in early childhood development, as outlined in the Themes.

Lack of prevention and early intervention

With less than 2 per cent of government spending on the prevention of social and health issues, and services typically only available where the need is acute, it is understandable that charities do what they can to respond to the most urgent need that their resources allow.

The interrelationship between the crises means that a worsening of one or more exacerbates another, and there is a domino effect. For instance, the rise in family and domestic violence fuels homelessness, mental health issues, child abuse and poverty, and weakens social cohesion.

Growing poverty and disadvantage lead to higher rates of family and domestic violence, child abuse, homelessness, mental health issues and lower social cohesion.

Increasing mental health issues generate poverty and disadvantage, homelessness, child abuse and lower social cohesion, which only lead to the escalation of the mental health issues in a vicious cycle.

In this crisis maelstrom, our charities are simply trying to keep up with the urgent day-to-day needs of those most at risk. In the words of the founder of the Brotherhood of St Laurence, Father Tucker, we are rushing ambulances to the bottom of the cliff, rather than building the fence at the top.

Despite every dollar invested in preventive health saving an estimated $14.30 in healthcare and other costs, and health expenditure in Australia being 70 per cent higher per capita than the OECD average, preventive health only accounted for 1.3 per cent of that total compared to an average of 2.8 per cent in OECD countries.

Whether it is preventing recidivism for young people leaving incarceration with in-prison qualifications, intervening earlier in family violence with 'wrap around services' to prevent domestic violence and family breakdown and children going into child protection and homelessness, reneging school leavers to complete their education and enabling a pathway to a job, or better designed neighbourhoods and capacity building for community groups to enable stronger social cohesion for less social isolation and mental health issues, we know that investment in prevention and early intervention realises multiple returns.

But, in Australia, we are spending more to intervene late. For children and young people, the cost of 'late intervention' crisis services until 24 years of age has increased by nearly half in the last 5 years to $22.3 billion. Spending on child protection comprises 43 per cent, followed by youth crime and justice (22 per cent), youth unemployment (11 per cent) and youth homelessness (8 per cent)[71].

As the Grattan Institute points out, 'experience here and around the world shows that when budgets are cut, prevention is often the first on the chopping block. Prevention is less painful to slash than other kinds of healthcare, because the payoff from prevention spending is in the future, when current Treasurers and Ministers will be long gone'[72].

In summary, prevention and early intervention seek to reduce the risk factors and improve the protective factors.

Risk factors are conditions or characteristics that may increase the likelihood of negative outcomes or behaviours among people. These factors can encompass various aspects of a person's life, including individual, family, peer, school, and community influences. Recognising these risk factors allows program designers to target specific areas of vulnerability and tailor interventions accordingly.

For instance, risk factors for young people include socio-economic disadvantage, family dysfunction, education disengagement, community violence, mental health issues, lack of positive role models, substance abuse, discrimination and racism.

Protective factors, on the other hand, are conditions or attributes that buffer people from the negative effects of risk factors and promote resilience and positive development. These factors serve as sources of strength and support, enhancing the ability to cope with adversity and thrive in challenging environments.

Protective factors for young people include supportive relationships, personal resilience, positive school engagement, access to opportunities, cultural identity and pride, community support, healthy peer relationships, mental health access, positive parent practices, and emotional regulation[73].

Prevention and early intervention can shift the distribution curve of the need to the left and so dramatically reduce the number of individuals at the high-risk end of the curve requiring an urgent response.

---

[71] O'Connell M (2025) *The Cost of Late Intervention 2024*, The Front Project, Melbourne

[72] https://grattan.edu.au/news/cuts-to-preventive-health-are-a-false-economy/

[73] https://www.publications.qld.gov.au/ckan-publications-attachments-prod/resources/0a691579-f1ff-467f-944e-b2a93c8dec28/03.-program-design-risk-and-protective-factors.pdf?ETag=7a614e4a8229a3222e1ccfe895c2e02b

OFF TO CHARITYLAND

'Congratulations!
Today is your day.
You're off to Great Places!
You're off and away!'

DR. SEUSS,
OH, THE PLACES YOU'LL GO![74]

Culturally, I've found that governments, businesses and charities are each very different countries (if not continents or planets) – they have their own time zone, language and customs.

The private sector operates on shorter timeframes, commercial terminology, clear metrics and business cycles, the combination of which can be incomprehensible, pushy and threatening to charities and government. The resultant urgency, strict deadlines, legal agreements and contracts can be foreign to the charity partner.

Charities, on the other hand, work on the basis of nurturing relationships, rather than transactional deals. After all, they have many stakeholders to consider – founders, Board, ambassadors, patrons, staff, volunteers, regulators, governments, communities, consumer groups, corporate partners, clients, supporters, (social) media, user groups, commentators, peak bodies, research institutions, education and training organisations, professional bodies and the general public.

---

[74]Off to Charityland
Seuss, D (1990) *Oh, the places you'll go!*, Random House, New York

With charities only able to operate with a social licence from any of these stakeholders, it is no wonder that charities spend a lot more time managing risk when one adverse appearance in the media could lead to the withdrawal of government, corporate, and donor support. Unfortunately, this means that charities can be funder blinkered, rather than spending time and resources on evaluating, measuring and reporting outcomes (not just contractual activities and outputs) to record and report lessons learnt, policy and service system improvements, innovation, pilot projects and advocacy.

Compared to governments and businesses, charities have fewer staff and system resources, which means they will be slower and more cumbersome in their responses, including being able to provide the level of information requested. There may also be an unvoiced subtext of pushing back on the level of involvement and information that the funder requires that the charity feels is not appropriate or challenges their authority.

We also have to remember that charities fiercely compete with each other to win donations, philanthropic funding and government grants, as well as, with the private sector to win tenders for government service contracts. This means that charities feel they must protect their 'intellectual property' in how they deliver services and so are highly circumspect with the information they give out. Sadly, this results in a lack of partnership and collaboration, external evaluation and published research of 'what works'.

Having said all that, virtually everyone I have worked with in the charity sector has been an absolute joy to work with. They are committed, passionate, compassionate and work extremely hard. It's a working culture that business and government would kill for.

So, if you really want to make a difference, pack your bags, take your passport and take a trip to *charityland*. You'll find amazing people, awe-inspiring beliefs, and maybe your life's purpose. Just don't expect good coffee.

Joining a Board

For years, I've had the privilege of presenting at Leadership Victoria's Board Orientation Series for those looking to join a charity Board. I come in after the legal presenter has scared them with jail time and losing their home over the compliance requirements of acting in the best interest of the organisation, worker compensation and insolvency. It's no wonder they had loaded up on the refreshments in the break.

I am there to reveal the reality of sitting on a charity board.

Firstly, I explain that charity boards operate on lengthy discussions that eventually lead to a consensus and decision. Typically, the level of discussion is inversely proportional to the importance of the matter. In my 30 years of reporting to, and sitting on, boards, I've only ever experienced 1 vote when a decision could not be made.

In 1996, the Liberal Government assumed power and abolished a great hands-on training program called *SkillShare*, mainstreaming and tendering out its employment services as the *Job Network* in 1998. With providers only getting paid for getting jobseekers into employment for a minimum period, with the more disadvantaged getting a higher payment to compensate for the non-vocational support needed, this 'payment-by-results' transferred the financial risk from government to the provider.

Although the homelessness charity had run a successful SkillShare program, the CEO declined to tender for the Job Network, arguing that its cohort would only be a small part of the job seekers that the organisation would need to take on. As a manager of the Brotherhood of St Laurence at the time, we had taken the opposite decision. I argued at the Board meeting that SkillShare had shown the efficacy of training and employment services to those who are homeless as the most impactful and long-term intervention the organisation could provide. If the charity provided the Job Network service, then its clients would be assured of a better service and outcomes than a private sector provider. Otherwise, the charity would lose the ability to provide government funded training and employment services.

After some heated discussion around the Board table, it became obvious there wasn't going to be an agreement. The Chair called for a vote. The Board was split 50:50. After some scurrying, someone found the constitution, which gave a casting vote to the Chair. She sided with the CEO.

It was a sliding doors moment, and nobody knows what would have happened otherwise. We do know, however, that the system led to difficult job seekers being 'parked' and offered minimal or no service by some Job Network providers, with the resources saved then invested in those job seekers most likely to generate an outcome payment[75]. As a result, the charity's clients got little or no assistance from the Job Network. Little has changed over the years in succeeding iterations.

---

[75] Thomas M (2007) *A review of developments in the Job Network*, Research Paper 15 2007-8

This means that board meetings can be slow, frustrating and even turgid at times. However, in my experience, there is thorough analysis and transparent decisions are taken.

Secondly, I advised that they should voice their own motivations and get to know the motivations of their fellow board members, as well as what skills and experience they bring. Ideally, the latter is detailed in a skills matrix that shows each board member's competency (eg low, medium, high) under specified skills. It may seem obvious, but many prospective Board members are 'tapped on the shoulder' by a friend to replace outgoing directors without knowing what is required of them. Others may be on the board for status.

Thirdly, I ask them to bring the same enquiry and rigour they have had in their working lives. I've seen charity boards with eminent people from business, academia and government who, once they enter the reception, 'leave their brain at the door'. Maybe the 'doing good' area of the brain overrides their prefrontal cortex as an evolutionary higher-order reflex. In any case, the boardroom becomes a no-go zone for critical enquiry and strategic thinking.

Board members have a sacred duty to carry the torch for the charity as management, staff, governments and supporters come and go. Above all, their responsibility is to ensure the charity lives out its belief and achieves its purpose in the context of an ever-changing external environment. Accordingly, the board's performance should be measured annually on this basis.

Fourth, the interesting work is done in sub-committees of the board or project groups where the managers are present, and, in my view, often a better application of the time and talents of experienced people wanting to make a lasting difference.

Back in the room, in the presentation's Q&A session, I invariably get questions about the Chair of the board being too close to the CEO and not allowing alternative views and discussion or not being able to run an effective meeting. In my experience, being Chair is a very different proposition to being a board member, as a CEO role is from being in the management team.

Most of my charity CEO colleagues would, at some point, have gripes about their board, especially those that seek to problem-solve operational issues at the board or discuss matters outside of board meetings without the knowledge of the CEO. 'Nose in, fingers out' is the role of board members and to hold management to account for resolving issues and delivering outcomes.

There are few recourses if the Chair is not suitable. A confidential independent Board performance review can report the concerns of board members for discussion at the meeting.

Unfortunately, there is no legal requirement for the Chair, or any board member, to be suitably qualified.

The Corporations Act and the ACNC Governance Standard 5 simply requires charities to ensure their board members are aware of their duties and comply with them, including acting with reasonable care and diligence, acting honestly and fairly in the best interests of the charity and for its charitable purposes, not misusing their position or information for gain, disclosing actual or potential conflicts of interest, ensuring that the financial affairs of the charity are managed responsibly, and not allowing the charity to operate while it is insolvent[76].

With 24 per cent of directors, and rising, now receiving payment[77], my view is that at least the Chairs of charity boards should be paid. They can donate their fee back to the charity if they wish, but I believe that it enables a higher level of accountability. The Chair should also have completed an appropriate company directors course, such as with the Australian Institute of Company Directors.

---

[76] https://www.acnc.gov.au/tools/factsheets/responsible-people-board-or-committee-members

[77] Australian Institute of Company Directors & commonwealth Bank (2025) *Not-for-Profit Governance & Performance Study 2024-25* p.13 at https://www.aicd.com.au/content/dam/aicd/pdf/news-media/research/2025/nfp-governance-performance-study-2024-25-web.pdf

WAYS TO MAKE AN IMPACT

'If I don't move on this now, then nothing will ever move me'

MICHAEL 'WIPPA' WIPFLI[78]

Donate money

Cash is king to charities. Gifts, bequests, workplace, and regular giving by credit card are the most cost-effective forms of raising funds. Given the cost of regulation, organisation and logistics, public events are the most costly.

Despite workplace giving being an easy way to donate pre-tax through payroll, and 85 per cent wanting it, only 2 per cent of employers offer it. The average participation rate for organisations with an effective and active employee giving program is 25 per cent, but for those employers who do not have a corresponding staff engagement program, the participation rate is less than four per cent.

Those annoying international students accosting you in the street or shopping centre with thick Celtic accents are called 'charity muggers' or 'chuggers', 80 per cent of whom are employed by outsourced companies and made famous by actor Samuel Johnson calling them 'snakes, slugs, and dogs'. The charity's self-regulation body, Public Fundraising Regulatory Association, reported in 2018 that chuggers raised over $120 million and signed more than 320,000 donors. However, charities won't see at least the first year's donations and about half of the donors cancel their payment plans within the first year.

---

[78] *Change Makers: Michael 'Wippa' Wipfli on how he convinced Australia to change its social media laws,* Radio National Breakfast, 30 January 2025 at https://www.abc.net.au/listen/programs/radionational-breakfast/michael-wipfli-convincing-australia-to-change-social-media-laws/104875828

For donors looking for a long-term commitment, community foundations offer the establishment and administration of Donor Advised Funds (DAFs) for as little as $2,000, which allow donors to set up an investment account, receive an immediate tax deduction and make charitable donations from the fund over time.

For larger amounts, Private Ancillary Funds (PAFs) are a type of charitable trust designed to provide individuals, families or associations with an investment structure for philanthropic purposes.

For charities, donations are treated as 'tied' to one or more deliverables agreed with the donor, or 'untied', which can be used for any expenditure. Tied donations must be documented in writing, ideally in an agreement, to satisfy accounting and audit requirements and are kept as a liability in the balance sheet until the related expenditure is made and the corresponding income recognised.

If the charity is a Gift Deductible Recipient (DGR), it will issue a receipt as evidence of the donation as a deduction in your annual tax return. Australian tax law requires the donation to have been paid on or before 30 June to be included in that financial year.

Campaign

Petitioning the Parliament is a long-established fundamental right of any citizen. It is the only direct means by which an individual or group can ask the Parliament to take action—all other processes involve communicating through a parliamentary representative (Member or Senator) or a parliamentary committee.

Around 300 petitions are submitted annually. Since the recording of signatures began in 1988, the petition with the greatest number of signatures was presented on 26 February 2014 concerning funding support for community pharmacies, with 1,210,471 signatures. The second largest was presented on 4 December 2000 concerning taxation and beer prices, with 792,985 signatures[79].

Politicians will only act if they see a significant proportion of their electorate feels the issue is important, so show your commitment to a cause by signing up to a campaign.

---

79 https://www.aph.gov.au/About_Parliament/House_of_Representatives/Powers_practice_and_procedure/00_-_Infosheets/Infosheet_11_-_Petitions

Participate

The cheap and relatively pure heroin that flooded the streets of Australia's capitals in the 1990s caused many deaths and led Premier Jeff Kennett to implement the recommendations of David Penington's 1997 *Turning the Tide* report[80], including Australia's first specialist youth drug and alcohol service, the Youth Substance Abuse Service. Thirteen years later, I went to work for YSAS.

Despite Bob Hawke breaking down in tears on camera about his daughter, Rosslyn's, heroin addiction, youth drug and alcohol misuse is not typically the subject of nice conversation around the BBQ or dinner table. When the common public perception of young people choosing to abuse drugs, how could YSAS publicly advocate and fundraise for this cohort?

Enter one Fiona Healy. At a barbecue with friends in late 2006, Fiona came up with a plan to atone for the silly season. The idea was to give up alcohol for the year's shortest month and donate funds raised from the challenge to combat youth alcohol and substance abuse. Fiona and a friend raised $910 at the first *febfast* in February 2007[81].

Fiona was camped in an office at the back of YSAS trying to run febfast on her own. We both saw the potential of investing in marketing, technology and partnerships to grow the campaign. Former marketing manager at Lonely Planet, Howard Ralley, came on board and febfast grew into one of Australia's top ten campaigns, engaging thousands of Australians in awareness and raising over $1 million annually.

With the success of challenge fundraising events, such as the World's Greatest Shave, CEO Sleepout, Push Up Challenge, Movember, Steptember and the Big Freeze, every charity is trying to come up with the next experiential event that engages new and existing supporters to get involved in their cause. This quest for this Holy Grail of fundraising has led to some really innovative month-themed campaigns, such as Veganuary, Red Feb, februDAREy, March Charge, Mindful in May, JulEYE, Dogtober and Decembeard (cleverly following on from Movember)[82].

---

80 Parliament of Victoria, Drugs and Crime Prevention /committee (1997) *Inquiry into the Victorian Government's Drug Reform Strategy. Interim Report*, December 1997 accessed at https://www.parliament.vic.gov.au/images/stories/committees/dcpc/Crime_trends/Interim_Report_Victorian_Govts_Drug_Reform_Strategy_1997.pdf

81 https://www.fpmagazine.com.au/how-sms-is-supporting-febfasters-340395/

82 https://www.ourcommunity.com.au/calendar/calendar_main.jsp

You will be pleased to know that colours are not left out with Big Red BBQ, Purple Day, Wear Green for Premmies, March into Yellow, Go Blue for Autism, White Shirt Day, Teal Ribbon Day, Wear White at Work, White Wreath Day, Red Apple Day, White Ribbon Night, Red Nose Day, Gold Bow Day, White Balloon Day, Pink Ribbon Day, Bright Pink Lipstick Day and Orange Day, not to mention a myriad of designated days throughout the year, including National Condom Day on Valentine's Day.

And for those of you wondering whether Global Wind Day in June recognises chronic digestive disorders that cause excessive flatulence, it actually celebrates renewable wind power.

Just in case anyone feels left out, there is International Charity Day on 5 September, or should that be 5 Liptember?

Employ

There is no better impact you can make than employing a person who otherwise would not have the opportunity to get a job because of their circumstances.

The Commonwealth Employment Services (CES) has had a number of rebrands over the years as Job Network, Job Active and is now called Workforce Australia. The current $1.3 billion a year employment service is contracted out to local charity and commercial providers which can be found at www.workforceaustralia.gov.au. The providers will liaise with your employer to offer suitable candidates for interview. Providers receive a star rating of their performance from the government which can be accessed at the DEWR website.

Applicable specialist employment services are also detailed in the Themes.

Buy

You can easily swap some of your current suppliers with those that offer a comparable product and price, but enable their profits to fund social and environmental outcomes. So-called 'social procurement' has the potential to create a more inclusive and equitable society, and best of all, it doesn't require additional cost. It is for this reason that social procurement continues to gain momentum across Australia as a mechanism to leverage social value from your existing spend.

Indigenous people make up around 3 per cent of the population but only own around 0.06 per cent of Australia's businesses. Becoming a member of *Supply Nation* enables you to purchase from certified Indigenous businesses across Australia. For every dollar you spend, these suppliers generate $4.41 of social return, including employing more Indigenous people. Since 2009, *Supply*

Nation has facilitated more than $20 billion in procurement spend between members and Indigenous businesses[83].

If 'give a person a fish and they'll eat for a day. Teach a person to fish and they'll eat for a lifetime', then social enterprise is the fish canning factory to scale up the impact, employ the community and enable long-term financial sustainability.

There are over 12,000 social enterprises contributing $21.3 billion to the Australian economy, accounting for 1 per cent of our Gross Domestic Product and employing over 200,000 Australians - as many people as the mining industry[84]. *Social Traders* certifies social enterprises and has a directory on their website[85]. Over the last 7 years, over $1 billion has been spent with certified social enterprises[86].

I know what you are thinking. It's going to cost me more, with more hassle and I'm going to have to put up with poor quality. I can't complain because they are trying to do good and then I'll feel guilty when I switch back to my usual supplier.

Admittedly, the Salvo's first café 20 years ago called *Burnt Toast* didn't instil confidence, but now social enterprises will give you the best coffee, catering, bicycles, stationery, marketing, videos, job candidates, systems design and installation, packaging, clothing, gifts, printing, architecture, furniture and furnishings, horticulture & arboriculture, repairs and maintenance, building products and materials, cleaning, financial services, IT, legal, venue hire, waste management, travel, merchandise, healthcare, training and education.

If you already buy your toilet rolls from *Who Gives a Crap* or soap from *Thankyou*, you will know that you don't need to compromise on quality or price, whilst the profits go to improving water and sanitation in developing countries, rather than to shareholders.

---

[83] Supply Nation (2025) *The Sleeping Giant Rises. Understanding the social value created by Indigenous businesses and its contribution to Closing the Gap* at https://supplynation.org.au/uploads/Supply-Nation-2025-The-Sleeping-Giant-Rises-report.pdf

[84] Social Enterprise Australia (2022) *Business for good: The size and economic contribution of social enterprise in Australia*

[85] https://www.socialtraders.com.au/find-a-social-enterprise

[86]Ways to make an impact
Social Traders (2025) *Impact Report Financial Year 2024*, p.4 at https://assets.socialtraders.com.au/downloads/Social-Traders-Impact-Report-FY24.pdf#asset:220024@1

Volunteer

Whether it is the cake stall at the school fete, registering runners at the park run, serving drinks at the footy club bar, selling Christmas trees at the scout hall, or coaching the under-10s, our communities simply wouldn't function without local volunteers.

Formal volunteering that involves an ongoing commitment is in decline in Australia, but it could be your most rewarding life experience by working with a group of talented and passionate colleagues and seeing the difference you can make over a period of time.

GoVolunteer and *SEEK Volunteers* (both administered by SEEK) are the largest platforms with over 10,000 volunteering opportunities across the country.

As the world's first (and best) organisation for volunteering for international development, AVI has over 70 years of experience in selecting, placing and supporting skilled Australians in government, businesses and charities in developing countries. Volunteers use their skills and experience to build capacity in these organisations. The cost of training, travel, insurance, local living and accommodation allowances is funded by the Australian Government[87].

Mentoring can be particularly rewarding, with the opportunity to directly improve someone's life. Charities that specialise in mentoring are Big Brothers Big Sisters[88], Raise[89], AMES[90], She Codes[91] and the ABCN[92].

Galvanise your workplace

With time and relationships, our workplace provides a fantastic opportunity to raise awareness, take action and effect change at personal and organisational levels. All the Themes outline ways in which you can engage your colleagues and influence organisational policies and practices for a wider impact.

Come over to the light side

How many of our brilliant minds are wasted on jobs that do not make our world a better place? Psychologists on more addictive social media algorithms; nutritionists on designing the next chocolate bar; lawyers fighting over the shade of colour in company logos; financial wizards on new collateralised debt

---

87 https://www.avi.org.au/

88 https://bigbrothersbigsisters.org.au/

89 https://www.raise.org.au/volunteers/volunteer-roles-and-projects/

90 https://www.ames.net.au/volunteering/volunteer-mentors

91 https://shecodes.com.au/mentor/

92 https://abcn.com.au/mentors-companies/

obligation derivatives; tax experts on offshore minimisation – when they could be working on building capacity in charities and leading better mental health practice, health food education in schools, tenancy legal rights for evicted families, connecting community members to improve social cohesion, wealth equality and tax reform.

If you are one of the nearly half of the workforce in sales, marketing, banking and PR who believe your job is pointless[93], I can guarantee you will never feel that way in a charity.

If you are unfulfilled from generating profits for others (as I was), use your skills to generate income that is used to change lives.

If you are not convinced that your life's priority in our capitalistic society is to generate wealth, then you can still live a comfortable life on a charity's salary.

If you are searching for meaning in your life, then become a life-long fighter for social, animal or environmental justice.

You can start with volunteering for a charity and experience the life changing impact of its services.

Unless you are a Buddhist, you've only got one life on Earth. A short time on this planet to leave a mark. In two generations, you'll be well and truly forgotten.

So, it's time to use your time and talents for good. Take a leap and go to work for a charity. Ethical Jobs[94] is a good place to start.

Or start your own charity.

Invest

With the purple bear staring down at me, I had been told to drop everything and head out to a distant ABC Learning childcare centre, one of the 260 that were considered unviable. I soon came to learn that the childcare industry is a numbers game.

Established in 1988 with only 18 centres, ABC Learning expanded to operate over 1,000 centres nationwide and provide more than 1/5th of all long day care places. Their share price increased more than 300 per cent in the 5 years since

---

[93] Dur & van Lent M (2019) *Socially Useless Jobs*, Industrial Relations: A Journal of Economy and Society: Volume 58, Issue 1 https://doi.org/10.1111/irel.12227

[94] https://www.ethicaljobs.com.au/

the company first floated on the Australian Stock Exchange in 2001 to a market capitalisation of $2.6 billion.

The corporatisation of childcare centres and the profit margin generated were controversial. An Australia Institute staff survey found that only 29 per cent of respondents from ABC Learning centres said they always have enough time to develop individual relationships with the children they care for, compared with 54 per cent of community-based centre staff, due to poorer staff ratios. Only 55 per cent of ABC Learning centre respondents said enough food was always provided for children, compared with 80 per cent of staff at community-based centres[95].

From 2005, the company started aggressively acquiring other childcare operators in the UK and US, accumulating $1.8 billion in loans. Unable to service its debt in the midst of the global financial crisis, the business went into administration and the receivers were selling off the centres in 2 tranches – 720 considered financially viable and 260 unviable.

Enter the formidable former co-founder and Executive Director of Macquarie Group's private equity arm, Michael Traill AM, who had jumped ship to become the founding CEO of Social Ventures Australia and become the father of impact investing in this country.

Late one Sunday night, Michael received a call from Evan Thornley, the ex-McKinsey creator of search engine LookSmart, MP and social entrepreneur. Evan talked about the opportunity to buy out the collapsed ABC Learning centres to provide quality early learning given that research at his thinktank, Per Capita, had shown that 'the absolute pivot point of social opportunity is very young children, 0 to 5. Help kids from tough circumstances early and you can change their lives'[96].

Michael co-opted 2 charity leaders he trusted - former investment banker and my boss, Toby Hall, CEO of Mission Australia and Richard Spencer, CEO of The Benevolent Society.

A year later, the Goodstart consortium of Social Ventures Australia, the Benevolent Society, the Brotherhood of St Laurence and Mission Australia was announced as the preferred bidder for its offer of $95 million for 678 centres.

---

[95] Rush E & Downie C (2006) *ABC Learning Centres A case study of Australia's largest child care corporation*, The Australia Institute, Discussion Paper Number 87 June 2006 ISSN 1322-5421 at https://australiainstitute.org.au/wp-content/uploads/2020/12/DP87_8.pdf

[96] Traill M (2016) *Jumping Ship*, P.151

As part of the financing, 41 individuals and foundations lent $22.5 million, the highest impact investment in Australia.

Then Australia's largest social enterprise, 2 objectives expressed Goodstart's mission: to provide high-quality, accessible, affordable, community-connected early learning in its centres; and to partner and openly collaborate with the sector to drive change for the benefit of all children[97].

Impact investments are investments made into organisations, projects or funds with the intention of generating measurable social and environmental outcomes, alongside a financial return[98].

Now worth over $1 trillion globally, impact investments unlock capital to address the world's most pressing challenges in sectors such as sustainable agriculture, renewable energy, conservation, microfinance, and affordable and accessible basic services, including housing, healthcare, and education.

In Australia, examples of impact investments are:

Humanitix - the first not-for-profit ticketing platform that directs 100 per cent of profits, currently over $10 million, from booking fees to education projects that help children experiencing poverty, disadvantage, or disability[99].

Hireup - an online platform that enables disabled people and their families to find, hire and manage support workers by harnessing technology and connecting people with shared interests. Hireup has empowered over 460,000 disabled Australians by providing genuine choice and control over their support[100].

Xceptional harnesses the strengths of autistic people to fill skills gaps in areas including data analytics to cyber security[101]. Similarly, *Australian Spatial Analytics* is a work-integrated, not-for-profit social enterprise providing professional data services and geospatial and digital engineering careers for young neurodivergent adults[102].

Maths Pathway supports teachers to have a greater impact in the classroom through a learning and teaching model that delivers truly engaging and personalised learning for each student. Data from more than 6 years of student

---

97 https://www.socialventures.org.au/our-impact/goodstart-a-story-of-impact-investing/

98 https://impactinvestingaustralia.com/new-to-impact-investing/

99 https://humanitix.com/au

100 https://hireup.com.au/

101 https://xceptionalacademy.org.au/

102 https://www.asanalytics.com.au/

usage shows a consistent 2-3 fold increase in the rate of student learning in mathematics across all socioeconomic sectors[103].

Impact Investing Australia is a charity dedicated to accelerating the growth of impact investing in Australia. Michael Traill AM has established charity *For Purpose Investment Partners* as a social impact investment fund manager, bringing private sector capital and capabilities into sizeable businesses and projects to create significant social impact[104].

Social Impact Bonds

As a type of impact investment (but not actually a bond), a social impact bond is a financial instrument or contractual arrangement that pays a return based on the achievement of agreed social outcomes. Private investors provide upfront capital to fund service delivery or to improve a particular social outcome. Achievement of this outcome should reduce the need for, and therefore government spending on, acute services. Part of the resulting public sector savings is then used to repay investors' principal investment and provide a financial return. The repayment of the principal and the level of return are dependent on the level of specified outcomes delivered.

SIBs are applicable for government services that are high-cost and ongoing, especially long-term residential costs, such as keeping recidivist young people in prison and accommodating children in residential out-of-home care.

Social impact bonds help to shift the role of government from paying for inputs into social services to paying for outcomes, encouraging innovation, and directing resources to early intervention rather than more expensive acute responses.

Uniting's *Newpin* (New Parent and Infant Network) program provides opportunities for parents to therapeutically address their personal and family issues and help their children transition out of care and into a positive, parental environment. The *Newpin Social Benefit Bond* in NSW was Australia's first SIB, maturing in 2020. Over 7 years, 61 per cent of children were restored, almost 3 times the counterfactual. However, replication of the model in Queensland was less successful, and the bond was terminated early[105]. The Newpin SIB in South Australia has promising early results with almost 3/4 of

---

103 https://mathspathway.com/

104 https://www.fpinvest.com.au/

105 https://www.socialventures.org.au/our-impact/a-guide-to-outcomes-contracting-and-social-impact-bonds/#:~:text=The%20Newpin%20Social%20Benefit%20Bond%20in%20NSW%20was%20Australia's%20first,and%20the%20bond%20terminated%20early.

children who reached their assessment point having been reunified with their families, compared to just 22 per cent assumed to be reunified in the absence of the program[106].

As Australia's first homelessness-focused SIB, the *Aspire SIB* funded the delivery of the Aspire Program in Adelaide by the Hutt St Centre, a specialist homelessness service provider, in partnership with public and community housing providers. Based on the 'housing first' intervention model, the program focuses on strengthening community engagement and economic participation. Participants are provided assistance in securing stable accommodation, job readiness, training, employment, and life skills development. Importantly, they also have the long-term support of a dedicated 'Navigator' to help them connect with wider support services and identify and achieve their aspirations.

Over the term of the SIB funding arrangement, the Aspire Program supported 575 people experiencing chronic homelessness in metropolitan Adelaide. The Program housed 81 per cent of participants, with 85 per cent maintaining their tenancies. Critically, participants experienced a significant reduction in the rates at which they accessed hospital, justice and emergency accommodation services, in comparison to the baselines against which program results are measured – by 29 per cent, 33 per cent and 73 per cent, respectively. These Outcomes were all above the Outperform scenario and, as a result, the Aspire SIB has delivered a financial return to investors of 14.1 per cent per annum[107].

Collective giving

Gaining popularity, a giving circle brings a group of people with shared values and interests together to discuss and decide where to make gifts collectively. Giving circles set a minimum amount, for instance $1,000, and the money is pooled before being distributed through a collective consensus. As well as leveraging individual donations, giving circles build belonging, awareness and engagement, including volunteering and joining boards. Individuals multiply their impact and knowledge, have fun, and connect with their cause and community.

With only 31 per cent of corporate givers and 40 per cent of philanthropic givers considering gender in their philanthropy, charity *Australians Investing In*

[106] Social Ventures Australia (2024) *Newpin SA Social Impact Bond*, Annual Investor Report, Period ending 31 December 2023, Issued April 2024 at https://www.socialventures.org.au/wp-content/uploads/2024/07/Newpin-SA-SIB-Annual-Investor-Report-2024.pdf

[107] Social Ventures Australia (2025) *Aspire Social Impact Bond*, Annual Investor Report Period ending 30 June 2024 at https://www.socialventures.org.au/wp-content/uploads/2024/12/SVA-Aspire-SIB-Annual-Report-2024.pdf

Women has been established to provide resources and advocacy to improve gender-wise philanthropy[108].

There are also a growing number of women's collective giving groups, such as *She Gives*[109], *100 Women*[110] and the *Women's Environmental Leadership Australia Giving Circle*[111].

Most larger charities now have their own giving groups as an additional way to raise funds.

Private Ancillary Funds (PAFs) and Public Ancillary Funds (PuAFs)

Philanthropic Trusts or Ancillary Funds have existed in Australia for over a 100 years and were traditionally exempt from income tax. Following a 1999 report by the *Business and Community Partnerships Working Group on Taxation Reform* about how to foster philanthropy in Australia, a new form of philanthropic structure was introduced by the Howard Government in 2001. The Prescribed Private Fund (PPF) was described by the Prime Minister as a philanthropic structure that 'allowed families and individuals to donate to a trust of their own, which then disburses funds to a range of other gift-deductible recipients'. Importantly, PPFs allowed tax deductions for donations, were exempt from ongoing income tax, permitted family control and had no public fundraising requirements.

Now called Private Ancillary Funds (PAFs), they require: corporate trustees (not individuals); a 6 per annum minimum distribution of the market value of the net assets (as at the end of the previous financial year); a formal investment strategy; annual auditing; and compliance obligations.

As well as creating a giving mechanism for life that allows the family to be involved, the main benefit of a PAF is to park the net proceeds of the sale of a business or asset so that it is not subjected to capital gains tax. As the PAF must be private in nature, there must be a close relationship between those who establish the fund and those who donate to it[112].

---

108 Deloitte Access Economics (2024) *Remaking the norm. In collaboration with Australians Investing In Women and Minderoo Foundation,* https://www.deloitte.com/content/dam/assets-zone1/au/en/docs/services/economics/au-dae-remaking-the-norm-2024.pdf

109 https://shegives.com.au/

110 https://100women.org.au/

111 https://wela.org.au/giving-circle/

112 Australian Tax Office, *Private Ancillary Fund Guidelines 2009* accessed at https://www.legislation.gov.au/Details/F2016C00435

Since 2001, most individual and family foundations established in the last 20 years have been PAFs. With over 2,000 now in existence in Australia and growing at an annual rate of 8 per cent, PAFs now distribute $500+ million a year to charities.

There are also over 1,000 Public Ancillary Funds (PuAFs) that can receive donations from the public, including some community foundations. PuAFs must also distribute at least 6 per cent of the market value of their net assets (as at the end of the previous financial year).

The wealth management companies offer the creation and management of PAFs as part of their philanthropic services. Alternatively, the *Australian Communities Foundation* can assist[113].

Donor Advised Funds (DAFs)

Don't have the million dollars needed to set up your own foundation? For as little as $2,000 you can establish your own account under a large existing fund that is responsible (as the trustee) for investing the money, compliance and administration for a fee. You receive the tax deduction upfront and are advised annually on how much of the fund (with the investment interest) you would like to donate (subject to minimum level requirements) to which tax-deductible charities, or, alternatively, leave standing instructions. You can add to the fund anytime as a tax-deductible donation.

DAFs, also called 'named funds', 'sub-funds' or 'charitable fund accounts', are great for community groups or families to accumulate their gift-giving, be engaged in the cause and provide the opportunity for intergenerational giving.

The *Australian Communities Foundation*[114] and the *Lord Mayor's Charitable Foundation*[115] offer DAFs starting at $2,000. Sub-funds under *Perpetual Trustees* and *Equity Trustees*[116] require at least $5,000. The minimum amount for the *Victorian Women's Trust* and *Sydney Women's Fund* is $20,000.

Crowdfunding

With the advent of the internet, global platforms such as *KickStarter* and *Indegogo* have enabled large numbers of people to fund thousands of projects

---

113 https://www.communityfoundation.org.au/giving/structured-giving/individuals-families/foundations

114 https://www.communityfoundation.org.au/giving/structured-giving/individuals-families/funds

115 https://www.lmcf.org.au/ways-to-give/give-to-the-foundation/charitable-funds

116 https://www.eqt.com.au/mediacentre/2025/05/26/new-campaign-launched-to-redefine-giving

and ventures. Over the last 10 years, Australian platform *chuffed.org* has raised funds for a new home for Edgar's Mission; saved the Sawtel movie house in NSW; created television adverts for marriage equality during the plebiscite; put #KidsOffNauru on the Sydney Opera House; facilitated cultural burning and land management projects with Firesticks Alliance Indigenous Corporation; enabled the Dja Dja Warrung to get back their land; and the Biloela family to stay in Australia.

Australian-based platforms, *StartSomeGood*[117], *GoFundMe*[118] and *Pozible*[119] also provide a crowdfunding service for social and environmental projects and causes with no platform fees (although payment fees apply).

Cause related marketing

In 1984, American Express introduced mass market cause-related marketing to the world - the promotion of a company's product or service to raise money for a cause - by donating 1 cent to the restoration of the Statue of Liberty every time someone used its charge card[120].

As well as cents donated per product or service purchased, Australians can make a donation or round up at the checkout, buy on a particular day when the company donates its profits to a cause, buy a sticker that gets stuck on the shop window, or buy a product so the company can donate the same product to those in need.

This can be powerful where the charity's cause fits with the corporate's brand and customer base, leading to increased product sales for the company and new or reactivated supporters for the charity.

A great fit was for *R U OK* day on 10 September 2020, when Nestlé launched its special KitKat bars to encourage its customers to 'take the time to have a break and check in with someone, can have more of an impact than you might think'.

With 57 per cent of consumers' purchasing decisions being belief-based, Foodbank's partnerships include Subway Australia's biggest event of the year,

---

[117] https://startsomegood.com/crowdfunding/

[118] https://www.gofundme.com/en-au

[119] https://www.pozible.com/

[120] Rozensher S (2013) *The Growth Of Cause Marketing: Past, Current, And Future Trends,* Journal of Business & Economics Research,related April 2013 Volume 11, Number 4

the Subway Live Feed, which donates fifty cents for each sub purchased on World Sandwich Day in November[121].

At no cost to the charity, this is a great way to raise funds and profile, notwithstanding the reputation risk of aligning themselves with the company. In 2017, South Australian brewery, Coopers, created a batch of 10,000 cartons of its light beer cans to commemorate the Bible Society's 200th year with the evangelical Christian organisation's logo and by-line 'Live light: Happy 200th birthday to Australia's longest-living charity, from Australia's longest-living family brewery. Bible Society 1817–2017'.

The subsequent release of a video posted on Facebook by the Bible Society featured Liberal MPs Tim Wilson and Andrew Hastie sipping Coopers Premium Light and having a 'light discussion on a heavy topic', Tim made the case for same sex marriage and Andrew defended traditional marriage, whilst the host thanked the Coopers family. The campaign website said the men were able to enjoy the debate because there was 'both a Bible and good beer on the table'.

Within minutes, all hell broke loose with a massive social media backlash accusing Coopers of sponsoring a religious organisation to make an explicitly political point. *#boycottcoopers* drinkers vowed never to drink the brand again, posting videos throwing Coopers beer bottles in the bin, and pubs around the country turned off their Coopers taps.

2 company press releases later failed to halt the controversy until Coopers Brewery directors Melanie Cooper and Dr Tim Cooper posted a video apologising and giving their support for marriage equality.

In the US, Blake Mycoskie founded the company TOMS in 2006 after a visit to Argentina, where he met children who were so poor that they had no shoes. Inspired to help, Mycoskie designed a shoe after the common Argentinian alpargata, and pledged that for each pair sold, TOMS would donate a pair.

Following TOMS shoes, the *buy one, give one* campaigns have had mixed success in Australia. Following US company Warby Parker's 'Buy a Pair, Give a Pair' program that has distributed 15 million pairs of glasses to developing countries[122], eyewear retailer Oscar Wylee was fined $3.5 million for

---

[121] https://www.foodbank.org.au/support-us/partner-with-us/cause-related-marketing/subway-live-feed/?state=au

[122] https://www.warbyparker.com/buy-a-pair-give-a-pair

advertising that for each pair of glasses a consumer purchased, it donated another pair of glasses to someone in need, when it did not do so[123].

The latest campaign is Red Tractor's donation of a bag of oats to Foodbank for every bag purchased at ALDI Australia[124].

Donate used goods

I remember with much affection (and trepidation) the volunteer ladies who ran the Brotherhood's 17 opportunity shops. They were a force to be reckoned with. The most profitable shops subsisted on donations dropped off at the shop, rather than relying on donations through the 700 bins across the state, which could yield as low as 5 per cent of suitable quality for the shops. When you had to drop off the clothes and look the ladies in the eye, you weren't going to give them rubbish to sell.

Opportunity shops are profitable businesses for charities that provide essential untied funding, with the Salvos alone operating 365 stores nationally, supported by 10,000 staff and volunteers.

So, please go into your local op shop with your donations. It saves the charity the cost of transport and sorting.

Donate products and services

Donations of trading stock are tax deductible to a charity that is a Deductible Gift Recipient (DGR). *Good360 Australia*[125] and *GIVIT*[126] provide an online marketplace for businesses to donate spare and excess goods and for charities to request them. You can buy and donate new products to charities, such as women's hygiene products to *Share the Dignity*[127] or new clothes and groceries to *Women's Community Shelters*[128].

Donate property

Property purchased and donated within 12 months to a DGR charity can be claimed as a tax deduction as the lesser of the market value of the property on

---

123 https://www.accc.gov.au/media-release/oscar-wylee-penalised-35m-for-buy-a-pair-give-a-pair-charity-claims#:~:text=Eyewear%20retailer%20Oscar%20Wylee%20has,breach%20of%20Australian%20Consumer%20Law.

124 https://www.redtractorfoods.com.au/farm-partnerships/buy-one-give-one-with-red-tractor-foodbank-aldi-australia#:~:text=For%20every%20bag%20of%201.6,the%20next%20two%20weeks%20alone.

125 https://good360.org.au/give-the-goods/

126 https://www.givit.org.au/

127 https://www.sharethedignity.org.au/

128 https://www.womenscommunityshelters.org.au/get-involved/donations-of-goods/

the day the gift is donated or the amount you paid for the property. Property purchased, won or inherited valued at over $5,000 can be donated at any time for a tax deduction.

Property can be physical things, such as land and objects, and rights and interests that can be owned and have a value, such as shares and ownership rights[129].

Under the Cultural Gifts Program, a culturally significant item donated to a public art gallery, museum or library may be entitled to a tax deduction for the market value of the gift[130].

Just Knit It

At the time, it was known as the 2nd worst place on the planet, next to Darfur in Western Sudan. I was standing in a field with 2,000 new refugees on the outskirts of Goma, eastern Democratic Republic of Congo, who had fled killing and rape in their villages in the previous two weeks. I was there designing a relief program and had brought baby blankets knitted by kindly aunts and grandmothers 13,000 kilometres away to give some comfort and warmth for the destitute children.

3 months before, I was sitting with the knitters as they packed out ABC's Ultimo studio. There were devotees of *Wrap With Love*, a network of thousands of volunteers, who knit, crochet and weave in knitting groups or at home to make 25cmx25cm squares and send them onto sewers to make them into multicoloured wraps. Since 1992, over 25,000 volunteers have spent 77 million hours making over half a million wraps for people in over 75 countries[131].

Following a particularly cold winter in Melbourne in 2004 and the sudden resurgence in the popularity of knitting scarves, Ros Rogers OAM had the idea of getting her friends and family to direct their knitting energy towards charity, resulting in 180 scarves being knitted and distributed by the Emerald Hill Mission to those experiencing homelessness. The following year Ros officially launched *Knit One Give One* which now has 20,000 knitters distributing over 100,000 knitted items to 400 charities[132].

---

[129] https://www.ato.gov.au/businesses-and-organisations/not-for-profit-organisations/gifts-and-fundraising/tax-deductible-donations/gift-types-requirements-and-valuation-rules/donating-recently-purchased-property-to-a-dgr

[130] https://www.ato.gov.au/businesses-and-organisations/not-for-profit-organisations/gifts-and-fundraising/tax-deductible-donations/gift-types-requirements-and-valuation-rules/donating-under-the-cultural-gifts-program

[131] https://www.wrapwithlove.org/about-wrap-with-love/

[132] https://www.kogo.org.au/

Other charities taking knitted items are *Knit4Charities*[133] and the *Australia Red Cross*, which has 600 volunteer knitters and knitting groups that hand knit 50,000 Trauma Teddies a year for children[134].

Donate care

As of 30 June 2025, over 43,000 children were living in out-of-home care in Australia, having been extracted from their families for their safety.

Out-of-home care is a temporary, medium or long-term living arrangement for children and young people who are deemed to be at risk of violence, neglect or abuse in their family environments. Foster care is an integral part of out-of-home care, but Australia is experiencing a shortage of foster carers with the number of carers declining 20 per cent over the last decade and the demand for help increasing. This means that more children have to be placed in residential care and temporary housing.

Foster carers create a safe and supportive home for a child while their parents and families get back on their feet for short-term (overnight to 6 months), long-term, respite (1 or 2 weekends a month or for a week during school holidays) or emergency care (immediate care due to concerns for their safety, usually at night). They are part of the child or young person's care team, which includes the foster care agency and the child's birth family. Foster carers can be any gender, singles or couples, parents or with no parenting experience, working or retired, renting or owning their home and from any cultural or religious background[135].

It takes 6-9 months to be vetted and trained to become accredited to provide care for children and young people. *Fostering Connections* will help you locate your local charity providers[136].

Donate yourself

The Australian Red Cross Blood Service, now called Lifeblood, is an amazing success story. The invention of refrigeration in the 1930s meant that the need to collect blood on demand during an operation was replaced by a blood bank, which led to supplying blood to the Defence Forces during World War II. The subsequent discovery of the extraction of plasma in the 1940s led to thousands of litres of blood, as serum and dried plasma, being used by injured troops overseas.

---

[133] https://www.knit4charities.org.au/

[134] https://www.redcross.org.au/teddy/

[135] https://fosteringconnections.com.au/whats-involved/who-can-provide-care

[136] https://fosteringconnections.com.au/enquire

Today, Lifeblood collects over 1.6 million blood and plasma donations annually to provide over 1 million litres of blood[137]. But, out of the 57 per cent of Australians aged 18–74 who are eligible to donate blood, only 5 per cent do so. A new blood donor is needed every 4 minutes. So please, if you haven't, roll up your sleeves and donate.

Lifeblood also now collects and pasteurises donated breast milk for premature babies in neonatal units.

Despite 1 organ donor saving the lives of up to 7 people and helping many more through eye and tissue donation, only 2 per cent of people who die in hospital each year can be considered for organ donation. They must die in hospital as the organs need to be functioning well to be considered for transplantation. This small number of potential donors is reduced further when nearly half of the families decline to consent to the donation. For the 1,800 Australians waitlisted for a transplant and another 14,000 Australians on dialysis, many of whom could benefit from a kidney transplant, please register at *Donate Life* and tell your family[138]. Families generally want to honour the wish of their dying or deceased relative. If they don't know what their relative wanted, then only 4 out of 10 families consent to donation[139].

Bequests

Even when you are pushing up the daisies, shuffled off this mortal coil and gone to the choir invisible, charities still want your money. Bequests have become big business for charities because of the large amounts bequeathed from the increase in property prices, compared to the relatively low cost of contacting existing donors (and hassling their legal and financial advisers) to leave the charity in their will.

As a result, charities offer free or low-cost simple will preparation and invitations to bequest clubs that offer the bequestors special events. Technology has now caught up with online platforms such as *EveryWill* offering free wills and a list of charities[140]. If you do use their funeral comparison service, please choose *Bethel Funerals*, a charitable social enterprise that was established in 1997 to generate funds for Bible translation in the face of declining donations[141].

---

137 https://www.lifeblood.com.au/news-and-stories/vital-reads/2023-stats-and-snacks

138 https://www.donatelife.gov.au/

139 https://www.abc.net.au/news/2025-02-25/organ-donation-more-donors-fewer-transplants/104972632

140 https://everywill.com.au/

141 https://www.bethelfunerals.com.au/

PORTFOLIO PHILANTHROPY

'For every complex problem there is a solution which is clear, simple and wrong'

H.L. MENCKEN

As I strode out of the lift into a sea of suits bounded by wall-to-wall marble, the 180° view across the city was spectacular. This wealth manager was obviously keen to display its wealth.

The conversation excitedly turned to clause 99A of the Income Tax Assessment Act, which I gather is how trust income is taxed, as I looked out of the window to see a man swimming three floors down in the adjacent building. The debate then went on to how family philanthropy for the next generation can ensure the continuity of the business for the advisers.

The growth in wealth in Australia, especially among the very rich, has more than tripled in the past 2 decades, from 8 per cent of Australia's GDP in 2004 to 24 per cent of GDP in 2024, which has seen wealth management and tax advisory companies grow their philanthropy services as an important offering to their clients.

In good news for the wealth management and philanthropy services industry, it is estimated that $1.1 trillion will be transferred across a generation between now and 2030, and $2.6 trillion by 2040 in Australia[142].

---

[142]Portfolio philanthropy
Philanthropy Australia (2022) *Giving Trends and Opportunities* at https://www.philanthropy.org.au/wp-content/uploads/2022/11/Giving_Trends_and_Opportunities_-_Philanthropy_Australia_Report_2022.pdf

Greek playwright Aeschylus coined the term philanthropy in the 5th century BCE, meaning *love of humanity*, and we know that philanthropy has existed in the ancient civilizations of the Middle East, Greece, and Rome, including an endowment which supported Plato's Academy for some 900 years.

Australia has a proud history of philanthropy, from Elizabeth Austin donating £6,000 in 1880 to start the Austin Hospital for Incurables, to the Ian Potter Foundation and the John T Reid Charitable Trusts funding the early proof of concept of the bionic eye at the Bionics Institute.

Former Greens leader, Dr Bob Brown used his Goldman Environmental Prize of $49,000 as a deposit and a combination of borrowed funds and donations to buy properties to set up the Australian Bush Heritage Fund, now known as Bush Heritage Australia.

Philanthropy in Australia has established world-leading organisations such as Orygen Youth Health Research Centre, Walter and Eliza Hall Institute of Medical Research, the Heart Foundation, Foundation for Rural and Regional Renewal, Centre for Women's Mental Health, National Marine Park Network, Epworth Hospital, Human Rights Law Centre, Murdoch Childrens Research Institute, St Vincent's Institute of Medical Research, as well as the Parkes Telescope, Miles Franklin Literary Award and the Walkley Awards[143].

More recently, philanthropic foundations have recognised the need to come together to pool resources and expertise to tackle our entrenched social crises to establish programs and organisations in collaboration with government to effect change. In 2022, the *Investment Dialogue for Australia's Children (IDAC)* was established as a $65 million commitment between Government and philanthropic partners to improve the wellbeing of children, young people, and their families by working with communities to make long-term, intergenerational change. One of their priorities has led to the establishment of *Partnerships for Local Action and Community Empowerment (PLACE)* in 2024.

In 2025, the Albanese Government and the IDAC invested $50 million each to build supply and capacity of integrated early years services that bring together early learning, child and maternal health services, and family and community supports[144].

---

[143] The Myer Family Company Ltd (2013) *Australia's Top 50 Philanthropic Gifts* at https://tomorrowtoday.com.au/wp-content/uploads/2022/11/Australias-Top-50-Philanthropic-Gifts.pdf

[144] https://ministers.education.gov.au/chalmers/historic-investment-help-deliver-universal-early-childhood-education-and-care

One example of the change philanthropy can make over time is Intrepid Travel's co-founder Darrell Wade, who invested a $50,000 donation into Good Cycles, a new social enterprise created by two social entrepreneurs to provide mobile bicycle servicing to corporates and enable unemployed, disadvantaged young people to gain the skills needed to gain employment in the bike industry. Darrell then spent ten years on the Board guiding the organisation. Today, the annual income Good Cycles exceeds $10 million from bike-based services in Victoria, NSW and Queensland and is one of the few social enterprises profitable enough to take on unemployed disadvantaged young people as wage-earning trainees up front.

As successful business people who are entrepreneurial and problem-solvers, it is tempting to want to devise solutions to societal problems, when their role as philanthropists should be to 'underwrite an open-ended process for change'. Philanthropists must also be conscious to avoid the paternalism that still pervades philanthropy, 135 years after Andrew Carnegie wrote 'the man of wealth [must become] the …. agent for his poorer brethren, bringing to their service his superior wisdom, experience and ability to administer, doing for them better than they would or could do for themselves'[145].

The skills that drive commercial success may not be those needed to inspire, empathise and empower others to mobilise and sustain effective and enduring social change. Shared Value creator, Mark Kramer warns that 'when social progress is led by the wealthy, philanthropy as a placebo, offering well-intentioned help at the margins while diverting attention from the more fundamental reforms that might be less palatable'[146].

Indeed, Kramer questions whether philanthropists can address the underlying problems, rather than just alleviate the symptoms, because of the structural changes that are needed. He also notes that 'the more we highlight philanthropy as the solution, the more we excuse government and corporations from the need to change'.

Another challenge for charities is the short-term nature of 1 or 2 year philanthropic grants. Charities have to contract or reassign staff and gear up quickly to implement the project, program or service and spend the grant, before the staff have to be let go if no more projects are available. This creates a loss of knowledge and morale, and an environment of uncertainty and anxiety. The

---

[145] Carnegie A (1889) *Gospel of Wealth*

[146] Kramer M & Phillips S (2024) *Where Strategic Philanthropy Went Wrong,* Standford Social Innovation Review, Volume 22, Number 3

project's recipients also go through the feast and famine of programs or services started and closed.

To enable a more consistent, longer-term approach, the *2024 Not-for-profit Sector Development Blueprint* has called for greater flexibility in the distributions of philanthropic funds to allow the smoothing of distributions to charities over a period of up to 3 years[147].

My view is that, to achieve lasting change on scale, many actors are needed in philanthropy, business, charities, research, voters and governments. Government policy changes have been won through the mobilisation of large numbers of Australians who lobby their MPs around the continued unacceptability of an issue. Charities can play a key role in coordinating campaigns and philanthropists can invest in their capacity to do so.

In my experience, the most successful philanthropists:

1. get to know, trust and invest in a small number of outstanding charity CEOs that have the potential to effect greater change, including building their personal capacity;
2. are curious and want to get to understand the area they support;
3. take a long-term approach with multi-year commitments, understanding that change is slow and non-linear, and that their children and future generations could carry the torch;
4. are rigorous in discovering and assessing the outcomes, not just the activities or outputs (or the marketing spin).

Over the years there have been many theories of philanthropy coming out of United States academia, including *impact philanthropy* (a focus on achieving social or environment impact), *strategic philanthropy* (aligned to the donor's goals), *trust-based philanthropy* (building open and trustful relationships between funders and grantees), *venture philanthropy* (using traditional venture capital financing principles), *impulse philanthropy* (driven by the recognition that the donor expects), *collaborative philanthropy* (combining giving from donors), *catalytic philanthropy* (the use of influence and leadership to leverage the giving), *big bet philanthropy* (putting large sums of money into high-risk and potentially high-reward initiatives); and *effective altruism* (uses evidence and reason to determine the most effective ways to benefit others).

[147] Blueprint Expert Reference Group (2024) *Not-for-profit Sector Distribution Blueprint*, p.67

Call me naive, but I would have thought that all philanthropy should be based on the medium-long-term measurable impact, working in trusting relationships with the charities and with periodic, reliable evidence to review, assess, and improve the activities and outcomes.

Having said that, I'm going to take this opportunity to introduce another theory.

Portfolio Philanthropy

'Well, how do we know it is going to work?' came the cry from the end of the table as the meeting of the foundation considered a range of grants recommended by management.

Like most foundations, the grants were presented under the themes that the foundation determined were most important. Typically, these themes include housing and homelessness, education and employment, children and young people, social enterprise, First Nations, gender violence, mental health, refugee women and community building.

I replied that the reality is that we don't know.

Chairs shifted. Tumbleweeds spun across the floor.

For the business people in the room, this uncertainty certainly felt uncomfortable.

Surely, the charities just need to achieve what we funded them to do. They either succeed or they don't, and if they don't, then we won't fund them again. I didn't mention that no charity in my knowledge would be brave enough to admit to not having fully succeeded.

With any social intervention made under a service theme, there are so many factors affecting someone's life that determine their state of health and wellbeing. In practice, all the themes are inter-related.

For instance, poverty can be a factor in domestic violence that causes homelessness for the mother and kids fleeing the home. Childhood abuse can lead to trauma-based mental health issues, leading to drug use and dependence as self-medication to dull the pain. A refugee experiencing ongoing racism and discrimination lacks the self-esteem and opportunity to get into the workforce, leading to disengagement, crime, and the perpetrator of family violence.

So, given this quandary, what charities or sectors should you give to?

Enter the economist Harry Markowitz, who founded the Modern Portfolio Theory in this 1952 paper,[148] which introduces the concept of a portfolio of investments with different risks and returns. For a higher level of risk, a higher return is expected.

It is the same with giving or 'investing' money in charities.

Some programs, projects or services, such as pilots or trials, are riskier than others that have more evidence, but, if successful, could be ground-breaking and achieve a greater scale of impact. Other activities may provide the traditional, proven way of addressing a need, but have less impact, or return, in tackling the underlying cause.

In my experience, donors are understandably risk adverse. Given the complexity of the needs, short-term perspective and the relative lack of evidence to base their decision on, donors can feel more comfortable with, and motivated by, easy to comprehend and visual 'solutions' – for instance, a gym run for young people coming out of jail run by a former offender who got his life back on track, a school breakfast program using left over food prepared by volunteers, a social enterprise café with migrant women.

In practice, meaningful and sustainable change takes time and a range of coordinated interventions that:

1. Develop and collaborate in networks and cross sector partnerships;
2. Gather evidence on efficacy and the improvement of services;
3. Research and advocate for a change in government policy, systems and funding;
4. Innovate and pilot new approaches to achieve better outcomes;
5. Scale up or replicate a proven pilot to more clients and/or other areas; and
6. Simply respond to the immediate and urgent humanitarian need.

Each of these activities will have different timeframes, risks and returns, in the same way as investments in a portfolio.

To maximise a donor's 'return', a balanced *philanthropy portfolio* contains charities that offer this range of projects, programs and services. Although some charities are large enough to undertake this range, they may not be as innovative

---

[148] Markowitz H (1952) *Portfolio Selection* The Journal of Finance. **7** (1): 77–91. doi:10.2307/2975974. JSTOR 2975974.

or vocal as smaller, newer charities, in the same way as an investment portfolio includes start-up businesses as well as large and established companies.

The weighting of the philanthropy portfolio can also mirror an investment portfolio. For instance, the donor may seek a bigger proportion of shorter-term and higher risk activities, such as start-ups, pilots, and trials, and less for longer-term research and policy development.

Alternatively, a donor may want to emphasise short-term, urgent humanitarian work that alleviates suffering today as their priority and less about any policy or system change in the future.

Like different sized companies in an investment portfolio, the philanthropy portfolio contains large charities – such as The Smith Family, which has evaluated services, but the investment is small in relation to the size of their funds raised – to the equivalent of 'penny stocks' as highly speculative investments in small, unproven, grass-roots, innovative charities with social and environmental entrepreneurs that could achieve an impact return in excess of its size.

For instance, a balanced philanthropy portfolio to end homelessness could have a mix of supporting:

1) a network working to end functional homelessness; 2) the evaluation of the 'housing first' model to influence practice; 3) a research project that identifies the effect on children of homeless parent(s) and recommends changes to government policies; 4) a project that develops a new model of social housing with unused land from local government, design from a pro-bono architect and tenancy management from a community housing association; 5) the roll out of a program providing financial literacy to families experiencing financial stress to reduce the risk of family violence leading to homelessness; and 6) a program providing personal hygiene items for women in refuges.

To tackle entrenched poverty, a balanced philanthropy portfolio could look like: 1) a campaign to raise the income support or research into reform of the tax system; 2) a program that supports children from low income households improve their education attainment and escape the cycle of poverty through qualifications and employment; 3) research on the those entering poverty as a result of the cost of living crisis with recommended government measures; 4) a new pilot program that provides direct cash to low income families; and 5) groceries provided by a food bank.

I HAVE A DREAM

'We refuse to believe that there are insufficient funds in the great vaults of opportunity of this nation. And so we've come to cash this check, a check that will give us upon demand the riches of freedom and the security of justice'

MARTIN LUTHER KING JNR,
I HAVE A DREAM SPEECH,
MARCH ON WASHINGTON, 28 AUGUST 1963

Justice in Australia means every Australian having the dignity and opportunity of at least the fundamental human rights that we, and the world, signed up to in 1948, along with the environmental justice to address climate change for a liveable planet for future generations – indeed, for our very species.

With a GDP of $1.78 trillion and 1 of the world's top 20 largest economies, it is unconscionable that we can't ensure that all Australians have a safe home with enough resources and opportunities to live life; schools, universities, workplaces and communities that are safe, inclusive and tolerant, free from racism and discrimination; adequate social and health services that include sufficient prevention and early intervention to reduce needless suffering; and our First Nations peoples get to enjoy the same rights.

In a country that is politically polarised by daily debates over government spending and taxes, this doesn't mean that government funding, or our taxes, need to rise. Like the tax and income support reform, we know that we need the evidence and political will to radically change the way we design and deliver the service system. And we all have a part to play in this change.

This book illustrates that our national crises are interrelated but that our service provision is siloed, typically focusing on one of the issues at a time. Costing billions of dollars, there are thousands of services around the country provided or contracted by service sector-based local, State/Territory and Commonwealth government departments and the charities and companies that operate in the corresponding service sectors. Each has different contract periods, funding levels, required activities and outputs, eligibility criteria and geographical area coverage. Even working in the sector, it is impossible to know all the programs and services that affect the target cohort or area, especially with the rate of change with short-term contracts and political cycles. Compounding the issue, there is little interaction within and between service sectors as charities compete for government tenders and donations and protect their intellectual property.

Even where Ministers have the courage and take the initiative to reform a sector in their portfolio to improve outcomes, they lack the jurisdiction in other Ministerial portfolios and government departments to make the changes needed outside of their responsibility.

Inevitably, this can create competition, confusion, duplication, overlap and a shortage of essential services. 1 result is that service users have to tell their story repeatedly to each service provider. In some cases, it is a full-time job for them to coordinate the services they need with different agencies and systems.

More of the same won't address the worsening crises that we face. The only solution is the co-design with users and communities and the place-based coordination of services, together with ongoing monitoring and evaluation, and adaptation of services to improve service delivery and outcomes, alongside evidence for advocacy.

From the richest place in the world 150 years ago to the most disadvantaged area in the State, I showed up to present on social enterprise to the *Go Goldfields Alliance*. With generational poverty, young children at risk, poor health, domestic violence, and a pervasive lack of aspiration, the local government had coordinated a business case that identified that, in overcoming generational poverty, all possible cross-departmental and support mechanisms are in place at all stages of child and young adult development. This includes the stages of health in pregnancy, early parenting, pre-school, primary and secondary education, employment/ career planning and post-compulsory education. In order to provide adequate support, a long-term, whole-of-community, whole-of-government approach is warranted to provide optimal development and learning support for our upcoming generations[149].

---

[149] I have a dream
Perry M (2008) *Gold Prospects. Business Case For Whole-Of-Community Planning & Development 2008/2016*, Central Goldfields Shire Council accessed at

As well as the new way of working, the Alliance believed that the work needed to focus on achieving desired community outcomes rather than on service outputs, and identified:

- A reduction in the incidence of notifications to Child Protection Services;
- Improved communication and literacy skills, opportunities and positive life experiences for children and their families;
- Improved community connectedness for children, youth and families;
- Improving youth connection to appropriate training and education to achieve employment outcomes; and
- Increased breastfeeding rates[150].

The State Government supported the initiative with flexible funding and multi-departmental engagement.

With the belief that 'our community needs to work together, to challenge and change any system that impedes our goal', the Alliance's hundred local experts in 5 working groups undertook to 'challenge ourselves to be dynamic, to continuously collaborate, to maximise the benefits of co-design, to be accountable and to ensure long-term sustainability in our work'[151].

The presentation was an amazing experience. The passion, drive and insights of the group were second to none and we ended up spending the afternoon modelling a range of social enterprises for young people for the area.

Go Goldfields has demonstrated that a program can work across many levels through the co-design of community services with the local community, local coordination of service delivery by providers supported by their government departments, accountability to the community based on outcomes, continuous improvements in services and systems, and the measurement and reporting of outcomes.

A similar approach is occurring in NSW with *Mid Coast 4 Kids*, a collective impact initiative focused on improving child and youth serving systems for

---

https://www.parliament.vic.gov.au/images/stories/committees/rrc/disadvantage_and_inequality/submissions/021_20100324_CentralGoldfieldsShire.pdf

[150] State of Victoria (2015) *Go Goldfields Alliance Evaluation Report 2012-2014*, Central Victorian Primary Care Partnership (CVPCP), Go Goldfields Evaluation Working Group accessed at http://youthlaw.asn.au/wp-content/uploads/2016/09/Go-Goldfields-Alliance-Evaluation-Report-4.pdf

[151] https://gogoldfields.org/visionaspirations/

children, young people and families in the Mid Coast by bringing together local organisations and stakeholders within and outside the community to create lasting and meaningful change by aligning efforts, sharing resources and leveraging the strengths of our community and our partners[152]. Founded by nine charities to enable collaboration to achieve systems change, *The Possibility Project* is a key partner in this and other place-based, collective impact projects[153].

Another example is *Our Place*, an initiative of the Colman Education Foundation, which led the thinking and design of a new integrated government school in Doveton, a low income suburb in south-east Melbourne to holistically meet the needs of children from birth to Year 9. The college incorporates a number of local early childhood and family services offered by charities which, lacking adequate scale and coordination, had been struggling to meet the high demand and complex needs of the area's residents.

Outcomes from Doveton College show a significant reduction (from 55 per cent to 37 per cent) in the number of children identified as developmentally vulnerable on 1 or more domains, as measured by the Australian Early Development Census over a 5-year period. Children attending Doveton Early Learning Centre have achieved significantly higher performance on Preparatory School entry testing in reading than those who did not attend. These children also achieved significantly higher performance on reading and numeracy measures at Year 3 level.

Following on from the success at Doveton College, in 2017 the Colman Education Foundation and Department of Education and Training signed a landmark agreement to implement the *Our Place* approach at ten disadvantaged areas across Victoria - Bridgewood, Carlton, Frankston North, Mooroopna, Morwell, Northern Bay, Robinvale, Seymour and Westall[154].

The urgent need for integrated, place-based approaches has recently been recognised by the new government and philanthropically funded Partnerships for Local Action and Community Empowerment (PLACE), which will support hundreds of communities and initiatives nationwide, working with local communities to address complex and persistent socioeconomic barriers. It is an independent not-for-profit organisation governed by an innovative community accountability model.

---

152 https://www.midcoast4kids.com.au/about/

153 https://www.thepossibilitypartnership.org.au/about-us

154 https://ourplace.org.au/about/our-history/

PLACE will initially focus on place-based initiatives in four priority areas, each including a dedicated First Nations focus: 1) entrenched socio-economic barriers; 2) early years childhood development; 3) employment support programs; and 4) Australia's energy transition to net 0[155].

The UK is leading the way with its *English Devolution White Paper* and associated legislation to devolve political, social and economic power to 'end the top-down micromanaging of individual decisions and approaches by local leaders and replace it with a principle of constitutional autonomy and partnership' by creating Strategic Authorities consisting of a number of councils working together to drive local economic growth and more joined-up delivery of public services[156].

The UK government's *Plan for Change* includes a $1bn Better Futures Fund to support up to 200,000 children and their families over the next 10 years by bringing together government, local communities, charities, social enterprises, investors, and philanthropists to work together to give children a brighter future.

My dream is that this placed-based, integrated, collaborative, long-term approach becomes ubiquitous in Australia. To do so, governments, businesses, academia, charities, and philanthropy need to devolve power and resources to communities that understand their needs and work together to respond.

Governments

In designing, procuring and being accountable for the annual $200+ billion taxpayer funding of social services, governments have the potential to make the biggest change to the lives of Australians in need through:

- Improving wealth equality through a fairer tax system and income support.
- Medium and long term outcomes measures which are agreed, recorded and reported by geographical area, such as a local government area or primary health network (PHN) area. PHNs have unrivalled access to governmental data. The Australian Bureau of Statistics also has three Statistical Area Levels.

  The measures should include a *Multidimensional Poverty Index* as a poverty measure that reflects the multiple deprivations that poor Australians face in the areas of education, health, and living standards,

155 https://www.paulramsayfoundation.org.au/news-resources/new-place-to-empower-local-communities-around-australia

156 https://www.gov.uk/government/publications/english-devolution-white-paper-power-and-partnership-foundations-for-growth/english-devolution-white-paper#executive-summary

as used by the United Nations. This would enable transparency and accountability, as well as encourage service improvement and innovation to improve outcomes.

- Outcome-based, multi-service, minimum 5-year service contracts with a consortium of providers that align with these outcome targets and areas. This would necessitate government departments working together on coordinating their service development and delivery. Given their local knowledge and relationships, local governments or PHNs could play a valuable role in facilitating and coordinating cooperation across service providers in their areas.

  For instance, whilst homelessness is not an official responsibility of local government, a recent survey found that 85 per cent reported actively contributing to homelessness responses, especially coordinating local services and resources[157].

- Recognising and harnessing the inherent strengths in communities, including local groups and networks, in program and service design and delivery.
- Increasing investment in evidence-based early intervention and prevention services to reduce the suffering, burden and cost of crisis responses, as well as break the cycle of disadvantage. Philanthropy can play an important role in funding research, innovation, monitoring and evaluation in early intervention and prevention.
- Enabling economic and social development together, especially in 'poverty postcodes' that have entrenched, intergenerational poverty and disadvantage.
- Provide adequate funding for crisis services, including homelessness, mental health, family and domestic violence.
- Funding a central open repository of research and evaluation.
- Including funding for external monitoring and evaluation in service contracts.

Charities

The 2025 Not-for-Profit Governance & Performance Study reports that 'many organisations continue to face challenges in articulating and measuring their

---

[157] Pawson H, Parsell C, Clarke A, Moore J, Hartley C, Aminpour F and Eagles K (2024) *Australian Homelessness Monitor 2024*, UNSW City Futures Research Centre, Sydney, p.110

impact, highlighting the need for clearer frameworks to enhance understanding and accountability'[158].

There really is no excuse. Irrespective of their government contracts stipulating activity and output targets, charities must be able to articulate, measure and report their outcomes and impact according to their theory of change to realise their belief and purpose, including macro changes to the communities they work with, lessons learnt and policy and service system changes needed. Otherwise, charities risk further decline in trust and donations.

For instance, a homelessness agency that has the purpose of ending homelessness needs to articulate its plans to achieve this goal and its progress, including the policy and system change required, and not just report the number of people assisted by their government-funded services in their annual 'impact' report.

The recent *Not-for-profit Sector Development Blueprint* has recognised the need to strengthen the charity sector's practice and public knowledge of its effectiveness by recommending the development of agreed sector standards for outcomes measurement[159].

Charities should also be able to demonstrate their networks, collaborations and partnerships within and with other related sectors to address the interrelated issues, as well as make public their advocacy positions.

Philanthropists

Philanthropy has the unrivalled impartiality, relationships, voice, resources, capital and knowledge to be the catalyst and continuity for this change. To do so, philanthropists need to be catalysts (not just grant givers) that work together to scale their effect; collaborate with governments, research institutions, and services sectors; and take at least a ten-year evidence-based, incremental approach.

After all, Bridgespan's *15 Success Stories of Audacious Philanthropy for Large-Scale Social Impact* found that 90 per cent of efforts took more than 20 years to complete (the median was 45 years); 80 per cent required changes to government funding, policies or action; 75 per cent required coordination of

---

[158] Australian Institute of Company Directors & Commonwealth Bank (2025) *Not-for-Profit Governance & Performance Study 2024-25,* p.20

[159] Blueprint Expert Reference Group (2024) *Not-for-profit Sector Development Blueprint,* p.17, initiative 14a.

actors across sectors; and 66 per cent required one or more philanthropic 'big bets' of more than US$ 10 million[160].

With the Themes in this book either stagnating or not improving, and virtually all resources absorbed by crisis responses, philanthropy has the opportunity to invest in place-based, community-coordinated and user-driven prevention and early intervention approaches and gather the evidence for their efficacy and cost effectiveness to advocate for corresponding changes in government policy, service systems and funding.

Business

Given that companies rely on a workforce that lives nearby, they are an integral part of the local community and its wellbeing by supporting local charities with procurement, sponsorship, workplace giving, donations and staff volunteering.

An alignment with the business's goods, expertise, and influence with a charity or sector can enable significant and lasting policy and system change.

When I was at Mission Australia, I met Mike Smith, then CEO of ANZ Bank.

Formed in 1951 from two banks established in London in the nineteenth century, the Bank of Australasia and the Union Bank of Australia, the Australia and New Zealand Banking Group operates in 33 markets, including across the Pacific Islands.

With the purpose 'to shape a world where people and communities thrive. That is why we strive to create a balanced, sustainable economy in which everyone can take part and build a better life'[161], 2 of ANZ's 4 target outcomes relate to improving the financial wellbeing of its customers and the community.

Financial literacy, as the 'ability to make informed judgements and to take effective decisions regarding the use and management of money', is central to this outcome with 'improvements in financial literacy can not only support social inclusion, but also enhance the contribution that the financial services sector makes to the nation's wellbeing'[162].

---

160 Wolf Ditkoff S & Grindle A (2017) *Audacious Philanthropy: Lessons from 15 World-Changing Initiatives,* Harvard Business Review, September-October 2017 at https://hbr.org/2017/09/audacious-philanthropy

161 https://www.anz.com/shareholder/centre/about/our-strategy/

162 Roy Morgan Research (2003) *ANZ Survey of Adult Financial Literacy in Australia*, Melbourne, Australia, p.2 accessed at https://financialcapability.gov.au/files/anz-survey-of-adult-financial-literacy-2003.pdf

The first comprehensive review of Australian adult financial literacy by ANZ in 2003 found that the lowest levels of financial literacy were associated with lower education attainment, those not working for a range of reasons or in unskilled work, those with household incomes under $20,000, and those with lower savings levels.[163]

The same year, at a conference organised by the Brotherhood of St Laurence, then ANZ CEO, John McFarlane, reiterated that 'improving savings, general education levels and financial literacy levels are perhaps more important in addressing the underbanked'[164].

The following year, ANZ developed and launched Australia's first comprehensive adult financial education program, *MoneyMinded*, with the NSW Department of Education and Training and an advisory committee featuring nominees from the Australian Financial Counselling and Credit Reform Association (AFCCRA) and the Australian Securities and Investments Commission.

Comprising 6 topics, separated into 17 workshops delivered by financial counsellors within community organisations, trained by ANZ staff, *MoneyMinded* covers planning and saving; easy payments; understanding paperwork; living with debt; everyday banking and financial products; and rights and responsibilities.

As a neutral and independent financial education program, not ANZ-branded and not promoting any specific financial institution's services or products, MoneyMinded was initially delivered in Victoria, NSW, and Queensland by Brotherhood of St. Laurence, Berry Street Victoria, Kildonan Child and Family Services, The Benevolent Society, and The Smith Family[165].

16 years later, *MoneyMinded* has educated over 667,000 people[166] and has been tailored to the Asia/Pacific countries in which ANZ works, including

---

[163] Roy Morgan Research (2003) *ANZ Survey of Adult Financial Literacy in Australia*, Melbourne, Australia, p.4 accessed at https://financialcapability.gov.au/files/anz-survey-of-adult-financial-literacy-2003.pdf

[164] Brotherhood of St Laurence (2003) *Banking on the Margins. Promoting a More Financially Inclusive Community*, Melbourne, Australia accessed at http://library.bsl.org.au/bsljspui/bitstream/1/6149/1/Banking_on_margins_conf.pdf

[165] Russell R & Nair A (2005) *Evaluation of MoneyMinded: an Adult Financial Education Program*, RMIT University, Melbourne, Australia, accessed at https://www.anz.com/resources/1/7/170b71804f1d3e8ca55eb558b54e5b8d/RMIT-Money-Minded-Evaluation-May-2005.pdf?MOD=AJPERES

[166] Russell R, Kutin J, Stewart M, Welwood M & Marriner T (2019) *MoneyMinded impact report: A report prepared for ANZ*, RMIT University, Melbourne, Australia, p.2 accessed at https://financialcapability.gov.au/files/anz-money-minded-impact-report-2019.pdf

MoneyMinded Business Basics to provide micro-entrepreneurs overseas with the financial and business skills to start and grow their enterprises, and *MoneyBusiness* to better respond to the cultural context of Indigenous Australians, particularly those in remote communities.

The 2016 evaluation concluded that '*MoneyMinded* contributes to the improvement of individual financial wellbeing and plays an important role in strengthening financial inclusion in the communities where it is delivered. The behavioural changes experienced by participants include increased saving, increased use of a budget, reduced spending leaks, setting financial goals and increased planning' [167].

The 2019 evaluation found that participants in Australia and New Zealand experienced a 33 per cent and 132 per cent increase in their financial wellbeing score, respectively[168].

ANZ didn't stop there. It decided to tackle the lack of savings that John McFarlane mentioned at the 2003 conference and approached the Brotherhood of St Laurence.

The result, *Saver Plus*, is arguably the largest and longest-running matched savings program in the world, with over 64,000 vulnerable Australians collectively saving over $30 million[169]. Over 8 in 10 are still saving more than 7 years after completing the program; 85 per cent agreed they are better able to provide for their families; and 52 per cent were meeting bill and credit commitments without any difficulty, up from 15 per cent before participating in the program[170].

Saver Plus represents a best practice example of the power of community-business-government partnerships, with each sector providing its unique

---

[167] Russell R, Kutin J, Stewart M & Godinho V (2016) *MoneyMinded Report 2015*, RMIT University, Melbourne, Australia, p.4 accessed at https://www.anz.com/resources/9/8/989dcfe9-9d40-44ae-9f2d-7739ee8cfffc/moneyminded15report.pdf?MOD=AJPERES&MoneyMinded

[168] Russell R, Kutin J, Stewart M, Welwood M & Marriner T (2019) *MoneyMinded impact report: A report prepared for ANZ*, RMIT University, Melbourne, Australia, p.4 accessed at https://financialcapability.gov.au/files/anz-money-minded-impact-report-2019.pdf

[169] https://ministers.dss.gov.au/media-releases/17596#:~:text=The%20Albanese%20Labor%20Government%20is,and%20better%20navigate%20financial%20crises.

[170] Porter E, Bowman D, Panchal M, Fairbrother P, Banks M (2024) *Saver Plus at 21. Building a Resilience That Lasts*, Brotherhood of St Laurence, ANZ at https://library.bsl.org.au/bsljspui/bitstream/1/13502/4/Porter_etal_ANZ_Saver_Plus_at_21_2024.pdf

expertise and resources to the mutual goal of increased financial well-being and capability for lower-income Australians.

In February 2025, the Commonwealth government announced a further $51.5 million to continue the delivery of *Saver Plus* until 2030.

Academia

Australia's research institutions play a critical role in 1) bringing charities, government and business together to collaborate; 2) enabling the expert evaluation of services to generate an evidence base for service improvement, better outcomes and advocacy; 2) co-designing new and improved programs and services; and 3) using their networks and influence to advocate for change.

This book highlights the urgent need to ensure the charity's service funding includes a sufficient budget for these activities to create a step change in the provision of all these functions, thereby achieving the change so desperately needed.

THEMES

On my study wall is a map. I stole it from the weekly security briefing. It shows the front lines in red with green arrows showing the direction of the fighting - Croatians versus Serbians, Serbians versus Muslims, Croatians versus Muslims, and even Muslims versus Muslims in north-west Bosnia.

The 3 surrounded enclaves stand out as little red circles, each with a '10' in the middle. At the bottom of the map, note 10 says 'the Srebrenica, Zepa and Gorazde pockets remained relatively calm, with small arms fire recorded'.

Nineteen months later, the red circle around the town of Srebrenica saw more than 8,000 Bosnian Muslims, mainly men and boys, under the protection of the United Nations Dutch peacekeepers, massacred by the Bosnian Serb Army in the worst case of genocide since the Second World War.

As we left the briefing, a colleague from another agency was in tears. His contract was ending and he wanted to give us a parting message. He begged us not to lose hope in our humanitarian work, lest we lose our own humanity. So how can we expect our country and community to be compassionate and fair if we don't show compassion and strive for fairness?

Although the twelve social Themes listed are complex, inter-related, 'wicked problems' that must be addressed holistically to achieve lasting change, can I please encourage you to adopt and take the time to delve into one Theme that particularly touches you. Discover for yourself how you can take easy actions that create real impact to not just change lives, but change populations through prevention, early intervention and the very policy and systems that perpetuate the issues.

Each Theme has a brief outline of the latest facts (WHAT), the underlying causes of the issue (WHY) and the many opportunities to get involved and make an impact (ACT) through participating, purchasing, donating, volunteering, employing, investing, mentoring, pledging and campaigning.

In doing so, you can join a movement that, together and standing of the shoulders of those before us, can achieve lasting change for people and planet.

I have not included medical conditions as a Theme, which tend to be a personal choice, such as cancer conditions. Diseases typically have well-defined charities that provide services to the sufferers and medical research to alleviate or eliminate the disease. After all, there can be no better belief than a cure. However, please bear in mind the principles in choosing a charity outlined above, especially demonstrating collaboration.

The charities mentioned in this book have demonstrated impact through their public reporting and are largely national, but there are many more for you to discover.

FIRST NATIONS

'We are perhaps the ethnic group Australians feel least connected to. We are not popular and we are not personally known to many Australians. Few have met us and a small minority count us as friends. And despite never having met any of us and knowing very little about us other than what is in the media….Australians hold and express strong views about us, the great proportion of which is negative and unfriendly. It has ever been thus. Worse in the past but still true today'

NOEL PEARSON 2022 BOYER LECTURE[171]

With only 1 of 6 Australians socialising with Aboriginal and Torres Strait Islander people in the last year[172] and with the premise that we can't start reconciliation without this first step, I started *Taste of Reconciliation* as an annual event which invited senior corporate people to come and have dinner at a five star CBD hotel to meet and ask questions of Aboriginal elders.

Four years earlier, I had joined Mission Australia, which had just won a tender with the Victorian government to redevelop a derelict site in inner Melbourne into a social enterprise cafe to train Aboriginal young people for jobs in the hospitality industry.

The Fitzroy site had had a colourful history, housing a VD clinic after the war and then the iconic Victorian Aboriginal Health Service (VAHS), the first dedicated Indigenous health service in the country. Indeed, this Melbourne

---

[171]First Nations
https://capeyorkpartnership.org.au/noel-pearson-boyer-lecture-one/

[172] Reconciliation Australia (2022) *2022 Australian Reconciliation Barometer*, p.5

suburb rivalled Redfern as the centre of Aboriginal activism in the late 1960s and 1970s after the failure of the 1967 Referendum to create real change for Aboriginal people.

African Americans have been through a similar journey. Their civil rights movement started when the Voting Rights Act of 1965 failed to legislate away racism. Aboriginal people clearly saw the parallels with their African American brothers and sisters and Australia's Black Power movement took inspiration from Malcolm X, whose autobiography showed young Kooris how to funnel their frustrations surrounding the treatment of Aboriginal people in Australian cities into constructive resistance[173].

Lying vacant for the past decade, the building had deteriorated into a shell. Crudely painted with red, yellow and red stripes, it was the site of the unofficial Aboriginal Embassy and numerous protests.

Standing on the dirt floor, surrounded by rubble and gazing skyward through the vacant roof, the Housing Minister, VAHS CEO and I felt overawed by the history and the task.

With sustainable employment the best possible intervention for disadvantaged young people, transitional labour market social enterprises are commercial businesses that provide training, employability skills development and real work experience to a cohort that would not otherwise be employable to enable their transition to mainstream employment. Crucially, from day one, it provides the environment that, for the first time, treats the young person as a worker, and not a welfare recipient. This, in itself, is life-changing, especially when coming from a workless family.

Instead of a café, I wanted to aim higher. With a shortage of qualified chefs, we had the opportunity to create a quality restaurant downstairs with trainees working alongside the professional team in the kitchen. A training kitchen upstairs, unseen by the public, gave Indigenous young people the time and support to build their skills over 18 months to start a career as chefs, rather than lower-paid and transient cooks. This also meant that the site would be a safe, one-stop shop for the trainees with visiting trainers and support workers. I was delighted that the leading culinary teaching school, William Angliss Institute of TAFE, agreed to come on board.

---

[173] Green N *Black and Bloody Beautiful*, Honours Thesis Harvard University, USA accessed at http://www.kooriweb.org/foley/resources/history/newstuff2016/new per cent20folder/Naima per cent20Green per cent20Black per cent20and per cent20Bloody per cent20Beautiful.pdf

I also wanted diners to experience Indigenous culture through the food, in the same way as my parents had done forty years before, as 10-pound POMs when they went out to the local Greek and Italian restaurants for the first time.

As we had no experience running a restaurant, I needed to find a strong hospitality business partner. I approached the State manager of the Accor Group, which owns well-known hotels, such as Sofitel and Mercure. He agreed to advertise the restaurant manager role internally as a secondment and development opportunity for one of their food and beverage managers, as well as providing work experience in their hotel kitchens.

With funding from the Victorian government for the building works and equipment, the next two years of consultation with the local Aboriginal community, together with the design, construction and fitting out of the restaurant, were challenging.

In commissioning an eel trap for a hanging light from one of the two communities in Victoria permitted to make them, we inevitably offended the other, but we had no more budget left. We learnt that Aboriginal art in Victoria is not the familiar dots and circles of central and northern Australia, but lines and curves, and we commissioned a signature piece from leading Indigenous photographer, Wayne Quilliam. Thankfully, he showed us a range of lightings of the female nude before we picked the tasteful version that sits behind the bar.

The next challenge arose under Victorian legislation, which stipulated that a company Director had to hold the liquor licence, which meant a Board member of Mission Australia. Not an easy sell to a charity with a long history of tackling the social harm of alcohol misuse in Australia[174], including family violence, child abuse and homelessness. Thankfully, the Victoria-based Director and entrepreneurial businessman took up the challenge with the look – you better know what you are doing. I didn't, so I quickly enrolled in the responsible serving of alcohol course which he would need to take.

It was important that the restaurant be commercially successful to avoid draining the resources of Mission Australia (and so necessitating a new State Director in the process), as well as, ensuring the closest possible work setting to a regular business. The smaller the gap, the better the chance the trainee would successfully transition to a mainstream employer.

I had learnt at The Body Shop that a strong commercial brand is crucial. But with six months to go to the launch, we still didn't have a name or theme for

---

[174] Australian Institute of Health & Welfare (2020) *Alcohol, tobacco and other drugs in Australia*

the restaurant. We urgently convened the advisory group, which introduced us to the history of the area, including a nearby laneway with a briquette factory where Aboriginal people worked and socialised, which had been colloquially known as *Charcoal Lane*, later made famous by Archie Roach's song[175].

Brilliant. We had a great name and a black and white palette for the decor.

Unfortunately, if Australians know a business is run by a charity, they will assume it is poorer quality and a higher price. Called the 'pity purchase', they buy once out of sympathy, but not again.

So, following the advice from *thankyou* – Rule 1: Make Great Product* (*Never Use a good cause to sell an average product) and Rule 2: Never Break Rule 1, it was crucial that Charcoal Lane be positioned as an excellent and unique dining experience first. I spent another month working with Mission Australia's Brand Manager to address the charity's brand absence in the restaurant's signage and to establish a dedicated website for business promotion.

To engage diners, we placed brief stories on cards in the middle of the table for them to read while waiting for their meals, along with more information on the website, as we needed to raise funds for the training and support costs of each trainee.

We respected and continued the Aboriginal colours on the building by shining black, red and yellow against three triangle motifs in the top windows.

We wanted to avoid a patronising Aboriginal-themed restaurant and set the menu as contemporary Australian cuisine infused with native flavours. Each Indigenous ingredient has its own story, such as the Kakadu plum, which has the highest natural source of vitamin C in the world and was traditionally used to treat colds, the flu, and headaches. Lemon myrtles have been used by Indigenous Australians for 40,000 years, by wrapping the leaves in paperbark to flavour fish dishes, and to treat headaches by crushing and inhaling the leaves.

A year later, Charcoal Lane earned a score of 14 out of 20 in *The Age Good Food Guide*. Not bad, since 1 more point would represent the awarding of a coveted hat. The team then appeared in *The Age Melbourne Magazine's Top 100*, celebrating the city's most influential people.

---

[175] City of Yarra and the Aboriginal Cultural Signage Reference Group (2002) *Snapshots of Fitzroy* accessed at https://aboriginalhistoryofyarra.com.au/SnapshotsofAboriginalFitzroy.pdf

Twelve years later, the Duke and Duchess of Sussex popped in.

Back to the dimly lit Sofitel Grand Ballroom, filled with excited guests for the *Taste of Reconciliation* dinner. Although it was a venue they had frequented before, there was a decidedly nervous buzz around the room.

Despite 90 per cent of Australians feeling our relationship with Aboriginal and Torres Strait Islanders is important[176], we can be reluctant to consciously engage with an Indigenous person for fear of saying the wrong thing or getting a guilt trip in the face of the many wrongs of the last 250 years.

There is no escaping that the European settlers have stolen the land and lives of Australia's Indigenous peoples, which has led to the unconscionable suffering and the ongoing disadvantage of the First Nations people today.

Every State has a history of massacres[177] and almost 70 per cent of Australians accept that Aboriginal people were subject to mass killings, incarceration, forced removal from land, and their movement was restricted. However, there is a massive gap in trust with nearly half of Aboriginal and Torres Strait Islander people believing they have high trust towards Australians in the general community, but only 27 per cent of non-indigenous Australians reciprocate the view.

This is another gap we urgently need to close if we are to progress reconciliation in this country.

To ease the guests into the event, the Sofitel provided the usual 5-star luxury with the menu designed by the young trainee chefs at Charcoal Lane, cooked by them with the hotel staff in the cavernous kitchen and served by them with the hotel's front of house team.

As the CEOs sat down, they found an Aboriginal elder sitting at their table. The guests were then informed that they would be moving tables between courses, allowing them to meet other elders. There was a distinct sound of shifting bottoms and shuffling chairs. Always good to get people out of their comfort zone.

To set the scene, then CEO of Telstra, David Thodey AO, warmed up the corporate leaders with a stirring, heartfelt speech on his passion for the rights

---

[176] Reconciliation Australia (2019) *2018 Australian Reconciliation Barometer* accessed at https://www.reconciliation.org.au/wp-content/uploads/2019/02/ra_2019-barometer-brochure_web.single.page_.pdf

[177] See https://www.theguardian.com/australia-news/ng-interactive/2019/mar/04/massacre-map-australia-the-killing-times-frontier-wars

of First Nations peoples and Telstra's use of digital technology to assist them, giving the example *Machado Joseph Disease (MJD)*, an incurable hereditary neurodegenerative condition. Each child of a person who carries the defective gene has a 50 per cent chance of developing the disease[178].

MJD starts with memory deficits, difficulty with speech and swallowing, weakness in arms and legs, clumsiness, frequent urination and involuntary eye movements, and gradually, and cruelly, leads to paralysis of the body whilst the mind remains intact. Progression to dependence occurs over five to ten years. Most people are wheelchair bound and entirely dependent for their daily living needs within 10-15 years of the first symptoms emerging.

MJD is particularly prevalent in the Aboriginal communities in East Arnhem Land. David discussed how Telstra provided computers to the MJD Foundation to create a speech bank of common phrases for individuals who had lost their ability to speak. They were then used to make films about bush tucker and record family histories and memories[179].

David gave his peers a role model, providing them with the permission and inspiration to get engaged.

As the wine flowed and the delicious food was served, questions like 'why aren't you black' (in reply, Wurundjeri Elder, Ron Jones, would say he was born in the daytime whilst his ancestors were born in the night[180]) gave the opportunity for the elders to explain the history and lineage of Indigenous families in Victoria.

I went on to work with David and his team at Telstra to establish their first Indigenous employment program to mainstream the recruitment, training, and mentoring of Indigenous people in their divisions in a supportive and culturally safe environment.

Our First Nations peoples represent the oldest continuous living culture on the planet. Indigenous Australians represent 3.8 per cent of the total Australian population as per the 2021 census, or 983,709 First Nations people.

The population and proportion by State and Territory in the 2021 census was: NSW has 339,710 or 36 per cent; Queensland has 273,119 or 28 per cent; WA has 120,006 or 12 per cent; Victoria has 78,696 or 8 per cent; NT 76,481 or 8

[178] https://mjd.org.au/2-what-is-mjd.html

[179] Booth G, Huggins J, Thodey D, Rigney L-I, Ganley L, Glanville J, Pearson L, O'Leary T (2014) *Making the Connection: Essays on Indigenous Digital Excellence,* Fontaine Publishing Group, p.60

[180] https://www.youtube.com/watch?v=hUG8qTSnhsA

per cent; SA has 52,069 or 5 per cent; Tasmania has 33,857 or 3 per cent; and the ACT has 9,529 or one per cent.

4 in 10 live in a major city, one in four reside in inner regional Australia and one in five dwell in outer regional Australia. 1 in 6, or over 150,000 Indigenous people, live in remote or very remote Australia (compared to one in seventy non-Indigenous Australians).

1/3rd are under 15 years of age, the median age is 24 years and 3/4 live in New South Wales, Queensland and Western Australia combined. Over 9 in 10 identify as Aboriginal, 4 per cent as Torres Strait Islander and 4 per cent as both[181].

The path to the Closing the Gap plan began in 2008 with the Rudd Government establishing the *National Indigenous Health Equality Council* and the State governments approving the *National Indigenous Reform Agreement* which set out Closing the Gap targets to: close the life expectancy gap within a generation; halve the gap in mortality rates for Indigenous children under five within a decade; ensure access to early childhood education for all Indigenous four year olds in remote communities within five years; halve the gap in reading, writing and numeracy achievements for children within a decade; halve the gap for Indigenous students in year 12 attainment rates by 2020; and halve the gap in employment outcomes between Indigenous and non-Indigenous Australians within a decade.

The progress against the targets is monitored by the Productivity Commission to ensure all parties to the National Agreement understand how their efforts are contributing to progress.

Today, only 4 are on track to meet their targets. A further 6 targets show improvement but are not on track to be met. Outcomes continue to worsen against four targets - children commencing school being developmentally on track, rates of children in out-of-home care, rates of adult imprisonment (which have gone up 30 per cent since 2019), and suicide. With no nationally agreed process to determine the relevant contributions required from each State and Territory towards the targets, Commissioner Selwyn Button noted, 'in our review of progress towards the National Agreement on Closing the Gap, we

181 Australia Bureau of Statistics (2013) *Estimates of Aboriginal and Torres Strait Islander Australians* at https://www.abs.gov.au/statistics/people/aboriginal-and-torres-strait-islander-peoples/estimates-aboriginal-and-torres-strait-islander-australians/latest-release

found that governments had not taken enough meaningful action to meet their commitments under the Agreement'[182].

The health and social disadvantage faced by our First Nations people is shocking and unconscionable, and perpetuated by unrelenting racism and discrimination.

After practising self-determination and self-government for tens of thousands of years before colonisation began, the *Uluru Statement from the Heart's* request to at least have a dedicated mechanism for the First Peoples of Australia to have a say in government policy and legislation that affects their daily lives was defeated in the Voice to Parliament referendum.

Placed-based disadvantage

About 1 in 3 Indigenous households, or over 120,000 Indigenous people, live in poverty, with nearly 1 in 2 living in the most disadvantaged areas[183], ranging from 66 per cent in the Northern Territory, to 34-55 per cent in the States, to 1 per cent in the ACT[184]. Approximately 50 per cent of Indigenous adults are reliant on some form of welfare payment.

Some remote Indigenous communities live in absolute poverty, measured by poor, unsanitary infrastructure, with diseases that are largely eradicated in other parts of Australia, such as Rheumatic Heart Disease[185].

We know that families relying on public or private rent are more vulnerable to poverty. For Indigenous people, nearly 3/4 are housed in some form of rental property.

According to data from the Australian Institute of Health and Welfare, a significant majority of Indigenous Australians experiencing the most disadvantage are concentrated in very remote areas, with around 71 per cent of Indigenous people living in these regions classified as being in the most disadvantaged quintile, compared to only one per cent in major cities.

---

182 Productivity Commission (2025) *Closing the Gap Annual Data Compilation Report*, July 2024 at https://www.pc.gov.au/closing-the-gap-data/annual-data-report

183 The lowest quintile according to the SEIFA index

184 Australian Institute of Health and Welfare at https://www.indigenoushpf.gov.au/measures/2-09-index-of-disadvantage

185 Aboriginal and Torres Strait Islander Commission (ATSIC) (2004) *Submission* 244, pp.9-10 to Commonwealth of Australia (2004) *A hand up not a hand out: Renewing the fight against poverty. Report on poverty and financial hardship*, The Senate Community Affairs References Committee, Canberra

Homelessness

At 24,930 Aboriginal and Torres Strait Islander people[186], the homelessness rate for Indigenous Australians is nearly nine times the rate for non-Indigenous Australians and comprises 1 in 5 of all those experiencing homelessness[187].

In 2024/25, around 82,900 First Nations people received support from specialist homelessness services or nearly 3 in 10 of all clients[188], a 6 per cent increase on the previous year, whilst 126,000 Indigenous Australians live in public housing[189].

First Nations children are overrepresented among children experiencing homelessness, making up a 3rd of homeless children nationally, despite comprising only 6.8 per cent of the population under 18.

Health

Aboriginal and Torres Strait Islander life expectancy at birth is 71.9 years for males, or 8.8 years less than for non-Indigenous males, and 75.6 years for females, or 8.1 years less than for non-Indigenous females[190], with First Nations people living in major cities expected to live around five years longer than those living in remote and very remote areas[191].

It is shameful that almost two-thirds of deaths of those aged under 75 were avoidable with disease prevention and population health initiatives or access to timely and effective health care[192].

---

[186] Australian Bureau of Statistics (2023) *Aboriginal and Torres Strait Islander peoples experiencing homelessness* at https://www.abs.gov.au/articles/aboriginal-and-torres-strait-islander-peoples-experiencing-homelessness

[187] Australian Bureau of Statistics (2018*) Census of Population and Housing: Estimating Homelessness 2016*

[188] Australian Institute of Health and Welfare (2025) *Specialist homelessness services annual report 2024–25. First Nations clients* at https://www.aihw.gov.au/reports/homelessness-services/specialist-homelessness-services-annual-report/contents/first-nations-clients

[189] Australian Institute of Health and Welfare (2024) *Housing assistance in Australia 2024* at https://www.aihw.gov.au/reports/housing-assistance/housing-assistance-in-australia/contents/occupants

[190] Australian Bureau of Statistics (2023*) Aboriginal and Torres Strait Islander life expectancy* at https://www.abs.gov.au/statistics/people/aboriginal-and-torres-strait-islander-peoples/aboriginal-and-torres-strait-islander-life-expectancy/latest-release#data-downloads

[191] Australian Institute for Health and Welfare (2025) *Health and wellbeing of First Nations people* at https://www.aihw.gov.au/reports/australias-health/indigenous-health-and-wellbeing

[192] Australian Institute for Health and Welfare (2018) *Aboriginal and Torres Strait Islander Health Performance Framework - Summary report. Leading causes of disease burden and mortality*

At more than double that of non-Indigenous Australians, the burden of disease means that First Nations people lose 239,942 years annually due to premature death or living with disease or injury.

The top disease groups contributing to the burden in Indigenous people are in order: mental health & substance use disorders (such as anxiety, depression, and drug use); injuries (such as falls, road traffic injuries, and suicide); cardiovascular diseases (such as coronary heart disease and rheumatic heart disease); cancer and other neoplasms (such as lung cancer and breast cancer).

Cardiovascular diseases accounted for the largest gap in mortality rates between Indigenous and non-Indigenous Australians, followed by cancer and other neoplasms; endocrine, metabolic and nutritional disorders, including diabetes; and respiratory diseases[193].

In particular, Acute Rheumatic Fever (ARF), as the main cause of Rheumatic Heart Disease (RHD), is almost exclusively found in First Nations people. Associated with socioeconomic and environmental factors such as poverty and overcrowded housing, and entirely preventable, the rates of RHD in remote communities are some of the worst in the world, despite straightforward treatment with antibiotics[194].

Established in 2014, the charity, END RHD Centre of Research Excellence has led a collaboration between researchers, Aboriginal Community Controlled Health Organisations (ACCHOs), Indigenous leaders, governments, communities and people with lived experience to produce and enact *The RHD Endgame Strategy: A Snapshot. The blueprint to eliminate rheumatic heart disease in Australia by 2031*[195].

---

at https://www.indigenoushpf.gov.au/report-overview/overview/summary-report/4-tier-1-%E2%80%93-health-status-and-outcomes/leading-causes-of-disease-burden-and-mortality#:~:text=Cancer%20(as%20a%20broad%20disease,of%20death%20for%20First%20Nations

193 Australian Institute for Health and Welfare (2019) *Aboriginal and Torres Strait Islander Health Performance Framework - Summary report. 1.23 Leading causes of mortality* at https://www.indigenoushpf.gov.au/measures/1-23-leading-causes-of-mortality

194 Haynes E, Marawili M, Marika MB, Mitchell A, Walker R, Katzenellenbogen JM, Bessarab D (2022) *Living with Rheumatic Heart Disease at the Intersection of Biomedical and Aboriginal Worldviews*. Int J Environ Res Public Health. 2022 Apr 12;19(8):4650. doi: 10.3390/ijerph19084650. PMID: 35457520; PMCID: PMC9025526.

195 Wyber R et al (2020) *The RHD Endgame Strategy: A Snapshot. The blueprint to eliminate rheumatic heart disease in Australia by 2031*, Perth, The END RHD Centre of Research Excellence, Telethon Kids Institute

Family and domestic violence (FDV)

Aboriginal and Torres Strait Islander people are overrepresented as both victim-survivors and perpetrators of family and domestic violence.

The true rate of FDV in Indigenous communities is unknown due to low rate of reporting to police. Estimates suggest that around 90 per cent of violence against First Nations women and most cases of sexual abuse of First Nations children are undisclosed[196].

The 2021 National Community Attitudes towards Violence against Women Survey found that the courts and police were not trusted with less than half agreeing that when First Nations men were accused of violence, fair treatment would be provided by the courts (45 per cent) or the police (40 per cent).

We do know that the rate of domestic homicides for Indigenous women is nearly 6 times higher than that of non-Indigenous women, with six in ten experiencing physical or sexual violence perpetrated by a male intimate partner. They are 32 times more likely to be hospitalised for family violence than non-Indigenous people[197].

The *National Plan to End Violence against Women and their Children 2022–2032* has recognised First Nations people as a priority group in their efforts to address, prevent and respond to gender-based violence in Australia, supported by Closing the Gap Target 13 to reduce the rate of all forms of family violence against First Nations women and children by at least 50 per cent by 2031, as progress towards zero.

Children and young people

Disadvantage for our First Nations people starts even before they are born, with the child mortality rate twice that of non-Indigenous children[198].

Indigenous children are overrepresented in areas where child safety and security are compromised. Indigenous children aged 0–17 have higher rates of hospitalisations and deaths due to injury than non-Indigenous children; are more likely to be victims of child abuse, neglect and sexual assault; and are over-represented in homelessness and youth justice statistics.

---

[196] Willis M (2011) *Non-disclosure of violence in Australian Indigenous communities- external site opens in new window,* trends & issues in crime and criminal justice no. 405, Australian Institute of Criminology.

[197] Australian Institute for Health and Welfare (2019) *Family, domestic and sexual violence in Australia: continuing the national story*

[198] Commonwealth of Australia (2020) *Closing the Gap Report 2020*, p.15

Nationally, over 4 in 10 children aged 0–17 years in out-of-home care are Aboriginal and Torres Strait Islanders, whilst the same rate of Indigenous children in their first year of full-time schooling were categorised as developmentally vulnerable, twice that of non-Indigenous children[199].

Young Indigenous people account for nearly half of young people under youth justice supervision and nearly 6 in 10 of young people in youth detention[200].

In August 2025, the Australian government appointed a new National Commissioner for Aboriginal and Torres Strait Islander Children and Young People, as national targets to reduce child removal and youth detention continue to slide backwards, despite a dedicated action plan aimed at reducing the rate of First Nations child abuse and neglect and its intergenerational impacts, the *Safe and Supported: Aboriginal and Torres Strait Islander First Action Plan 2023–2026*[201].

Discrimination and racism

In June 2025, the Law Enforcement Conduct Commission found that a senior NSW police officer's decision not to call an ambulance after an Indigenous man was found self-harming in a prison cell was driven by 'unconscious racism'. He thought Aboriginal people tried to 'manipulate the system'[202].

Sadly, this is not an isolated incident. A 2023 Australian Institute of Health and Welfare report concluded that 'experiences of racism and racial discrimination are common for Aboriginal and Torres Strait Islander people regardless of gender, age and geographic location' and 'are associated with negative impacts on mental health and wellbeing outcomes, including psychological distress, stress and depression'[203].

Furthermore, *Jumbunna Institute* Director Professor Lindon Coombes notes that in 2025 'racism remains an insidious and all too common aspect of life for Indigenous people in Australia', noting that racist views were emboldened during the Voice referendum, with racist abuse and harmful and derogatory language being spread online and in person.

---

199 Australian Institute for Health and Welfare (2017) *Australia's welfare 2017: in brief*

200 Australian Institute for Health and Welfare (2017) *Australia's welfare 2017: in brief*

201 https://www.dss.gov.au/child-protection/resource/safe-and-supported-aboriginal-and-torres-strait-islander-first-action-plan-2023-2026

202 https://www.theguardian.com/australia-news/2025/jun/24/unconscious-racism-nsw-police-indigenous-prisoner-ntwnfb?CMP=Share_iOSApp_Other

203 Truong M and Moore E (2023) *Racism and Indigenous wellbeing, mental health and suicide*, Catalogue number IMH 17, Australian Institute of Health and Welfare, Australian Government at https://www.indigenousmhspc.gov.au/publications/racism

Other research has found that a third of Indigenous Australians aged 15 years and over have experienced unfair treatment in the previous year because they were Aboriginal and/or Torres Strait Islander[204], and 42 per cent of Indigenous Australians aged 18 years and over report experiencing everyday racial discrimination[205].

The unconscious bias against First Nations peoples is pervasive. A 2020 study found that 3 in 4 Australians unconsciously hold a negative prejudice against Aboriginal and Torres Strait Islander peoples, which indicates that experiences of discrimination amongst Indigenous Australians may reflect an implicit bias inherent in Australian society[206].

Worryingly, this racism appears to be growing. The last Australian Reconciliation Barometer found that 60 per cent of First Nations people had experienced at least 1 form of racial prejudice, compared to 52 per cent in 2020 and 43 per cent in 2018[207].

The third report from the *Call It Out project*, covering the 453 reports of racism against Aboriginal and Torres Strait Islander people reported on the *Call It Out First Nations Racism Register* from March 2023-March 2024 found that the most common forms of racism were stereotyping (23 per cent) and discrimination (15 per cent), followed by hate speech (13 per cent) and non-recognition of cultural rights (11 per cent). Aggressively racist behaviour – including physical violence, verbal abuse, hate speech, threats, intimidation, bullying and damage to property – made up over 1 in 3 of the reports. The analysis found racism was most likely to take place online and in the media (1 in 3 reports), followed by public places (13 per cent) and in the workplace (12 per cent)[208].

---

[204] Australian Bureau of Statistics (2017) *Stressors, by sex and remoteness, Aboriginal and Torres Strait Islander persons aged 15 years and over 2014–2015, Proportion of persons [Table 14.3]*, National Aboriginal and Torres Strait Islander Social Survey 2014–2015, https://www.abs.gov.au/AUSSTATS/abs@.nsf/DetailsPage/4714.02014-15?OpenDocument

[205] Thurber K, Colonna E, Jones R, Gee G, Priest N, Cohen R, Williams D, Thandrayen J, Calma T, Lovett R and Mayi Kuwayu Study Team (2021) *Prevalence of everyday discrimination and relation with wellbeing among Aboriginal and Torres Strait Islander adults in Australia*, International Journal of Environmental Research and Public Health, 18(12):6577, doi:10.3390/ijerph18126577

[206] Shirodkar S (2019) *Bias against Indigenous Australians: Implicit Association Test results for Australia*, Australian Journal of Indigenous Issues: Vol. 22, No. 3-4, Dec 2019: 3-34

[207] Reconciliation Australia (2022) *2022 Australian Reconciliation Barometer* at https://www.reconciliation.org.au/wp-content/uploads/2022/11/Australian-Reconciliation-Barometer-2022.pdf

[208] Allison F, Cunneen C, Coombes L and Selcuk A (2025) *"If you don't think racism exists come take a walk with us". The Call It Out Racism Register 2023-2024*, Jumbunna Institute for

16 years after Nicky Winmar pointed proudly to his skin in a gesture of defiance at racial abuse, in 2019, racism in sport was again in the spotlight with Channel Ten screening *The Final Quarter*, showcasing the shameful treatment of Adam Goodes over the final 3 years of his AFL career with the Sydney Swans.

In 2021, AFL great Eddie Betts spoke out for the first time. He told The Age newspaper 'racism does exist in Australia, and over the past 10 years of playing AFL footy, I have been racially abused every single year. It happened last week. It happened the week before that and the week before that."

In 2024, Former Kangaroos players Jimmy Krakouer and Phil Krakouera lodged a Supreme Court statement of claim on behalf of former AFL and VFL players who experienced racial vilification, harassment or humiliation on the basis of race between 1975 and 2022.

Despite their natural talent and exciting skills, racism towards Indigenous players in sport is widespread with every second First Nations person experiencing racism at sports events[209].

Recognising the growing issue, in March 2026, Indigenous Affairs Minister, Malarndirri McCarthy, announced an inquiry into rising racism, hate and violence against First Nations people to examine the forms, impacts and drivers of racism experienced by First Peoples, and the changes needed to address it.

Education and employment

The proportion of Indigenous teenagers (aged 15 to 19 years) not fully engaged in work or education is 3 times that of non-Indigenous people, whilst approximately 70 per cent of young Indigenous adults (aged 20-24 years) are not fully engaged with work or education.

It is no wonder then that Indigenous unemployment rates are well over twice that of non-Indigenous people in cities and regional centres, and are much higher in remote areas, with Indigenous people in full-time employment or education of around 30 per cent of each age cohort, compared to at least 50 per cent of non-Indigenous people.

Indigenous Education and Research, University of Technology Sydney at https://callitout.com.au/wp-content/uploads/2025/02/Jumbunna-Call-It-Out-Annual-Report-2023-2024-Final.pdf

[209] Victorian Health Promotion Agency (2012) *Mental health impacts of racial discrimination in Victorian Aboriginal communities Experiences of Racism survey: a summary*

With 'you can't be what you can't see', the lack of role models is a challenge, as Indigenous Australians hold less than 1 per cent of senior leadership roles across corporate Australia. More than half have endured racism at work[210].

Justice

Rather than incarceration rates decreasing towards the Closing the Gap target, they've increased over time, and Indigenous people continue to be grossly over-represented in Australian prisons. Incredibly, nearly 1 in 20 of all Aboriginal and Torres Strait Islander adult males are imprisoned today, make up over a 3rd of all prisoners, and have increased 20 per cent since 2019[211].

The Royal Commission into Aboriginal Deaths in Custody recognised that the fundamental causes for the over-representation of First Nations people in custody are not factors associated completely within the criminal justice system, but are symptomatic of the broader social and economic inequality faced by First Nations people outlined above, including early school leaving, low school performance, and low educational attainment; high rates of unemployment and low-quality employment; lack of secure accommodation; hearing impairment, cognitive impairment/disability or mental and physical illness; risky use of alcohol and illicit drugs; the trauma associated with colonisation, being a member of the Stolen Generations, and the forced removal of First Nations children; and a greater risk of being neglected or abused, and being a victim of family violence for children, young people and women.

Tragically, 33 First Nations people died in custody in 2024-25, the largest number since the first year of the national monitoring program in 1979-1980 and brings the total number of Indigenous deaths in custody since the 1991 royal commission into Aboriginal deaths in custody to 600. Of that figure, 397 have been in prison custody, 6 in youth detention, and 197 in police custody[212].

Research by the University of NSW reported that upwards of 90 per cent of Indigenous prisoners in New South Wales have complex health and disability support needs[213].

---

[210] Minderoo Foundation (2022) *Australian Indigenous Employment Index 2022 National Report* at https://cdn.minderoo.org/content/uploads/2022/05/22105150/Woort-Koorliny-Australian-Indigenous-Employment-Index-2022.pdf

[211] Australian Bureau of Statistics (2025) *Corrective Services, Australia. National and state information about adult prisoners and community-based corrections, including legal status, custody type, Indigenous status and sex* at https://www.abs.gov.au/statistics/people/crime-and-justice/corrective-services-australia/mar-quarter-2025

[212] https://www.aic.gov.au/statistics/deaths-custody-australia

[213] Baldry E, McCausland R, Dowse L and McEntyre E (2015) *A predictable and preventable path: Aboriginal people with mental and cognitive disabilities in the criminal justice system,*

WHY

As this 'racism is an ongoing consequence of colonisation, systematic oppression and the exclusion and disempowerment of Indigenous Australians'[214], we need to face up to our nation's history.

In the words of the country's first dedicated Indigenous legal service, the Victorian Aboriginal Legal Services, 'the impact of systemic racism on Aboriginal communities is a direct product of this country's violent and racist history. The legal system is built on a foundation of violence and dispossession, denial of sovereignty and humanity, with the colonial project continuing through policies of protection and assimilation'[215].

There were between 300,000 and 950,000 Aboriginal people living in Australia when the British arrived in 1788 with 260 distinct language groups and 500 dialects[216].

After circumnavigating New Zealand, the *HMS Endeavour* arrived at Point Hicks in Gippsland, Victoria on 20 April 1770. Cook's voyage had 3 aims: to establish an observatory at Tahiti to record the transit of Venus (when the planet passed between the earth and the sun); to record natural history, led by 25-year-old Joseph Banks; and a final, secret goal was to continue the search for the Great South Land.

His instruction was 'you are also with the consent of the Natives to take Possession of Convenient Situations in the name of the King of Great Britain; or, if you find the Country uninhabited, take Possession for His Majesty by setting up Proper Marks and Inscriptions, as first discoverers and possessors'.

He sailed north to Botany Bay and raised the Union Jack on 29 April 1770, before continuing northward along the Australian coastline, narrowly avoiding shipwreck on the Great Barrier Reef, before Cook raised it again on 22 August 1770 on Possession Island, off Cape York, when he claimed the east coast of

---

UNSW, Sydney at https://www.unsw.edu.au/content/dam/pdfs/unsw-adobe-websites/yuwaya-ngarra-li/2023-06-yn/2023-07-a-predictable-and-preventable-path-final.pdf

214 Truong M and Moore E (2023) *Racism and Indigenous wellbeing, mental health and suicide,* Catalogue number IMH 17, Australian Institute of Health and Welfare, Australian Government, p.vi

215 https://www.vals.org.au/wp-content/uploads/2022/01/Community-fact-sheet-Systemic-Racism.pdf

216 Australian Institute of Health and Welfare (2023) *Aboriginal and Torres Strait Islander Health Performance Framework - Summary report* https://www.workingwithindigenousaustralians.info/content/History_2_60,000_years.html#:~:text=They%20were%20a%20hunter%2Dgatherer,language%20groups%20and%20500%20dialects.

Australia in the name of King George III. The crew was sworn to secrecy about the lands they had discovered.

Australian historian Henry Reynolds argues that, in itself, the claim would have mattered no more than Tasman's 1642 claim over Tasmania or the claim over Western Australia made by a French expedition in 1772. A claim based on discovery could be the basis for an assertion of sovereignty only when it is accompanied by actual possession[217]. This began when the First Fleet arrived and Governor Phillip hoisted the Union Jack again on 26 January 1788 at Sydney Cove, marking the first European settlement of Australia.

Phillip was instructed to establish a penal colony on the basis of a proposal to the government from Banks and James Matra, who noted that New South Wales was 'peopled only by a few lack inhabitants who, in the rudest state of society, knew no other arts than such as were necessary to their mere animal existence'. Despite admitting that he knew nothing of the vast inland, he argued that 'we may have liberty to conjecture that [it is] totally uninhabited'.

Phillip soon found that 'the natives are far more numerous than they were supposed to be', but it would take 2 centuries for Eddie Mabo to successfully overturn the myth that at the time of colonisation Australia was *terra nullius* or land belonging to no one with the High Court recognising that Indigenous peoples had lived in Australia for thousands of years and enjoyed rights to their land according to their own laws and customs. 12 months later, the *Native Title Act 1993* was passed.

15 months after the First Fleet landed, 70 per cent of the Aboriginal people in and around Sydney Cove were killed by smallpox, followed by up to a 3rd of the population of the eastern Australian tribes as the pandemic spread.

While the European population had a strong resistance to diseases such as bronchitis, measles, scarlet fever, chicken pox and even the common cold, exposure to these diseases was often fatal to Aboriginal populations. Added to this were other diseases such as smallpox, tuberculosis and venereal disease (such as syphilis) that were deadly for European and Aboriginal populations alike.

Changes to diet also became a source of ill health and disease. Some changes were caused by restricted access to traditional food, from land being fenced off, native animals being shot for sport, and the introduction of hoofed animals such as sheep (which trampled and destroyed native plants that had served as staple foodstuffs). For some, these changes led to starvation, for others to the adoption

---

[217] Reynolds H (2021) *Truth-Tellin. History, Sovereignty and the Uluru Statement*, Sydney, p.17

of a European-style diet including refined sugar, flour, and offal, replacing what had been a high-protein diet. The impact of a diet based on these introduced foodstuffs was made worse by the provision of rations that consisted of the worst quality and cheapest grains and meats available[218].

We now know that more than 10,000 Aboriginal and Torres Strait Islander people were killed in 403 massacres. Before 1830, most of the massacres were carried out by foot soldiers from British regiments posted to New South Wales, Tasmania and Western Australia to protect the frontiers from Indigenous attack. They were often part of joint operations with settlers and convicts and led by magistrates. As European settlement expanded into the north and west after 1860, most of the massacres were conducted by employees of major companies who were bankrolling big pastoral or mining leases[219].

By 1900, the population of Indigenous people had fallen by 84 per cent to 117,000[220].

Missionaries often settled in remote areas where they would build churches, schools, and other facilities to convert souls and serve the local Aboriginal community. The first mission was established at Wellington Valley in New South Wales in 1832 by the Church Missionary Society. Life on the missions was strictly regulated with Indigenous residents typically required to attend religious services, adopt Western dress codes, and speak English. Children were often separated from their families to be educated in mission schools, a practice that contributed to the loss of Indigenous languages and cultural practices[221].

To quell the violence on the frontiers of early Australia, to reduce devastation by disease and to provide Aborigines with a 'humane' environment while their race died out, colonial governments introduced systems of 'protective' legislation. The first was in 1860 in South Australia, where a Chief Protector was appointed to watch over the interests of Aboriginal people and to 'smooth the dying pillow'. Similar legislation was passed in Victoria (1869), Queensland (1897), Western Australia (1905) and New South Wales (1909)[222].

---

218 https://aboriginalhistoryofyarra.com.au/9-disease/

219 https://www.abc.net.au/news/2022-03-16/aboriginal-people-genocidal-killings-massacre-map-nt-wa/100913106

220 https://www.creativespirits.info/aboriginalculture/people/aboriginal-population-in-australia

221 https://www.historyskills.com/classroom/year-9/yr-9-reserves-and-missions-reading/#:~:text=Aboriginal%20missions&text=They%20were%20established%20by%20religious,by%20the%20Church%20Missionary%20Society.

222 https://researchdata.edu.au/smoothing-pillow-dying-race/1431627

The Aboriginal Protection Act 1869 made Victoria the first colony to create an act that allowed the government to totally regulate the lives of Aboriginal people, including where they could live and work, who they could marry, and when they were allowed to go to the local towns.

The Act changed the definition of 'Aboriginal' to exclude those who were 'half-caste' (only one parent was counted as Aboriginal), which led to half-caste children being removed from missions and placed in white families or institutions, leading to the start of the 'Stolen Generations'.

Between 1910 and 1970, thousands of Aboriginal and Torres Strait Islander children were forcibly removed from their families and communities by churches, welfare organisations and governments. Whilst the exact number is not known, it is estimated that over 100,000 and anywhere from 1 in 10 to 1 in 3 Indigenous children were forcibly removed from their families and fostered or adopted by non-Indigenous families or raised in institutions. Many experienced neglect, physical and sexual abuse and exploitative labour, and were denied contact with their families[223].

Today, over 20,000 Aboriginal and Torres Strait Islander children have been removed from their families to go into out-of-home care. They represent 43 per cent of the total number of children in out-of-home care[224].

When I was born, First Nations people were counted as fauna and flora. Section 127 of Australia's Constitution stated that 'in reckoning the numbers of the people of the Commonwealth, or of a State or other part of the Commonwealth, Aboriginal natives should not be counted'. This changed with the landmark 1967 referendum, which saw the highest ever yes vote of over 90 per cent.

In 1970, in Redfern, Aboriginal activists and lawyers established the first Aboriginal Legal Service staffed by volunteers who provided free legal advice and representation to the Aboriginal people of inner Sydney. Today, there are dedicated services in each State and Territory which provide legal advice, assistance, representation, community legal education, advocacy, law reform activities, and prisoner through-care to Aboriginal and Torres Strait Islander peoples in contact with the justice system.

A year later, Redfern was also the site of the first Aboriginal Community Controlled Health Organisation (ACCHO) established in response to

---

223 Commonwealth of Australia (1997) *Bringing them Home. National Inquiry into the Separation of Aboriginal and Torres Strait Islander Children from Their Families,* Australian Human Rights Commission, Canberra

224 https://www.snaicc.org.au/our-work/child-and-family-wellbeing/family-matters/

experiences of racism in mainstream health services and an unmet need for culturally safe and accessible primary health care. There are now more than 140 ACCHOs across Australia with peak representative organisations across all states and territories[225]. ACCHOs not only have an essential role in addressing immediate healthcare needs but also invest in driving change in the more entrenched structural determinants of health[226].

In 1988, the leaders of the Central and Northern land councils, artist Wenten Rubuntja and activist Galarrwuy Yunupingu, presented then Prime Minister Bob Hawke with the Barunga Statement, which called on Hawke to honour his earlier promises to deliver national land rights legislation and a treaty. Hawke signed the statement and promised a treaty by 1990.

In 1991, *the Royal Commission into Aboriginal Deaths in Custody* report called for a process of national reconciliation. The Australian Parliament passed the Council for Aboriginal Reconciliation Act 1991, launching a process of national reconciliation and establishing the Council for Aboriginal Reconciliation with the vision for 'a united Australia which respects this land of ours; values the Aboriginal and Torres Strait Islander heritage; and provides justice and equity for all'[227]. But few of those proposals have been implemented, and Indigenous people continue to die at alarming rates in prison cells, police vans, or during arrest.

In the middle of the 2025 Reconciliation Week, a young, disabled Warlpiri man died following a scuffle in a Coles supermarket in Alice Springs after he was 'placed' on the floor by 2 plain-clothed policemen.

Since the Royal Commission, 600 Indigenous Australians have died in custody[228].

However, we have seen the welcome emergence of an early intervention approach to Indigenous youth offending called *justice reinvestment.*

The interest in justice reinvestment grew when the United States was facing high and rising costs of building and staffing prisons. They began to ask whether addressing the social causes that underlay the jailing of people would

---

225 https://www.naccho.org.au/acchos/

226 Pearson, O., Schwartzkopff, K., Dawson, A. *et al.* Aboriginal community controlled health organisations address health equity through action on the social determinants of health of Aboriginal and Torres Strait Islander peoples in Australia. *BMC Public Health* **20**, 1859 (2020). https://doi.org/10.1186/s12889-020-09943-4

227 https://www.reconciliation.org.au/reconciliation-timeline-key-moments/

228 https://www.theguardian.com/australia-news/2025/jul/31/closing-the-gap-report-goals-targets-worse-ntwnfb

be cheaper and more effective. They argued that the money spent on programs to keep people out of prison would be more than equal to that necessary to build more prisons.

In Australia, justice reinvestment is a way of reducing Aboriginal People's interactions with the criminal justice system by Aboriginal communities developing their own solutions for change, making them safer and more just, as well as contributing to broader systemic reform in education, health, care, and child protection.

Award-winning *Just Reinvest NSW* was formed in 2012 as a coalition united around wanting to take action to reduce the number of Aboriginal children and young people being locked up has been a leader in developing. Its first project, Maranguka, is the first Aboriginal-led place-based model of justice reinvestment in Australia. Maranguka takes a 'life-course' approach, targeting issues likely to push Aboriginal people into the justice system that arise from a child's earliest years into adulthood.

The justice reinvestment projects have shown that self-determination and culture are foundational for community empowerment and essential to delivering better First Nations justice outcomes[229].

Today, justice reinvestment projects take place in Halls Creek (WA), Port Adelaide (SA), Moree, Mt Druitt, Bourke (NSW), Rockhampton, Cherbourg (QLD), and Alice Springs (NT).

In 2023, the Australian government commenced its National Justice Reinvestment Program, offering $69 million in grants to support up to 30 community-led Justice Reinvestment initiatives[230].

Hawke's successor, Paul Keating's Redfern speech in 1992 was the first ever public acknowledgement by the Commonwealth Government of the dispossession of the country's First Nations peoples:

> *'the problem starts with us non-Aboriginal Australians.*
> *It begins, I think, with that act of recognition.*
> *Recognition that it was we who did the dispossessing.*
> *We took the traditional lands and smashed the traditional way of life.*

---

229 Allison F and Cunneen C (2022) *Justice Reinvestment In Australia. A Review Of Progress And Key Issues,* Jumbunna Institute for Indigenous Education and Research, University of Technology Sydney, Justice Reinvestment Network Australia, July 2022 at https://www.justreinvest.org.au/community/jrnsw-na/

230 https://ministers.ag.gov.au/media-centre/now-open-national-justice-reinvestment-program-15-09-2023

We brought the diseases. The alcohol.
We committed the murders.
We took the children from their mothers.
We practised discrimination and exclusion.
It was our ignorance and our prejudice.
And our failure to imagine these things being done to us.'

Following the High Court recognising native title in the landmark Mabo v Queensland (No.2) case, the Native Title Act was enacted in 1993 to recognise the rights and interests of Aboriginal and Torres Strait Islander people in land and waters according to their traditional laws and customs. For native title to be recognised, the laws and customs observed by Aboriginal and Torres Strait Islander people when Australia was colonised must have been acknowledged and observed in a 'substantially uninterrupted' way from the time of settlement until now.

Native title may be claimed in areas where it has not been extinguished, such as vacant (or unallocated) Crown land, parks and public reserves, beaches, some leases (such as non-exclusive pastoral leases), land held by government agencies and oceans, seas, reefs, lakes, rivers, creeks and other waters that are not privately owned. Native title rights cannot be claimed in relation to minerals, gas or petroleum under Australian law and native title in tidal and sea areas can only be of a non-exclusive nature, as exclusive native title is considered inconsistent with other common law rights regarding marine access and navigation.

And then, the types of rights that are recognised in a native title determination depend on the particular laws and customs of the native title claim group, and what they can prove[231] with native title only recognising the right to perform certain activities, such as maintain and protect sites, camping, hunting, fishing and ceremonies, which come from traditional laws and customs. It does not recognise those traditional laws and customs themselves.

Typically, native title is found to exist alongside other non-Indigenous property rights, such as pastoral leases. In some cases, native title rights may include possession of an area to the exclusion of all others or the right to take resources, such as fish, but do not amount to full legal ownership of land or waters, and they cannot be sold.

The requirements for proof are significant and burdensome. Once a claim has been successfully filed and registered with the National Native Title Tribunal, applicants can claim the right to negotiate against the development of the land.

---

[231] https://nativetitle.org.au/learn/native-title-and-pbcs/native-title-rights-and-interests

However, if the rights of pastoralists, mining companies, the federal government, or private owners come into conflict with native title rights, they supersede the native title rights[232].

Native title holders are entitled to compensation for activities which diminish or damage their native title rights and interests for acts which occurred on or after 31 October 1975, when the Racial Discrimination Act 1975 came into effect. However, the Act does not allow for discrimination on the basis of race, colour, descent or national or ethnic origin. Compensation claims have only recently come before the court, with the Ngaliwurru and Nungali peoples awarded $2.5 million in 2016 in compensation for the losses suffered by the damage and extinguishment of their native title in and around the town of Timber Creek in the Northern Territory.

Currently, 647 native title claims have been approved by the courts covering 3.7 million square kilometres of land and waters across Australia.

In 1995, the Australian Government officially recognised the Aboriginal and Torres Strait Islander flags. 27 years later, the Aboriginal flag flew on Sydney Harbour Bridge.

The landmark 1997 *Bringing Them Home* report by the *National Inquiry into the Separation of Aboriginal and Torres Strait Islander Children from Their Families*, found that 'in institutions and in foster care and adoptive families, the forcibly removed children's Aboriginality was typically either hidden and denied or denigrated. Their labour was often exploited. They were exposed to substandard living conditions and a poor and truncated education. They were vulnerable to brutality and abuse. Many experienced repeated sexual abuse'[233].

Ten years later, Prime Minister Kevin Rudd offered a formal apology to Australia's Indigenous peoples, particularly the Stolen Generations, on behalf of the nation at the Australian Parliament House. He acknowledged that 'the laws and policies of successive Parliaments and governments had resulted in the forcible removal of Aboriginal and Torres Strait Islander children from their families and 'inflicted profound grief, suffering and loss on these our fellow Australians'.

In echoes of the lack of consistent commitment of governments to progress the Closing the Gap targets, another 18 years later, in 2025, the Healing Foundation

---

[232] https://aiatsis.gov.au/about-native-title

[233] Human Rights and Equal Opportunity Commission (1997) *Bringing them Home. Report of the National Inquiry into the Separation of Aboriginal and Torres Strait Islander Children from Their Families,* Part 3 Consequences of Removal, Chapter 11 The Effects

found that only 6 per cent of the *Bringing Them Home* report recommendations have been clearly implemented[234].

Following the Council for Aboriginal Reconciliation's Australian Declaration Towards Reconciliation and the Roadmap for Reconciliation in 2001, *Reconciliation Australia* was established as the lead body for reconciliation in Australia to promote and facilitate reconciliation by building relationships, respect and trust between the wider Australian community and Aboriginal and Torres Strait Islander peoples[235].

In 2007, the Howard government's Intervention in the Northern Territory followed the *Sacred Little Children* report, which found 'clear evidence that child sexual abuse is a significant problem across the Territory'. The report noted that 'a number of underlying causes are said to explain the present state of both town and remote communities. Excessive consumption of alcohol is variously described as the cause or result of poverty, unemployment, lack of education, boredom and overcrowded and inadequate housing. The use of other drugs and petrol sniffing can be added to these. Together, they lead to excessive violence. In the worst case scenario, it leads to sexual abuse of children'[236]. The Intervention lasted until 2022.

In 2008, Prime Minister Kevin Rudd and the founder of Fortescue Metals, Andrew Forrest, launched the *Australian Employment Covenant* with the goal of creating 50,000 jobs for Indigenous Australians within 2 years. Despite the Australian Government assisting 73 employers with up to $132 million for 20,000 job pledges, only 2,800 Indigenous job placements were achieved in that time[237]. Despite the range of government-backed specialist Indigenous employment services, at the last census, the employment rate for First Nations people aged 25–64 was 56 per cent, compared to 75 per cent of non-Indigenous

---

234 Healing Foundation (2025) *'Are you waiting for us to die?' The unfinished business of Bringing Them Home* at https://cdn.healingfoundation.org.au/app/uploads/2025/02/11171935/BTH_Report_Are-you-waiting-for-us-to-Die-Final-2025-1.pdf

235 https://www.reconciliation.org.au/our-work/

236 Northern Territory Government (2007) *Report of the Northern Territory Board of Inquiry into the Protection of Aboriginal Children from Sexual Abuse*

237 Jordan K. & Macec D. (2010) *Corporate Initiatives In Indigenous Employment: The Australian Employment Covenant Two Years On*, ANU Centre For Aboriginal Economic Policy Research, CAEPR Working Paper No. 74/2010 at https://dspace-prod.anu.edu.au/server/api/core/bitstreams/838a416f-c4fa-4126-8def-701497d3b4ae/content

people of the same age range. Outcome area 8 of the Closing the Gap Agreement has a target of 62 per cent by 2031[238].

In 2009, Australia finally supported the United Nations *Declaration on the Rights of Indigenous People*. Previously, Australia had been 1 of only 4 nations to oppose the Declaration. 8 years later, the UN *Special Rapporteur on the Rights of Indigenous Peoples* reported that 'it is woefully inadequate that, despite having enjoyed over 2 decades of economic growth, Australia has not been able to improve the social disadvantage of its Indigenous population. The existing measures are clearly insufficient as evidenced by the lack of progress in achieving the 'Close the Gap' targets'. The extraordinarily high rate of incarceration of Aboriginal and Torres Strait Islanders, including women and children, is a major human rights concern'[239].

In 2015, the 16 member Referendum Council jointly appointed by the Prime Minister, Malcolm Turnbull, and Leader of the Opposition, Bill Shorten, was set up to advise the government on steps towards a referendum to recognise Aboriginal and Torres Strait Islander peoples in the Australian Constitution, which led to the *Final Report of the Referendum Council* published on 30 June 2017 with the *Uluru Statement* as a preface.

The Uluru Statement states that sovereignty has never been ceded or extinguished and co-exists with the sovereignty of the Crown. It called for the establishment of a First Nations Voice enshrined in the Constitution and a Makarrata Commission to supervise a process of agreement-making between governments and First Nations, as well as truth-telling about Indigenous history[240].

Then in October 2017, Prime Minister Turnbull issued a joint statement with the Attorney-General, George Brandis, and the Indigenous Affairs Minister, Nigel Scullion, rejecting the Uluru Statement, saying 'the government does not believe such a radical change to our Constitution's representative institutions has any realistic prospect of being supported by a majority of Australians in a majority of states'.

Turnbill was right. The 2023 Voice referendum failed to gain a majority in any State and nationally with less than 40 per cent of Australians voting yes. Despite

---

[238]Australian Institute of Health and Welfare (2023) *Employment of First Nations people* at https://www.aihw.gov.au/reports/australias-welfare/indigenous-employment

[239] https://antar.org.au/issues/undrip/australia/#:~:text=On%203%20April%202009%2C%20the,carefully%20announcing%20the%20nation's%20commitment.

[240] https://ulurustatement.org/the-statement/view-the-statement/

the result, 86 per cent of Australians agree or strongly agree that 'the relationship between Aboriginal and Torres Strait Islanders and the wider Australian community is very important for Australia as a nation'[241].

State governments offer more hope with Victoria leading the way.

After more than 4 years and over 1,300 submissions, Australia's first Indigenous-led truth-telling inquiry, Victoria's *Yoorrook Justice Commission* handed down its final report. It found that the First Peoples of Victoria have endured crimes against humanity and genocide since the beginning of colonisation in Victoria, and they are still being impacted by systemic injustice today as a result. The Commission concluded that colonisation involved widespread massacres, cultural destruction, forced child removals and economic exclusion[242].

Shortly afterwards, the Victorian government became the first jurisdiction in Australia to sign a treaty with its Indigenous people. The treaty includes a permanent representative and deliberative body for First Peoples in Victoria called *Gellung Warl* ('tip of the spear' or 'pointed spear' in Gunaikurnai language) comprising the continuation of the First Peoples' Assembly of Victoria; a new Outcomes and Justice Commission (called *Nginma Ngainga Wara* - 'you will do' in Wadi Wadi language) to evaluate and monitor how effective the Victorian Government is in achieving better outcomes for First Peoples; and *Nyerna Yoorrook Telkuna* to continue the truth-telling and healing process[243].

Meanwhile, NSW, Tasmania and SA governments are progressing with their truth-telling and treaty processes, albeit at varying speeds. Following the defeat of Labor, Queensland repealed the *Path to Treaty Act 2023*, putting an end to the process.

Western Australia has not committed to a treaty process. However, the Noongar native title agreement could be seen as 'Australia's First Treaty' with the Indigenous people receiving a $1.3 billion package relating to land, resources,

---

[241] O'Connell J (2023) *Mapping Social Cohesion 2023*, Scanlon Foundation Research Institute, p.66 at https://scanloninstitute.org.au/sites/default/files/2023-11/2023%20Mapping%20Social%20Cohesion%20Report.pdf

[242] Yoorrook Justice Commission (2025) *Truth Be Told* at https://cdn.craft.cloud/06ad3276-b3d9-4912-bcbb-37795aade9a8/assets/documents/Yoorrook_Official-Public-Record_Accessible.pdf

[243] https://www.treatyvictoria.vic.gov.au/what-treaty-will-deliver#gellung-warl-an-ongoing-representative-and-deliberative-body

governance, finance and cultural heritage in exchange for surrendering native title rights and interests.

2017 also saw the establishment of the *Recognition in Anthem Project* to work on a new version of our national anthem, with lyrics written by poet and former Victorian Supreme Court judge, Peter Vickery. Written by Scottish-born Australian composer Peter Dodds McCormick, the song was first performed as a patriotic song in Australia in 1878 and was readopted as our national anthem in 1984 by the Hawke government after 51.4 per cent of Australians voted for it in the 1977 plebiscite, replacing *God Save the Queen.*

'We are *young* and free' clearly ignored the 60,000 years of human occupation. Vickery's proposed lyrics replaced 'young' with 'one'. With criticism growing, including several National Rugby League football players deciding not to sing the anthem before the first match of the State of Origin series in 2019, the change was made on 1 January 2021.

Ultimately, the ongoing negative stereotyping, cultural bias, discrimination and racism towards our First Nations peoples emanates and perpetuates from our lack of education, engagement, awareness, recognition and appreciation for the Indigenous traditions, values and knowledge around us.

Please take the actions below to find out how you can be inspired to close this gap.

ACT

Former Deputy Leader of the Labor government, Hon Jenny Macklin AC, notes that the problem in addressing Indigenous rights is that 'not enough non-Indigenous Australians know Indigenous Australians. As a result, not enough Australians are personally invested in closing the gap'[244]. You can change this.

Workplace

Over 5 million Australians now work or study in an organisation with a Reconciliation Action Plan (RAP) approved by Reconciliation Australia[245]. RAPs follow four graduating stages: Reflect, Innovate, Stretch, and Elevate, and outline the organisation's commitment to Indigenous rights and reconciliation through Indigenous recognition, employment, and procurement.

---

244 Macklin J & Deane J 92025) *Making Progress. How Good Policy Happens,* p.106

245 https://www.reconciliation.org.au/wp-content/uploads/2023/12/2023-RAP-Impact-report.pdf

To help you manage your reconciliation strategy and plan, Biripi man, Kieran Shirey, and Natalia Florez have developed an online platform, *Weavr*[246].

A one-day cultural awareness training provides you and your colleagues with introductory knowledge of Aboriginal culture and respectful ways of working with Aboriginal clients, consumers, partners and colleagues. It is important to understand your local history and traditions with face-to-face training from your local Australian Community Controlled Health Organisation (ACCHO)[247] or Aboriginal organisation. The Centre for Cultural Competence Australia provides online cultural capability courses[248].

Employ

The commitment to employ Indigenous people in your organisation requires the development of a culturally aware, safe, and respectful workplace with culturally appropriate policies and procedures actively implemented to acknowledge and value their cultural identity, experiences, and perspectives, as well as preventing any assault, challenge, or denial of their culture. This includes incorporating Acknowledgement of Country, a smoking ceremony to cleanse the building and people, a plaque on the building acknowledging the traditional owners (buy from KINYA LERRK[249]), cultural awareness training, and respectful communication practices tailored to Aboriginal cultures.

Another accommodation is *Sorry Business*, the mourning of the loss of a family or community member, by following traditional ceremonies and practices, which necessitates flexibility in the organisation's bereavement leave policy. See the Fair Work Ombudsman's fact sheet[250].

A note of warning. I've seen many talented Aboriginal workers crushed by the expectation of their co-workers that they are the representative and expert in Indigenous culture, as well as trying to perform their day jobs. There is a danger that they are pulled into workshops, consultations or development processes to seek their inclusion and advice. At best, they can only advise on the cultural aspects of their birth area, if they are aware, which may not be where the organisation operates. This 'cultural load'[251], combined with the many cultural and community obligations in their lives that they balance every day, makes the

---

246 https://weavr.au/

247 https://www.naccho.org.au/locations/

248 https://www.ccca.com.au/

249 https://kinyalerrk.com.au/

250 https://www.fairwork.gov.au/sites/default/files/2024-06/fd-first-nations-people-supporting-sorry-business-fact-sheet.pdf

251 https://www.apsc.gov.au/working-aps/diversity-and-inclusion/diversity-inclusion-news/cultural-load-its-real-thing

job impossible. It is no wonder, then, that governments have a high representation of Indigenous employees.

Minderoo Foundation's *Indigenous Employment Index – Employer Roadmap*[252] is a useful tool.

CareerTrackers is a national charity that supports pre-professional First Nations university students and links them with employers to participate in paid, multi-year internships. Students perform their internships with sponsor organisations with the aim of converting from intern to full-time employee upon completion of their university degree. Over 80 per cent of CareerTrackers students are in full-time employment within 3 months of completing their studies. In addition to creating lasting employment opportunities, the organisation provides interns and their sponsor organisations with year-round support to prepare students for success at university and in their chosen professions and their communities[253].

To attract Indigenous employees, you can post your jobs for First Nations job seekers at Aboriginal-owned and Supply Nation certified companies such as Indigenous Employment Australia[254] or First People Recruitment Solutions[255], or become a host employer with *AFL SportsReady* to train 16-24 year-old Indigenous school students, recent school leavers or adults returning to work[256].

Volunteer

Indigenous organisations need your time and talents. Select 'Indigenous Australians' on *SEEK Volunteer* or *GoVolunteer*[257].

Community First Development recruits volunteers in Perth, Adelaide, Darwin and Far-North-Queensland with skills in business development, communications, strategic planning, website design and development, youth work, plumbing and carpentry[258].

The *AIATSIS Volunteer Program* provides an opportunity to contribute to the work of a world-renowned research, collecting and publishing organisation of

---

252 https://www.minderoo.org/publications#:indigenous-employment-index-employer-roadmap
253 https://careertrackers.org.au/
254 https://atsijobs.com.au/
255 https://www.fprs.com.au/
256 https://aflsportsready.com.au/hire-a-trainee/
257 https://govolunteer.com.au/indigenous-australians-volunteering
258 https://www.communityfirstdevelopment.org.au/volunteers

Aboriginal and Torres Strait Islander cultures, traditions, languages and stories[259].

Buy

Join over 850 organisations and sign up to *Supply Nation* to access Australia's leading database of 5,000+ verified Indigenous businesses to purchase goods and services in construction, food and hospitality, office supplies and printing, facilities management, graphic design, recruitment and labour hire, sustainability and IT[260].

Indigenous-owned social enterprises include *Gawun Supplies* which sells unique, Indigenous designed hi-vis workwear and corporate polos[261], *Dreamtime Artistry* supplies Authentic Indigenous arts and crafts[262], *Saltwater People* is a full-service creative agency that delivers strategic design communications and cross-cultural engagement[263].

We all use toilet paper – buy yours from *Yarn'n* which is FSC-certified, made from 100 per cent recycled materials and manufactured in Australia using 50 per cent less water and 90 per cent less energy. Half of the profits go to the *Yalari Foundation* to provide full boarding scholarships to Indigenous children from regional and remote communities around Australia[264].

Participate

Every year on 26 May, *National Sorry Day* remembers and acknowledges the mistreatment of Aboriginal and Torres Strait Islander people who were forcibly removed from their families and communities, which we now know as the 'Stolen Generations'.

Starting the day after, National Reconciliation Week is a time for all Australians to learn about our shared histories, cultures, and achievements, and to explore how each of us can contribute to achieving reconciliation in Australia. This is a time for non-Indigenous Australians to organise or attend an event. Resources are on the Reconciliation Australia website[265].

National NAIDOC Week celebrations are held across Australia in the first week of July each year (Sunday to Sunday), to celebrate and recognise the history,

---

259 https://aiatsis.gov.au/about/work-us/volunteer

260 https://supplynation.org.au/

261 https://gawunsupplies.com.au/

262 https://dreamtimeartistry.com/

263 https://saltwaterpeople.com.au/

264 https://yarnn.au/

265 https://www.reconciliation.org.au/our-work/national-reconciliation-week/

culture and achievements of Aboriginal and Torres Strait Islander peoples. It is an opportunity for non-Indigenous Australians to get to know their local Aboriginal and/or Torres Strait Islander communities through activities and events held across the country[266].

There is no substitute for experiencing Indigenous culture firsthand with an Aboriginal elder guide on-county. *Discover Aboriginal Experiences* has 200 tours, trips and retreats[267]. Additionally, the Australian and each State and Territory government tourism website has a selection of Indigenous tours.

Campaign

In 1888, the New South Wales premier at the time, Henry Parkes, was asked which activities would be included for Aboriginal people in the celebrations marking a centenary of British colonisation of Australia. He replied: "And remind them that we have robbed them?"[268]. If you feel that it is wrong to celebrate our national day on the date that the First Fleet sailed into Sydney Cove to start the European colonisation and the subsequent dispossession, killing and suffering of our First Nations peoples, then you can participate in alternative 'Invasion Day' or 'Survival Day' events. Pledge and buy a 'Not a Date to Celebrate' T-shirt at *Clothing the Gaps*[269].

Additionally, your organisation can join hundreds of others that stay open and give their staff an option to work on the Australia Day public holiday each year, whilst taking a day off at another time. Register with *Change it Ourselves*[270].

Donate

Since 2011, the *Indigenous Literacy Foundation* has worked with over 400 remote Communities, gifted nearly 800,000 books, supplied 100 playgroups with early literacy *Book Buzz* resources, and published 109 books reflecting 31 Aboriginal and Torres Strait Islander languages[271]. As well as donating, primary school students can take part in *Busking for Change* by learning a song in a local NT language and 'busking' or performing the song collectively or individually to their friends, family, school, or posting a video online[272].

---

266 https://www.naidoc.org.au/about/naidoc-week

267 https://www.discoveraboriginalexperiences.com/home-page

268 https://www.theguardian.com/australia-news/2018/jan/19/what-our-leaders-say-about-australia-day-and-where-did-it-start-anyway

269 https://www.clothingthegaps.com.au/pages/not-a-date-to-celebrate?srsltid=AfmBOoqVVmD7wsWpjAKAFYKJSHTu-B6QEAa9x4uIxHs-w62G8xZjtqtT

270 https://www.changeitourselves.com.au/

271 https://www.indigenousliteracyfoundation.org.au/

272 https://buskingforchange.ilf.org.au/

As an Indigenous organisation that supports Aboriginal and Torres Strait Islander students to realise their full education and employment potential, the *Aurora Education Foundation* has demonstrated double the rate of Year 12 completion, triple the ATAR attainment, and double the transition to university for high school students supported compared to other Indigenous students nationally[273].

Established by Aboriginal footballers, Adam Goodes and Michael O'Loughlin in 2009, the *GO Foundation* provides scholarships to Indigenous young people attending school or university, to learn more about their own culture and identity with other Indigenous young people, and enable access to jobs, internships, and work experience[274]. By becoming a partner employer, you can enable a pathway to a life-changing career.

Established in 2009, the *National Aboriginal and Torres Strait Islander Women's Alliance* champions the voices of Aboriginal and Torres Strait Islander women. They advocate through their representation of over 180 women's charities and organisations across the country[275].

---

[273] https://aurorafoundation.com.au/our-impact/

[274] https://www.gofoundation.org.au/

[275] https://natsiwa.org.au/

CHILD SAFETY

'Every child deserves a champion. An adult who will never give up on them. Who understands the power of connection and insists that they become the best that they can possibly be'

RITA PIERSON[276]

As I look at Kate in the activity room at the YSAS day centre, her arms covered in scars from self-harm alongside the bruised veins from daily heroin injecting, it is inconceivable to comprehend what she has already been through in her short life.

Sexually and physically abused by her mother's boyfriends from 5 years old, she was glad of the variety of drugs they gave her to numb the pain. Never knowing her father, she got good at pushing the boyfriends' drugs around the housing estate. After all, who would suspect a ten-year-old? Her payment was in drugs and the beatings stopped.

She was introduced to a local adult gang and soon became adept at jimmying locks of houses and cars. She felt useful, belonging and valued. Even respected at times. She never liked the violence of house invasions, and got caught on the CCTV. Her piercings were a real give away.

Juvie was a badge of honour, and she got to meet some cool older kids in the months she was detained on remand (due to the bottleneck in the courts caused by the government's hard-on-crime stance). These kids regaled her with their

---

[276]Child safety
Pierson R (2024) *Every child needs a champion* – video at https://www.ted.com/talks/rita_pierson_every_kid_needs_a_champion?language=en.

daring exploits in between being in and out of child protection and youth detention.

Released on a good behaviour bond, Kate never made it to the appointment with the social worker. Instead, she lived in a squat with friends of the kids she met in remand. The next few years were a blur of squats, sex, shooting up, drinking, stealing, violence, suicide attempts and stays at Her Majesty's pleasure.

Kate has had enough. She wants to go straight. The YSAS youth worker heard this the last time she came in, before she disappeared for three months.

We are now discovering more about the effects of complex developmental trauma of children's exposure to traumatic events on their development and long-term outcomes. It is thought that, in this context, the neurological development of the brain becomes distorted such that the 'survival' mechanisms of the brain and body are more dominant than the 'learning' mechanisms, resulting in wide-ranging impairments in arousal, cognitive, emotional and social functioning[277].

As a result, YSAS has been a leading practitioner of trauma-informed practice, including ERIC (Emotional Regulation, Impulse Control). This evidence-based, psychological intervention assists adolescents and young adults in developing skills to regulate their emotions better and manage impulsivity.

In 2017, the Royal Commission into Institutional Responses to Child Sexual Abuse report stated 'the sexual abuse of a child is a terrible crime. It is the greatest of personal violations. It is perpetrated against the most vulnerable in our community. It is a fundamental breach of the trust that children are entitled to place in adults. It is one of the most traumatic and potentially damaging experiences and can have lifelong adverse consequences'.

Eight years later, child safety was again in the spotlight with a 26-year-old childcare worker charged with 70 offences including sexually abusing eight children, aged between 5 months and 2 years old, in his care. Distressingly, 2,000 children were advised to undergo testing for sexually transmitted infections.

Tragically, this is not an isolated incident. As the Human Rights Commissioner explained, 'this is not the first time and it won't be the last, unless governments across the federation take urgent action to implement the evidence-based

---

[277] Atkinson J (2013). *Trauma-informed services and trauma-specific care for Indigenous Australian children* (Closing the Gap Clearinghouse Resource 21), Canberra, Australian Institute of Health and Welfare

recommendations from numerous inquiries over the past decades that will help keep our children safe'[278].

In the past 10 years, Australia has seen 39 inquiries, reviews and Royal Commissions committed to reducing child abuse and neglect. Meanwhile, cases continue to rise.

Perpetrators can be anyone - family members, family friends, coaches, teachers, clergy, babysitters, and any other acquaintances. They can be any age, race, gender, religious belief, sexual orientation, education level, or financial status. They may have sexual feelings towards children, or not.

Some 60 years after the first research into child maltreatment in Australia, the Australian Child Maltreatment Study has obtained the first evidence of the national prevalence of all 5 forms of child maltreatment (physical abuse, sexual abuse, emotional abuse, neglect, and exposure to domestic violence), and of multi-type maltreatment, determining that child maltreatment is endemic in Australia[279].

Children and young people in Australia have the right to grow up safe, connected and supported in their family, community and culture. They have the right to grow up in an environment that enables them to reach their full potential[280].

The World Health Organisation defines child maltreatment as the abuse and neglect that occurs to children under 18 years of age, including all types of physical and/or emotional ill-treatment, sexual abuse, neglect, negligence and commercial or other exploitation, which results in actual or potential harm to the child's health, survival, development or dignity in the context of a relationship of responsibility, trust or power[281].

The scale of child abuse in this country is truly horrific.

Some 2.7 million Australians aged 18 years and over, or 1 in 7, have experienced childhood physical and/or sexual abuse before the age of 15 perpetrated by an adult. Of these, 1.7 million are women. 9 in 10have known

[278] https://humanrights.gov.au/about/news/media-releases/national-childrens-commissioner-calls-urgent-action-safer-childcare

[279] Mathews B, Thomas H and Scott J (2023) *A new era in child maltreatment prevention: call to action*, The Medical Journal of Australia, Volume 218 No 6, 3 April 2023

[280] Commonwealth of Australia (2021) *Safe and Supported: the National Framework for Protecting Australia's Children 2021–2031* at https://www.dss.gov.au/sites/default/files/documents/12_2021/dess5016-national-framework-protecting-childrenaccessible.pdf

[281] https://www.who.int/news-room/fact-sheets/detail/child-maltreatment

their abuser, with 7 in 10 having experienced abuse by a family member, 1 in 5 by another known person, 1 in 7 by someone within an institutional setting, and less than 1 in 10 by a stranger[282].

When child sexual abuse occurs, it rarely happens only once, with almost 2.5 million adults experiencing sexual abuse more than 6 times as children[283].

Almost 1 in 10 Australian men has admitted to committing child sexual abuse offences, even if they have not been caught. These men were 3 times more likely than the general population to work with children[284]. Many perpetrators of child sexual abuse are never charged, and even fewer are successfully prosecuted. With only 27 per cent of people with Working with Children Checks not continuously verified[285], they are not a fail-safe way of identifying if an adult actually poses a risk to the safety of children. Predators know this and rely on it to keep hurting children[286].

Online sexual abuse is high and escalating in Australia. In 2023-24, the Australian Federal Police's *Australian Centre to Counter Child Exploitation* received 58,503 reports of online child abuse, or 160 per day, a 45 per cent increase over the previous year. Every one of these reports contains images and videos of real children being sexually abused or exploited for the sexual gratification of offenders[287].

If someone is worried that a child is being seriously harmed or neglected, or is at risk of being seriously harmed or neglected, they can make a report to their State/Territory child protection department. Mandatory reporting legislation requires occupations who are likely to interact with children in the course of

---

[282] Australian Bureau of Statistics (2023) *2021-22 Personal Safety Survey* at https://www.abs.gov.au/statistics/people/crime-and-justice/personal-safety-australia/latest-release

[283] Mathews B (2023) The Australian Child Maltreatment Study: National prevalence and associated health outcomes of child abuse and neglect, Med J Aust 2023; 218 (6 Suppl): S1-S51

[284] Salter M (2023) *Identifying and understanding child sexual offending behaviours and attitudes among Australian men*, UNSW Australian Human Rights Institute at https://www.humanrights.unsw.edu.au/news/worlds-largest-child-sexual-abuseperpetration-prevalence-study-recommends-significant-investment-early-interventionmeasures

[285] https://www.theage.com.au/national/victoria/loopholes-in-national-child-safety-reforms-raise-red-flags-about-sex-abuse-risks-20251230-p5nqq0.html

[286] Hakansson E, Tucci J and Mitchell J (2024) *Hear us now, act now. First insights on prevention and early intervention from those with lived and living experience of child sexual abuse*, Australian Childhood Foundation at https://www.childhood.org.au/app/uploads/2024/02/Our-Collective-Experience-Project-%E2%80%93-First-Report.pdf

[287] https://www.afp.gov.au/news-centre/media-release/reports-child-exploitation-afp-led-accce-increase-45-past-financial-year

their work, for example, teachers and early childhood educators, welfare practitioners, medical practitioners, police and religious ministers, to report cases of suspected child abuse and neglect.

2/3rds of notifications are made by school, police or health workers. The notification triggers an intake process where child protection workers evaluate the notification and determine what action to take. An investigation occurs when a notification of alleged abuse meets the threshold for further action. If the investigation substantiates the abuse, a care and protection order is used to give child protection departments some responsibility for a child's welfare.

In 2024–25, excluding Queensland, nearly 250,000 children were subjects of notifications of alleged maltreatment, or 6 per cent of all children, with over 45,000 under care and protection orders and nearly 40,000 children investigated had their maltreatment substantiated[288]. With 81,000 investigations completed in 2024-25 and 32 per cent of child protection notifications resulting in an investigation, it appears that it takes a year on average to conclude an investigation, which would correlate to the shortage of child protection workers in many states due to a lack of qualified applicants, high turnover, and burnout through high caseloads[289].

Out-of-home care refers to temporary, medium, or long-term living arrangements for children and young people who cannot live safely in their family homes.

Under a care and protection order, the department can put in place family support services to address the underlying causes of the abuse or remove the child from their family and place them into out-of-home care, a temporary, medium or long-term living arrangement for children and young people who cannot live in their family home, comprising:

- *Foster care*: a child is taken into care by a foster carer who has been trained and approved to look after children. There are over 9,000 foster carer households with placements with over half having multiple children;
- *Kinship care*: a child is taken into care by a relative or family friend allowing them to remain within the family or local network. There are

[288] Australian Government (2026) *Report on Government Services 2026, Part F, Section 16, 16 Child protection services*, Productivity Commission at https://www.pc.gov.au/ongoing/report-on-government-services/community-services/child-protection/

[289] For example, see NSW https://www.abc.net.au/news/2024-04-12/casework-shortage-out-of-home-care-first-nations-children/103697212

over 15,000 relative/kinship carer households with placements with a third having more than one child;

- *Permanent care*: a child is placed into the care of a permanent carer, including foster or kinship carers where it is intended the child will remain in their care until age 18 or beyond;
- *Residential care*: a young person is placed into a residence, typically run by a not-for-profit organisation, including family group homes that are typically run like a family home, with a limited number of children who are cared for around-the-clock by resident carers; and
- *Independent living.*

As of 30 June 2025 (excluding Queensland), a total of 42,446 children were in out-of-home care in Australia at an annual cost of $7 billion, with nearly 7 in 10 in out-of-home care for 2 years or more. With 9 in 10 in home-based care (foster care, relative/kinship care and other home-based care), over 4,000 children are kept in residential units.

Testament to the lack of early intervention in this country, the majority of children and young people who live in residential care have been known by the child protection system since their first year of life[290].

Residential care is meant to be a safe and supportive environment, but the inadequacy of government funding results in inadequate staffing levels to provide the needed therapeutic trauma-informed services. Exposure to trauma often results in kids displaying challenging behaviour which should be managed with an intensive, therapeutic care response. But all too often, residential care facilities have to resort to calling police instead, leading to a cycle of involvement with the criminal justice system, which often has lifelong impacts[291].

Instead of a place where they can heal from harm, state care often inflicts more harm. Children are moved often, their placements – especially in residential care – are unsafe, and there are not enough supports to help them recover from trauma[292].

The Queensland government notes that children may experience a range of emotional, psychological and physical problems as a result of being harmed,

---

[290] https://professionals.childhood.org.au/prosody/2016/11/residential-care-in-australia/

[291] https://www.legalaid.vic.gov.au/care-not-custody-keeping-kids-residential-care-out-courts

[292] Commission for Children and Young People (2019) *'In our own words': Systemic inquiry into the lived experience of children and young people in the Victorian out-of-home care system* at https://ccyp.vic.gov.au/assets/Publications-inquiries/CCYP-In-Our-Own-Words.pdf

including low self esteem; increased fear, guilt and self-blame; distrust of adults or difficulty forming relationships with others; disrupted attachments with those who are meant to keep them safe; mental health disorders such as anxiety, attachment, post-traumatic stress and depression disorders; self-harming or suicidal thoughts; learning disorders, including poor language and cognitive development; developmental delay, eating disorders and physical ailments; permanent physical injuries or death; violent, aggressive or criminal behaviour or other behavioural problems; drug and alcohol abuse and high-risk sexual behaviour.

This was vividly brought to light in 2016 when the Four Corners *Broken Homes* programme reported on a house run by a national child welfare charity which was 'crammed with adolescents who had been in and out of courts and hospitals and police stations for much of their short lives, kids hardened by a lifetime of neglect. Police were called to the house frequently. Fires were lit in the backyard. Holes were put through walls. The children often felt desperate and alone'. The programme also cited an inspector acting for the NSW Ombudsman reporting that girls, aged under 16, were using dating apps to meet strange men before disappearing for days on end[293].

Seven years later, a University of Melbourne report noted that 'one form of abuse that children and young people in residential care are particularly vulnerable to is child sexual exploitation. This involves mostly adult perpetrators targeting children and offering them something – drugs, money, attention, 'love' – in exchange for sexual activity'. The report includes an example from a case worker on just how quickly a vulnerable young person can be targeted:

"One case that I have at the moment, where a young person moves into a new residential house. They use an app with location sources – so, like, a dating-type app. This young person has spoken to me about the timeframe between landing in the new house and actively having sex with an older man in exchange for cannabis – the timeframe was 10 minutes[294].

Today, the out-of-home system is still failing our most vulnerable children.

---

293 https://www.abc.net.au/news/2016-11-14/four-corners-broken-homes-child-protection/7987450

294 McKibbin G, Humphreys C and Green J (2023) *We must act now to stop child sexual exploitation in residential care*, University of Melbourne at https://pursuit.unimelb.edu.au/articles/we-must-act-now-to-stop-child-sexual-exploitation-in-residential-care

Children in residential homes know that they can abscond with little consequence. An inquiry by Victoria's Commission for Children and Young People found that the 9,000 children in out of home care were being suspended or expelled from schools at five times the rate of other children, only a quarter were progressing from year 10 to 12, compared to 80 per cent of other students. No child in care completed their Year 12 qualification[295].

In December 2023, a 12-year-old girl was charged with murdering a woman in Melbourne after being reported missing 275 times and accused of a series of violent attacks[296]. In 2026, it was reported that a 13-year-old girl became pregnant after leaving residential care and being raped by 17 and 19-year-old men[297]. Another report disclosed that children in residential care in Victoria are openly using drugs, including ice[298].

A 2024 review by the NSW government found 'the out-of-home care system in NSW is not fit for purpose and fails to meet the needs of children and young people at an efficient cost'[299].

A University of Sydney study has found that the widespread impact of child abuse and neglect in Australia causes nearly half of the common mental conditions. Childhood maltreatment was found to account for 41 per cent of suicide attempts in Australia, 35 per cent for cases of self-harm and 21 per cent for depression. The study finds that if childhood maltreatment were eradicated

---

[295] Commission for Children and Young People (2023) *Let us Learn. Systemic inquiry into the educational experiences of children and young people living in out-of-home care* at https://ccyp.vic.gov.au/assets/Publications-inquiries/let-us-learn/CCYP-Education-inquiry-report-FINAL.pdf

[296] https://www.abc.net.au/news/2024-02-05/victoria-government-failures-state-care-children-murder-case/103425904

[297] https://www.abc.net.au/news/2026-01-06/13-year-old-pregnant-sexual-assaults-state-residential-care/105980432?utm_source=abc_news_app&utm_medium=content_shared&utm_campaign=abc_news_app&utm_content=other

[298] https://www.abc.net.au/news/2026-01-07/berry-street-residential-care-drug-use-staff/106129258?utm_source=abc_news_app&utm_medium=content_shared&utm_campaign=abc_news_app&utm_content=other

[299] NSW Department of Communities and Justice (2024) *System review into out-of-home care. Final report to the NSW Government* at https://dcj.nsw.gov.au/documents/service-providers/out-of-home-care-and-permanency-support-program/about-permanency-support-program-and-overview-childstory-and-oohc-resources/System-review-into-out-of-home-care-Final-report-to-the-NSW-Government.pdf

in Australia, more than 1.8 million cases of depression, anxiety, and substance use disorders could be prevented.[300]

Furthermore, Australians who had experienced child maltreatment were 4 times more likely to have self-harmed in the previous year, 4 times more likely to have attempted suicide in the previous year, and 6 times as likely to be dependent on cannabis[301]. Adults who suffered childhood maltreatment have about 3 times the odds of any mental disorder, generalised anxiety disorder, major depressive disorder and severe alcohol use, and almost 5 times the odds of post-traumatic stress disorder[302].

WHY

In this country, child abuse is widespread. It occurs across all socio-economic, religious and ethnic groups and is due to a combination of societal attitudes, family environment, institutional settings and online access.

Four other Themes of this book are also contributors – family and domestic violence, gender inequality, mental health and poverty and disadvantage.

Societal ignorance and stigma

Child sexual abuse thrives on disempowerment, secrecy, isolation and disbelief.

There is a pervasive belief that children's voices, views and feelings hold less weight than those of adults with power over them, whilst children are not considered to have inherent rights of their own. Their developmental immaturity is treated as a weakness that can be exploited, and they are often betrayed by the very adults who are supposed to care for, support and teach them. Adult perpetrators impose secrecy to deny children their voice and create isolation to keep children hidden from view in ways that enable abuse to continue with minimal risk of discovery.

---

[300] Grummitt L, Baldwin JR, Lafoa'i J, Keyes KM, Barrett EL. (2024) *Burden of Mental Disorders and Suicide Attributable to Childhood Maltreatment, JAMA Psychiatry.* Published online May 08, 2024. doi:10.1001/jamapsychiatry.2024.0804

[301] Lawrence DM, Hunt A, Scott JG, et al. (2023) *The association between child maltreatment and health risk behaviours and conditions throughout life in the Australian Child Maltreatment Study*, Medical Journal of Australia; 218 (6 Suppl): S34 - S39 .

[302] Scott J, Malacova E, Ben Mathews B, Haslam D, Pacella R, Higgins D, Meinck F, Dunne M, Finkelhor D, Erskine H, Lawrence D, Thomas H (2023) *The association between child maltreatment and mental disorders in the Australian Child Maltreatment Study*, The Medical Journal of Australia, Volume 218 No 6, 3 April 2023

The combination of these factors leads to the most egregious violation of what should be safe and trusting relationships[303].

Repeatedly, in research undertaken by the *Australian Childhood Foundation*, child abuse is perceived to be a problem in some other family, some other neighbourhood or in another community. There is inadequate recognition that abuse occurs at the scale that it does. It is minimised and repeatedly ignored. The effect is that children are not always believed. 1 in 3 adults would not believe a child who made a disclosure about abuse to them. Another 1 in 3 is unsure whether or not to believe a disclosure[304].

Perpetrators

At least 9 out of 10 perpetrators of child abuse are male. Most child sexual abuse is perpetrated by someone known to the child.

The Australian Government's National Office for Child Safety notes that 'there is no typical profile of a person who sexually abuses children and young people. Not all perpetrators have the same traits, behaviours or motivations, and they come from different backgrounds and circumstances. There is often very little that makes perpetrators stand out from the general population. They often have secure, well-paying jobs; have strong social networks (including partners, families, and friends); and can be considered well-respected members of communities[305].

A variety of complex factors may influence an adult to sexually abuse a child in any setting, including: adverse experiences in childhood, such as physical, emotional and sexual abuse and neglect; interpersonal, relationship and emotional difficulties, including difficulty connecting with other adults, intimacy problems and poor social skills, and emotional affiliation with children; distorted beliefs and 'thinking errors' that may facilitate child sexual abuse; indirect influences, such as contextual or 'trigger' factors[306].

---

303 Hakansson E, Tucci J and Mitchell J (2024) *Hear us now, act now. First insights on prevention and early intervention from those with lived and living experience of child sexual abuse*, Australian Childhood Foundation at https://www.childhood.org.au/app/uploads/2024/02/Our-Collective-Experience-Project-%E2%80%93-First-Report.pdf

304 Tucci J and Mitchell J (2022) *Still unseen and ignored: Tracking Community Knowledge and Attitudes about Child Abuse and Child Protection in Australia*, Frontiers in Psychology, 2 September 2022, Volume 13 – 2022 at https://doi.org/10.3389/fpsyg.2022.860212

305 https://www.childsafety.gov.au/about-child-sexual-abuse/who-perpetrates-child-sexual-abuse

306 Commonwealth of Australia (2017) *Royal Commission into Institutional Responses to Child Sexual Abuse*, Final Report: Volume 2, Nature and cause, p.14, Canberra

Organisations

The *Royal Commission into Institutional Responses to Child Sexual Abuse* found that 'the extent of child sexual abuse in institutional settings in Australia is significant. Child sexual abuse has occurred across a wide range of institutions and has affected tens, if not hundreds, of thousands of people over many years'. Many organisations in Australia have failed to protect children from abuse, failed to listen to children who tried to disclose abuse, and failed to respond appropriately when abuse came to light[307].

Home

With 2 in 5 children also exposed to domestic violence, there is no denying that home is unsafe for many Australian children. The effects of violence (for instance, pain, distress, anger, irritability, fear, reduced mobility, hospitalisation) may affect a mother's parenting capacity, as may mental illness or substance misuse problems that emerge as a consequence of domestic violence. Furthermore, domestic violence may result in mothers being emotionally distant, unavailable or unable to meet their children's needs[308].

Children living with domestic violence display physical, developmental, psychological and behavioural effects, as well as the impact of trauma and developmental regression, with significantly poorer outcomes on 21 childhood psycho-social, developmental and behavioural dimensions. Behavioural problems include acting out, violence and aggression towards others. Outcomes for child witnesses were similar to those where children were also directly physically abused[309].

Furthermore, children living in families dealing with mental illness, substance problems and economic hardship are twice as likely to be at risk of multi-type maltreatment[310]. Children are particularly vulnerable to cumulative harm in families with multiple and complex problems in which the unremitting daily impact of multiple adverse circumstances and events has a profound and

---

[307] Commonwealth of Australia (2017) *Royal Commission into Institutional Responses to Child Sexual Abuse*, Final Report: Volume 2, Nature and cause, Canberra

[308] Holt S, Buckley H and Whelan S (2008) *The impact of exposure to domestic violence on children and young people: A review of the literature. Child Abuse and Neglect*, 32, 797-810.

[309] Kitzmann K, Gaylord N, Holt A, and Kenny E (2003). *Child witnesses to domestic violence: A meta-analytic review. Journal of Consulting and Clinical Psychology*, 71(2), 339-352.

[310] Higgins D, Mathews B, Pacella R, Scott J, Finkelhor D, Meinck F, Erskine H, Thomas H, Lawrence D, Haslam D, Malacova E and Dunne M (2023) *The prevalence and nature of multi-type child maltreatment in Australia, JAMA Psychiatry.* Published online May 08, 2024, doi:10.1001/jamapsychiatry.2024.0804

exponential impact on children and diminishes their sense of safety and wellbeing[311].

Online

The increase in young people (including children and infants) accessing the internet has seen a corresponding upward trend in cases of online child sexual exploitation, including grooming, image-based abuse, and the spread of self-generated sexually explicit material.

Improvements to downloading speeds and the proliferation of smartphones have made accessing pornography easier, faster, and more anonymous than ever before. Exposure to violent pornography is especially a concern in relation to harmful coercive sexual behaviour among adolescents, which can lead to abuse[312].

The Australian Medical Association has voiced the concern that the internet is exposing children to sexually explicit content that teaches that sex is about 'use and abuse'[313]

There is also increasing pressure on young people (particularly young women) to take and send sexually explicit images, with potential for intentional harm by others, including cyber bullying, harassment, sexual abuse, and pornographic use of the images[314].

Worryingly, research by the *Australian Centre to Counter Child Exploitation (ACCCE)* found that only one in five parents and carers thought there is a likelihood that online child sexual exploitation can happen to their child; only 3 per cent listed online grooming as a concern; and over half did not know what they could do to keep children safe from online child sexual exploitation.

The ACCCE concluded that 'poor knowledge, existing myths and misconceptions and lack of confidence in knowing what to do are reducing the community's ability to respond effectively to the prevention of online child sexual exploitation, and that current social norms are hampering proactive vigilance, guidance and oversight, including: the prioritisation of preventative measures for physical safety over online safety; the desire to preserve privacy

---

311 https://aifs.gov.au/resources/policy-and-practice-papers/issues-safety-and-wellbeing-children-families-multiple-and

312 https://aifs.gov.au/resources/short-articles/children-and-young-peoples-exposure-pornography

313 https://professionals.childhood.org.au/prosody/2016/07/melinda-tankard-reist/

314 https://psychology.org.au/inpsych/2015/april/sampson

of the child/young person when online; and the tendency to assign blame to victims in instances of online sexual exploitation[315].

The rise of Generative Artificial Intelligence is accelerating child sexual abuse by unlocking the ability for a single child predator to quickly create child sexual abuse material at scale by adapting original images and videos into new abuse material, re-victimising the child in that content, or manipulating benign material of children into sexualised content, or creating fully AI-generated material[316].

The result is a growing number of schoolboys exposed for creating and disseminating sexually explicit, AI-generated images of female students[317].

Government

More children are being removed from their homes due to violence, abuse and neglect than ever before. The State and Territory government child protection systems are stretched to their limits, struggling to meet the demand and support children and families. There is a shortage, high turnover, and burnout of child protection workers as governments struggle with the sheer number of child protection notifications[318].

As *The Australian Centre for Social Innovation* notes 'the current approach to resolving child protection challenges at scale is to reactively tinker with procedures and tools, roll out new pilots, adopt out-of-context programs, restructure organisations, displace blame, and continue to hope this change, this reform, will be the one that works. But even noble and novel good-intentioned initiatives operate within and reinforce our existing structure — we're patching holes but forcing new leaks[319].

Australia is in the midst of a severe foster carer shortage, with the trend of more carers exiting the system than have come in due to a generational change in

---

[315] Australian Centre to Counter Child Exploitation (2020) *Online Child Sexual Exploitation: Understanding Community Awareness, Perceptions, Attitudes And Preventative Behaviours*, Research Report, February 2020 at https://www.accce.gov.au/sites/default/files/2021-02/ACCCE_Research-Report_OCE.pdf

[316] Thorn (2024) *Safety by Design for Generative AI: Preventing Child Sexual Abuse* at https://info.thorn.org/hubfs/thorn-safety-by-design-for-generative-AI.pdf

[317] https://www.theguardian.com/australia-news/article/2024/jun/12/schoolboy-arrested-after-allegedly-posting-fake-explicit-images-of-female-students-ntwnfb

[318] https://www.theguardian.com/australia-news/article/2024/may/08/children-in-danger-as-nsw-child-protection-reaches-crisis-point-striking-caseworkers-say

[319] The Australian Centre for Social Innovation (2016) *Generation by Generation Pragmatic approaches to reducing intergenerational cycles of reliance on child protection services* at https://www.tacsi.org.au/file/ll3e31kzt/TACSI_Generation%20by%20generation%20report_2016.pdf

attitudes and the cost-of-living crisis[320]. This effectively means that more children need to be placed in residential care units.

As we have seen with the other Themes of this book, the service system is in crisis, dealing with an ever-growing, complex, interrelated need. Without an investment in prevention and early intervention, the system will be in perpetual crisis. A report by *Social Ventures Australia* showed that investing $193 million every year over a 10-year period in early intervention services to prevent situations from escalating would prevent 1,460 children from entering out-of-home care or progressing to residential care every year and deliver cumulative net savings of at least $1.8 billion to the child protection and out-of-home care system in Victoria[321].

ACT

It is up to all of us to ensure children are safe in our families, network of friends, sports clubs, community groups, schools and online.

For your (grand)children and young people

The National Office for Child Safety's *One Talk at a Time* aims to help prevent child sexual abuse by encouraging adults to learn about the issue and have ongoing, proactive, preventative conversations with children, young people and other adults. The campaign is aimed at adults with children and young people in their lives[322].

The *Alannah & Madeline Foundation* has a range of online tools for parents on digital safety, reporting child abuse and AI[323].

Ensure yours is a child-safe organisation

More important than CCTVs and Working with Children Checks is an organisational culture that puts the best interests of children and young people first.

---

[320] https://www.eqt.com.au/about-us/media-centre/news-items/whats-new/more-support-for-foster-carers-as-numbers-continue-to-decline#:~:text=Australia%20is%20in%20the%20midst,network%20for%20at%2Drisk%20children.

[321] Social Ventures Australia (2020) *The economic case for early intervention in the child protection and out-of-home care system in Victoria* at https://www.socialventures.org.au/wp-content/uploads/2024/07/Keeping-families-together-through-COVID-Report-Summary-2020.pdf

[322] www.childsafety.gov.au

[323] https://www.alannahandmadeline.org.au/learning-resources?types=19377

The *National Office for Child Safety* website provides practical tools and training resources to help organisations implement the *National Principles for Child Safe Organisations*, help parents and carers learn about child safe organisations and how to report child abuse[324]. Training is available with the *National Association for Prevention of Child Abuse and Neglect (NAPCAN)*[325].

Child Safe also provides assistance with policies and procedures, child safe audit and roadmap, training and risk management tools[326].

Bravehearts provides child protection online training courses to equip those supporting and working with children with the knowledge and tools to create and maintain child-safe environments[327].

Become a foster carer

Foster carers are part of the child or young person's care team, which includes the foster care agency and the child's birth family and creates a safe and supportive home for a child while their parents and families get back on their feet.

Anyone over 21 years can apply to become a foster carer. Foster carers come from all backgrounds and walks of life - single, part of a family, married, young or old, working full or part-time or have children of their own, from multicultural and multifaith backgrounds and LGBTIQ+ people.

Foster carers care for one child or more at any one time, for just a couple of nights a month up to 6 months or more. The assessment, accreditation and training process typically takes six months.

Participate

Attend an event in *National Child Protection Week* in September and pledge your support[328].

Volunteer

Young people aged 16 who are transitioning from out-of-home care to independence often need to develop independent living skills and manage on their own. As well as the opportunity to volunteer as a mentor with young people leaving care, lead tenant services provide a safe, semi-independent living environment in which young people are supported by 1 or 2 approved

---

324 https://www.childsafety.gov.au/

325 https://www.napcan.org.au/programs-training/

326 https://www.childsafe.org.au/

327 https://bravehearts.org.au/education/online-courses/

328 https://www.napcan.org.au/national-child-protection-week-pledge/

adult volunteer lead tenants who provide day-to-day guidance and mature role-modelling. The lead tenant volunteer also works collaboratively with program staff members in monitoring and responding to the wellbeing of young people.

Contact your local charity out-of-home provider, such as *Berry Street*[329], *McKillop*[330] or *OzChild*[331].

Campaign

Started nearly 30 years ago, the *Australian Childhood Foundation* is the national leader in understanding and developing trauma-informed practice to support children hurt by abuse, neglect and family violence to heal. Their *Our Collective Experience Project* collates and reports the shared wisdom of survivors of sexual abuse during childhood to inform policy and practice[332]. Sign their petition to establish a Federal Minister for Children[333].

Invest

As outlined above, there is an urgent need to increase the investment in preventing children from entering out-of-home care. The proven Uniting's Newpin (New Parent and Infant Network) program involves parents and their children regularly attending a centre-based program for up to 18 months to engage in a range of activities that promote wellbeing, improve parenting capacity and support the development of positive family relationships.

This successful program in NSW became the basis of Australia's first Social Impact Bond (SIB). Please see the 'Ways to Make an Impact' chapter.

Donate

Established in 1993 and originally the Australian Association of Children and Young People in Care, the *CREATE Foundation* is the national consumer body for children and young people with an out-of-home care experience which supports 26,000 children and young people with a care experience as clubCREATE members. CREATE is at the forefront of research and advocacy for policy and system change, including position papers, submissions and campaigns, as well as a podcast which provides a platform for young people to share their experiences and shed light on the care system[334].

---

329 https://www.berrystreet.org.au/you-can-help/become-a-mentor

330 https://www.mackillop.org.au/programs/lead-tenant-program

331 https://www.ozchild.org.au/service/lead-tenant/

332 https://www.childhood.org.au/app/uploads/2024/02/Our-Collective-Experience-Project-%E2%80%93-First-Report.pdf

333 https://www.childhood.org.au/minister-for-children/

334 https://create.org.au/

Bravehearts was founded by Hetty Johnston AM following her young daughter's disclosure of sexual abuse. Its research supports lobbying and legislative reform initiatives to promote the protection of children[335].

We know that investment in early intervention programs could prevent thousands of children from entering out-of-home care and save the government $2 for every $1 spent. Operating since 2014 and in 6 regions across Victoria, *Anglicare Victoria's* Rapid Response model has been highly successful at keeping families together by providing families with short-term and intensive face-to-face support. A safety-focused plan is developed with child protection and the family, and provides intensive, in-home support to address the crisis[336].

---

335 https://bravehearts.org.au/research-lobbying/reform/

336 https://www.anglicarevic.org.au/our-services/family-and-parenting-support/rapid-response/

HOMELESSNESS

'Homelessness is no longer confined to the most vulnerable. With the housing crisis forcing working families into homelessness, this should be a wake-up call for action'

KATE COLVIN, CEO HOMELESSNESS AUSTRALIA[337]

Sitting around the Board table, the excitement was palpable, if not surreal, when the CEO reported that, in the last week, he had received calls from a number of Australian government Ministers and MPs to come and visit. Any politician taking an interest in homelessness was a highlight of the year, so we felt all our Christmases had come at once.

On coming to power, Prime Minister Kevin Rudd had told his team to go and visit local homelessness agencies to understand the issues and services. He declared homelessness a 'national obscenity' and committed to halve the number of homeless in Australia and accommodate all those sleeping rough by 2020. 'A country like this should not have this problem, so large and long-standing without being addressed. It's time we had a decent solution to this problem that has been around for a long time,' he stated[338].

Brotherhood of St Laurence Executive Director Tony Nicholson said the plan was 'by far the most substantial commitment to tackling homelessness that we have ever seen in Australia. After many years, Australians have become accustomed to glib, political promises attached to grab bags of initiatives, and this stands in great contrast to that approach.'

---

[337] https://www.brisbanetimes.com.au/national/rudd-promises-urgent-action-for-homeless-20080128-ge9lpx.html

[338]Homelessness https://www.smh.com.au/national/rudds-2020-homeless-pledge-welcomed-20081221-72rw.html

For the first time, we felt that homelessness was getting the high-level political attention it deserved and eagerly prepared for a sea-change in the government's commitment.

We were delighted with the depth and breadth of the subsequent white paper, *The Road Home: A National Approach to Reducing Homelessness*, which was, and remains, the only national comprehensive plan to tackle homelessness. Under the plan, the Australian and State/Territory governments pledged $1.2 billion over four years with $800 million to the National Partnership Agreement on Homelessness and $400 million to the National Partnership on Social Housing for stepped-up early intervention, better homelessness services and an expanded supply of affordable housing, representing a 55 per cent increase in funding.

The media applauded the commitment and the Leader of the Opposition, Malcolm Turnbull, promised bipartisan support (but said the main focus should be on providing jobs for Australians).

We hoped that now the scourge of homelessness had the political will with sufficient funding to be tackled with conviction.

There was some progress with a 13 per cent decrease in rough sleepers, but a 31 per cent increase in people living in overcrowded houses largely accounted for the number of homeless Australians rising from 89,728 in 2006 to 105,237 in 2011.

Prophetically, the Council of Australian Governments (COAG) Reform Council's housing affordability report for 2010-2011 showed that there was no indication that housing affordability had improved, and the private rental market had actually worsened significantly for the lowest income households. Dr John Falzon, CEO of the St Vincent de Paul Society, stated that 'this problem is not going to go away unless we tackle the problem of public housing'.

At the 2012 National Homelessness Conference, Federal Homelessness Minister Brendan O'Connor reaffirmed the government's pledge to halve homelessness and provide supported accommodation for all rough sleepers by 2020. However, the Leader of the Opposition, Tony Abbott, refused to commit, saying it was unrealistic and couldn't be met. His win in 2013 put an end to the dream.

WHAT

The Australian Bureau of Statistics defines homelessness as 'when a person does not have suitable accommodation alternatives, they are considered homeless if their current living arrangement is in a dwelling that is inadequate; or has no tenure; or if their initial tenure is short and not extendable; or does not allow them to have control of, and access to space for social relations'.

The rate of homelessness in Australia has fluctuated between 51 people per 10,000 population in 2001 to 48 per 10,000 in 2021. From the last available data on census night in 2021, a total of 122,494 Australians were estimated to be experiencing homelessness, an increase of 5 per cent from 2016.

Of these, 2 in 5 were living in 'severely' crowded dwellings (a 6 per cent decrease from 2016); 1 in 5 were in supported accommodation for the homeless (a 14 per cent increase from 2016); and 1 in 6 were living in boarding houses (a 27 per cent increase from 2016); and 7,636 were living in improvised dwellings, tents, or sleeping out (rough sleepers) with nearly a third being in WA, a doubling over the previous 5 years.

A 'severely' crowded dwelling is one that needs 4 or more extra bedrooms to adequately accommodate the people living there[339].

As an upside of the COVID pandemic, during 2020 at least 12,073 rough sleepers benefited from COVID-19 Emergency Accommodation programs staged by NSW, South Australia, Queensland, and Victoria. By 2022, these placements and move-on housing programs in NSW and Victoria alone facilitated safe, secure and supported accommodation pathways for around 3,500 former rough sleepers with complex needs, at least partially relieving the growing backlog of chronic rough sleepers built up over previous years[340].

Since then, there has been a 22 per cent increase in people experiencing rough sleeping in the 3 years to 2023-24[341]. In New South Wales, rough sleeping has surged by 51 per cent since 2020, largely driven by an increase in regional communities. A survey of Victoria's councils in 2025 also found a sharp rise in

---

[339] https://www.ahuri.edu.au/analysis/brief/when-dwelling-considered-crowded-and-severely-crowded

[340] Pawson, H., Martin, C., Thompson, S., Aminpour, F. (2021) *COVID-19: Rental housing and homelessness policy impacts*, ACOSS/UNSW Poverty and Inequality Partnership Report No. 12, Sydney

[341] Pawson H, Parsell C, Clarke A, Moore J, Hartley C, Aminpour F, Eagles K (2024) *Australian Homelessness Monitor 2024*, City Futures Research Centre, UNSW School of Social Science, University of Queensland at https://homelessnessaustralia.org.au/wp-content/uploads/2024/12/AHM_final.pdf

rough sleepers across Melbourne suburbs, with each council rating the issue as severe or very severe[342].

In what CEO of Homelessness Australia, Kate Colvin, described as 'deaths of needless poverty and despair', almost 1,500 Australians die in homelessness each year, with nearly half aged 35-54 years[343].

Modelling estimates that in 2022, there were between 2.7 million and 3.2 million Australians at risk of homelessness, where one negative shock could result in them losing their home. This represents a 63 per cent increase between 2016 and 2022 in the number of Australians at risk of homelessness[344].

In 2024–25, the number of people assisted by State/Territory-based homelessness services (SHS) increased to almost 289,000, or over 1 in 100 Australians, with 49 per cent experiencing homelessness and 51 per cent at risk of becoming homeless. Applicants newly assisted by services and classed as homeless (as opposed to 'at risk of homelessness') have risen by 16 per cent over the last 5 years to 132,542[345].

Homelessness is becoming more persistent. More than 3 in 5, or 183,000, SHS clients either continued to access support in 2024–25 after having received it in 2023–24 or returned to SHS support after a period without assistance.

The number of Australians experiencing persistent homelessness (those who have been homeless for more than 7 months out of 24 months whilst a client of the specialist homelessness service) has risen by a 3rd over the last 5 years to 41,100. Almost half are children and young people.

SHS clients had around 492,000 support periods, an average annual increase of 1.8 per cent since 2011–12. The median days supported is steady at 58, whilst he median number of nights accommodated increased to 34 nights, up from a low of 28 nights in 2019–20. This means that Australians are stuck in

---

[342] The Municipal Association of Victoria (2025) *Homelessness in Victoria. Summary Report* at https://www.mav.asn.au/__data/assets/pdf_file/0007/42874/Homelessness-in-Victoria-MAV-Summary-Report-Jun-2025.pdf

[343] https://homelessnessaustralia.org.au/homelessness-crisis-claiming-more-lives-at-a-younger-age/#:~:text=%E2%80%9CThese%20are%20deaths%20of%20needless,national%20crisis%20demands%20immediate%20action.%E2%80%9D

[344] Impact Economic and Policy (2024) *Call Unanswered. Unmet Demand For Specialist Homelessness Services*, Homelessness Australia, p.5 at https://homelessnessaustralia.org.au/wp-content/uploads/2024/11/Impact-Economics-Call-Unanswered.pdf

[345] Australian Institute of Health and welfare (2025) *Specialist homelessness services annual report 2024–25* at https://www.aihw.gov.au/reports/homelessness-services/specialist-homelessness-services-annual-report/contents/clients-services-and-outcomes

homelessness for longer, subject to longer periods of support and/or more repeated periods of short-term support[346].

In recent years, the number of SHS clients sleeping rough at the start of their support has risen from 25,000 clients in 2019–20 to 34,800 in 2024–25.

These figures only report those seeking and being provided a homelessness service from a provider. They exclude the 129,000 requests made for SHS support, on average, or around 350 unassisted requests per day, turned away due to a lack of capacity in these services, especially due to a lack of crisis accommodation. This represents an increase of 17 per cent on 2023-24.

A survey with 23 Specialist Homelessness Services over 2 weeks in September 2024 revealed that: 39 per cent of services were forced to close their doors to people seeking help at least once during the fortnight; 83 per cent of services were unable to answer phone calls for some period during the survey, leaving people in crisis without immediate assistance; and 74 per cent of services were unable to reply to emails during the survey, impacting housing referrals and support requests[347].

This meant that families with children who had no accommodation failed to get assistance 20 per cent of the time and unaccompanied young people and children with no accommodation were turned away 11 per cent of the time.

Additional evidence that these figures are an underestimate of homelessness is provided by the most recent Australian Bureau of Statistics General Social Survey which found that only a third of homeless people sought help during their most recent experience of homelessness[348].

Recently, providers report a new wave of homelessness among low and middle-income earners who have never accessed services previously and are now seeking support due to rent rises and other cost-of-living pressures. This is reflected in a nearly 50 per cent increase in the proportion of employed persons receiving homelessness services over the 5 years [349].

On any given night, 1 in 7 people experiencing homelessness is a child under 12. While homelessness is devastating for anyone regardless of their age, the

---

[346] ibid

[347] Ibid

[348] Australian Bureau of Statistics (2015) *General Social Survey: Summary Results, Australia* at https://www.abs.gov.au/statistics/people/people-and-communities/general-social-survey-summary-results-australia/2014

[349] Australian Institute of Health and welfare (2025) *Specialist homelessness services annual report 2024–25*

experience has detrimental effects on children and young people well into their adult lives[350].

In 2024-25, nearly 1 in 7, or 40,500, requesting assistance from specialist homelessness services was an unaccompanied young person, many fleeing violence or neglect at home. Over 7 in 10 were not in education or training. Of the 2/3rds seeking accommodation, only half were successful[351].

Children who experience homelessness are particularly vulnerable and are at an increased risk of being homeless as adolescents and adults. They are more likely to experience mental health, emotional, and behavioural challenges than housed children. Children facing homelessness are also more likely to report food insecurity and to go hungry, negatively impacting developmental and health outcomes[352].

Homelessness also makes it difficult to focus on study. For young people, it is hard to enrol or stay enrolled in a course when you don't know where you will be living in the future. For children, the impact of homelessness on their development and connection to school is particularly harmful. Homelessness significantly disrupts children's participation in education, leading to learning difficulties and disengagement[353].

As a result, most homeless children have poor academic records and few skills which would assist them to obtain even unskilled employment in a competitive labour market[354], leading to intergenerational poverty and disadvantage and their own risk of homelessness as adults.

WHY

Three other themes of this book - family and domestic violence, poverty and disadvantage, gender inequality and mental health are significant causes of homelessness. Australians experiencing homelessness are in the perfect storm

350 https://www.missionaustralia.com.au/stories/safe-homes/homelessness-and-its-lasting-impact-on-children-and-young-people

351 Australian Institute of Health and welfare (2025) *Specialist homelessness services annual report 2024–25*

352 https://streetsmartaustralia.org/creating-change-for-children-in-homelessness/#:~:text=Child%20and%20youth%20homelessness%20in%20Australia&text=They%20are%20more%20likely%20to,impacting%20developmental%20and%20health%20outcomes.

353 https://www.launchhousing.org.au/ending-homelessness/research-hub/employment-and-education

354 https://humanrights.gov.au/sites/default/files/Chapter%2022.pdf

of the interrelatedness of these issues, together with shortages in support services and crisis, transition, social, and affordable accommodation.

As the leading cause, family and domestic violence was given as the main reason in nearly 3 out of 10 presentations to homelessness services, amounting to 76,500 women, with over a 3rd experiencing homelessness at the time[355]. Additionally, over 2 in 5 of those experiencing persistent homelessness were women and children affected by family and domestic violence.

Tragically, only 3 per cent of women and children victims of family and domestic violence receive the long-term housing solutions they need.

Mental health issues are also a major cause of homelessness. Nearly a 3rd, or 80,000 Australians with a current mental health issue presented to homelessness services in 2024/25 and half of those experiencing persistent homelessness, or 20,500 having a current mental health issue[356]. Poverty is a major factor, with nearly 4 in 5 receiving some form of government assistance as their main source of income[357].

With women over 45 the fastest-growing age group of people experiencing homelessness in Australia – often the result of financial insecurity, relationship breakdown, and limited access to affordable housing – financial avoidance, as the complex interplay of financial insecurity, social norms, and behaviours, can increase a woman's risk of experiencing homelessness[358].

Sitting on the Board of a leading homeless agency for 10 years, it was so frustrating to see successive governments unwilling to tackle the chronic shortage of crisis, transition, social and affordable accommodation that would have provided a responsive, housing first approach that enabled wrap-around support services and pathways out of homelessness. Instead, the system seemed to keep people in a state of homelessness (as getting a job would only move you down the priority list to get into public housing) until, after many years, they qualified for a place in social housing. Their reward is often appalling living conditions in areas of high unemployment with little prospect of a job.

Those experiencing homelessness, such as being evicted from their house or escaping family violence, contact their State or Territory's homelessness service system through one designated phone number to be referred to a

---

[355] Australian Institute of Health and Welfare (2025) *Specialist homelessness services annual report 2024–25*

[356] ibid

[357] ibid

[358] https://www.sefa.com.au/project-daffodil

homelessness service provider in their area to access crisis (also called 'emergency') accommodation where they can stay for a few weeks.

More than 3 quarters of homelessness services reported finding it 'much harder' to find suitable housing for clients in mid-2024 compared with 12 months earlier, which saw 190 requests per day on average turned away, or 71,000 per annum, meaning that for nearly a 3rd of Australians who needed short-term or emergency accommodation no accommodation could be found, nor were they referred to another agency for help[359].

Worryingly, the proportion of unassisted requests made by people presenting alone rose from 56 per cent of requests in 2018–19 to 65 per cent in 2024–25.

This lack of government-funded crisis beds means that providers are funded to purchase short-term crisis accommodation from private operators of boarding houses, hotels, motels, hostels, and caravan parks. This accommodation is often unsanitary, unsafe and inappropriate and provides inadequate support for those who receive it[360]. As a result, people are moved between venues. In 2019, 50 homelessness and family violence organisations in Melbourne took the unprecedented step of turning homeless people away rather than referring people to unsafe and squalid motels and boarding houses as a form of emergency housing[361].

The next step is transitional housing for up to 2 years, or however long a permanent public housing place is available. Transitional accommodation is government-funded and operated by the government or by a charity community housing association (CHO), which, with tailored support services, helps people to stabilise their lives before moving into longer-term housing in the private rental market, affordable or social housing. Again, there is a shortage of places and, again, they are likely to be moved between facilities. In Victoria, this means that women and children spend, on average, three months in unsafe and inappropriate motels before transitional accommodation places are available[362].

---

359 Australian Institute of Health and Welfare (2024) *Specialist homelessness services annual report 2023–24. Unassisted requests for services* at https://www.aihw.gov.au/reports/homelessness-services/specialist-homelessness-services-annual-report/contents/unassisted-requests-for-services

360Northern and Western Homelessness Network (2023) *A Crisis in Crisis. The appalling state of emergency accommodation in Melbourne's north and west* at https://womenshousing.com.au/app/uploads/2023/03/a-crisis-in-crisis-doc.pdf

361 https://www.theage.com.au/national/victoria/no-more-referrals-to-dodgy-crisis-housing-warn-homelessness-services-20190214-p50xu7.html

362 Launch Housing (2025) *BUILDING FUTURES. A New Support System for Families with Children Experiencing Homelessness* at https://www.launchhousing.org.au/wp-content/uploads/2025/07/Launch-Housing-Insights_BuildingFutures.pdf

As a result, people are becoming stuck in homelessness for longer, requiring longer periods of agency support, and/or more repeated periods of short-term support.

Social housing is government funded and either managed by government or CHOs. With 75 per cent of the rent subsidised by the Commonwealth Rent Assistance program up to a set amount, the rent paid is 25-30 per cent of the renter's income, including benefits.

Affordable housing is accommodation typically built, owned and run by CHOs and is designed for key workers on low incomes, such as teachers, firefighters and nurses, with rent set at 75-80 per cent of market value.

The CHO movement was born in the late 19th century in England, when philanthropists set up charitable housing trusts to help homeless people and alleviate poverty. State governments picked up the model in the 1990s encouraging their establishment and regulation.

CHOs have the advantage of working locally with many partners, such as local governments and religious groups, who have 'lazy land'[363] that can be utilised, as well as partnerships with for-profit builders to include a proportion of affordable housing in larger projects in order to get planning benefits. With State governments transferring some of their housing stock to the CHOs, the CHOs can borrow against this capital and further develop affordable accommodation.

Post the Global Financial Crisis in 2008, the Rudd Government established the National Rental Affordability Scheme to increase the supply of affordable rental homes for low-to-moderate income households. Property investors who are accepted into the program were offered financial incentives each year (for up to 10 years) when they rented out their property at a minimum of 20 per cent below market rate to eligible residential tenants. The Scheme was designed to minimise rental stress for low-to-middle income-earners, especially key workers, and to fuel large-scale investment into the construction of affordable housing to create employment. In 2014, the Abbott government scrapped new deals under the Scheme.

As of 2022, 160+ CHOs own over 40,740 homes, comprising 14 billion in land and buildings, and manage 132,000 social and affordable housing tenancies[364].

---

[363] Thanks to Rob McGauran for this term

[364] Community Housing Industry Association (2024) *Australia's Community Housing Industry In Profile 2022* at https://www.communityhousing.com.au/wp-content/uploads/2024/05/CHIA-2022-Data-Digest-pub-042024.pdf?x97340

The long-term underinvestment by governments in social housing, which has declined to 4.1 per cent of all homes in 2025, down from 4.7 per cent in 2013[365], has resulted in longer waiting lists and homelessness, and a bottleneck causing longer stays in crisis and transitional accommodation, which are also insufficient.

As of June 2023, there were 298,000 public housing dwellings owned and managed by State/Territory governments, plus 114,000 community housing dwellings. Because of government policy to grow CHOs, the number of community housing dwellings increased almost fourfold, whilst the number of public housing dwellings decreased by 13 per cent since 2006[366].

In the meantime, the 2024 Productivity Commission's Report on Government Services reported that 224,326 households are on the waiting list for social housing across Australia, with the greatest need increasing by four per cent to 106,534 compared to last year's figures[367].

Australia and State/Territory government funding of housing and homelessness services is governed by the *National Housing and Homelessness Agreement (NHHA).* In 2022, the Productivity Commission concluded that the NHHA is ineffective, failing to foster collaboration between governments or hold governments to account. As a funding contract, the NHHA is not a blueprint for reform'[368].

It notes that 'as funding is largely untied, State and Territory Governments have wide discretion about how they use NHHA funds. The NHHA is a highly transactional agreement that focuses on State and Territory Government accountability to the Australian Government, rather than all levels of government being accountable to the Australian community. There is also little connection between need and the allocation of NHHA funding between States and Territories. Homelessness funding is distributed according to outdated data (from the 2006 Census) and general funding is based on population. Funding is not based on need nor the different costs of providing services in each jurisdiction'[369].

Because all governments need to agree to the co-funding arrangements, the negotiation of the NHAA has been torturous and often exceeded the deadline,

---

365

366 Everybody's Home (2025) *Out of Reach Australia's Rental Crisis and the Decline of Social Housing* at https://everybodyshome.com.au/resources/out-of-reach/

367 Productivity Commission (2024) *Report on Government Services 2024*, Part G, Section 18

368 Productivity Commission (2022) *In need of repair: The National Housing and Homelessness Agreement*, Study Report, Canberra

369 Ibid, p.9 & 13

resulting in homelessness services not knowing their budgets well into the financial year.

From 1 July 2024, the National Agreement on Social Housing and Homelessness (NASHH) which replaced the NHHA funds the States and Territory governments an additional $423 million over 5 years for social housing and homelessness services. For this new Agreement, the Commonwealth doubled its dedicated funding allocation for homelessness services to $400 million a year, provided the States and Territories matched the funding[370].

Managed by the Future Fund, in 2023, the Australian government created the $10 billion Housing Australia Future Fund (HAFF) as a dedicated investment vehicle to support the delivery of 20,000 new social homes and 10,000 new affordable homes across Australia over a 5-year period through co-investment grants administered by Housing Australia, whilst still earning a return of CPI plus 2-3 per cent per annum, net of investment fees over the long term. The holy grail is to use this fund to attract sustainable co-financing from the $4 trillion superannuation funds. IFM Investors estimates that only 0.5 per cent of the industry super funds would be needed to realise $15 billion in investment to create 100,000 additional homes[371].

However, as the Grattan Institute points out, social housing – where rents are typically capped at 30 per cent of tenants' incomes – is unlikely to create an attractive return.

Murray Barr was a bear of a man, an ex-marine, 6 feet tall and heavyset, and when he fell down— which he did nearly every day—it could take 2 or 3 grown men to pick him up. He had straight black hair and olive skin. On the street, they called him Smokey. He was missing most of his teeth but he had a wonderful smile. People loved Murray.

His chosen drink was vodka. On the streets of downtown Reno, where he lived, he could buy a 259 millilitre bottle of cheap vodka for a $1.50. If he was flush, he could go for the 750 millilitre bottle, and if he was broke he could always do what many of the other homeless people of Reno did, which is to walk through the casinos and finish off the half-empty glasses of liquor left at the gaming tables.

370 https://www.ahuri.edu.au/analysis/news/whats-2024-budget-housing-and-homelessness

371 https://www.ifminvestors.com/en-au/news-and-insights/media-centre/investing-in-australia-accelerating-industry-super-investment-and-growing-australias-housing-supply/

"If he was on a runner, we could pick him up several times a day," Patrick O'Bryan, who is a bicycle cop in downtown Reno, said. "And he's gone on some amazing runners. He would get picked up, get detoxed, then get back out a couple of hours later and start up again. A lot of the guys on the streets who've been drinking, they get so angry. They are so incredibly abrasive, so violent, so abusive. Murray was such a character and had such a great sense of humour that we somehow got past that. Even when he was abusive, we'd say, 'Murray, you know you love us,' and he'd say, 'I know'—and go back to swearing at us."

"I've been a police officer for 15 years," O'Bryan's partner, Steve Johns, said. "I picked up Murray my whole career. Literally."

Johns and O'Bryan realised that if you totted up all his hospital bills for the 10 years that he had been on the streets—as well as substance abuse treatment costs, doctors' fees, and other expenses— "it cost us one million dollars not to do something about Murray".

Malcolm Gladwell's article in the New Yorker concluded 'but, of course, Reno didn't have a place where Murray could be given the structure he needed. Someone must have decided that it cost too much' [372].

Million-Dollar Murray was Gladwell's argument for *Housing First*, a then-novel approach to the homelessness problem. Gladwell's point was that a small percentage of the homeless population—generally, those classified as chronically homeless—account for most of the costs. Therefore, it would be cheaper to provide housing first for stability and the foundation to provide wrap-around services.

Established in 1990 in New York City, *Common Ground* exemplified Housing First by creating high-quality permanent and transitional housing for the homeless with the philosophy that supportive housing costs substantially less than homeless shelters, and many times less than jail cells or hospital rooms. Nearly 30 years later, the Times Square Common Ground remains the largest supportive residence in the country, and thousands of people have been able to escape or avoid life on the streets by finding a home in one of its 652 apartments. Today, the charity operates nearly 4,000 units of housing across New York City[373].

---

[372] Gladwell M (2006) *MILLION-DOLLAR MURRAY*, New Yorker, 0028792X, 2/13/2006, Vol. 82, Issue 1

[373] https://breakingground.org/who-we-are/

In 2006, the first Common Ground model of permanent supportive housing was opened in Adelaide. By 2008, the Australian Common Ground Alliance came together as a group of homelessness and housing organisations that worked to advocate for the establishment of other Common Grounds in city centres around Australia. The construction company, Grocon, made a commitment to build a Common Ground at cost for Melbourne, Sydney, and Brisbane.

Elizabeth St Common Ground in Melbourne opened in 2010; the Camperdown Common Ground opened in Sydney in 2011; the Brisbane Common Ground in 2012; and Common Ground Tasmania opened two buildings in 2012[374].

Another Housing First model is the *Youth Foyer*. Originating in France in the 1890s, Youth Foyers provide a safe and stable home with integrated education, employment and living skills support for young people aged 15–24. 2/3rds gain secure, decent employment[375]. The Foyer Foundation lists the current 17 Youth Foyers[376]

In an example of the power of giving, The Foyer Foundation established *FoyerInvest*, a consortium of not-for-profits, investors and philanthropists working toward the goal of fifty Accredited Youth Foyers in Australia by 2030. Charity *Hand Heart Pocket* initiated FoyerInvest's Queensland Working Group which brought together the 6 youth services and community housing providers already expert in delivering Foyers, along with Foyer tenants, with the aim of advocating for more in the state. This initiative has resulted in a $320 million commitment from the Queensland state government that was announced earlier in 2024[377].

Throughout this book, community-based integrated responses are shown to be highly effective. Homelessness is no exception. Under US charity *Destination: Home*, in 2020, 200 stakeholders in Santa Clara came together- representatives of community-based service organisations, local government, philanthropy,

---

[374] https://www.mercyfoundation.com.au/our-focus/ending-homelessness/common-ground-permanent-supportive-housing/#:~:text=In%202006%20the%20first%20Common,part%20of%20Housing%20Choices%20Australia.

[375] Foyer Foundation (2022) *Under One Roof. The social and economic impact of Youth Foyers* at https://foyer.org.au/wp-content/uploads/2023/04/FYF_UnderOneRoof_Summary_singlepagesfinal.pdf

[376] https://foyer.org.au/

[377] https://www.philanthropy.org.au/news-and-stories/how-a-philanthropic-consortium-is-helping-young-people-out-of-homelessness/?apcid=0063926383921fccc67cbb00&utm_campaign=4-20-7-june-2024-public&utm_content=4-20-7-june-2024-public&utm_medium=email&utm_source=ortto

business, healthcare, and people with lived experience - to develop a 5-year Community Plan to End Homelessness.

The Plan has 3 strategies - address the root causes of homelessness through system and policy change; expand homelessness prevention and housing programs to meet the need; and improve the quality of life for unsheltered individuals and create healthy neighbourhoods for all. To achieve a 30 per cent reduction in the annual inflow of people becoming homeless, the Homelessness Prevention System was established to provide temporary financial assistance, legal support and other services to help at-risk families and individuals maintain their housing and avoid falling into homelessness. Of the over 7,000 households at imminent risk of homelessness, 94 per cent remained stably housed.

To house 20,000 people, a US$950 million affordable housing bond was raised that earmarked over 70 per cent of the funds for housing that targets homelessness, creating 59 new developments with 5,200 affordable housing units[378].

With housing affordability stress as the main driver of homelessness increasing by 36 per cent in the three years to 2023-24[379], we can't leave homelessness without mentioning the ever-widening housing divide in Australia.

After all, homelessness can be seen ultimately as a housing problem.

A CEO of a local government once mentioned to me that the principal objective of his council was to ensure house prices increase. In a basic supply and demand equation, limiting new supply and creating scarcity leads to higher prices, creating a win-win: NIMBY residents are happy, house owners are wealthier, council rates are higher, there is less pressure on local services, management gets its bonuses, and the councillors are re-elected.

In 2020–21, dwelling approvals in Australia surged to 221,974, driven by pandemic stimulus and ultra-low interest rates, marking the highest level since 2017–18, followed by a steady decline through to 162,892 dwellings in 2023–24, the lowest financial-year total since 2011–12, despite a growth in population of 1.8 million people.

In 1990 and through the entirety of the decade that followed, the median dwelling across Australia was worth around 9.5 times that of annual household

---

378 https://osh.santaclaracounty.gov/affordable-housing/2016-measure-affordable-housing-bond/measure-housing-bond-progress

379 Pawson H, Parsell C, Clarke A, Moore J, Hartley C, Aminpour F and Eagles K (2024) *Australian Homelessness Monitor 2024*, Sydney, UNSW City Futures Research Centre at https://homelessnessaustralia.org.au/wp-content/uploads/2024/12/AHM_final.pdf

income per capita. But then in 2000, the government introduced the 50 per cent capital gains discount, which, combined with negative gearing, made housing speculation very profitable. This was then followed by the introduction and soon doubling of the First Home Owner Grant which likewise served only to spur demand for housing.

By 2020, the median household income was 13.5 times dwelling prices, and by the end of 2025, it was 16.1 times[380].

The resultant 6 per cent compound annual growth in the value of houses over the past twenty-three years versus 3 per cent annual growth in average incomes has meant that house ownership is becoming ever more unaffordable.

The lack of affordable housing has produced record low vacancy rates and record high rentals. Housing stress, when lower-income households spend more than 30 per cent of their gross income on housing costs, can push them into homelessness. With tenants now paying, on average, a 3rd of their pre-tax income on rent[381], over 2 in 5 low-income households renting private homes were in housing stress and at risk of being pushed into homelessness in 2022-23, despite receiving Commonwealth Rent Assistance[382].

With national rents climbing 44 per cent in the 5 years to September 2025, compared with wage growth of 17.5 per cent over the same period, Anglicare Australia's 2025 Rental Affordability Snapshot surveyed rental listings across Australia and found that affordability has crashed to record lows. Out of 51,238 rental listings, it found that only 352 rentals (0.7 per cent) were affordable for a person earning a full-time minimum wage, 28 rentals for those on a Disability Support Pension, and only 3 rooms for rent in shared houses were affordable for a person on Job Seeker[383].

After the RBA's 13 rate rises, households deemed 'extremely at risk' – based on their share of household income being spent on repayments and outstanding debt – topped 1.016 million, about 20 per cent of mortgage holders[384].

---

380 https://australiainstitute.org.au/post/housing-affordability-is-so-bad-that-2020-now-looks-good/

381 Cotality (2026) Quarterly Rental Review Report September 2025

382 Productivity Commission (2024) *Report on Government Services 2024*, Part G, Section 18

383 Anglicare Australia (2025) *Rental Affordability Snapshot National Report 2025 \ Sixteenth Edition* at https://www.anglicare.asn.au/wp-content/uploads/2025/04/Rental-Affordability-Snapshot-National-Report.pdf

384 https://www.roymorgan.com/findings/9517-mortgage-stress-risk-march-2024

It is not surprising then that housing affordability is the most rapidly growing cause of homelessness over the past 4 years[385].

Governments have responded, but Treasury briefings have revealed that Australia will have to build housing at a significantly faster rate than it has in the last couple of decades to meet the government's target of 1.2m new homes between June 2024 and 2029.

This means about 240,000 new dwellings every year. However, the most recent State of the Housing System report predicts we will fall short of the target by more than 262,000 homes, an even bigger miss than was predicted the year before[386].

ACT

Campaign

Launched in 2018 by a coalition of housing, homelessness and welfare organisations to achieve the change needed so everybody has a safe and decent place to live, *Everybody's Home* is a national campaign to fix the housing crisis. Sign their petition to the Government to fund a pipeline of at least 25,000 social and affordable homes each year[387], as well as an additional 16,810 social housing units for women and children escaping family and domestic violence[388].

With the evidence that children and young people are more vulnerable when experiencing homelessness, sign onto *Home Time*'s national campaign to unlock Australia's housing system for almost 40,000 children and young people with nowhere to live[389].

---

385 Launch Housing (2022) *Australian Homelessness Monitor 2022* at https://www.launchhousing.org.au/ending-homelessness/research-hub/australian-homelessness-monitor-2022

386 National Housing Supply and Affordability Council (2025) *State of the Housing System 2025* at https://nhsac.gov.au/sites/nhsac.gov.au/files/2025-05/ar-state-housing-system-2025.pdf

387 https://everybodyshome.com.au/take-action/petition/

388 Equity Economics (2021) *Nowhere to Go. The Benefits Of Providing Long-Term Social Housing To Women That Have Experienced Domestic And Family Violence,* Everybody's Home, p.5

389 https://www.hometime.org.au/

To challenge the NIMBYs and advocate for more housing development in your area, join the YIMBY (Yes In My Back Yard) movement in your city, including Melbourne[390], Sydney[391] and Brisbane[392].

Participate

In 2006, financial planner Bernard Fehon was on the organising committee for the Vinnies annual gala dinner, targeting CEOs and business owners who would have the most money to bid on the auction items secured for the event. But he felt uncomfortable having a feast to raise money for those who can't afford their next meal. With his kids doing a Sleepout for Vinnies at their school, he came up with a *CEO Sleepout* version[393].

With no allowance for their status, the participants spent a cold winter night with only cardboard between them and the concrete. Since then, the event has raised over $30 million and inspired similar events in the UK, South Africa, USA, Taiwan and New Zealand.

Launch Housing's *The Roughin' It Challenge* dares you to go 24 hours with no bed, 1 bag and $10 a day[394], Melbourne City Mission runs *Sleep At The 'G*[395], Stepping Stone House runs *Sleep Under the Stars* at Barangaroo on the edge of Sydney Harbour[396] and the *Coast Shelter Sleepout* is on the NSW Central Coast[397]. Mission Australia invites you to Sleepout at anytime, anywhere[398], the *Salvos Sleepout* is held in Launceston & Hobart, Brisbane and Sydney[399] and The Property Industry's *Sleep Out* is held in Queensland and NSW[400].

Join an event in National Homelessness Week in August or hold your own event[401].

Donate

Speaking at the 2016 Homelessness Conference in Adelaide, former Adelaide Thinker in Residence, Rosanne Haggerty, outlined how she viewed

---

[390] https://www.yimby.melbourne/
[391] https://www.sydney.yimby.au/
[392] https://yimbyqld.com.au/
[393] https://www.ceosleepout.org.au/
[394] https://www.roughinitchallenge.org.au/why-rough-it
[395] https://www.mcm.org.au/get-involved/sleep-at-the-g
[396] https://www.sleepunderthestars.com.au/
[397] https://www.coastsheltersleepout.com.au/
[398] https://act.missionaustralia.com.au/sleepout
[399] https://www.salvationarmy.org.au/get-involved/salvos-sleepout/
[400] https://give.pif.com.au/sleepout
[401] https://homelessnessaustralia.org.au/event-category/homelessness-week-events/

homelessness as a solvable problem that Adelaide is uniquely placed to solve. Rosanne issued a challenge to put in place a plan to end street homelessness and organisations from across the public, private, community and university sectors have collectively taken up that challenge. As a coalition of more than forty charities, government agencies, private organisations and service providers, the *Adelaide Zero Project* is a collective response to this call to action and the first city outside North America to implement an approach that has seen seven communities achieve Functional Zero homelessness for veterans, and three communities for chronically homeless people[402]. Functional Zero will be achieved when there are enough services, houses, and crisis beds for everyone who needs them. As a result, homelessness is rare, and for those who experience it, it is short-lived and one-off.

Since then, other States have started similar 0 projects with collaborations of local governments and providers in NSW (Sydney, Northern Rivers), Victoria (Port Phillip, Melbourne, Frankston, Dandenong, Stonnington, Geelong, Yarra, and Merri-bek); Queensland (Brisbane, Gold Coast, Logan) and WA (Perth, Fremantle, Rockingham, Mandurah, Geraldton, Kwinara and Bunbury). Learn more, sign up or donate to these projects, which are listed at *The Australian Alliance to End Homelessness*[403].

Another early intervention, place-based model is the *Community of Schools and Services (COSS)* approach where at-risk or homeless young people are identified in schools, and a team of school staff, local homelessness agencies and youth services come together to monitor students and provide interventions, such as short-term counselling and wraparound case management for more complex cases. COSS has halved the number of young people at risk of homelessness in Albury, New South Wales, after similar results in Geelong, Victoria[404].

Notwithstanding the immense work being done by charities to provide services to Australians experiencing homelessness, given the sheer scale of the challenge to end homelessness, keeping up the pressure on governments to adequately fund housing and homelessness services is critical.

The charities that have a track record of evidence-based research and national advocacy include:

---

402 https://www.dunstan.org.au/adelaide-zero-project/background/

403 https://aaeh.org.au/local-communities

404 https://yesunlimited.com.au/the-albury-project/

Homelessness Australia	homelessnessaustralia.org.au
Streetsmart Australia	streetsmartaustralia.org
Mission Australia	missionaustralia.com.au
St Vincent de Paul Society	vinnies.org.au
National Shelter	shelter.org.au
Council to Homeless Persons	chp.org.au
Launch Housing	launchhousing.org.au
Sacred Heart Mission	sacredheartmission.org

Buy

Based in the UK, since its founding in 1996, about 7,000 street vendors experiencing homelessness, marginalisation and disadvantage have sold more than 14 million copies of *The Big Issue*, collectively earning more than $38 million. Today, the magazine sells for $9 and vendors get half[405].

Purchase from social enterprises that support people experiencing homelessness, such as mobile plans with *Better Life Mobile*[406]; real estate services to property owners and investors in Brisbane with *Elevate Residential*[407] and Melbourne with *Homegound*[408]; coffee from *Ground+Co* at the State Library of WA[409]; sorting and packing, decluttering, rubbish removal, furniture removals, storage, cleaning and home maintenance with *Removals For Hope* in Greater Sydney[410]; clothing from *HoMie*[411], and gift boxes from *Mettle*[412].

Volunteering

Typing 'homeless' into *GoVolunteer* yields a variety of volunteering requests, including for hairdressers and barbers for homeless people with Short Back & Sidewalks in Geraldton.

---

405 https://thebigissue.org.au/our-programs/the-magazine/
406 https://betterlifemobile.com.au/
407 https://www.elevateresidential.com.au/
408 https://www.homegroundrealestate.com.au/
409 https://theunderground.org.au/
410 https://removalsforhope.org.au/
411 https://homie.com.au/
412 https://www.mettlegifts.com/

Donate goods

You can donate goods to *Women's Community Shelters*[413] or local homelessness service providers near you directly[414] or through *GIVIT*[415].

[413] https://eu3gbhyx3of.exactdn.com/wp-content/uploads/2024/10/Shelter-Donation-Wish-List-October-2024_web.pdf
[414] Type 'homelessness' into https://askizzy.org.au/
[415] https://www.givit.org.au/

POVERTY AND DISADVANTAGE

'We need to ensure collectively as Australians that the fair go is the defining part of our future and not just the defining part of our past'

DR JIM CHAMBERS, INTERVIEW WITH DAVID SPEERS, INSIDERS, ABC, 24 AUGUST 2025[416]

In a cold, draughty church hall the executive team of the Brotherhood of St Laurence sat down to devise the vision and mission of the venerable organisation. A much-loved national institution, the Brotherhood was founded in 1930 by Anglican priest and social activist Father Gerard Tucker.

Famous for his preventative approach – 'it is better to have a fence at the top of the cliff than an ambulance at the bottom' - the Brotherhood has had a long history of evidence-based research into the causes of poverty and disadvantage and influencing government policy and programs.

From making films in the 1940s showing the appalling living conditions of the slums in inner Melbourne, to an open letter to Prime Minister Bob Hawke citing the nearly 1 million children in poverty published on the front page of the newspaper, the Brotherhood has been at the forefront of public advocacy and new responses, such as family planning clinics, family day care and social housing.

The weight of this heritage and expectation was not lost on the group. The astute Executive Director at the time, Bishop Michael Challen, had a keen sense of,

[416] Poverty and disadvantage https://ministers.treasury.gov.au/ministers/jim-chalmers-2022/transcripts/interview-david-speers-insiders-abc-10

and respect for, the Brotherhood's tradition and we spent the morning talking about the ethos that underpinned the organisation.

In the end, we deliberately avoided workshopping a new vision and mission. We settled on the one overriding belief that Father Tucker enshrined for the organisation from the start *-an Australian free of poverty.*

But, nearly 100 years after Father Tucker chose a saint who had been barbequed to death for stopping the Roman emperor Valerian grabbing the riches of the Church (when ordered to give up the church's treasures, he brought forward the poor, the crippled, the blind and the suffering, saying that these were the true treasures), poverty and disadvantage are entrenched and robbing millions of Australians their basic rights, dignity and opportunity.

WHAT

Along with the other 190 United Nations Member States, Australia is a signatory to the Sustainable Development Goals (SDG). SDG1 aims to 'end poverty in all its forms everywhere' by 2030, including to 'reduce at least by half the proportion of men, women and children of all ages living in poverty in all its dimensions according to national definitions'.

But for an affluent country, the latest Sustainable Development Report for Australia notes our score for SDG1 is declining and 'significant challenges remain'[417].

It is a national disgrace that over 3 million Australians live below the poverty line, with a similar number experiencing food insecurity. At 12.7 per cent, poverty in Australia is higher than the OECD average of 11.9 per cent and worse than many of our peer countries, such as Finland (5.7 per cent), the Netherlands (8.2 per cent), Canada (8.6 per cent), and the UK (11.2 per cent).

The extent of poverty in Australia was highlighted recently by the 2024 *Social Cohesion Index* which reported that 41 per cent of adults say they are at best 'just getting along' financially, 11 per cent describe themselves as 'poor' or struggling to pay bills and 28 per cent say they often or sometimes could not pay for meals, medicine or healthcare in the last 12 months, or could not pay their rent or mortgage on time[418].

---

[417] Allen C, Mendoza Alcántara A, Dechrai I & Hehir M (2025) *Transforming Australia: SDG Progress Report 2024*, Monash Sustainable Development Institute, Monash University. P.8 at https://www.monash.edu/__data/assets/pdf_file/0010/3898900/MSDI-Transforming-Australia-SDG-Progress-Report-2024.pdf

[418] Scanlon Foundation Research Institute (2024) *Mapping Social Cohesion* at

Poverty is cruel, unrelenting and dehumanising. Poverty is a daily battle to meet daily essential needs that are basic human rights - struggling to pay for food, housing, clothing, education, health care, utilities, transport and recreation.

The son of a family that owned a spinning and weaving factory in Dundee, Ronald Henderson studied economics at Cambridge University and was supervised by John Maynard Keynes, but it was his social work undertaken during university vacations, notably in Wales, where he lived for a while with an unemployed family, that was his motivation. After economists at the University of Melbourne sought his advice on the need for independent research in economic policy in Australia, he became the founding Director of the Institute of the University's Applied Economic Research.

After being elected to the Social Science Research Council, he published a groundbreaking study into poverty in Melbourne and led the McMahon government to establish the Commission of Inquiry into Poverty in 1972, with Henderson as chair. The resulting report set a benchmark for what was considered poor – the *Henderson Poverty Line*, which is the disposable income required to support the basic needs of a 2-adult, 2-child household, and was set at $62.70 a week and has been indexed over time. As Australia does not have an official poverty line, we continue to rely on this 1972 definition.

The legacy of Henderson didn't end there with 2 of his doctoral students producing a blueprint for a universal health care system, which was implemented by the Whitlam government in 1975[419].

Despite 646,000 Australians temporarily escaping poverty with the supplementary government income payments during COVID, poverty rates have since increased to the highest level recorded in the last 20 years, with the current cost of living crisis further exacerbating the level of poverty in Australia[420].

Whilst half of those experiencing poverty do so for less than a year, multi-year persistent poverty accounts for nearly 1 in 7 Australians, with those previously experiencing poverty 2 and a half times more likely to re-enter poverty, and half

[419] https://adb.anu.edu.au/biography/henderson-ronald-frank-29836#:~:text=Henderson%20was%20elected%20to%20the,to%20measure%20poverty%20in%20Australia.

[420] Commonwealth of Australia (2024) *Fairly Equal? Economic mobility in Australia*, Productivity Commission, July 2024

of Australians in the bottom 2 deciles of wealth remained there over 2 decades[421].

The 761,000 Australian children (or over 1 in 6) living in poverty today suffer constant stress, hardship and deprivation from insecure housing conditions, lack of food, absence of healthcare and basic amenities. Social isolation and exclusion occur through the lack of funds for school excursions, sporting activities and what many Australians regard as normal social activities enjoyed by families. In the long term, poor educational achievements limit employment opportunities and may sentence those who have suffered child poverty to a lifelong struggle just to survive.

Meanwhile, nearly 1 in 3 of the million single-parent households live in poverty and account for nearly half of children living in poverty, compared to a quarter a decade ago, as successive governments have forced single parents – predominantly mothers – off parenting payments and on to lower unemployment benefits[422].

This has significant economic impacts for the government, undermines social cohesion, and reduces our overall national capabilities[423]. It is little wonder then that a child who lives in poverty is 3 times as likely to live in poverty as an adult.

UNICEF's latest Report Card found that one in six children in Australia has been left in a plateau of poverty for nearly a decade, and we rank 26th out of 38 OECD countries. UNICEF noted that 'the period from 2012-14, following the recession, saw economic recovery and stable economic growth in most high and upper-middle income countries. This period presented as an opportunity to tackle child poverty, which some countries took, such as the UK, and others, like Australia, did not'[424].

In 2024, research from the *Bankwest Curtin Economics Centre* reported that child poverty rates rose sharply post-COVID, with 823,000 Australian children living under the poverty line in 2022. An additional 102,000 children fell below

---

421 Commonwealth of Australia (2024) *Fairly Equal? Economic mobility in Australia*, Productivity Commission, July 2024, p.15

422 Laß I, Botha F, Peyton K and Wilkins R (2025) *The Household, Income and Labour Dynamics in Australia Survey: Selected Findings from Waves 1 to 23*, Melbourne Institute of Applied Economic and Social Research, The University of Melbourne

423 Commonwealth of Australia (2004) *A hand up not a hand out: Renewing the fight against poverty. Report on poverty and financial hardship*, The Senate Community Affairs References Committee, Canberra

424 https://www.unicef.org.au/media-release/1-in-6-children-in-australia-stuck-in-plateau-of-poverty

the poverty line between 2021 and 2022, with the evidence of rising living costs and falling household incomes suggesting this number will have grown even further through 2023 and into 2024[425].

With just 12 per cent of people strongly agreeing that 'Australia is a land of economic opportunity where, in the long run, hard work brings a better life', the working poor are growing, with 1.3 million Australians in a job living in poverty. 10 percent of postcodes in Australia account for half the country's highest levels of disadvantage (including low income, crime, family violence, poor air quality, early school leaving, lack of post-school qualifications, prison admissions, juvenile convictions, long-term unemployment, households with no parent in paid work, public housing and no internet access), largely unchanged for decades, creating entrenched, place-based intergenerational disadvantage[426].

With less than 4 in 10 believing that 'people living on low incomes in Australia receive enough financial support', the Australian government's Economic Inclusion Advisory Committee reports that the current rate for the JobSeeker is too low and recommends increasing the JobSeeker payment to 90 per cent of the Age Pension, with a return to society of $1.24 for every dollar invested. Indeed, a single person on Jobseeker is living about 40 per cent below the poverty line. The Committee notes that 'the long-run benefits far outweigh any potential costs from reduced work incentives due to an increase in JobSeeker'[427].

Article 25 of the Universal Declaration of Human Rights states 'everyone has the right to a standard of living adequate for the health and well-being of himself and of his family, including food, clothing, housing, medical care and necessary social services.' And yet more than 2.3 million households are severely `food insecure', meaning they are actively going hungry – reducing their food intake, skipping meals or going entire days without eating[428]. 7 out of every 10 tenants are in rental stress (paying over 30 per cent of their income on rent)[429]

Back to Henderson. In 2019, the United States Census Bureau launched a multidimensional deprivation index, which took into account the official

---

[425] Bankwest Curtin Economics Centre (2024) *Child Poverty in Australia 2024. The lifelong impacts of financial deprivation and poor-quality housing on child development* at https://bcec.edu.au/assets/2024/08/BCEC-Child-Poverty-in-Australia-2024-web.pdf

[426] Jesuit Social Services (2021) *Dropping Off The Edge. Persistent and multilayered disadvantage in Australia*

[427] Economic Inclusion Advisory Committee 2025 Report to Government, p.8 at Economic Inclusion Advisory Committee 2025 Report to Government

[428] Foodbank, *Foodbank Hunger Report 2023*

[429] InfoChoice (2024) *InfoChoice Rent Crisis Survey*, January 2024

income measure together with education, health, housing quality, neighbourhood quality, and economic security. It found the income poverty rate for the US for 2017 was 13.4 per cent, but the rate of deprivation was 15.4 per cent. And they weren't all the same people – the new tool had exposed entirely new cohorts of people in need, including those who were not income poor but were significantly deprived in other ways – in total, 18 per cent of the population[430].

In submissions to the federal Senate inquiry on the nature and extent of poverty in Australia last year, multiple organisations, including the Australian Council of Social Service, the thinktank Per Capita, Anglicare, and the Antipoverty Centre, advocated for a multidimensional poverty index.

Poverty and disadvantage have an insidious causal relationship with many other Themes in this book, notably homelessness, family and domestic violence, mental health, youth justice, and social cohesion, and cause a vicious intergenerational cycle of poor childhood development, educational attainment, employment prospects, mental and physical health, violence and substance dependence.

In particular, we know that poverty experienced in the first 5 years of life is especially harmful to children's development. Nearly 1 in 3 children from low socioeconomic families is not developmentally ready when they enter primary school[431], a rate that has remained largely unchanged in the last 15 years[432].

Once they reach school, the pattern of children from advantaged backgrounds outperforming children from disadvantaged backgrounds has become evident and the gap continues to widen[433].

---

430 Gassman B (2019) *Multidimensional Deprivation in the United States: 2017*, American Community Survey Report, May 2019, United States Census Bureau at https://www.census.gov/content/dam/Census/library/publications/2019/demo/acs-40.pdf

431 Lamb S et al (2020) *Educational opportunity in Australia 2020. Who succeeds and who misses out, Centre for* International Research on Education Systems, Victoria University, for the Mitchell Institute: Melbourne at https://vuir.vu.edu.au/42362/1/educational-opportunity-in-australia-2020.pdf

432 Commonwealth of Australia (2021) *Australian Early Development Census* at https://www.aedc.gov.au/early-childhood/findings-from-the-aedc

433 Tham M, Leung C, Hurley P, Pilcher S, & Prokofieva M (2025) *Unequal from the start: The achievement gap and the early years,* Mitchell Institute, Victoria University at https://content.vu.edu.au/sites/default/files/documents/2025-04/unequal-from-the-start-report-march-2025.pdf

This means that children who start behind too often stay behind[434].

WHY

As Nobel Laureate Joseph Stiglitz notes – 'inequality is a policy choice. The negative trends can be reversed'. He reports that 83 per cent of countries have high income inequality, accounting for 90 per cent of the world's population. Wealth inequality is far higher than income inequality. Globally, between 2000 and 2024, the richest 1 per cent captured 41 per cent of all new wealth, in contrast to just 1 per cent being captured by the bottom half of humanity.

We are the 3rd richest country per adult in the world, behind only Switzerland and the US, and like to think of ourselves as the land of the 'fair go' and the 'lucky country'. But Australia has a number of stubborn structural factors that embed poverty and disadvantage.

Globalisation and corporate power

Capitalism has lifted innumerable people out of poverty over the last 2 centuries, significantly increased standards of living, and resulted in innovations that have radically improved human well-being. But, as the 'the worst economic system, except for all the others', its shortcomings have been ever more exposed when the interests of short-term profit are put before people.

In Australia, the abuse of market power can keep prices (and profits) high and disadvantaging those on low incomes the most. With a relatively small population and the concentration of companies, it is not surprising that there is a wide range of 'exploitative business pricing practices that enable the extraction of extra dollars from consumers in a way that would not be possible in markets that are competitive'[435].

An example is the pervasive unethical, harmful and fraudulent conduct by bank staff to drive their commissions and record profits that has cost over half the Australian population up to $201 billion between 2025-2019[436] exposed by the Banking Royal Commission.

---

[434] Weiss E & Garcia E (2017) *Education inequalities at the school starting gate. Gaps, trends, and strategies to address them* at https://www.epi.org/publication/education-inequalities-at-the-school-starting-gate/

[435] Fells A (2024) *Inquiry Into Price Gouging And Unfair Pricing Practices*, Final report, ACTU

[436] Breidbach C, Culnane C, Godwin A, Murawski C & Sear C (2019) *How Australians feel about their finances and financial service providers 2019*, University of Melbourne, Melbourne at https://www.unimelb.edu.au/finfuture?a=3145613

The lack of effective competition and higher prices is evidenced by the fact that we have some of the most profitable supermarket, banking, airline and insurance sectors in the world.

Meanwhile, Australia has one of the highest levels of casual employment in the world, with 2.75 million casual workers, or nearly 1 in 5 employees[437]. An estimated 687,500 casuals want a permanent job, but only a small minority – barely 1 in 15 – have been able to secure it. Up to 1/3rd of casual workers report receiving no loading and at least 875,000 casual workers, or again, about 1 in 3, are paid below the national minimum wage. This creates a lack of basic employee entitlements like paid leave and superannuation, income insecurity, and poor mental and physical health due to precarious working conditions and lack of job security.

It is not surprising that the 2020 Edelman Trust Barometer found that 56 per cent of respondents agreed that capitalism 'is doing more harm than good in its current form'. The report also found that high inequality is linked to less trust in government. The 2025 report confirms the decline in trust of Australians in their employer, especially amongst low income workers[438].

Wealth inequality

Wealth inequality is twice as high as income inequality in Australia and continues to worsen. The share of the nation's wealth of the bottom 40 per cent declined by around a third since 2004 to around 5.5 per cent. Today, Australia has 48 billionaires who hold more wealth than the bottom 40 per cent of the population combined[439]. Furthermore, close to 24 per cent of wealth is held by the top 1 per cent of Australians, well above peer countries such as the Netherlands (13 per cent), Finland (18 per cent), and the UK (21 per cent)[440]. Wealth inequality is getting worse in Australia with the income share of the top 1 per cent nearly doubling since 1980[441].

---

437 Australian Council of Trade Unions (2025) *Escaping The Casual Employment Trap*, Melbourne

438 2025 Edelman Trust Barometer (2025) *Trust and the Crisis of Grievance. Australia Report* at https://www.edelman.com.au/sites/g/files/aatuss381/files/2025-03/2025%20Edelman%20Trust%20Barometer_Australia%20Report.pdf

439 Oxfam International (2026) *Resisting the Rule of the Rich: Defending Freedom Against Billionaire Power*, Oxford, UK

440 Allen C, Mendoza Alcántara A, Dechrai I & Hehir M (2025) *Transforming Australia: SDG Progress Report 2024*, Monash Sustainable Development Institute, Monash University, p.8

441 https://www.theguardian.com/australia-news/2025/may/19/labor-andrew-leigh-focus-productivity-after-us-inequality-warning?CMP=Share_iOSApp_Other

With over 8 in 10 people agreeing that 'in Australia today, the gap between those with high incomes and those with low incomes is too large'[442], the top 10 per cent of households ranked by wealth possess 44 per cent of all wealth in Australia[443]. However, we grossly underestimate just how much the big end of town out-earns the rest of us, with survey respondents thinking CEOs (of publicly listed companies) typically earned 7.1 times an average full-time salary. In fact, the figure is a staggering 103 times[444].

The increase in house prices and rents, especially since COVID, has meant that property ownership is the main factor in widening the wealth gap, especially between older home and investment property owners, and young Australians on low and modest incomes who are shut out of home ownership and struggle with escalating rents.

As Alan Kohler notes in his Quarterly Essay, 'it's destructive because of the inequality that results: with so much wealth concentrated in the home, it stays with those who already own a house and within their families. For someone with little or no family housing equity behind them, it's virtually impossible to break out of the cycle and build new wealth'[445].

The result is that from 2003 to 2021 home ownership among people aged 25 to 29 fell from 44 per cent to 38 per cent and for people aged 30-34 it dropped from 57 per cent to 50 per cent, whilst the proportion of median household disposable income required to pay the median rent rose from 26 per cent to 31 per cent.

Australians are facing a rental market that has never been less affordable. Anglicare Australia's *2025 Rental Affordability Snapshot* surveyed rental listings across Australia and found that, out of 45,115 rental listings, only 0.7 per cent were affordable for a person earning a full-time minimum wage; 0.3 per cent were affordable for a person on the Age Pension; 0.1 per cent were

---

442 O'Connell J (2023) *Mapping Social Cohesion 2023*, Scanlon Foundation Research Institute, p.43 at https://scanloninstitute.org.au/sites/default/files/2023-11/2023%20Mapping%20Social%20Cohesion%20Report.pdf

443 Australian Council of Social Service and University of New South Wales (2024) *Inequality In Australia 2024: Who Is Affected And How*, April 2024

444 Hoy C , Page L , Eckel C , Grossman P and Goldstein D (2025) *Political Polarization, Wage Inequality and Preferences for Redistribution*, Working Paper No. 08/25, Melbourne Institute of Applied Economic and Social Research at https://melbourneinstitute.unimelb.edu.au/__data/assets/pdf_file/0004/5361052/wp2025n08.pdf

445 Kohler A (2023) *The Great Divide. Australia's housing mess and how to fix it*, Quarterly Essay no. 92, November 2023

affordable for a person on the Disability Support Pension; and none were affordable for a person on Youth Allowance[446].

Place-based, intergenerational disadvantage

In Australia, over 1 in 10 of the 2,188 SA2s (Statistical Area 2, averaging 10,000 people) have long-term, multilayered disadvantage with jobless parents; youth not in education, training, or employment; and low-income indicators prevalent. The most overrepresented indicators in the most disadvantaged 3 per cent of areas in NSW, Victoria, and Queensland relate to public housing, crime, family violence, and unemployment.

If you are born in Logan, Mandurah, Glenorchy, Christie Downs, Mt Druitt or Broadmeadows, you are highly likely to follow in the footsteps of previous generations and be out of school, unskilled or unemployed; a victim of family violence or abuse; a public housing tenant, suffer from drug and alcohol dependence; mental health issues; and be incarcerated[447].

These areas are characterised by high unemployment, low-paid, casualised manual jobs, waves of migrants and refugees, social housing, disaffected youth, and higher crime rates. Unsurprisingly, research shows that people who live in these neighbourhoods are trapped in poverty[448].

This persistent poverty is a significant phenomenon in Australian society, with over 1 in 8 of the population found to be persistently poor, especially amongst women, single-parent families, the elderly, and people living in more disadvantaged areas[449].

Research shows low household income during childhood is a key predictor of disadvantage in later life. Children from households that experienced several years of income poverty, compared with those who did not, are 2.4 times less likely to get a university degree, 1.8 times less likely to be full-time employed, and 1.3 times less likely to have a permanent, ongoing job. They are also more likely to suffer early adult poverty (3.3 times more likely), to live in social

---

446 Anglicare Australia (2025) *Rental Affordability Snapshot. National Report*, sixteenth edition 2025 at https://www.anglicare.asn.au/publications/2025-rental-affordability-snapshot/

447 Tanton R, Dale L, Miranti R, Vidyattama Y, Yule A and McCabe M (2021) *Dropping Off the Edge 2021: Persistent and multilayered disadvantage in Australia*, Jesuit Social Services, Melbourne

448 Commonwealth of Australia (2024) *Fairly Equal? Economic mobility in Australa*, Productivity Commission, July 2024, p.49

449 Vera-Toscano E. and Roger Wilkins R. (2022) *The Dynamics of Income Poverty in Australia: Evidence from the HILDA Survey, 2001 to 2019*, Melbourne Institute: Applied Economic & Social Research, The University of Melbourne

housing (up to 2.5 times), and to experience financial stress (2.5 times more likely) than children from non-poor households[450].

Ironically and sadly, in my experience, the international development approach in the poorest countries on Earth, with place-based, strengths-focused, community-owned and led development, is well ahead of our current top-down, siloed and individualised social services and healthcare interventions.

However, we are seeing some green shoots.

In 2019, the Australian and state and territory governments established a small ($5m a year) project called *Stronger Places, Stronger People* as a community-led, collective impact initiative in 10 communities across Australia (Logan, Rockhampton and Gladstone in Queensland; Bourke and the Macleay Valley (including Kempsey) in New South Wales; Mildura in Victoria; Burnie in Tasmania; the Far West Region of South Australia (including Ceduna); and the Barkly Region (including Tennant Creek) and Gove Peninsula in the Northern Territory to 'disrupt disadvantage and create better futures for children and their families through locally tailored and evidence-driven solutions to local problems, in partnership with local people'[451], but no evaluation has been published.

After initial development work by the University of Queensland, Australia and New Zealand School of Government and the Collaboration, in October 2024, the Australian Government and 5 philanthropic partners (Minderoo, Paul Ramsay, Ian Potter and Bryan Foundations and the Dusseldorp Forum) committed $38 million to establish *Partnerships for Local Action and Community Empowerment (PLACE)*, a not-for-profit organisation to act as a one-stop-shop to identify, support and enhance place-based programs in areas like the early years, youth development, health, education, employment and youth justice. PLACE will focus on strengthening the capacity of communities to design and deliver programs, promote evidence sharing and improve data governance across place-based initiatives[452].

The UK has led this approach since 2010 with its *Big Local*, the largest example of community-led place-based change the country has ever seen. The program has demonstrated the value of building community capacity and investing in

---

[450] Vera-Toscano E and Wilkins R (2020) *Does poverty in childhood beget poverty in adulthood in Australia?* Melbourne Institute: Applied Economic & Social Research, University of Melbourne.

[451] Australian Government Department of Social Services (2019) *Stronger Places, Stronger People Model*, October 2019 at https://platformc.org/sites/default/files/spsp/spsp-model.pdf

[452] https://ministers.dss.gov.au/speeches/16556

local social infrastructure in 150 disadvantaged communities in England over 10-15 years by supporting residents to lead lasting change in their neighbourhoods through a genuine transfer of power and responsibility to local people. The 2025 findings show that Big Local areas perform better overall than benchmark areas across all the indicators measured, particularly in crime reduction, business growth, and relative child poverty outcomes[453].

Government income support

Around 2.4 million Australians receive income support payments (excluding the Age Pension), including: JobSeeker Payment for adults of working age; Youth Allowance for jobseekers aged 16 to 21 years; Carer Payment to reflect duties that reduce the capacity for paid work; Parenting Payment for principal carers of young children; Disability Support Pension (DSP) for those with defined impairments to work; and Student payments for those in defined education and training (including for students, Youth Allowance, Austudy, ABSTUDY).

The system includes other payments, benefits, allowances, and supplements such as Commonwealth Rent Assistance, Family Tax Benefit, Paid Parental Leave, Remote Area Allowance, and utilities and pharmaceutical allowances, and various concessions such as health cards.

The unemployed are lazy, don't want to work, are happy to live off welfare and are too choosy in the face of a labour shortage. In political rhetoric and tabloid headlines, they are dole bludgers ripping off taxpayers, culminating in Scott Morrison's 'if you're having a go you'll get a go…. we will always be backing in those Australians who are looking to make a contribution not take one' and Joe Hockey's declaration in his budget speech of that year that Australia was a nation of "lifters and leaners".

As Minister for Social Services, Christian Porter, explained to the National Press Club in 2016, one of (Jobseeker's predecessor) Newstart's 'design features' was 'to make it challenging to subsist'.

Despite social safety nets having a long history as a protective mechanism for the poor that can be traced back as far as Ancient Egypt and the Roman Empire with almost 100 out of 186 countries having some form of social protection scheme covering 47 per cent of the planet's population, the demonisation of

---

[453] Local Trust (2025) *Everybody needs good Neighbourhoods 2. A counterfactual analysis of the impact of resident-led neighbourhood-based initiatives in deprived communities,* July 2025 at https://localtrust.org.uk/wp-content/uploads/2025/06/Everybody-needs-good-neighbourhoods-2.pdf

unemployed Australians suits governments that seek to limit spending on benefits.

For instance, the rates of Job Seeker and Youth Allowance have not increased in real terms for 25 years. For 740,800 Australians[454], Job Seeker is just 20 per cent of the average wage, 43 per cent of the minimum wage and 69 per cent of the pension. The payment is the second lowest in the OECD. Consequently, 60 per cent of households relying on Job Seeker live below the poverty line[455].

The inadequacy of income support payments harms people's mental and physical health. More than 8 in 10 respondents to a 2024 survey said that receiving income support negatively affected their physical health, and 9 in 10 said it negatively affected their mental health. 3/4 said they could not access healthcare and medicine because they cannot afford them.

The survey also found that sufficient food is a discretionary item for people receiving income support. More than 2/3rds of people reported reducing their intake of fresh fruit, vegetables, meat, and other expensive items, with nearly two-thirds (twice)stating that they skipped meals or ate less to get by (or both).

People on benefits go to great lengths to pay their energy bills. Nearly 7 in 10 reported reducing their use of heating and cooling to afford energy bills, and 6 in 10 said they go without food or medicine to be able to pay their energy bill. 1 in 3 said that they have an energy debt[456].

Adding injury to insult, the Australian government's *Robodebt* program, designed to recover overpaid welfare payments, forced thousands of Australians to repay debts they did not owe. The debts were often calculated using averaged income figures rather than actual data, leading to significant overestimates. As a result, many recipients were falsely accused of owing money and some took their lives. In 2020, the Federal Court ruled that the method used to calculate debts was unlawful and the government was forced to refund over $1.7 billion to affected people.

Australia's income support system should play a key role in poverty prevention. However, many income support payments are inadequate on their own to prevent poverty. Consequently, where income support is the main source of

[454] Australian Institute of Health and Welfare (2023) *Unemployment payments* at https://www.aihw.gov.au/reports/australias-welfare/unemployment-payments

[455] ACOSS (2024) *Woefully low' JobSeeker payment just 20% of average wage. The solutions to poverty are clear* at https://www.acoss.org.au/media_release/woefully-low-jobseeker-payment-just-20-of-average-wage-the-solutions-to-poverty-are-clear/

[456] ACOSS (2024) *Raise the Rate Survey 2024*, p.7

income for a household, there is a very high risk of that household living in poverty.

Education, training and employment

Education is a lifeline to escaping poverty.

The Smith Family notes that 'children and young people living in disadvantage have access to fewer books and learning materials in the home. In many cases, the parents of disadvantaged children may not have the skills or experience to support their child's education. As these children get older, they have fewer role models and access to mentors and networks that are critical for creating educational opportunities to help them build their aspirations and be motivated to learn[457].

With those who have only completed Year 12 or below twice as likely as those with a bachelor's degree to end up in the lowest 10 per cent of income, only around 60 per cent of young people growing up in poverty complete Year 12, compared to 83 per cent in high socioeconomic areas[458].

Indeed, the relationship between education and poverty is 'one of double jeopardy: not only are the poor unlikely to participate in all levels of the education system to the same extent as the advantaged, but their experience in education is less likely to result in favourable outcomes'. This 'double jeopardy' perpetuates the cycle of poverty[459].

This lack of educational attainment inhibits progress towards gaining the training and skills needed to enter the workforce, with the Australian Government expecting that over the next 10 years, more than 9 out of 10 new jobs created will require post-secondary qualifications[460].

In short, people with low levels of education are more likely to be unemployed and to be unemployed for longer.

The historic mismatch between the skills employers need and those that the education and training systems produce is another barrier.

---

457 https://www.thesmithfamily.com.au/poverty-in-australia

458 The Smith Family (2022) *Pathways, Engagement and Transitions: Experiences of early school leavers* at https://www.thesmithfamily.com.au/-/media/files/programs/pet/pet-report3-web.pdf

459 Foster L & Hawthorne L (1998) *Poverty, Education and Training,* in Fincher R & Nieuwenhuysen J, *Australian Poverty: Then and Now,* Melbourne University Press, 1998, p.204.

460 ibid p.ix

For people already in poverty, low wages are cited as one reason that the completion rate for apprentices and trainees has stayed around 50 per cent, with female enrolments in apprenticeships in core trades such as carpentry, automotive and electrical remaining below 2 per cent[461].

With skills development seen as the responsibility of government, PwC found that 78 per cent of Australian CEOs see the availability of key skills as the top threat to growth, yet only 38 per cent are establishing employee upskilling programmes, and only 13 per cent have made significant progress doing so, despite 3/4 of staff wanting to learn[462].

The Australian Government notes that the 'tertiary system must adjust to meet future workforce needs by providing greater support for disadvantaged students and increasing collaboration across higher education, vocational education, industry and governments. Finally, a culture of lifelong learning, supported by greater workplace training, will ensure people can upskill to take advantage of future opportunities in the labour market'[463].

In its post-European history, Australia has always needed skills, as my father experienced when he came out in the 1950s to work as a cost accountant for Volkswagen. But we have relied on short-term migration to fill skills gaps rather than taking a longer-term approach to education and training, despite knowing what skills we will need in the future.

In recognition, before the 2022 Jobs and Skills Summit, the Business Council of Australia and the Australian Council of Trade Unions signed an agreement endorsing the principle that 'migration needs to complement domestic skills and training – not act as a substitute for it – and workers in Australia should have a first opportunity for jobs on offer[464].

The next challenge to enable those with lower educational attainment and non-vocational barriers to get into employment. Enter the Australian government's $2 billion a year employment services, now called Workforce Australia. A 2023 Parliamentary Inquiry was damning, finding that 'Australia no longer has an effective, coherent national employment services system; we have an

---

[461] Australian Government Department of Employment and Workplace Relations (2022) *Australian Apprenticeship Services and Supports Discussion Paper*

[462] PricewaterhouseCoopers (2024) *27th Annual Global CEO Survey - Australian insights*

[463] Commonwealth of Australia (2023) *Working Future. The Australian Government's White Paper on Jobs and Opportunities*, The Treasury, October 2023, p.x

[464] Australian Council of Trade Unions and Business Council of Australia (2023) *Agreement between the Australian Council of Trade Unions and the Business Council of Australia* at https://assets.nationbuilder.com/bca/pages/6904/attachments/original/1661956110/ACTU_BCA_Jobs_Summit_Agreement_1_September_2022.pdf?1661956110

inefficient, outsourced, fragmented social security compliance management system that sometimes gets someone a job against all odds. The system does not effectively serve job seekers or engage service partners'[465].

The Inquiry goes on to conclude that 'it is clear that the overwhelming majority of unemployed people want to work. But the current rigid approach to mutual obligations is killing unemployed people's intrinsic motivations and efforts to seek work, by drowning them and those paid to help them in a mountain of red tape, compliance requirements and pointless mandatory activities. People are made to do silly things that don't help them get a job—such as pointless training courses or applying for jobs they won't get—and are then harshly and repeatedly sanctioned for trivial or inadvertent breaches of prescriptive'.

Meanwhile, the relatively low reported official unemployment rates mask that nearly three million Australians are either underemployed or out of work, equivalent to 1 in 5 of the current workforce[466].

Even for those in work, the rise in the casualisation of jobs to around 25 per cent of employment has resulted in an increase in the working poor with 2.6 million casual employees earning $11.59 less per hour than their permanent counterparts, a pay gap of 28.6 per cent which has been growing steadily since 2016 and is now the highest on record[467].

Tax system

With around 2 in 3 of Australians saying the tax system either does nothing to reduce income and wealth inequality, or actually makes it worse[468], the regressive nature of Australia's tax system does not help those in poverty.

Personal income taxes are progressive, whereby tax rates increase with income. Households in the lowest 20 per cent pay only 4 per cent of their overall income in income taxes on average, compared with 15 per cent for the middle 20 per cent and 26 per cent for the highest 20 per cent.

---

[465] Parliament of Australia (2023) *Rebuilding Employment Services*, Final report on Workforce Australia Employment Services, House of Representatives Select Committee on Workforce Australia Employment Services, p.xi at https://parlinfo.aph.gov.au/parlInfo/download/committees/reportrep/RB000017/toc_pdf/RebuildingEmploymentServices.pdf

[466] Commonwealth of Australia (2023) *Working Future. The Australian Government's White Paper on Jobs and Opportunities*, The Treasury, October 2023

[467] Australian Council of Trade Unions *Media Release*, 22 May 2023 at https://www.actu.org.au/media-release/casual-workers-earn-11-59-less-per-hour-than-permanent-employees/

[468] Dawson E (2025) *2024 Per Capita Tax Survey*, Per Capita at https://percapita.org.au/our_work/per-capita-tax-survey-2024/

However, the progressive impact of income taxes is largely offset by the regressive impact of other taxes, such as the Goods and Services Tax, which raises almost twice the share of household income from the lowest 20 per cent of households compared to the top 20 per cent[469].

Furthermore, we have a tax system that gives preferential treatment to income from assets, such as discounts to capital gains tax, negative gearing, superannuation tax concessions and family trust arrangements, which are used most by older and wealthier Australians[470].

Introduced by the Howard government in 1999, the 50 per cent capital gains tax discount applies to any investment held longer than 12 months, will cost Australia $250 billion over next decade, more than twice as much as the concession has cost in its entire 25-year history, with the top 1 per cent of taxpayers will receive nearly 60 per cent of the benefit this financial year, as estimated by the Parliamentary Budget Office[471].

As superannuation earnings and withdrawals are not taxed over the age of 60, a retiree household, earning $100,000 per annum, can pay less than half of the tax of a working household with the identical income, purely based on age[472].

The result is that, in the past 10 years, the Australians over 60 have earned an income around 11 per cent higher than those aged 18-30.

Indeed, we have a system where each year the richest 10 per cent get nearly $22 billion a year in tax breaks to use superannuation – nearly double the $12.2 billion the government spends funding public schools and $5 billion more than the $16.9 billion spent on jobseeker[473].

As well as older Australians earning significantly more private income, government expenditure targeting older Australians – such as the age pension, aged care and health care – has increased significantly in real, per-person terms.

---

469 Australian Council of Social Service (2015) *Tax Talks 5: The effects of a higher GST on households*, NSW

470 https://www.abc.net.au/news/2024-02-12/tax-reform-unavoidable-income-tax-workers-ageing-population/103445138

471 https://www.theguardian.com/australia-news/2026/feb/05/capital-gains-tax-discount-to-cost-australia-250bn-over-next-decade-with-retirees-and-high-income-earners-to-benefit-most?CMP=Share_iOSApp_Other

472 https://grattan.edu.au/news/a-better-tax-system/

473 https://www.theguardian.com/business/grogonomics/2025/dec/18/the-stats-dont-lie-australias-tax-system-is-designed-to-benefit-the-wealthiest-and-the-rest-of-us-pay-for-it?CMP=Share_iOSApp_Other

In contrast, net expenditure targeting younger households remains relatively constant.

This combination of tax and government spending policies means that Australians over 60 have an average after-tax income 60 per cent higher than those aged 18-30[474].

This intergenerational inequity in our tax system was front and centre at the Commonwealth government's August 2025 economic reform roundtable. The Treasurer, Dr Chambers, now recognises that 'intergenerational fairness is one of the defining principles of our country, but also of our government'[475].

Globally, there are calls to tax the super-rich. Nearly 400 millionaires and billionaires from 24 countries have signed onto the *Time to Win* campaign which recognises that 'decades of innovation have gone hand in hand with decades of inequality, environmental destruction, and wasted opportunity. The richest 1 per cent now own more than 95 per cent of the world's population put together'[476].

With over a quarter of large companies not paying income tax[477] and technology companies paying a fraction in tax compared to their revenue[478], it is not surprising that 3/4 of Australians believe big corporations don't pay enough tax and nearly 2/3rds support the implementation of a Windfall Profits Tax[479].

The last major review of the tax system by Ken Henry recommended an equitable, transparent and simplified personal income tax with a much higher tax-free threshold[480]. In 2024, he commented that the 'cost-of-living pressures people are feeling today are the consequence of a lack of genuine tax reform over the last 15 years'[481].

---

474 Varela P, Breunig R & Smith M (2025) *Measuring the changing size of intergenerational transfers in the Australian tax and transfer system*, Working Paper 7/2025, Tax and Transfer Policy Institute, Crawford School of Public Policy, Australian National University, May 2025 at https://crawford.anu.edu.au/sites/default/files/2025-04/Complete%20WP%20Varela%20Breunig%20Smith_2025%20compressed.pdf

475 https://www.abc.net.au/listen/programs/radionational-breakfast/radio-national-breakfast-full-episode-22nd-august-2025/105684448

476 https://timetowin.world/

477 Australian Tax Office (2025) *ATO Corporate tax transparency report 2023–24*

478 https://www.afr.com/politics/federal/the-australian-companies-paying-the-most-tax-20241021-p5kjve

479 Dawson E (2025) *2024 Per Capita Tax Survey*, Per Capita, p.3

480 Commonwealth of Australia (2010) *Australia's future tax system—Report to the Treasurer. Part 1 Overview*, December 2009, p.xix & xx

481 https://www.abc.net.au/news/2024-02-15/ken-henry-australias-tax-system-in-worse-position-after-15-years/103465044

The Grattan Institute has proposed the halving of the capital gains tax discount, limiting negative gearing in line with most other comparable countries, and including home equity above $750,000 in the Age Pension assets test. But with the heavy political cost of tax reform (most recently with Bill Shorten's Labor losing the 'unlosable election' in 2019 on an election platform that included changes to both negative gearing and the Capital Gains Tax (CGT) discount), any party risks angering a significant proportion of the electorate.

With Australians set to inherit an estimated $3.5 trillion over the next 20 years, in the greatest wealth transfer in the nation's history, there are calls for the reinstatement of an inheritance tax which was abolished in the 1970s in line with 24 of the 38 OECD countries[482].

Cost of living crisis

The recent rise in interest rates and prices of essential goods and services, such as fuel, mortgage payments, rents, utilities, and healthcare, has caused the recent cost of living crisis. Whilst wealthier households have managed their higher expenses by cutting back on discretionary spending and dipping into savings, lower income households spend a much larger portion of their income on housing and other essentials.

The cost of living crisis has made it harder for low-income households to afford basic necessities like food, housing, and utilities, leading to increased food insecurity, housing stress, and a rise in child poverty, with the most vulnerable experiencing a decline in living standards and increased financial hardship; and, ultimately, pushing more people below the poverty line.

Gambling

At a record $31.5 billion and rising, so large are Australia's annual gambling losses that they now eclipse what governments spend on aged care and what is spent on the National Disability Insurance Scheme[483]. This represents the largest per capita losses in the world[484].

An estimated 3.1 million Australian adults are engaged in some form of harmful gambling, which is linked to financial stress, family violence and poor mental

---

[482] Anglicare Australia (2025) *Paying It Forward. Tackling Wealth Inequality in Australia* at https://www.anglicare.asn.au/2025/02/14/anglicare-australia-calls-for-tax-reform-to-curb-wealth-divide/

[483] Equity Economics (2025), *Gambling in Australia's cost-of living crisis*, Alliance for Gambling Reform and Wesley Mission at https://www.equityeconomics.com.au/report-archive/gambling-in-australias-cost-of-living-crisis-the-black-hole-in-household-budgets

[484] Australian Institute of Health and Welfare (2023) *Gambling in Australia* at https://www.aihw.gov.au/reports/australias-welfare/gambling

health. Nearly 2 in 3 of Australian adults have gambled at least once in the past 12 months, a 14 per cent rise in the last 5 years. Nearly 1 in 3 adults gamble at least monthly[485].

Younger adults are particularly affected with 18–24 year-olds who gamble regularly nearly twice as likely to be at high risk of harm compared to older age groups.

With 2 in 3 of 74 teams across the NRL, AFL, Rugby Australia, Football Australia, Cricket Australia, Netball Australia and the NBL receiving money from gambling companies[486], Chair of the Parliamentary committee examining gambling in 2023, the late Peta Murphy MP, commented that 'we have a culture where sport and gambling are intrinsically linked. These behaviours are causing increasingly widespread and serious harm to individuals, families, and communities'. She went on to say 'gambling advertising and simulated gambling through video games, is grooming children and young people to gamble and encourages riskier behaviour. The torrent of advertising is inescapable. It is manipulating an impressionable and vulnerable audience to gamble online'[487].

After recommending a phased, comprehensive ban on online gambling advertising within three years, and despite over 3 in 4 of AFL fans in favour of a ban[488] and the AFL CEO criticising the volume of gambling ads, the AFL lobbied against a blanket ban, raising the potential of higher ticket prices, less funding for integrity initiatives the risk of pushing gambling underground or offshore to unregulated markets. The AFL CEO then went to head up Australia's largest gambling company.

This is not surprising given that the AFL has a financial stake in its fans' gambling habits, receiving a cut of each bet or a percentage of a gambling company's turnover, receiving at least $30 million a year, compared to the NRL's gambling take of $50 million[489].

---

[485] Tillman G, Irving R, Wickramasinghe S, Pappu T, Budinski M, Greer N, Whitlock B & Sakata K (2025) *National Gambling Prevalence Study Pilot 2024: Key findings*, Australian Gambling Research Centre, Australian Institute of Family Studies

[486] https://www.abc.net.au/news/2025-02-28/gambling-sponsorship-australia-sport-revenue-advertising-betting/104975050

[487] https://www.aph.gov.au/About_Parliament/House_of_Representatives/About_the_House_News/Media_Releases/Report_released_You_win_some_you_lose_more

[488] https://www.theguardian.com/australia-news/2023/jun/30/afl-fans-back-gambling-advertising-ban-and-caution-against-three-year-delay

[489] https://grattan.edu.au/news/pm-should-rebuff-nrl-and-afl-on-gambling-ads/

Among the 550,000 high-risk gamblers in Australia, over 2 in 3 have cognitive, behavioural or mental health conditions, 2 in 3 experience financial hardship (such as going without meals) and 1 in 6 experienced suicidal thoughts. 1 in 5 of those whose partner gambled weekly or more experienced intimate partner violence[490].

More concentrated in low income areas, poker machines account for the most gambling losses in Australia at $12 billion with gamblers in poorer suburbs losing more than 3 times the money to poker machines compared to gamblers in more advantaged areas[491].

Lower-income households are particularly vulnerable, as the rising cost of essential goods and services further squeezes already tight budgets, leaving even less room for unexpected expenses, emergencies, or discretionary spending.

Gamblers who had problems spent much more of their households' income on gambling than other regular gamblers, with those experiencing severe problems in low-income households spending an average of 27 per cent of their disposable household income on gambling - equivalent to 4 times their yearly household utility bills, or more than half the grocery bills for that income group[492].

Intimate partners and children of gamblers are worst hit, and the ripple effects of gambling on families include emotional and mental health impacts, physical health problems and addiction, breakdown of family and social relationships, conflict, intimate partner violence, and child maltreatment[493].

Climate change

Climate change exacerbates existing socioeconomic disadvantages by disproportionately impacting low-income Australians, who often live in areas most vulnerable to extreme weather events like heatwaves, floods, and bushfires, while lacking the financial resources to adapt, leaving them more

---

[490] Tillman G, Irving R, Wickramasinghe S, Pappu T, Budinski M, Greer N, Whitlock B & Sakata K (2025) *National Gambling Prevalence Study Pilot 2024: Key findings*, Australian Gambling Research Centre, Australian Institute of Family Studies, Melbourne at https://aifs.gov.au/sites/default/files/2025-09/2509-AGRC-National-Gambling-Prevalence-Report.pdf

[491] https://www.abc.net.au/news/2016-07-07/government-study-finds-pokie-gambling-hits-poor-suburbs-harder/7574548

[492] Armstrong A & Carroll M (2017) *Gambling activity in Australia*, Australian Gambling Research Centre, Australian Institute of Family Studies, Melbourne

[493] Equity Economics (2025), *Gambling in Australia's cost-of living crisis*, Alliance for Gambling Reform and Wesley Mission, p.6

susceptible to housing insecurity, increased energy costs, and health risks due to poor housing conditions[494].

ACOSS estimates that there are about 1.8 million low-income households in Australia that cannot afford to escape extreme temperatures because they're stuck in inefficient homes that are expensive to warm or cool. With very hot days and heatwaves becoming more common, Australians experiencing financial and social disadvantage are worst impacted through homes with poor energy efficiency, high energy prices, low incomes, and health conditions.

ACOSS' *2024 Heat Survey* found that more than half the respondents could not cool their home because they do not have air conditioners or fans, have them but they are broken, or could not afford to run them. 8 in 10 reported that exposure to high temperatures in the home had negative physical and mental health impacts, making them unwell. For many, the heat seriously aggravated existing chronic health conditions[495].

Lack of government targets

Unlike other countries, and possibly deterred by the Prime Minister's promise at a speech at the Sydney Opera House that 'by 1990, no Australian child will be living in poverty' and the continued lack of progress to the Close the Gap targets, our governments have avoided measuring, setting, and reporting on targets.

Worse, as the Australian government notes, and unlike 160 other countries, we have no official poverty measure in Australia and no single, agreed, objective indicator of poverty[496].

We only need to look to our neighbours. New Zealand has legislated a target to halve child poverty to less than 10 per cent by 2028[497]. Similarly, the UK has a target to reduce the rate of children in poverty by 2027/28 to 6 per cent on the material hardship measure; 5 per cent on the before-housing-costs income poverty measure; and 10 per cent on the after-housing costs income poverty measure.

---

494 https://www.acoss.org.au/climate/#:~:text=Climate%20change%20will%20affect%20low%20income%20households,on%20energy%20and%20water%20than%20wealthier%20households.

495 ACOSS (2024) *ACOSS Summer Heat Survey 2024* at https://www.acoss.org.au/wp-content/uploads/2024/03/ACOSSHeatSurveyReport2024.pdf

496 Department of Foreign Affairs and Trade (2018) *Report On The Implementation Of The Sustainable Development Goals*, Canberra, p22 at https://www.dfat.gov.au/sites/default/files/sdg-voluntary-national-review.pdf

497 Child Poverty Reduction Act 2018

ACT

Campaign

With Australian billionaire wealth 71 per cent higher than it was in 2020 and 16 more billionaires today than there were in 2020, *Oxfam* has calculated that a wealth tax of 2-5 per cent on Australian multi-millionaires and billionaires alone would raise $33 billion annually. To show your support for this measure, join the *Bill the Billionaires* campaign[498].

We know that raising the rate of income support enables millions to escape poverty and live a life of more dignity. This occurred with the Labor Government's 2009 'Secure and Sustainable Pension Reforms' to 3.3 million age pensioners, disability pensioners, carers, wife pensioners and veteran income support recipients lifted over a million Australians out of poverty. More recently, the $550 supplement provided by the government during COVID sharply reduced poverty among people on income support. Poverty among people in households on the JobSeeker Payment fell from 76 per cent in 2019 to 15 per cent in June 2020, lifting 646,000 people (including 245,000 children) out of poverty[499].

Anglicare Australia calculates that the cost of raising JobSeeker, Parenting Payment, and Carer Payment to the poverty line, and pulling almost 2.3 million Australians out of poverty, including 840,000 children, is $161 billion over the coming decade[500]. This is less than the $165 billion cost of negative gearing and capital gains tax discounts over the same period[501].

Join the *Raise the Rate for Good*[502] campaign to increase the rate of Jobseeker and other income support payments to at least $80 a day 'so everyone can keep a roof over their head and food on the table'.

---

498 https://www.oxfam.org.au/what-we-do/advocacy-and-campaigns/make-tax-fair/bill-the-billionaires/

499 Australian Council of Social Service and University of New South Wales (2022) *COVID, Inequality And Poverty In 2020 & 2021: How Poverty & Inequality Were Reduced In The Covid Recession And Increased During The Recovery,* Build back fairer series, report no. 3, an ACOSS/UNSW Sydney Poverty and Inequality Partnership Report, March 2022 at https://povertyandinequality.acoss.org.au/wp-content/uploads/2022/03/Build-back-fairer-report-3_FINAL.pdf

500 https://www.anglicare.asn.au/2025/03/24/anglicare-australia-seeks-commitments-as-election-is-called-3/#:~:text=Costings%20showing%20that%20JobSeeker%2C%20Parenting,tax%20concessions%20for%20housing%20investors

501 https://www.theguardian.com/australia-news/article/2024/jul/01/negative-gearing-and-capital-gains-tax-discounts-to-cost-australian-budget-165bn-over-10-years-analysis-reveals

502 https://www.raisetherate.org.au/

As well as increased income support, a more equitable tax system is urgently needed to share Australia's considerable wealth more fairly. Call on the next parliament to reform our tax system by signing *Think Future's* online open letter[503] or signing Oxfam Australia's petition to get big corporations and high-income earners to pay more tax[504].

The *Valuing Children Initiative* has a campaign to end child poverty in Australia and invites pledges and signatures to its petition[505].

Participate

For more than 20 years, *Anti-Poverty Week* has operated in Australia around mid-October, the *UN Day for the Eradication of Poverty* to help Australians understand poverty and to take action collectively to end it. Get involved in one of the many events held during the week[506].

Employ

A job is the most impactful intervention for people living in poverty. As well as income, it gives identity, self-esteem, belonging, confidence, relationships and skills development.

A job brings a future.

Search for your local *Workforce Australia* providers, whose role it is to find you suitable candidates[507].

Donate goods

Religion-based charities have their purpose in helping the poor, so there is no shortage of charities that will take your donation of money or goods. Having run the Brotherhood of St Laurence's donated goods, the opportunity shops are a valuable source of income for charities, especially where donations are made directly to the shop. The bins may be more convenient, but you can avoid the significant cost that charities incur in collection, sorting, and waste disposal.

With 1 in 5 women forced to improvise on period products just to make ends meet, *Share the Dignity* distributes period products to women and girls and

---

503 https://www.thinkforward.org.au/taxwealthnotwork

504 https://www.oxfam.org.au/what-we-do/advocacy-and-campaigns/make-tax-fair/

505 https://www.endchildpoverty.com.au/supportus

506 https://antipovertyweek.org.au/

507 https://www.workforceaustralia.gov.au/individuals/coaching/providers/

campaigns to end the shame and stigma that surrounds periods with *Period Pride*[508]. You can set up a collection box to collect period products[509].

Buy

Many social enterprises enable disadvantaged Australians to gain the work experience and skills needed to enter mainstream employment. See the Social Traders' directory of certified social enterprises[510].

Mentor

The *Australian Business and Community Network (ABCN)* connects volunteers from member companies with students from low socio-economic backgrounds to provide workplace-based mentoring programs that develop students' confidence, skills and aspirations vital for thriving in the workplace of the future[511]. In Tasmania, Victoria, WA and NSW, *EdConnect Australia* recruits, trains and supports skilled volunteers to provide support to students in local schools[512].

Donate or volunteer

National charities that demonstrate an evidence-based approach, lasting impact and advocate for policy and system change to poverty in Australia through their programs and research include:

- *The Smith Family* enables better education outcomes for children in poverty. Their evidence-based services support 200,000 children, young people, parents, carers and community professionals across Australia[513]
- *Brotherhood of St Laurence* are the leaders in social research and advocacy through its Social Policy and Research Centre [514]
- *Schools Plus* supports over 350 schools and 7,000 teachers to design, deliver and evaluate their projects, help to build leadership capacity and encourage knowledge sharing within and between schools, and enable early intervention for children where learning gaps are occurring and

508 https://www.sharethedignity.org.au/period-pride
509 https://www.sharethedignity.org.au/shop/viewitem/collection-box-4
510 https://www.socialtraders.com.au/find-a-social-enterprise
511 https://abcn.com.au/about/what-we-do/
512 https://www.edconnectaustralia.org.au/volunteer/
513 https://www.thesmithfamily.com.au/programs
514 https://www.bsl.org.au/

provide access to future-focused skills in literacy, numeracy and STEM, to help children develop lifelong learning[515]

- The *Country Education Foundation* is a national charity helping rural and regional youth access education, training and jobs through grants, scholarships, support services and resources[516]
- *The Australian Literacy and Numeracy Foundation* is a national charity assisting First Nations, refugee and other vulnerable Australians in our most marginalised communities to gain vital language, literacy and communication skills[517]
- *Good Shepherd* is the leader in financial inclusion for over a million low-income Australians with financial counselling and 400,000 No Interest Loans with nab over the last twenty years[518].
- *St Vincent de Paul*[519] *and Anglicare*[520] have a long history of research and submissions tackling policy and system change to reduce poverty, including advocating for a fairer and welfare tax system

With lower income households proportionally more affected by higher prices and the health effects from climate change and unable to afford to adapt their homes, disadvantaged Australians are excluded. A 'just transition' to net zero means a fair and socially equitable transition where communities, trade unions, businesses, and governments work together to develop and implement carefully planned policies to support those directly impacted by low-carbon policies[521]. At COP27 at Sharm el-Sheikh, the Australian government signed the *Just Transition Declaration.* Its second principle requires 'the development of effective, nationally coherent, locally driven and delivered just transition plans within countries is dependent on effective and inclusive social dialogue'.

The just transition includes (re)skilling workers for the lost and new jobs created in the transition, including 8,500 jobs expected to be lost and the communities that have come to depend on the coal energy industry. The *Brotherhood of St Laurence* carries out policy and systems transition research,

---

515 Schools Plus (2023) *Impact Report 2023* at https://www.schoolsplus.org.au/wp-content/uploads/2023/06/Schools-Plus-Impact-Report-2023_Final-Digital-Version.pdf

516 https://cef.org.au/

517 https://alnf.org/

518 https://goodshep.org.au/

519 https://www.vinnies.org.au/advocacy/low-income-support

520 https://www.anglicare.asn.au/

521 Global Compact Network Australia (2019) *Leaving no one behind Planning for a Just Transition*, Discussion paper, August 2019 at https://unglobalcompact.org.au/wp-content/uploads/2019/08/2019.08.27_Just-Transition-Discussion-Paper.pdf

for instance, 'reframing the role of Australia's VET system for climate and environmental action'[522].

The *Next Economy* supports communities across regional Australia to develop plans and strategies that reduce carbon emissions while simultaneously creating good social and economic outcomes, as well as connecting them to the resources and expertise they need to implement those plans[523].

522 https://library.bsl.org.au/bsljspui/bitstream/1/13370/1/Longley_Skilling_for_green_transition_NCVER_NoFrills_conf_Jul2023.pdf

523 https://nexteconomy.com.au/what-we-do/

CLIMATE CHANGE

'We are the first generation to feel the effect
of climate change and the last generation who can do
something about it.'

BARACK OBAMA, UNITED STATES PRESIDENT

WHAT

The World Meteorological Organization's *State of the Climate Update for COP30* reveals that the past 11 years (2015-2025) have been the warmest on record, with each year surpassing previous temperature highs. With 2023, 2024 and 2025 officially the hottest years in recorded history at 1.6°C warmer than the 1850-1900 pre-industrial level, the United Nations Secretary General has acknowledged that it is now inevitable that humanity will overshoot the target in the Paris climate agreement, with 'devastating consequences for the world'[524].

With carbon emissions setting a new record in 2025[525], the world is currently on track for a catastrophic 2.6°C of global heating by the end of the century[526].

The world faces a number of interconnected tipping points, including the collapse of the Atlantic Meridional Overturning Circulation (the ocean current system in the Atlantic that transports warm water north and cold water south which is a critical component of the global climate system, distributing heat and affecting weather patterns, sea levels, and marine ecosystems) and the collapse

[524] Climate change https://www.theguardian.com/environment/2025/oct/28/change-course-now-humanity-has-missed-15c-climate-target-says-un-head

[525] https://globalcarbonbudget.org/fossil-fuel-co2-emissions-hit-record-high-in-2025/

[526] https://climateactiontracker.org/global/emissions-pathways/

of the Greenland and west Antarctic ice sheets, which would lead to a twelve metre sea level rise affecting one billion people[527].

According to an international report from 160 scientists in 23 countries, the first tipping point for the Earth has already been reached with the widespread dieback of the planet's warm water coral reefs[528].

The ANU's *Global Water Monitor Report* notes that rising temperatures are changing the way water moves around the planet and wreaking havoc on the water cycle. The report found that rising sea surface temperatures intensified tropical cyclones and droughts in the Amazon Basin and southern Africa. Global warming also contributed to heavier downpours and slower-moving storms, as evidenced by deadly flash floods in Europe, Asia and Brazil.

The most damaging water-related disasters in 2025 included flash floods, river floods, droughts, tropical cyclones and landslides. Water-related disasters have killed more than 8,700 people, displaced 40 million people and caused economic losses exceeding US$550 billion[529].

The intensity of events is rising. 4 years after experiencing a one-in-100-year flood, in May 2025, parts of NSW's mid-north coast experienced a 1-in-500-year flood, according to Natural Hazards Research Australia. At the same time, the agricultural regions of South Australia and north-west Victoria experienced drought.

Flooding in 2025 was marked by unprecedented rainfall, glacial lake outbursts, and storm surges that devastated communities in the United States, Afghanistan, Brazil, Nigeria, East Africa, South Africa, Pakistan, India, Nepal and north-east Queensland with thousands killed, tens of thousands of homes and farms destroyed, millions displaced and billions of dollars in damage[530].

Typhoons Kalmaegi and Fung-wong in Vietnam and the Philippines, Tropical Cyclone Ditwah in Sri Lanka and Southern India, Cyclone Dikeledi in Madagascar and Mozambique, Cyclone Alfred in South East Queensland and Northern New South Wales, and Hurricane Melissa in Jamaica left hundreds dead, millions affected and costs in the billions.

---

527 Stokes C.R., Bamber J.L., Dutton A. *et al. Warming of +1.5 °C is too high for polar ice sheets,* Commun Earth Environ 6, 351 (2025). https://doi.org/10.1038/s43247-025-02299-w

528 Lenton T M et al (2025) *The Global Tipping Points Report 2025*, University of Exeter, Exeter, UK

529 Van Dijk, A et al (2025) *Global Water Monitor 2024, Summary Report*, Global Water Monitor Consortium at www.globalwater.online

530 https://sustainabilityglobal.org/flood-disasters-in-2025/

As well as absorbing between a 3rd and a half of the CO_2 and slowing the rate of climate change, our oceans absorb over ninety per cent of the heat, reducing their cooling effect on the Earth's climate and causing a 26 per cent increase in acidification, leading to less capacity to absorb CO_2 and substantial changes in ocean ecosystems.

The resultant increase in sea surface temperature leads to an increase in the amount of atmospheric water vapour over the oceans, fuelling more intense cyclones and severe storms, as well as increased ice melt at the poles.

In both the Arctic and Antarctic, ice loss compounds ice loss. This is because while bright sea ice reflects most of the Sun's energy back to space, open ocean water absorbs it. With more of the ocean exposed to sunlight, water temperatures rise, further delaying sea ice growth.

The very low Antarctic sea ice extent throughout the last 4 years is unmatched in historical observations[531] with the height of the Antarctic sea ice 30 per cent below the 1981-2010 average[532].

Ice-sheet melting and deep-ocean warming are likely to continue to fuel sea-level rise in the centuries to come. If the Earth warms by 2°C, irreversible melting will be triggered across nearly all of Greenland and much of West Antarctica, committing the planet to 12-20 metres of sea level rise over the coming centuries. For context, over a quarter of a billion people currently live on land less than 2 meters above sea level[533] whilst Australia has about 160,000 to 250,000 Australian properties at risk of coastal flooding with a sea level rise of 1 metre[534].

In turn, higher background water levels mean that deadly and destructive storm surges push farther inland and ever more frequent high-tide flooding.

According to the UNHCR, the UN's refugee agency, an annual average of 21.5 million people were forcibly displaced each year by weather-related events – such as floods, storms, wildfires and extreme temperatures – between 2008 and 2016. Climate refugees are expected to surge in the coming decades, with international thinktank, the Institute for Economics & Peace, predicting that 1.2

---

531 https://climateextremes.org.au/record-low-antarctic-sea-ice/

532 https://nsidc.org/sea-ice-today/analyses/antarctic-sea-ice-minimum-hits-near-record-low-again

533 Gergis J (2024) *Highway to Hell. Climate Change and Australia's Future*, Quarterly Essay, Issue 94, p.15 & 26

534 Australian Academy of Science (2021) *The risks to Australia of a 3°C warmer world*, p.10

billion people could be displaced globally by 2050 due to climate change and natural disasters.

Recognising that atoll Pacific Islands, such as Tuvalu and Kiribati, are already facing sea inundation, on 9 November 2023, Australia and Tuvalu signed an unprecedented cooperation agreement to offer 280 Tuvaluans, or 2.5 percent of the island's population, permanent residency in Australia each year. In July 2025, nearly a 3rd of Tuvalu citizens entered the ballot for the first batch of visas.

According to the Australian lead author on the United Nations' Intergovernmental Panel on Climate Change's *Sixth Assessment Report*, Dr Joëlle Gergis, 'even if nations make good on their net 0 promises there is a 90 per cent chance that we are still on track for 2.4°C of global warming which will lock in centuries of irreversible changes to the climate system'.

The Australian government notes that 'as climate hazards change in frequency and increase in severity, it is likely we will experience more compounding, cascading and concurrent hazards in the future'[535].

At 3°C, Australia's east coast will have to life-threatening levels of heat with temperatures regularly exceeding 50°C in summer, combined with longer and more intense bushfires and droughts[536] which will accelerate the loss of productive farmland and threaten our food security. Storms and flooding will have violently reshaped our coastlines, and unique ecosystems have been damaged beyond recognition – including the Great Barrier Reef, which no longer exists[537].

The Australian government warns that health and social support services may not keep up with more frequent, severe and longer duration events, particularly where the events also compromise critical infrastructure.

Over 10 million Australians live in areas facing extreme heat-related risks with more Australians dying from heatwaves than all other extreme weather events combined[538]. According to the ACOSS Heat Survey, heatwaves were

---

[535] Australian Climate Service (2025) *Australia's National Climate Risk Assessment Report 2025, p.34*

[536] Gergis J (2024) *Highway to Hell. Climate Change and Australia's Future*, Quarterly Essay, Issue 94, p.19 & 24

[537] Australian Academy of Science (2021) *The risks to Australia of a 3°C warmer world* at https://www.science.org.au/supporting-science/science-policy-and-analysis/reports-and-publications/risks-australia-three-degrees-c-warmer-world

[538] L Coates et al (2014) *Exploring 167 years of vulnerability: an examination of extreme heat events in Australia 1844–2010*' in Environmental Science & Policy, vol. 42, pp. 33– 44

responsible for 36,000 deaths between 2006 and 2017 in Australia[539]. At 3°C, this heat-related mortality is expected to rise by 444 per cent in Sydney and 259 per cent in Melbourne, and as many as 2.7 million extra days of work will be lost in agriculture, construction, manufacturing and mining, hitting productivity[540].

By 2050, more than 1.5 million people living in coastal areas will be hit by rising sea levels and coastal flooding. By 2090, over a 3rd of coastal communities could be at high or very high risk, representing over 3 million people[541]. Brisbane, Melbourne, and Sydney will see coastal flood risks rise to 300 days a year.

Globally, concentrations of all major long-lived greenhouse gases in the atmosphere continue to increase. Global annual mean carbon dioxide (CO_2) concentrations reached 426.91 parts per million (ppm) in 2024 (up from 419.2 ppm in 2023), and the global average annual CO_2 concentrations reached a record high of 424.61 ppm[542].

The last State of the Climate Report reported that Australia's climate has warmed by an average of 1.51 ± 0.23°C since national records began in 1910 which has led to an increase in the frequency of extreme heat events over land and in the oceans, as well as heavy short-term rainfall events becoming more intense. With sea surface temperatures rising by an average of 1.08°C since 1900, sea levels are rising around Australia, leading to more frequent extreme high levels that increase the risk of inundation and damage to coastal infrastructure and communities[543].

The CSIRO notes that the future for Australia is the continued increase in air temperatures, with more heat extremes, fewer cold extremes and the continued decrease, on average, in cool season rainfall across many regions of southern and eastern Australia, which will likely lead to more time in drought. There will also be more intense short-duration heavy rainfall events even in regions where the average rainfall decreases or stays the same, a continued increase in the

---

539 ACOSS (2023) *ACOSS 2023 Heat Survey. How hotter days affect people on lowest incomes first, worst and hardest* at https://www.acoss.org.au/wp-content/uploads/2023/02/Heat-Survey-Report_20230228.pdf

540 Australian Climate Service (2025) *Australia's National Climate Risk Assessment Report 2025*

541 Australian Climate Service (2025) *Australia's National Climate Risk Assessment Report 2025, p.44* at https://www.acs.gov.au/pages/41f9b35a4c7041c68d33ee41552b0dce

542 https://gml.noaa.gov/ccgg/trends/

543 Commonwealth of Australia (2024) *State of the Climate 2024*, CSIRO and Bureau of Meteorology at https://www.csiro.au/en/research/environmental-impacts/climate-change/State-of-the-Climate p.2

number of dangerous fire weather days, and a longer fire season for much of southern and eastern Australia[544].

At 3°C of global warming, many of Australia's ecological systems would be unrecognisable. Our agricultural production would decline, creating widespread food insecurity through increasing desertification, declining river flows, reducing water availability for irrigated agriculture, heat stress for livestock, erosion of grazing land, or loss of livestock from flooding and storms.

Climate change in Australia already has a huge economic cost. Australia has some of the highest per capita losses from natural catastrophes in the world, consistently coming in only behind the United States.

Over the past 5 years, insurers have incurred $22.5 billion in claims due to natural disasters, a 67 per cent increase on the last 5 years period, not counting the $1.4 billion cost of Cyclone Albert in March 2025. The resultant 14 per cent increase in home insurance premiums in 2024 has added to the cost-of-living crisis. Analysis by the Climate Council shows that over half a million properties may be uninsurable by 2030 due to their exposure to extreme weather events from climate change[545]. This could rise to 1.5 million homes by 2050. In the meantime, 77 per cent of properties at extreme risk of flooding do not have insurance cover[546].

The Australian government predicts that increased natural disasters could cost the country up to $200.6 billion a year. Economic modelling shows climate damage will deliver a 14 per cent annual hit to Australia's Gross Domestic Product (GDP) if current global climate policies continue, wiping out $6.8 trillion from our economy between now and 2050[547].

Climate change also presents a major public health concern in Australia.

A 2022 study found more than 80 per cent of Australians have experienced a disaster in the past five years. Of those, half said they had experienced a mental

---

[544] Ibid p.3

[545] e Climate Council of Australia Limited (2022) *Uninsurable Nation: Australia's Most Climate-Vulnerable Places*

[546] Insurance Council of Australia (2025) *Insurance Catastrophe Resilience Report 2024/25* at https://insurancecouncil.com.au/wp-content/uploads/2025/10/21340_ICA_CAT-Report_2025_Final-spreads.pdf

[547] https://igcc.org.au/6-8-trillion-gdp-hit-if-renewable-energy-transition-is-delayed/#:~:text=New%20economic%20modelling%20shows%20climate,of%20the%20pockets%20of%20Australians.

health issue as a result[548]. Psychological distress has been documented in increased domestic violence and alcohol and substance abuse which has persisted for years following extreme weather events in Australia. Clinically diagnosed post-traumatic stress disorder (PTSD), anxiety disorders, depression and suicide increase in communities impacted. Even without direct exposure, the mere awareness of the unfolding threat of climate change has mental health impacts, including feelings of anxiety, grief, hopelessness, frustration and anger[549].

Meanwhile, poor air quality, especially from bushfire smoke, creates a range of health problems, especially for those with pre-existing heart or lung conditions, whilst infectious diseases, such as Ross River virus and other vector-borne diseases, will shift in their geographical distribution and intensity of transmission as weather patterns change.

WHY

We have known for over 100 years that the main driver of a warming world is carbon dioxide and the greenhouse effect. In essence, some gases in the Earth's atmosphere act a bit like the glass in a greenhouse, trapping the sun's heat and stopping it from leaking back into space to cause global warming.

In 1896, a seminal paper by Swedish scientist Svante Arrhenius first predicted that changes in atmospheric carbon dioxide levels could substantially alter the surface temperature through the greenhouse effect. Then in 1938, Guy Callendar connected carbon dioxide increases in Earth's atmosphere to global warming. In 1956, Gilbert Plass formulated the Carbon Dioxide Theory of Climate Change, which stated that, as the amount of carbon dioxide increases, the atmosphere becomes opaque over a larger frequency interval, and the outgoing radiation is trapped more effectively near the Earth's surface, and the temperature rises[550].

Without the presence of these Greenhouse Gases (GHGs), the Earth could not sustain its livable temperature. However, with rapid industrialisation of the

---

548 https://www.climatecouncil.org.au/resources/climate-change-mental-health-toll-australians/#:~:text=In%20December%202022%2C%20the%20Climate,health%20issue%20as%20a%20result.

549 Doctors for the Environment Australia (2021) *How Climate Change Affects Mental Health In Australia*

550 Plass G (1956) *The Carbon Dioxide Theory of Climatic Change,* Tellus, Volume 8, Issue 2, p.140-154

global economy and the resulting release of great volumes of human-made GHGs, the planet has experienced abnormal levels of warming.

How much any one greenhouse gas influences global warming depends on 3 key factors:

1. How much of the gas exists in the atmosphere. Concentrations are measured in parts per million (ppm) - 1 molecule of that gas in every 1 million molecules of air;
2. How long the gas remains in the atmosphere, otherwise known as its lifetime; and
3. How effective the gas is at trapping heat, referred to as its *global warming potential (GWP)*, as a measure of the total energy that a gas absorbs over a given period of time (usually 100 years) relative to the emissions of 1 ton of carbon dioxide.

Carbon dioxide accounts for almost 80 per cent of global human-caused emissions, with 40 per cent remaining after 100 years, 20 per cent after 1,000 years, and 10 per cent as long as 10,000 years later. About 90 per cent comes from the burning of fossil fuels, nearly three-quarters of which comes from coal and oil. 4 regions accounted for about 2/3rds of global fossil-fuel carbon emissions: China at 31 per cent; the USA at 14 per cent; the European Union at 7 per cent; and India at 7 per cent. Industrialised countries represent just 20 per cent of the world's population but account for 80 per cent of cumulative carbon dioxide emissions since the beginning of the industrial revolution[551].

From natural gas production and livestock, *methane* comprises 12 per cent. It persists in the atmosphere for around 12 years, but its global warming impact is almost 30 times greater than that of carbon dioxide over a 100-year period.

From sources like fertilizers, *nitrous oxide* represents 6 per cent with a GWP of 270 times that of carbon dioxide on a 100-year time scale, and it remains in the atmosphere, on average, a little more than a century.

Emitted from a variety of manufacturing and industrial processes, *fluorinated gases* - hydrofluorocarbons (HFCs), perfluorocarbons (PFCs), sulphur hexafluoride (SF6), and nitrogen trifluoride (NF3) account for 3 per cent, but the GWP for these gases can be in the thousands to tens of thousands. They have long atmospheric lifetimes, in some cases lasting tens of thousands of

[551] https://www.csiro.au/en/research/environmental-impacts/climate-change/climate-change-qa/sources-of-co2#:~:text=In%202022%2C%20most%20of%20the,sources%20(2%20per%20cent).

years. HFCs are used as a replacement for ozone-depleting chlorofluorocarbons and hydrochlorofluorocarbons, usually in air conditioners and refrigerators[552].

It is standard practice when measuring GHGs to convert all emissions to CO_2 equivalent (CO_2e). Each gas is measured, multiplied by its global warming potential and then aggregated to give total GHG emissions in CO_2 equivalents.

It is estimated that between 1750 and 2019, atmospheric concentrations of carbon dioxide increased by 47 per cent, methane by 156 per cent, and nitrous oxide by 23 per cent. Of all the human-driven emissions of carbon dioxide, approximately half were generated in the last 30 years alone.

In 1977, 24-year-old Jonathan Shanklin saw an advert for a job at the British Antarctic Survey, which read Wanted: physicist with an interest in

meteorology and programming skills'

Feeling he ticked all the boxes, Shanklin applied and was offered the role.

1 of Shanklin's tasks was checking and correcting all of the data from the Dobson ozone spectrophotometer in Antarctica. This instrument measures the amount of ultraviolet light reaching Earth, providing an accurate picture of how much ozone there is in the atmosphere. He faced a huge backlog as scientists had, until then, simply scrawled the data on sheets of paper.

About this time, the organisation was planning to have an open day at their Cambridge headquarters to show the latest Antarctic science to eminent scientists, politicians and the public. Shanklin recalls that there had been concern at the time that exhaust gases from Concorde (the supersonic passenger aircraft) or chlorofluorocarbons (CFCs) from spray cans might damage the ozone layer. He thought this unlikely, so he decided to present that year's data and compare it with values his boss had computed from a decade earlier, expecting them to be the same.

The only problem was that they weren't the same.

Surprised and slightly alarmed, Shanklin continued to work through the backlog to try and see if that year was just a one-off. It wasn't. The results were clear: since the late 1970s there had been a systematic decline in the amount of spring ozone. By 1984, the ozone layer over Halley Research Station in Antarctica was only about 2/3rds as thick as it had been in earlier decades.

---

552 https://www.nrdc.org/stories/greenhouse-effect-101#gases

Less than 2 years after publishing the results to the shock of the world, the *Montreal Protocol* became the first globally agreed environmental action agreement, succeeding in eliminating nearly 99 per cent of ozone-depleting substances and setting the model for future climate action.

5 years later, on the 20th anniversary of the first Human Environment Conference in Sweden, the world's celebrities - Richard Branson, Robert Redford, Sir Paul McCartney, Penelope Cruz, Pele, John Denver, Placido Domingo, Jeremy Irons, Ted Turner and Jane Fonda (where was Bono?) - joined the world's political leaders, charities and scientists from 179 countries to gather at the *1992 Rio Earth Summit*.

The resultant *Rio Declaration On Environment And Development* declared that 'human beings are at the centre of concerns for sustainable development' (Principle 1); 'States have, in accordance with the Charter of the United Nations and the principles of international law, the sovereign right to exploit their own resources pursuant to their own environmental and developmental policies, and the responsibility to ensure that activities within their jurisdiction or control do not cause damage to the environment of other States or of areas beyond the limits of national jurisdiction' (Principle 2); 'the right to development must be fulfilled so as to equitably meet developmental and environmental needs of present and future general' (Principle 3); 'in order to achieve sustainable development, environmental protection shall constitute an integral part of the development process and cannot be considered in isolation from it' (Principle 4); and 'States shall cooperate in a spirit of global partnership to conserve, protect and restore the health and integrity of the Earth's ecosystem' (Principle 7)[553].

A key achievement of the Summit was the establishment of *the United Nations Framework Convention on Climate Change (UNFCCC)* as an international environmental treaty to combat 'dangerous human interference with the climate system' and to stabilise greenhouse gas concentrations in the atmosphere, together with its decision-making body, the Conference of the Parties (COP), meeting annually to assess progress in dealing with climate change.

At COP3 in Japan, for the first time, developed nations reached an agreement on actions to cut GHG emissions in an attempt to stabilise global climate change by adopting the Kyoto Protocol with Annex B setting out binding emission

---

[553] United Nations (1993), *Report of the United Nations Conference on Environment and Development, Volume I Resolutions Adopted by the Conference*, Rio de Janeiro, 3-14 June 1992, A/CONF.151/26/Rev.l (Vol. I), New York at https://documents.un.org/doc/undoc/gen/n92/836/55/pdf/n9283655.pdf?token=kZfA026XhLz1p20iAh&fe=true

reduction targets for 37 industrialised countries and economies in transition and the European Union. Overall, these targets added up to an average 5 per cent emission reduction compared to 1990 levels over the 5 year period 2008–2012. In 2012, the Doha Amendment to the Kyoto Protocol was adopted for a second commitment period, starting in 2013 and lasting until 2020.

However, in the lead-up to Kyoto, the Howard Government repeatedly threatened that it would refuse to sign any international agreement that did not meet its demands. The result was the 'Australia Clause', which granted extraordinary concessions in the last hours of the Kyoto Climate Change Conference. In addition to an 8 per cent increase over 1990 levels of emissions, Australia's base year emissions were inflated by 30 per cent by the inclusion of net emissions from land clearing.

Australia signed the *Kyoto Protocol* in 1998, but the Howard government decided not to ratify it, leaving Australia and the United States as the only major industrialised nations not to do so, despite the fact that, unlike almost every other nation, Australia gave itself the ability to increase its emissions. The ratification came with Kevin Rudd's victory in 2007 as the first official act of the new Government. Meanwhile, the sharp fall in land clearing emissions turned Australia's 8 per cent target into a 'three-inch putt'[554].

At COP 15 in Copenhagen in 2009, it was hoped that a new legally binding agreement would be reached to follow on from the *Kyoto Protocol*. Although that meeting fell short of those expectations, the *Copenhagen Accord* did recognise the need to reduce global GHG emissions to limit the increase in global temperature to below 2°C.

In the lead up to COP 21 in 2015 in Paris, nations submitted Nationally Determined Contributions (NDCs), which set out each country's plan for addressing climate change, including a target for reducing GHG emissions and how the countries intend to achieve that target. The resultant *Paris Agreement* agreed to the parties 'holding the increase in the global average temperature to well below 2°C above pre-industrial levels and pursuing efforts to limit the temperature increase to 1.5°C above pre-industrial levels, recognizing that this would significantly reduce the risks and impacts of climate change' (Article 2)

[554] The Australia Institute (1998) *A Poisoned Chalice Australia and the Kyoto Protocol*, Background Paper No. 13, Canberra, at https://australiainstitute.org.au/wp-content/uploads/2020/12/WP13_8.pdf

[555] with NDCs to be reviewed and updated every five years under the 'transparency framework'.

Australia's NDC at the time was to reduce GHG emissions by 26-28 per cent below 2005 levels by 2030, compared to the UK and European Union's 53 and 40 per cent reduction in emissions by 2030 from 1990 levels, respectively[556].

Needless to say, climate policy has been a polarising and highly politicised issue in Australia with more twists and turns than a Le Carré novel.

Cabinet documents released on 1 January 2024 by the National Archives show that in 2003 the Howard government backflipped on its moves towards a trading scheme that had been supported by ministers, including then Treasurer Peter Costello and Foreign Minister Alexander Downer.

Then, in 2007, under pressure to respond to climate change, Prime Minister Howard announced a carbon trading scheme would be set up if he won the 2007 federal election. Beaten by 'Kevin07', the Rudd Government announced the introduction of a cap-and-trade system under the *Carbon Pollution Reduction Scheme (CPRS)* in 2008. The European Union had set up the world's first international emissions trading system three years previously.

Under the CPRS, the government would issue permits for the 'cap' of emissions for about one thousand of the highest emitting companies. If the companies produced more emissions than their permits, then they could buy permits from other companies that had reduced their emissions under their cap, estimated at $20-$40 per tonne.

The *Climate Action Summit*, representing 140 climate groups, condemned the CPRS, including the government's unambitious target of only 5 per cent below 2000 levels by 2020, and agreed to campaign to prevent it becoming law. Meanwhile, industry groups (particularly the Minerals Council of Australia, which warned that the scheme would cause massive job losses) and the Opposition campaigned on the resultant higher prices faced by Australian households and small businesses. As a result, the CPRS legislation failed to pass the Senate in 2009, creating a double-dissolution trigger. However, Kevin Rudd negotiated a deal with Opposition Leader Malcolm Turnbull on amendments to the CPRS, who then urged Coalition MPs to support the revised scheme. But on 1 December 2009, Tony Abbott replaced Turnbull as leader

---

[555] United Nations (2015) *Paris Agreement* at https://unfccc.int/sites/default/files/english_paris_agreement.pdf

[556] https://www.carbonbrief.org/paris-2015-tracking-country-climate-pledges/

and withdrew Coalition support for the scheme. The CPRS was voted down in Parliament for a second time.

2 years later, following her overthrowing of Kevin Rudd and stating that 'there will be no carbon tax under the government I lead', Prime Minister Julia Gillard, supported by the Greens, introduced a carbon pricing scheme, before Kevin Rudd returned to the prime ministership announcing he would terminate the carbon tax and move to an emissions trading scheme (ETS) in 2014.

The Abbott government, campaigning that ditching the tax would save households $550 per year, won in 2014 and repealed the scheme, in favour of the *Direct Action Plan* which included an *Emissions Reduction Fund*. While electricity prices did fall slightly after the carbon price was removed in 2014, two years later they were higher than when the carbon price was in place.

Gillard's scheme ran for 2 years and achieved a 2 per cent reduction in emissions, before emissions subsequently rose for the next four years under Prime Minister Abbott.

In 2015, after beating Abbott in a leadership spill, Malcolm Turnbull had to back down on the emissions reduction target in his *National Energy Guarantee* to bring in a carbon emissions reduction target in the energy sector of 26 per cent by 2030, in the face of opposition from the right of his party. Australia's NDC in 2015 set a target of 26-28 per cent below 2005 levels by 2030. However, this target was 'developed into an emissions budget covering the period 2021–30', meaning that meeting the target would be judged on whether total emissions over this period remain within the target budget, not whether the actual emissions level in 2030 is 26-28 per cent below the emissions in 2005[557].

Now a mainstay in Australia's emissions reduction plan, in 2016, the Turnbull Government introduced the Safeguard Mechanism to limit greenhouse gas emissions from Australia's largest industrial facilities by setting emissions baselines for high-polluting facilities, which were required to acquire and surrender Australian carbon credit units (ACCUs) or reduce emissions if they exceeded their baseline.

Under Scott Morrison's government, the Liberals coalition partner, the Nationals, resisted public pressure to set a net 0 commitment by 2050 (despite all States and Territories having done so) until a deal was struck just days before

557 https://www.aph.gov.au/About_Parliament/Parliamentary_departments/Parliamentary_Library/pubs/BriefingBook47p/ClimateChangeEmissionsReduction

COP26 in Glasgow where Morrison stated that Australia was 'ahead of the pack'[558] on emissions reductions and described his policy of 'technology not taxes' to be the core of 'the Australian way'[559]. Unlike other countries at COP26, there was no increase to Australia's NDC target.

The Albanese Labor government's win in 2022 put in place Australia's NDC 2030 emissions reduction target of 43 per cent below 2005 levels, as both an emissions budget target and a single year target.

However, remember that our unique definition of emissions includes land use which is the main sectoral trend driving the long-term decrease in Australia's total emissions and does not include the combustion of Australian-produced fossil fuels which generate at least 5 per cent of global emissions. The carbon emissions from our exports are almost triple the emissions from our domestic use of fossil fuels[560]. Due to expire in 2003, the recent government approval of Woodside's North West Shelf gas extension to 2070, all of which will be exported, locks in more than 4 billion tonnes of climate pollution, equivalent to a decade of Australia's annual emissions,[561] and at a time when our gas exports need to fall by 90 per cent to align with 1.5°C of warming according to the government[562]. Similarly, studies by the United Nations and International Energy Agency have found that demand for gas will drop as much as 62 per cent and 78 per cent, respectively[563].

The next battleground is Woodside's proposed plans to drill offshore in the Browse Basin, some 425 kilometres from Broome, the largest discovered untapped gas reserve in Australia. But the site is only 3 kilometres from Scott Reef, a richly diverse coral reef system that lies in both state and federal waters. Greenpeace has over half a million signatures on an e-petition to stop the project[564].

Currently, Australia's emissions are 28 per cent below the 2005 level. This fall has taken place almost entirely in the land sector, together with a decline in the

---

558 https://tasmaniantimes.com/2021/11/scott-morrison-address-to-cop-26/

559 https://theconversation.com/the-australian-way-how-morrison-trashed-brand-australia-at-cop26-171670

560 https://www.humanrights.unsw.edu.au/research/australian-climate-accountability-project

561 https://www.climatecouncil.org.au/resources/labor-approves-woodside-extension/

562 Australian Government (2024) *Future Gas Strategy*, May 2024 at https://www.industry.gov.au/sites/default/files/2024-05/future-gas-strategy.pdf

563 Wilkinson M (2025) *Woodside vs The Planet. How a company captured a country*, Issue 99, Quarterly Review, p.25&26

564 https://www.greenpeace.org.au/act/woodside

electricity sector as renewable energy has been replacing coal-fired generation[565].

The Climate Change Performance Index 2025 ranks Australia a lowly 52 out of 63 countries in terms of emissions, renewables, energy use and climate policy[566]. Furthermore, our 2030 NDC target of 43 per cent is not aligned with the Paris Agreement target of 1.5°C and needs to be significantly improved to do so[567]. It is not surprising then that the *Climate Action Tracker* rates Australia's performance as 'insufficient'.

In the meantime, in 2023–24, Australian governments have provided $14.5 billion worth of funding and tax breaks to assist fossil fuel industries, a 31 per cent increase on 2022-23 largely due to the increase in the Federal Government's Fuel Tax Credits Scheme (FTCS) to $9.6 billion in 2023–24 and concessions on aviation fuel growing by $430 million, or 36 per cent to a total of $1.6 billion. Subsidies in the forward estimates increased from $57 billion to a record $65 billion[568].

The FTCS refunds fuel excise - a Federal government tax of about 50 cents on every litre of petrol or diesel that you buy - in part, or in full, paid by eligible business users of fuel. Since the implementation of the Fuel Tax Act in 2006, Australia has generated over $147 billion in cumulative fuel taxation to 2021-22, whilst the Federal Government has provided over $95 billion in fuel tax credits.

As the 18th largest Government expense program in 2023-24, the FTCS means that no fuel tax is payable for vehicles that only drive off-road, such as trucks on mine sites, and a reduced rate of fuel tax is payable for on-road vehicles heavier than 4.5 tonnes, such as semi-trailers, B-doubles, and passenger buses.

---

565 Climate Change Authority (2024) *Annual Progress Report 2024* at https://www.climatechangeauthority.gov.au/sites/default/files/documents/2024-11/2024AnnualProgressReportAtAGlance.pdf

566 Burck J, Uhlich T, Bals C, Höhne N, Nascimento L, Wong J, Beaucamp L, Weinreich L, RuAt L (2024) *Climate Change Performance Index 2025*, Germanwatch, NewClimate Institute, and Climate Action Network International at https://ccpi.org/wp-content/uploads/CCPI-2025-Results.pdf

567 https://climateactiontracker.org/countries/australia/

568 The Australia Institute (2024) *Fossil fuel subsidies in Australia 2024* at https://australiainstitute.org.au/wp-content/uploads/2024/05/P1543-Fossil-fuel-subsidies-2024-FINAL-WEB.pdf

The Grattan Institute argues that there is no business reason why larger vehicles should pay less than smaller vehicles – in fact, quite the reverse, since heavy vehicles do far more damage to roads[569].

Mining accounts for 21 per cent of Australia's total emissions in 2021 and has played a central role in undermining our progressive emissions reduction goals, rising by 65 per cent since 2005. The growth in emissions is a result of the steadily increasing use of imported diesel in mining equipment[570]. The government's approval of 7 new coal mine projects in 2023 and 2024 will allow coal mining and exports to continue for many decades to come.

Moreover, the emissions generated by our exports of coal and gas are not counted in our NDC emissions reduction targets submitted to the United Nations.

The need to reduce our emissions also represents our economic future. For a country that relies on international trade, from 2026, the European Union's Carbon Border Adjustment Mechanism will impose a charge on the embedded carbon content of certain imports, including fertilizers, cement, aluminium, iron and steel, so the ability to produce goods and services at a lower carbon intensity than our international peers increasingly presents a competitive advantage.

But there is hope. CSIRO's modelling shows that Australia can use existing technologies to reduce emissions by 52 per cent from 2020 levels by 2030, including reducing fossil fuel use in electricity generation from 70 to 10 per cent by 2030[571]. After all, we have the highest rooftop solar uptake in the world, accounting for over a quarter of total renewable energy generation.

In response to a journalist's question at COP28, Climate Change Minister, Chris Bowen, stated 'Australia's biggest economic potential is as a renewable energy superpower, and this transition, of phase out of fossil fuels, is Australia's economic opportunity as a renewable energy superpower'[572].

---

[569] Terrill M, Burfurd I and Bradshaw N (2023) *Fuelling budget repair: How to reform fuel taxes for business*, Grattan Institute at https://grattan.edu.au/wp-content/uploads/2023/02/Fuelling-budget-repair-Grattan-report.pdf

[570] Pollard M and Buckley T (2024) *Fuel Tax Credit Scheme and Heavy Haulage Electric Vehicle Manufacturing in Australia*, Climate Energy Finance at https://climateenergyfinance.org/wp-content/uploads/2023/09/Fuel-Tax-Credit-Scheme-and-Heavy-Haulage-Electric-Vehicle-Manufacturing-in-Australia.docx.pdf

[571] Brinsmead T, Verikios G, Cook S, Green D, Khandoker T, Kember O, Reedman L, Rodriguez S and Whitten S (2023) *Pathways to Net Zero Emissions – An Australian Perspective on Rapid Decarbonisation*, CSIRO, Australia

[572] https://minister.dcceew.gov.au/bowen/transcripts/press-conference-cop28-dubai-0

The 2024 re-elected Labor government defeated the Coalition's nuclear policy and committed to 82 per cent of renewables by 2030, up from 46 per cent today, assisted by the *Cheaper Home Batteries Program* which started on 1 July 2025, as well as additional investment $8 billion in renewable energy and low emissions technologies through a $2 billion expansion of the Clean Energy Finance Corporation.

This was followed in September 2025 by the Australian government's NDC required for the UN climate conference, COP30 in Brazil, to an emissions reduction of 62-70 per cent on 2005 levels by 2035 at its 'maximum level of ambition'. The range is below the 65-75 per cent cut advised by the government's Climate Change Authority as 'ambitious, but achievable' in April 2024.

The Climate Council notes that achieving a stronger target of 70 per cent and above would unlock investment and greater economic growth, with modelling indicating that a 75 per cent cut by 2035 could deliver $370 billion to GDP, 69,000 new jobs annually, and $190 billion in export revenue by 2050[573].

But even at a reduction target of 62 per cent, we have a mountain to climb.

In the 5 years to 2023-24, Australia reduced emissions by an average of 9 megatonnes (Mt). In the last financial year, emissions reduced by 7Mt. To meet the government's 2030 target, emissions reductions need to more than double that, cutting 16Mt per year. They need to go further still to hit the new 2035 goal, cutting 19-24Mt annually.

And remember the Australia Clause negotiated by John Howard in Kyoto that advantageously included carbon emissions from land use and forestry in our emissions calculations. Between 2005 and March 2025, Australia's emissions decreased by 28 per cent. However, when you remove the land use sector, emissions have only dipped by a small 4 per cent, led by the switching of coal-fired power stations to renewable electricity.

Even the government's own Environment Department is sceptical, reporting that, whilst Australia is on track to reach a 42 per cent reduction in emissions by the end of this decade, just shy of its target, on current projections emissions will fall by just 48 per cent by 2035[574].

---

573 https://www.climatecouncil.org.au/resources/australias-2035-climate-target-is-one-of-the-most-critical-decisions-were-making/

574 DCCEEW (2025) *Australia's emissions projections 2025*, Department of Climate Change, Energy, the Environment and Water, Canberra, p.4

To reach at least the 62 per cent reduction target, the Climate Change Authority modelling includes the need for 20 times as many electric vehicles, twice as many rooftop solar panels and the quadrupling of wind capacity[575].

The ongoing political climate wars will not help with the Coalition abandoning its commitment to net 0 by 2050. At the same time, the proportion of Australians who think that climate change is happening and is caused by human activity is declining and now sits just above half. Furthermore, those who think the world will be able to prevent dangerous levels of global warming caused by climate change is less than four in ten[576].

In the meantime, communities and regulatory bodies in Australia are resorting to legal action to achieve change after the *Urgenda Foundation* and 886 people took the Dutch government to court for not doing enough to prevent climate change and won. The courts ordered the Dutch government to take immediate steps to cut greenhouse gas emissions.

However, success to date has been limited.

On 28 July 2022, the critical need to address the effects of climate change led the UN General Assembly to adopt a historic resolution declaring that access to a clean, healthy and sustainable environment be a universal human right. 2 months later, the Torres Strait 8 made international legal history after the United Nations Human Rights Committee found that the Australian Government is violating its human rights obligations to Torres Strait Islanders by failing to act on climate change. In 2025, the Federal Court found that the Commonwealth does not owe a duty of care to Torres Strait Islander peoples to protect them from the impacts of climate change or fund adaptation measures, ruling that Australia's greenhouse gas emissions targets should be decided by the parliament, not the courts.

In 2023, a small volunteer environment group, the Environment Council of Central Queensland, unsuccessfully took our federal Environment Minister and 2 big coal companies to Court to protect our living wonders from climate harm.

Legal action against Australia's 'largest companies obstructing and delaying Australia's transition to net 0 and lobbying against climate action despite having made repeated public declarations in support of limiting global warming

---

575 https://www.abc.net.au/news/2025-09-19/the-task-ahead-to-reach-2035-emissions-target/105789538?utm_source=abc_news_app&utm_medium=content_shared&utm_campaign=abc_news_app&utm_content=other

576 https://www.theguardian.com/australia-news/2025/nov/25/guardian-essential-poll-only-a-quarter-of-older-australians-believe-climate-change-can-be-prevented?CMP=Share_iOSApp_Other

to 1.5°C and the goals of the Paris Agreement'[577] has been more successful with government regulation agencies and charities, such as the *Environmental Defenders Office*, holding companies accountable for their environmental impacts and greenwashing, such as Parents for Climate successfully suing EnergyAustralia over its claims about 'carbon neutral' products.

Then, in July 2025, the International Court of Justice declared that all countries have a legal obligation to protect and prevent harm to the climate. Countries are now bound to rapidly reduce their emissions below 1.5 degrees of warming. Failure to do so could result in developed countries like Australia having to pay monetary compensation to developing countries or being required to rebuild infrastructure and restore ecosystems damaged by climate change[578].

We know that we can't rely on governments and companies to save our species and environment. We all need to play our role.

ACT

We have a brief and rapidly closing window to secure the future of our species, our families and our communities. Whilst individually we are highly unlikely to influence the emissions of other countries, we can take responsibility for our own emissions and advocate for our organisations and networks to take action. After all, we have the highest per capita GHG emissions of all OECD countries.

Calculate and reduce your emissions

Carbon Neutral[579] and *Carbon Positive Australia*[580] have easy-to-use online carbon calculators that estimate your (and your organisation's) carbon footprint for vehicles, energy, waste, water and transport.

As energy will typically be your highest source of emissions, draught-proofing, insulation, energy efficient appliances, LED lighting and double-glazed windows will reduce your energy usage. More actions to reduce energy usage can be found at the Australian government's energy.gov.au website[581].

As food production is responsible for 26 per cent of global GHG emissions, a change in diet can reduce your footprint, especially beef, which emits 60

---

577 Climate Integrity (2024) *Risky Influence: The legal implications of misaligned climate-related lobbying by Australian companies* at https://climateintegrity.org.au/risky-influence-report

578 https://www.theguardian.com/commentisfree/2025/jul/24/the-icjs-ruling-means-australia-and-other-major-polluters-face-a-new-era-of-climate-reparations?CMP=Share_iOSApp_Other

579 https://carbonneutral.com.au/

580 https://carbonpositiveaustralia.org.au/

581 https://www.energy.gov.au/households/household-guides/reduce-energy-bills

kilograms of CO2e per kilogram due to its resource intensity, land use, water and energy resources, as well as producing methane during its digestive processes. Lamb is 24kg of CO_2e, prawns are 12kg, pork is 7kg and poultry is 6kg CO_2e[582].

Dairy milk produces 3 times the emissions of plant milks and much higher water use[583], which means cheese is a high emitter at 21kg of CO_2e.

Unfortunately, dark chocolate emits 19kg of CO_2e due to the land clearance from planting the cacao trees. However, citrus fruits, apples and nuts are almost carbon neutral because of the carbon sequestered in their trees. So, maybe buying fruit and nut chocolate is a good compromise?

Buying local will save on the emissions produced by the transportation of imported products.

Electrify

Household, vehicle and industry electrification is the fastest way to reduce carbon emissions, supported by a clean energy grid. It means healthier homes and workplaces, a fairer energy system and lower bills.

In transitioning away from burning fossil fuels to renewable electricity to reduce emissions, businesses and households should replace gas heating and appliances with electric alternatives. To generate your own renewable electricity, join the 3 million Australian households with solar panels on their roof (there are Federal and State government subsidies available) and purchase renewable electricity from your energy retailer at no extra cost.

Guidance can be found at *Rewiring Australia*[584]. The incentives to electrify vary with each State and Territory. Search for your jurisdiction's subsidies at www.energy.gov.au.

To encourage the take-up of electric cars, the Australian government currently allows you, as an employee, to salary package the lease of an electric car by paying the lease cost pre-tax[585].

Community-based household electrification is gaining popularity. In 2025, the *Australian Renewable Energy Agency (ARENA)* provided $5.4 million in

582 https://www.visualcapitalist.com/ranked-foods-with-the-largest-environmental-impact/

583 https://ourworldindata.org/environmental-impact-milks

584 https://www.rewiringaustralia.org/

585 https://www.ato.gov.au/businesses-and-organisations/hiring-and-paying-your-workers/fringe-benefits-tax/types-of-fringe-benefits/fbt-on-cars-other-vehicles-parking-and-tolls/electric-cars-exemption

funding to electrify 500 households in NSW's north Illawarra area, with other communities currently under consideration[586].

Buy

After reducing your GHG emissions as far as possible, becoming net carbon neutral (or net zero) requires the purchase of carbon offsets for your remaining emissions.

Developed as a project of *The Foster Foundation* to offer Australian motorists a tree-planting program to re-capture GHG emissions and promote fuel-efficient technologies, *Greenfleet* is a charity that has planted over 10 million trees and created over 500 native biodiverse forests, restoring 10,000 hectares to native Australian ecosystems and offsetting four million tonnes of CO_2e. You can purchase offsets for your household, car or business[587].

Carbon Neutral and *Carbon Positive Australia* also offer tree planting offsets for purchase.

If you would like to purchase offsets that also enable international community development outcomes, the *Gold Standard marketplace* details projects that are accredited by the world-leading carbon accreditation, Gold Standard, established by WWF and other charities[588].

Join

First Nations peoples in Australia have been custodians of this land for tens of thousands of years and are disproportionately impacted by the increasing effects of climate change. Governments and others increasingly recognise how Indigenous knowledge can help us better monitor and adapt to a warmer world.

You can become a member of the *First Nations Clean Energy Network*, which brings together cultural leaders, community organisations, academics, technical advisors, and renewables companies to create pathways for First Nations communities to actively participate in and benefit from the clean energy transition[589].

For grant givers, the *Australian Environmental Grantmakers Network (AEGN)* is a network of 180+ members are trusts, foundations and individual donors that

---

[586] https://www.abc.net.au/news/2025-01-28/chris-bowen-expands-household-electrification-scheme/104868630
[587] https://www.greenfleet.com.au/
[588] https://marketplace.goldstandard.org/
[589] https://www.firstnationscleanenergy.org.au/membership_org

provides a safe, trusted space to share environmental funding opportunities, insights and experience[590].

Your organisation can benefit from joining *Global Compact Network Australia*, the Australian arm of the *United Nations Global Compact*, the world's largest corporate sustainability initiative, with over 20,000 participating businesses and 3,800 non-business organisations based in over 160 countries. Their resources include the *Climate Ambition Accelerator*[591].

Invest

You have the choice to exclude companies that significantly contribute to emissions, or that are not taking action to reduce their emissions, through selecting ethical options in your superannuation and investment funds. Given the urgency to decarbonise our energy generation, there are funds that specifically invest in renewable energy, such as the *Australian Renewables Income Fund* managed by the *Foresight Group*, which has attracted investment from the *Clean Energy Finance Corporation*[592].

Campaign

Australia's environmental charities have led the way in campaigning.

Get involved in *Environmental Justice Australia's* public interest litigation and legal advocacy campaigns[593], sign *Greenpeace's* petition to 'protect Scott Reef's native whales, dolphins, turtles - and our climate - from Australia's dirtiest offshore gas drilling project'[594] and Oxfam's petition to Make Big Polluters Pay[595]. The *Australian Marine Conservation Society* has several petitions, including cutting plastics entering the oceans, standards for imported seafood, and protecting Ningaloo[596] and *360 Australia* (named for 350 parts per million of CO_2 which has been identified as the upper limit to avoid a climate tipping point) has 'rise-up' events to join[597].

---

590 https://www.aegn.org.au/about-us/

591 https://unglobalcompact.org.au/environment-climate-change/climate-ambition-accelerator/

592 https://www.cefc.com.au/case-studies/green-light-for-australian-renewables-income-fund/

593 https://envirojustice.org.au/

594 https://www.greenpeace.org.au/act/woodside

595 https://www.oxfam.org.au/what-we-do/advocacy-and-campaigns/make-big-polluters-pay-email/

596 https://www.marineconservation.org.au/campaigns/

597 https://350.org.au/rise-up/

Volunteer

Join your local *Australian Conservation Foundation Community* group[598], local *Landcare* or *Coastcare* group[599], a local project with *Conservation Volunteers Australia*[600], *Australian Wildlife Conservancy* projects[601] or look for environmental volunteering opportunities on *GoVolunteer*[602] or *SEEK Volunteer*[603].

Train in non-violent direct action to become a *Climate Activist* with *Greenpeace*[604].

For natural disasters, apply to the *Salvation Army Emergency Services*[605], Blaze Aid[606] or see Australian Red Cross advertised opportunities for volunteers for emergencies[607]. Queenslanders can sign up to the *Emergency Volunteering Community Response to Extreme Weather (EV CREW)* that matches volunteers with disaster and emergency management agencies when and where they are needed[608]. Those living in WA can register with *Emergency Volunteers*[609].

Donate

First Nations organisations are at the forefront of the climate movement in Australia, working to advocate for climate justice, empower communities, and protect Country. The *Firesticks Alliance Indigenous Corporation* is an Indigenous-led network that seeks to revitalise cultural burning practices and promote sustainable land management by providing training, implementing on-ground works, and conducting scientific monitoring to enhance ecosystem health[610].

Chaired by one of the world's most respected environmental leaders, and former Deputy Premier of Victoria, Professor John Thwaites AM, *Climateworks* is an independent not-for-profit centre within Monash University

598 https://www.acf.org.au/community-groups
599 https://landcareaustralia.org.au/landcare-get-involved/findagroup/
600 https://volunteerportal.conservationvolunteers.com.au/s/make-booking
601 https://www.australianwildlife.org/support-us/volunteer/
602 https://govolunteer.com.au/
603 https://www.volunteer.com.au/environment-conservation-volunteering
604 https://www.greenpeace.org.au/get-involved/volunteer/action-training/
605 https://www.salvationarmy.org.au/emergency-services/volunteering/
606 https://blazeaid.com.au/volunteer-information
607 https://www.redcross.org.au/act/how-can-i-help/volunteering-in-an-emergency/
608 https://emergencyvolunteering.com.au/emergency-volunteering/
609 https://emergency.volunteer.org.au/
610 https://firesticks.org.au/

that leads in research and modelling to present solutions to decarbonisation across Australian industries, energy systems and households.

An active public advocate is *The Climate Council*, the reincarnation of the Climate Commission, which was abolished by the Abbott government, and is crowdfunded by 16,000 Australians, which produces a range of topical news and research[611].

611 https://www.climatecouncil.org.au/

MENTAL HEALTH

'This feeling will pass. The fear is real but the danger is not.'

CAMMIE MCGOVERN, *SAY WHAT YOU WILL*[612]

It was a proud day when we launched the latest *headspace* centre at the old Collingwood football club ground, Victoria Park, on the first floor of the Bob Rose stand that looked onto the ground.

Headspace is a 'soft entry' enhanced primary care service system for 12–25-year-olds who present with a range of health and social issues, predominantly mental health-related. As a one-stop-shop, it offers horizontal integration of health and social services, with codesign from young people to create and safeguard a youth-friendly culture of care. It has inspired widespread global reform in youth mental health primary care.

After the launch, then President of Collingwood, Eddie Macquire, visited the team and regaled us with stories of his heroes.

In true Collingwood style, Bob Rose was 'hard as nails' – a fierce, almost brutal competitor who thrived on physical contact and whose shirtfronts left many an opponent reeling. Rose possessed seemingly boundless courage and a will-to-win that bordered on fanaticism. Time and again he would lift Collingwood from seemingly hopeless positions. With the Pies down to only 16 fit players in the 1952 preliminary final against Fitzroy, Rose produced a stunning 15-minute frenzy in which he kicked 3 goals and set up 2 others for teammates, giving his team a lead that they would hang on to for the rest of the brutal encounter.

After 7 years with Wangaratta Rovers, he returned to a hero's welcome at Victoria Park as coach for the 1964 season. The Pies had finished 7th in 1962

---

[612] Mental health
McGovern C (2014) *Say What You Will*, HarperCollins

and 8th in a horrid 1963 season marked by infighting and a board upheaval. But Rose took essentially the same list all the way to a Grand Final in his first season as coach, and went within 2 minutes of winning the flag. In 1974, his son Robert, himself a VFL footballer and Victorian cricketer, was tragically left a quadriplegic after a car crash. Bob looked after Robert in the years that followed, during which he returned to Victoria Park as a board member.[613]

Each year, Collingwood and the Western Bulldogs play for the Robert Rose Cup to raise awareness for people living with disability.

Whilst Bob Rose's story was inspirational, what was remarkable was Eddie's recollection, passion and personal association with the Collingwood heroes. At the age of 6, as a migrant kid from the tough Melbourne suburb of Broadmeadows, Eddie found identity, belonging and a community at the Collingwood football club[614]. He has found his tribe. I can't imagine the heartbreak, 51 years later, when he was forced from his beloved club a week after he said the release of the club's *Do Better* report – which found evidence of systemic racism at the Magpies – was a 'proud day' for the club.

Eddie's genuine and very personal care for his Collingwood club community inspired us to remember that, although the headspace centre was a team of clinicians providing medical treatment, it could be a thriving community of young people that we cared deeply about and that could help each other. So, we encouraged the young people to build an active group that provided mutual support, especially for young LGBTQI+ people who experience stigma, discrimination, bullying, violence, and exclusion. As a result, a higher number of people in LGBTQ+ communities experience poorer social, emotional and psychological wellbeing and mental health.

The group was a great success, enabling them to find safety and thrive in their tribe.

Sadly, millions of Australians do not feel this safety or support. They feel daily distress.

WHAT

Mental health is a state of mental well-being that enables people to cope with the stresses of life, realise their abilities, learn well and work well, and contribute to their community. It is an integral component of health and well-

613 https://forever.collingwoodfc.com.au/players/bob-rose/

614 https://www.youtube.com/watch?v=Yn7PE0zHDPI

being that underpins our individual and collective abilities to make decisions, build relationships and shape the world we live in.

Mental health conditions, on the other hand, are characterised by a clinically significant disturbance in an individual's cognition, emotional regulation, or behaviour[615]. In this country, 1 in 5 people has had a mental disorder in the last year,[616] and around 1 in 2 Australians will struggle with their mental health during their lifetime[617]. Roughly 60 per cent of these people won't seek help[618].

Everyone feels anxious from time to time. When anxious feelings don't go away, happen without any particular reason, or make it hard to cope with daily life, it may be a sign of an anxiety condition. Anxiety conditions include Post-Traumatic Stress Disorder (after experiencing a traumatic event); Generalised Anxiety Disorder (feels anxious on most day); Obsessive Compulsive Disorder (ongoing unwanted or intrusive thoughts and fears that cause anxiety); panic attacks (intense, overwhelming and often uncontrollable feelings of anxiety); and social anxiety disorder (an intense fear of being criticised, embarrassed or humiliated)[619].

Anxiety is the most common mental health condition affecting 3.4 million Australians and rising.

We all feel sad, moody or low sometimes. It's a normal part of life. If these feelings come and stay for more than 2 weeks, it might be a sign of depression, including feeling numbness and emptiness, overwhelmed, irritation and frustration (including with small things), miserable and sad, unhappy, guilt, indecisive, and disappointed. Depression affects one in seven people in Australia[620].

The proportion of Australians aged over 15 years old with anxiety or depression has nearly doubled from 2009 to 2021 to almost 1 in 5[621].

Every year in Australia, more than 3,000 people die by suicide—nearly 9 people a day. Suicide remains the leading cause of death for people aged 15-44

615 https://www.who.int/news-room/fact-sheets/detail/mental-disorders

616 Australian Bureau of Statistics (2007) National Survey of Mental Health and Wellbeing: Summary of Results

617 https://www.beyondblue.org.au/mental-health

618 https://www.blackdoginstitute.org.au/about/who-we-are/

619 https://www.beyondblue.org.au/mental-health/anxiety

620 https://www.beyondblue.org.au/mental-health/depression

621 https://www.aihw.gov.au/mental-health/overview/prevalence-and-impact-of-mental-illness

and the second leading cause of years of life lost, with over 159,000 years of potential life lost to suicide in Australia each year.

But suicide deaths are only the tip of the iceberg.

Over 1 in 3 of young people report having suicidal thoughts and behaviours by 18–19 years of age[622], and 1 in 6 people aged 16-85 in Australia (around 3.3 million people) have experienced suicidal thoughts or behaviour at some point in their lives. Furthermore, over 1.7 million people aged 16-85 had self-harmed in their lifetime. The same research showed that around 55,000 people in Australia attempt to take their own lives each year, or about 150 people each day[623].

Suicide, suicide attempts, or suicidal distress will impact most Australians at some point in their lives. It is estimated that over 7 million Australian adults are close to someone who has died by suicide or attempted suicide and 1 in 2 young people are impacted by suicide by the time they turn 25[624]. The effects are devastating for families and communities. People who are bereaved by suicide are also at greater risk of dying by suicide themselves, with children of a parent who dies by suicide being three times more likely to take their own lives than children whose parents die by other causes.

Those who care for people who have attempted suicide can experience high levels of distress and their own risk is increased. The impact on emergency and health service personnel who care for people who have attempted suicide is also long-lasting. Beyond the human impacts, the economic cost of suicide and suicide attempts is estimated to be $30.5 billion each year.

One in 30 adult Australians experiences bipolar disorder each year[625]. They experience alternating depressive episodes with periods of manic symptoms, including euphoria or irritability, increased activity or energy, increased talkativeness, racing thoughts, increased self-esteem, decreased need for sleep, distractibility, and impulsive recklessness[626]. Bipolar disorder is largely inherited through genetics and can be triggered by factors including stress,

---

622 Swami N, Faulkner A, Slade T, Vukusic S & Hoq M (2025) *Suicidal thoughts and behaviours in adolescence*, Growing Up in Australia Snapshot Series – Issue 14, Australian Institute of Family Studies at https://aifs.gov.au/sites/default/files/2025-08/2507_Snapshot14_suicide-behaviours.pdf

623 National Suicide Prevention Office (2024) *Advice on the National Suicide Prevention Strategy. Consultation draft* at https://haveyoursay.mentalhealthcommission.gov.au/draft-advice-national-suicide-prevention-strategy

624 https://www.suicidepreventionaust.org/news/statsandfacts

625 https://www.bipolaraustralia.org.au/bipolar-information

626 https://www.who.int/news-room/fact-sheets/detail/mental-disorders

pregnancy, and illicit drug use. Although there is no cure for the condition, it can be well managed. People who receive timely treatment are generally able to work, have families, and participate in all aspects of community life.

Affecting 1 in a 100 Australians, schizophrenia is characterised by significant impairments in perception and changes in behaviour, including persistent delusions, hallucinations, disorganised thinking, highly disorganised behaviour, or extreme agitation. Antipsychotic medications are used to treat the psychotic symptoms.

Called a silent epidemic, an estimated 1.1 million Australians are currently living with an eating disorder, a 21 per cent increase over the last 12 years, with 1 in 10 experiencing an eating disorder at some point in their lifetime. Less than a 3rd receive treatment or support. In 2023, over a thousand deaths were due to an eating disorder[627].

Eating disorders, such as anorexia nervosa and bulimia nervosa, involve abnormal eating and preoccupation with food, as well as prominent body weight and shape concerns. Approximately a 3rd of Australian adolescents engage in disordered eating behaviours within any given year, such as restrictive dieting, binge eating, vomiting, and laxative use, that do not meet criteria for an eating disorder[628].

A 2025 report from *Liptember* called for more gender-targeted services to set a better standard of mental health care for Australian women due to high levels of depression (52 per cent), anxiety (44 per cent) and body image issues (39 per cent).

Whilst the prevalence of people experiencing mental illness is similar across the nation, it has been suggested that the comparable rates of mental illness in rural areas and major cities mask a high prevalence of psychological distress and untreated (or undiagnosed) mental illness. Rates of self-harm and suicide increase with remoteness and people who experience suicidality are more likely than the general population to have a mental health disorder or condition.

---

[627] Butterfly Foundation (2024) *Paying the Price. The economic and social impact of eating disorders in Australia*, Second Edition, Deloitte Access Economics at https://butterfly.org.au/wp-content/uploads/2024/03/Paying-the-Price-Second-Edition-25-March-2024.pdf

[628] https://nedc.com.au/eating-disorders/eating-disorders-explained/eating-disorders-in-australia

The mental health of young Australians is declining[629]. For instance, the rates of psychological distress in 15-24 year-olds more than doubled from 18 per cent in 2011 to 42 per cent in 2021[630]; almost half of females aged 16-24 years and almost 1/3rd of males aged 16-24 years had mental disorder in the previous year[631]; and the rate of hospitalisation for intentional self-harm has also surged by 70 per cent in young women aged 15-19 between 2008–09 to 2021–22[632] with more than 1 in 4 females aged 16–24 years self-harming in their lifetime[633].

Untreated mental health conditions cost Australian workplaces approximately $10.9 billion per year, comprising $4.7 billion in absenteeism, $6.1 billion in productivity, and $146 million in compensation claims[634].

WHY

Many other Themes of this book contribute to the mental health issues, including family and domestic violence, child abuse, social cohesion, racism and discrimination, and poverty and disadvantage.

Suicidal distress is a human response to overwhelming suffering. It is complex with many factors at play rather than a single isolated cause, including social determinants (such as income, education, employment, housing, early childhood development, social inclusion, and access to healthcare) and individual factors, including contextual factors (such as stressful life events, trauma and abuse, and discrimination), clinical factors (for example, mental illness, drug and alcohol use, chronic physical illness), personality factors, genetic factors and demographic factors (such as age, gender, sexual orientation, ethnicity, cultural heritage). It is often the impact of social

---

[629] McGorry P, Coghill D and Berk M (2023) Mental health of young Australians: dealing with a public health crisis, Med J Aust | | doi: 10.5694/mja2.52047 at https://www.mja.com.au/journal/2023/219/6/mental-health-young-australians-dealing-public-health-crisis

[630] https://psychology.org.au/about-us/news-and-media/media-releases/2024/federal-budget-falls-short-of-addressing-australia

[631] Australian Bureau of Statistics (2022) *National Study of Mental Health and Wellbeing* at https://www.abs.gov.au/statistics/health/mental-health/national-study-mental-health-and-wellbeing/2020-21

[632] https://psychology.org.au/about-us/news-and-media/aps-in-the-media/2024/australian-teens-trapped-by-social-media-apps-as-t#:~:text=More%20than%20four%20in%2010,%E2%80%9309%20to%202021%E2%80%9322.

[633] Australian Institute of Health and Welfare (2024) *Deaths in Australia* at https://www.aihw.gov.au/reports/life-expectancy-deaths/deaths-in-australia/contents/leading-causes-of-death

[634] PwC (2014) *Creating a mentally healthy workplace: return on investment analysis* Accessed at http://www.headsup.org.au/docs/default-source/resources/beyondblue_workplaceroi_finalreport_may-2014.pdf

determinants interacting with a person's individual risk factors that leads to a person experiencing suicidal distress.

The key themes that emerged from interviews with approximately 3,000 people with lived and living experience of suicide included suicidal thoughts and behaviours tracing back to early life experiences of abuse, violence, trauma, family conflict or bereavement, as well as experiences with alcohol and other drug problems, discrimination and concurrent and complex life stressors closer in time to a suicide attempt[635].

The Australian Government's Advice on the National Suicide Prevention Strategy recognises that most suicides are preventable and that a holistic and upstream approach is needed by addressing social and economic drivers like disadvantage, as well as better support for the mental health system.

This includes reducing the prevalence and impact of child abuse and family and sexual violence, bringing down unemployment, enhancing access to education and providing better support for families who have been impacted by suicide.

The chapter on Social Cohesion shows that communities in which people feel safe, healthy, economically secure and connected to others are associated with higher levels of wellbeing, lower levels of distress and lower suicide rates. Improving the community's baseline wellbeing enhances opportunities to thrive and has a protective effect by 'buffering' the impact of suicidal risk factors.

This holistic approach has led the NSW government to enact the Suicide Prevention Bill 2025, placing suicide prevention at the centre of government decision-making and embedding accountability across agencies, including NSW Police[636].

The COVID pandemic's disruption to work and social functioning has been linked with the changing mental health of many Australians, elevating symptoms of depression and anxiety and increasing the risk of stress, loneliness, depression, anxiety and self-harm[637].

---

[635] National Suicide Prevention Adviser (2020) *Compassion First: Designing our National Approach from the Lived Experience of Suicidal Behaviour*, Canberra: National Mental Health Commission at https://www.health.gov.au/resources/publications/national-suicide-prevention-adviser-compassion-first-designing-our-nationalapproach-from-the-lived-experience-of-suicidal-behaviour

[636] https://www.nsw.gov.au/ministerial-releases/world-leading-suicide-prevention-bill-passes-nsw-parliament

[637] Bower M, Donohoe-Bales A, Smout S, Ngyuen AQH, Boyle J, Barrett E, Teesson M (2022) *In their own words: An Australian community sample's priority concerns regarding mental health*

The HILDA Survey follows the lives of more than 17,000 Australians each year, over the course of their lifetime, collecting information on many aspects of life in Australia, including household and family relationships, income and employment, and health and education.

During the COVID pandemic in 2021, HILDA found that 29 per cent of women and 23 per cent of men were in psychological distress, compared to 18 per cent and 15 per cent respectively in 2007. While psychological distress had risen across all age groups, the increase had been most significant in younger Australians with 42 per cent experiencing psychological distress, up from 18 per cent in 2011[638].

Today, 5 years after COVID, Australians are experiencing even higher levels of distress.

The *2024 Suicide Prevention Australia Community Tracker* reports that 74 per cent of Australians are feeling elevated levels of distress beyond normal levels compared to the previous year due to: cost of living and personal debt (49 per cent); family and relationship breakdown (24 per cent); housing access and affordability (24 per cent); unemployment and job security (22 per cent); and social isolation and loneliness (22 per cent). The top causes of elevated distress for young people (18-24 years) are similar with the addition of social media, self-image and bullying (38 per cent)[639].

For people with mental health issues, the social stigma and discrimination they experience can make their problems worse and make it harder to recover, avoiding getting the help they need because of the fear of being stigmatised. A 2022 national survey estimated that over four million Australians experienced mental health-related stigma and discrimination in the prior twelve months. Most commonly, this came from people close to them with 1 in 3 people reporting unfair treatment by family and friends, and 1 in 4 reporting unfair treatment by their spouse or partner.

Experiences of discrimination in the workplace are also common, with 1 in 3 people reporting unfair treatment in the workplace[640]. Whilst over 90 per cent

---

in the context of COVID-19. PLoS One. 2022 May 19;17(5):e0268824. doi: 10.1371/journal.pone.0268824. PMID: 35588438; PMCID: PMC9119542

[638] Wilkins R., Vera-Toscano E. and Botha F. (2024) *The Household, Income and Labour Dynamics in Australia Survey: Selected Findings from Waves 1 to 21*, Melbourne Institute: Applied Economic & Social Research, the University of Melbourne

[639] https://www.suicidepreventionaust.org/young-australians-struggling-as-advice-on-the-national-suicide-prevention-strategy-released-today/

[640] Australian government Department of Prime minister and Cabinet (2022) *National Survey of Mental Health-Related Stigma and Discrimination* at

of employees believe mental health in the workplace is important, only half feel that their workplace is mentally healthy and that their most senior leader values mental health[641]. 3 in 4 of people feel uncomfortable telling their employer they are experiencing a mental illness[642].

When Australians do seek help, the mental health care service landscape is complex, under-resourced, and inconsistent. The government's *National Mental Health Commission* notes that the mental health system's ability to provide effective care is not improving[643]. The Productivity Commission concludes that 'the mental health and suicide prevention system is fragmented and out of reach for many people' and the National Mental Health and Suicide Prevention Agreement signed by all governments 'has fundamental flaws, meaning it is not supporting progress towards a person-centred, integrated mental health and suicide prevention system'[644].

Mental health care services are provided in the private sector via the Medicare Benefits Schedule-subsidised system, utilising private health insurance rebates and patient contributions, among other funding streams. Non-government organisations (sometimes with state or federal government funding, for example, through Primary Health Networks and other departmental programs) also deliver ambulatory and residential mental-health-specific services. State and territory health and hospital services and private hospitals deliver both community and hospital-based services[645].

There are significant shortages of all professions in the mental health workforce, especially in the public system. *SANE Australia* called the mass resignation of psychiatrists in NSW public health in 2025 an 'entirely predictable reflection of the fragile state of our mental health system. It

---

https://behaviouraleconomics.pmc.gov.au/sites/default/files/projects/stigma-survey-report.pdf

641 TNS (2014) *State of Workplace Mental Health in Australia*, Beyond Blue accessed at https://www.headsup.org.au/docs/default-source/resources/bl1270-report---tns-the-state-of-mental-health-in-australian-workplaces-hr.pdf?sfvrsn=8

642 https://mhaustralia.org/media-releases/mental-health-still-taboo-workplace-september-2013

643 National Mental Health Commission (2024) *Monitoring the performance of Australia's mental health system. National Report Card 2023* at https://www.mentalhealthcommission.gov.au/sites/default/files/2024-07/national-report-card-2023_0_0.pdf

644 Productivity Commission (2025) *Mental Health and Suicide Prevention Agreement Review Interim report*, p.2 & 3 at https://www.pc.gov.au/inquiries/current/mental-health-review/interim/mental-health-review-interim-overview.pdf

645 https://www.ruralhealth.org.au/sites/default/files/publications/nrha-mental-health-factsheet-july2021.pdf

highlights the broader issue of inadequate investment in mental health services and the urgent need for comprehensive reform'[646].

The cost of living crisis has meant that nearly 1 in 5 Australians delayed seeing, or did not see any, mental health professional in the last months due to cost, a 60 per cent increase in 3 years.

Since the pandemic, the government has returned the number of Medicare-rebated psychology sessions to 10 per calendar year under a Mental Health Treatment Plan, from twenty in COVID. Anyone who has, or knows someone who has, a mental health issue knows that 10 sessions are not enough. Even when a psychologist can be found, the average fee of $235 for a 45-60 minute session[647], or $2,350 for another 10 sessions, is prohibitive for many people. 10 sessions is an arbitrary number that may lead to higher costs in the long run, as accessing crisis services could be necessary. Waiting until the next calendar year for the next 10 sessions could see symptoms spiral in the meantime. Research shows between 13 and 18 sessions are required for half of people to reliably improve in psychological therapy[648].

The Australian Psychological Society's *Healthcare Index* survey shows the severe pressure the mental health sector is under since the pandemic. Almost 2 in 3 of patients had to wait more than 12 weeks to receive care, and 1 in 3 psychologists were unable to see new clients due to heightened demand, an increase from 1 in 5 in June 2021[649].

Leading mental health research organisation, *Orygen*, has pointed out that 2 million Australians are in the 'missing middle' whose needs are not being met by current mental health services. They are often too unwell for primary care, but not unwell enough for state-based services. They may have accessed services in the past year; however, these services were not able to deliver either the duration of care or the level of specialist care appropriate for more complex and serious mental ill-health[650].

---

646 https://www.sane.org/news/mass-resignation-of-psychiatrists-in-nsw

647 https://www.helplink.com.au/f/cost-of-seeing-psychologists-sydney/#:~:text=Average%20Cost%20of%20a%20Psychology%20Session&text=While%20the%20Australian%20Psychological%20Society,on%20our%20data%20is%20%24235.

648 Hansen, N. B., Lambert, M. J., & Forman, E. M. (2002). The psychotherapy dose-response effect and its implications for treatment delivery services. *Clinical Psychology: Science and Practice, 9*(3), 329–343. https://doi.org/10.1093/clipsy.9.3.329

649 Healthengine Limited (2024) *Australian Healthcare Index*, August 2024 at https://australianhealthcareindex.com.au/australian-healthcare-index-august-report/

650 https://www.orygen.org.au/Orygen-Institute/Policy-Areas/Government-policy-service-delivery-and-workforce/Service-delivery/Defining-the-missing-middle/orygen-defining-the-missing-middle-

The latest headspace *National Youth Mental Health Survey* found more than half of young people believe their mental health is getting worse, with one in four citing social media as the main reason for the decline. 1 in 3 young people is experiencing problematic social media use and would like to disconnect, but the fear of missing out is stopping them.

The survey also found that over half of young people feel fearful of the future due to climate change, with one in five saying climate change is affecting their daily lives. The same proportion also identified financial instability and cost of living, including housing affordability[651].

Bullying is linked to poor mental health, including an increased risk of developing depression and anxiety, and overall poorer psychological and emotional functioning. Bullying is also a risk factor for suicidal thoughts and behaviours, with bullied young people being almost 10 per cent more likely to consider suicide than non-bullied youth. A recent Australian study looking at risk profiles of adolescents who have been admitted to hospital for suicidal behaviour found that 60 per cent reported a history of bullying[652].

Bullying in Australian schools is a serious problem, with over 1 in 5 males and 1 in 6 females aged 8 to 18 years reporting being bullied at least once a week. Another source reports that approximately 1 in 4 Year 4 to Year 9 Australian students are being bullied every few weeks or more often.

The internet and smartphones have only served to make online bullying ubiquitous.

According to Australia's eSafety Commissioner, online bullying amongst children is reaching 'concerning levels' with cyber-bullying prevalent. 1 in 5 young school students experiences online bullying in any one year, and 1 in 2 Australian young people has experienced some form of cyberbullying in their lifetime[653].

With the march of artificial intelligence (AI), we have seen that generative AI makes it easier for people to bully others in ways that are fast, realistic, targeted

---

pdf?ext=#:~:text=The%20'missing%20middle'%20is%20a,enough%20for%20state%2Dbased%20services.

651 https://headspace.org.au/our-impact/evaluation-research-reports/youth-mental-health-statistics/

652 https://www.unsw.edu.au/newsroom/news/2020/03/the-long-term-negative-effects-of-bullying

653 headspace (2020) *insights: experiences of cyberbullying over time headspace National Youth Mental Health Survey 2020* at https://headspace.org.au/assets/Insights-experiences-of-cyberbullying-over-time-National-Youth-Mental-Health-Survey-2020.pdf

and humiliating, intensifying the risk of children and young people being seriously harmed, including explicit AI-generated images. In 2022, the *Online Safety Act* gave the eSafety Commissioner new powers to address the cyberbullying of children. The act reduced the time online platforms have to respond to eSafety removal notices from 48 hours to 24 hours, and also granted the Commission new powers to require individual users to take specific actions.

Recent research by Assistant Minister Dr Andrew Leigh and health economist Dr Stephen Robson found that, since the first touchscreen phones and social media platforms in 2007-2020, 'the mental wellbeing of young Australians has worsened considerably with young people reporting a mental disorder rising by 50 per cent, the rate of self-harm hospitalisations increasing by 35 per cent and the suicide rate rising by 34 per cent'. They concluded that social media has played a key role in worsening mental health in this country and 'delaying access to smartphones and social media until the middle teenage years is supported by the available evidence' [654].

Alongside parental overprotection in the real world, the underprotection of children in the virtual world post the smartphone is also cited for the global 'great rewiring of childhood' and the tidal wave of adolescent anxiety, depression self-harm and suicide[655].

Enter Nova FM's radio host Michael 'Wippa' Wipfli. In 2024, he and Rob Galluzzo founded the *36 Months* campaign to raise the age Australians can access social media from 13 to 16 years, reflecting the mental health issues, cyberbullying, anxiety, depression, self-harm and suicide in Australian teenagers caused by social media, especially during the critical phase of psychological development - the 36 months between ages 13-16.

KitKat came on board with a new campaign, 'Have a Break…until 16', with a mobile digital billboard parked at Parliament House, over 130,000 Australians signing the online petition, opposition leader Peter Dutton committing to the change in the radio studio, and a meeting with the Prime Minister, gaining his support.

In only 6 months, the campaign gained bipartisan support and achieved a remarkable change in government policy. On 29 November 2024, the Australian Parliament passed the *Online Safety Amendment (Social Media Minimum Age) Bill 2024*. The Bill sets 16 as the minimum age for social media

[654] Leigh A and Robson S (2024) *The Rise of Social Media and the Fall in Mental Wellbeing Among Young Australians*, CESifo Working Paper No. 11563, ISSN 2364-1428

[655] Haidt J (2024) *The Anxious Generation. How the Great Rewiring of Childhood is Causing an Epidemic of Mental Illness*, Penguin Random House UK, London

access, requiring age-restricted social media platforms to take reasonable steps to prevent underage users from having social media accounts. The ban on Facebook, Instagram, TikTok, Snapchat, X (Twitter), YouTube, Reddit, Twitch, Kick, and Threads for under 16s came into force on 10 December 2025.

ACT

Participate

October is Mental Health Month with the World Mental Health Day on 10 October. Join Mental Health Australia's campaign[656] and walk, run, or roll 40km, 60km, 100km or 150km virtually for the Black Dog Institute's *One Foot Forward* during the month of October to show those experiencing symptoms of mental illness they are not alone and to help raise funds for crucial mental health research and support services[657].

Other days are the *National Day of Action against Bullying and Violence* in August[658], *Body Image and Eating Disorders Awareness Week* during the first full week of September[659] and *R U OK? Day* in September[660]. *BodyKind August* is the Butterfly Foundation's free annual awareness celebration for schools, homes, and sporting/activity clubs, encouraging everyone to be kind to their own and all bodies.

Walk 9 km anywhere for the 9 Australians who die every day by suicide on *World Suicide Prevention Day* on 10 September and raise funds for crisis support and suicide prevention services[661]. *Suicide Prevention Australia* has a range of resources to take action on the day[662].

Created by her parents following the loss of their 14-year-old daughter to suicide after ongoing bullying, go blue on *Do It for Dolly Day* in May[663] to help change the culture of bullying by addressing the impact of bullying, anxiety, depression and youth suicide, through education and direct support to young people and families.

---

656 https://worldmentalhealthday.com.au/

657 https://www.blackdoginstitute.org.au/news/national-mental-health-month-join-in-with-black-dog-institute/

658 https://bullyingnoway.gov.au/preventing-bullying/national-week-of-action

659 https://butterfly.org.au/get-involved/campaigns/biedaw/

660 https://www.ruok.org.au/r-u-ok-day

661 https://www.outoftheshadowswalk.org.au/

662 https://www.suicidepreventionaust.org/world-suicide-prevention-day/

663 https://www.dollysdream.org.au/event/do-it-for-dolly-day-2024/do-it-for-dolly-day-2025

Designed with, and specifically for, young people, and accessed by more than 2 million people in Australia each year, *ReachOut* is an online safe place where young people can openly express themselves, get a deeper understanding and perspective on what's happening in their lives, connect with people who will provide judgement-free support, and build the resilience to manage their challenges now and in the future. Resources for carers, parents and schools are also provided[664]. Enter ReachOut's *Laps for Life* to swim and raise funds in March[665].

Workplace

Workplace Health and Safety laws require employers to eliminate or minimise risks to the health and safety of workers. 'Health' includes psychological health.

A mentally healthy workplace is generally one in which there is a positive workplace culture and an understanding that mental health is everyone's responsibility; stress and other risks to mental health are managed; people feel safe and supported to talk about mental health; and mental health support is tailored for individuals and teams. The benefits to your organisation include attracting and retaining staff, less staff absenteeism and lost working days, increased productivity and greater job satisfaction[666].

You can use October as Mental Health month to introduce mental wellbeing initiatives, such as mindfulness training into the workplace. The *Black Dog Institute* offers a workplace mental health toolkit and workplace mental health programs and services· It is a partner in the new Australian government's *Mentally Healthy Workplaces* website that contains a range of tools and resources[667].

Volunteer

Since 2008, *Raise* has delivered more than 1,000 early intervention youth mentoring programs across Australia by recruiting, screening and training over 8,800 volunteer mentors who give 2 hours a week (at the same time on the same day) for 20 weeks to support more than 13,500 young people in years 7-9[668]. Raise's *2023 Evaluation Report* found that 91 per cent of corporate mentors felt more confident to support the wellbeing of others at work, and 89 per cent of

---

664 https://au.reachout.com/

665 https://www.lapsforlife.com.au/

666 https://business.gov.au/risk-management/mental-health/create-a-mentally-healthy-workplace

667 https://beta.mentallyhealthyworkplaces.gov.au/

668 https://www.raise.org.au/

the mentees improved in at least one of the four outcome areas – asking for help, hope for the future, resilience, and school belonging[669].

Campaign

Australians for Mental Health has two online petitions that call on the Australian government to make the reform and investment in mental health care a top priority for our nation at National Cabinet, and the creation of a new Mental Health and Wellbeing Commissioner within the Australian Human Rights Commission[670].

Donate

In 1997, then Premier of Victoria, Jett Kennett's daughter came to him after 2 of her friends lost their lives in totally unrelated, separate car accidents. 'She was very upset, and she asked me what I could do to stop [young people] dying on the roads. I thought she was challenging me to reduce the road toll, but when we found out more about these two young men's deaths, we came to the conclusion that while they died as a result of a motor vehicle accident, both of them had been emotionally depressed and both had used their cars to take their lives. That led me to realise that we needed to set up a body to look at depression on a national rather than a state basis and try to educate people about depressive illnesses and encourage them to seek help early and to remove the stigma associated with the illness'[671].

He founded what has been a highly effective organisation in raising the awareness, understanding of, and responses to depression and other mental disorders 'as a reliable source of mental health information, support, and hope' for millions of Australians – *Beyond Blue*[672].

Founded in 1985 as the Mood Disorders Unit at Sydney's Prince Henry Hospital, the *Black Dog Institute* is the only medical research institute in Australia to investigate mental health across the lifespan. As well as world-leading research, they have developed a range of digital tools for self-assessment and self-help[673].

SANE is for people with recurring, persistent or complex mental health issues and trauma, and for their families, friends and communities, including 24/7 online community forums that provide a safe, non-judgmental space to share

---

669 https://www.raise.org.au/about/submissions-reports/

670 https://www.afmh.org.au/

671 https://www.hopechannel.com/read/how-jeff-kennett-beats-the-blues

672 https://www.beyondblue.org.au/about

673 https://www.blackdoginstitute.org.au/

experiences, seek advice and receive support; digital and telehealth support; information and resources; and referrals with qualified counsellors and peer support workers[674].

The *Butterfly Foundation* is the national charity for all Australians impacted by eating disorders and body image issues, and for the families, friends and communities who support them. Butterfly provides evidence-based support services, treatment and resources, prevention and early intervention programs, and advocating for the needs of the community[675].

Started by 2 siblings in 2006, Rosie and Lucy Thomas, *Project Rockit* has engaged close to 600,000 Year 3–12 students in over 2,500 schools in youth-led workshops to reduce the prevalence and impact of bullying. External evaluation by Western Sydney University demonstrated that before the program, only 49 per cent of young people felt confident enough to challenge bullying, but after completing the program 96 per cent felt confident to stand up[676].

---

674 https://www.sane.org/

675 https://butterfly.org.au/

676 https://www.projectrockit.com.au/our-impact/

Racism and discrimination

RACISM AND DISCRIMINATION

'In many conversations with migrants, refugees and other diverse Australians, I've heard a common refrain: they don't just want to be statistics in a census or smiling faces in government brochures. They want to be part of the decision-making. They want to be trusted with stories, with strategy, with steering the future.'

SHADI KHAN SAIF,
AFGHAN JOURNALIST BASED IN MELBOURNE[677]

As I talked to a group of articulate Sudanese young people in a park one day, they pointed out the circling unmarked police car. One of them had taken a video on their phone of the abusive treatment of their friend by a policeman, who then demanded their phone. He fled in fear. Clearly still petrified, having brought back the trauma of the unimaginable violence at the hands of the authorities that he had experienced in his home country, he pleaded with us to take his phone.

They had found themselves living in another police state.

Unfortunately, this was by no means an isolated case.

In the first case of its type, the Flemington Kensington Community Legal Centre and 6 young men took the Victoria Police to the Federal Court alleging that they were stopped, harassed and racially abused by several individual

677 https://www.theguardian.com/australia-news/commentisfree/2025/jul/14/australias-multiculturalism-lives-mostly-on-the-surface-inclusion-without-voice-is-tokenism?CMP=Share_iOSApp_Other

police officers and that these incidents were part of a pattern of racial profiling that unlawfully discriminated against them in contravention of the Commonwealth Racial Discrimination Act 1975[678].

6 years after the case began, on the eve of an eight week trial as the Chief Commissioner was expected to give evidence, it was settled. Victoria Police acknowledged in a joint statement read out in the Federal Court that it had, in fact, received many complaints of racial discrimination.

To his credit, the Chief Commissioner subsequently released a three year '*Equality is not the same…*' plan to eliminate racial profiling, including a review of field contact policies, a trial of 'stop & search' receipting, unconscious bias training and the setting up of stakeholder advisory groups, including the Chief Commissioner's Human Rights Strategic Advisory Committee and Young People's Portfolio Reference Group. As head of a youth agency, I was a member of the latter and it was illuminating to talk to senior police about the issue.

We were involved in trialling one of the measures in the Commissioner's plan, the piloting of stop and search receipts. The police officer provided a receipt that included the police officer's number and the reason that he or she had stopped the person. The aim was to prevent arbitrary and racially discriminatory stop and searches by police, as well as assist in tracking and documenting any racial disparities in stop and search patterns.

The upshot was that young African people were still racially profiled and stopped. Now they had a pink piece of paper to show for it. We pointed out the obvious weaknesses and thankfully, the trial was abandoned shortly after.

An embedded culture of racism and discrimination is hard to change. A year later, a sergeant and 2 constables were sacked over producing a police station branded stubby holder mocking African migrants[679].

And 10 years later, research by the Centre Against Racial Profiling showed a disproportionate number of police searches against Aboriginal, African, Middle Eastern and Pacific Island communities. First Nations Victorians, and those with African, Middle-Eastern and Pacific Islander backgrounds, were 15, 10, 5

---

678 Kelly A (2013) *An end to racial profiling in sight*, Crime and Justice Insight 8, VCOSS accessed at https://insight.vcoss.org.au/wp-content/uploads/2013/06/Insight8.AnthonyKelly.Final_.pdf

679 https://www.theage.com.au/national/victoria/three-police-officers-sacked-others-disciplined-over-racist-sunshine-stubby-holders-20140305-346mq.html

and 5 times more likely to be searched than White Victorians and 10, 7, 2 and 5 times more likely to have force used against them, respectively[680].

WHAT

We like to think of ourselves as a world-leading, successful multicultural country. But racism occurs every day in Australia and is endemic in our organisations, schools, media, governments, and communities[681].

The fact is that we are a racist country with a system of oppression and hierarchies between social groups based on perceived differences – place of origin, race, and cultural background, exacerbating societal inequalities structurally, institutionally, and interpersonally[682].

Despite the *Racial Discrimination Act 1975* making it unlawful to treat someone unfairly because of their race, colour, descent, national or ethnic origin or immigrant status, racism in Australia is, according to our Race Discrimination Commissioner, 'entrenched in the systems, structures, and institutions of Australia since colonisation. It is pervasive and causes real harm to people every single day. It leads to worse health outcomes, poorer educational outcomes, over representation in the justice system, negative representation in the media, and consistent roadblocks in employment'[683].

Racism is more than just prejudice between people or groups of people. Racism occurs when prejudice is accompanied by the power to harm, oppress or discriminate, either by individuals, organisations or systems. Racism can take many forms, including systemic racism, institutional racism, societal racism and individual/interpersonal racism[684]. Racism can be conscious or unconscious, active or passive, obvious or subtle[685].

Even though mistreatment and discrimination are commonly experienced by people from African and Asian backgrounds with nearly half made to feel different or as if they did not belong in the last 12 month, the Australian-born

---

680 https://www.racialprofilingresearch.org/keyfindings-2024

681 Fozdar F (2022) *Racism in Australia today,* Journal of Intercultural Studies, 43(5), 686–688. https://doi.org/10.1080/07256868.2022.2060991

682 Ben J et al (2022) *Racism in Australia: a protocol for a systematic review and meta-analysis. Systematic Reviews,* 11(1), 47–47. https://doi.org/10.1186/s13643-022-01919-2, p.2

683 Australian Human Rights Commission (2024) *The National Anti-Racism Framework: A roadmap to eliminating racism in Australia* at https://humanrights.gov.au/sites/default/files/2024-11/NARF_Full_Report_FINAL_DIGITAL_ACCESSIBLE.pdf

684 https://alltogethernow.org.au/racism/racism-in-australia/

685 https://www.dca.org.au/research/racism-at-work

population are at least as likely as overseas-born Australians to recognise racism as a problem. In 2025, nearly 7 in 10 Australian-born adults believe that racism is a fairly or very big problem in Australia, a similar proportion to those born in Asia or Africa[686].

It's often said, especially by our politicians, that Australia is a world-leading multicultural country. Since the arrival of the first Europeans, the country has accepted in an estimated ten million migrants, including nearly a million refugees and others in humanitarian need[687].

Despite the longstanding racism and discrimination, and perhaps because most of us, or our family, are migrants to this country, with a majority of us born overseas or having at least one parent born overseas, we continue to view multiculturalism and diversity as good for Australia. Today, 2 in 3 of Australians agree that accepting immigrants from many different countries makes Australia stronger, while more than 4 in 5 agree that multiculturalism has been good for Australia, that immigrants are generally good for Australia's economy, and that immigrants improve Australian society by bringing new ideas and cultures[688].

However, the explosion of migrant arrivals post-COVID to record 737,000 migrant arrivals in 2023-24, up 73 per cent from the year before, has resurfaced the issue of immigration, with the influx being blamed for exacerbating cost-of-living pressures, the housing crisis, overstretched health services, and congested cities.

With the number of temporary migrants in the country at any one time at a record nearly 2.5 million[689], over half of Australians now believe that the number of immigrants accepted into Australia at present' is 'too high' (as opposed to 'too low' or 'about right'), a rate that has doubled in the last 3 years.

Among those who think immigration is too high, nearly 6 in 10 think the economy or housing shortages and affordability is the most important problem facing Australia in 2025. This is corroborated by a 2024 survey of 2,000 voting-age Australians which found that nearly 2 in 3 of Australians either agree or

---

686 Scanlon Foundation Research institute (2025) *Mapping Social Cohesion 2024*, p.15

687 https://immi.homeaffairs.gov.au/what-we-do/refugee-and-humanitarian-program/about-the-program/about-the-program

688 Scanlon Foundation Research institute (2025) *Mapping Social Cohesion 2024*, p.10

689 https://www.abc.net.au/news/2025-11-07/effect-of-migration-on-housing-in-several-starts/105980904?utm_source=abc_news_app&utm_medium=content_shared&utm_campaign=abc_news_app&utm_content=other

strongly agree that 'the current rate of immigration is making housing less affordable'[690].

The fact is that it doesn't. Modelling by Monash University and RMIT found that the cost of housing grew by 1.1 per cent more to in each year between 2006 and 2016 than would have happened if there was no migration[691]. This is only a small fraction of the 6 per cent annual house price growth that occurred over that period.

Since the 2023 peak, net migration has fallen sharply to 2009 levels and is expected to fall further, but this is unlikely to stop the right wing's political playbook stance over demonising migrants and against a 'Big Australia'.

Blaming migrants is not new. But, as Australia's race discrimination commissioner, Giridharan Sivaraman, notes, 'taking the easy but misleading route of blaming migrants for economic insecurity only serves to stoke the already smouldering fires of racism'[692].

Despite studies consistently finding that ethnic diversity improves business performance[693] with diverse and inclusive workplaces being more profitable, innovative, creative, and engaging[694], a 2023 study showed that discrimination is widespread in the Australian job market. A team of experts designed more than 12,000 identical resumes for more than 4,000 job applications, altering the applicant's name to represent different ethnicities. The applications were made across 12 different occupations, ranging from high-skilled jobs needing a university degree, medium-skilled jobs where a qualification was required, and low-skilled jobs where only previous experience was desirable.

Despite their resumes being almost identical, with the same level of experience and qualifications, applicants with non-English names were 57 per cent less likely to receive a positive response for a leadership role and 45 per cent less likely to be considered for a non-leadership role[695].

---

690 RedBridge (2024) *Concern over immigration, attitudes towards politics and government, and vote intention. A RedBridge Public Opinion Snapshot*

691 Moallemi M & Melser D (2019) *The impact of immigration on housing prices in Australia,* Pap Reg Sci. 2020;1–14. https://doi.org/10.1111/pirs.12497

692 https://www.theguardian.com/commentisfree/2025/nov/25/giridharan-sivaraman-australia-doesnt-need-another-migration-debate-tackle-inequality?CMP=Share_iOSApp_Other

693 https://www.mckinsey.com/featured-insights/diversity-and-inclusion/diversity-matters-even-more-the-case-for-holistic-impact

694 https://www.dca.org.au/resources/di-planning/business-case-for-di

695 Adamovic M and Leibbrandt A (2023) *Is there a glass ceiling for ethnic minorities to enter leadership positions? Evidence from a field experiment with over 12,000 job applications,* The

Our workplaces are also racist. In its 2023 survey of over 1,500 workers from various sectors and organisations across Australia, the Diversity Council of Australia found that 93 per cent felt that Australian organisations needed to take action to address racism whilst only 27 per cent reported that their organisations had been proactive in preventing workplace racism[696].

Furthermore, the latest *Inclusion@Work Index* reports that under half of workers felt their teams are inclusive and just 3 in 10 reported their manager is inclusive, representing a steady decline since 2019[697].

Based on a succession of research reports, racism is also widespread in Australia's educational settings[698] and racism within Australian schools remains a significant barrier to accessing, engaging and succeeding in education[699].

The seminal 2017 *Speak Out Against Racism* study found that 43 per cent of students saw incidents of racial discrimination directed towards other students by teachers, and over 40 per cent of Aboriginal and/or Torres Strait Islander students or students from culturally and linguistically diverse communities experienced racial discrimination from their peers. Many teachers reported feeling underprepared to respond to racism in the classroom[700].

A 2019 research report found that 40 per cent of non-white Australian students are victims of racial discrimination at school and that many of these students are left feeling as if racism has become a part of their everyday life[701]. Furthermore, a 2020 study reiterated that it is common for non-white Australian

---

Leadership Quarterly, Volume 34, Issue 2, 2023, 101655, ISSN 1048-9843, https://doi.org/10.1016/j.leaqua.2022.101655

[696] Diversity Council of Australia (2022) *Racism at Work* at https://www.dca.org.au/wp-content/uploads/2023/06/infographic_racism_at_work_final_1.pdf

[697] Diversity Council Australia (2024) *Inclusion@Work Index 2023–2024: Mapping the State of Inclusion in the Australian Workforce*, Synopsis Report at https://www.dca.org.au/wp-content/uploads/2024/10/DCA_Inclusion_Index_2023-2024_Synopsis.pdf

[698]Bosco Ngendakurio J, (2024) *Report: Racism in Australian Schools Impacts and Possible Solutions*, Ethnic Communities Council of Queensland, Scanlon Foundation, Griffith Centre for Social and Cultural Research

[699] Gibbs J, Paradies Y, Gee G & Haslam N (2022). *The effects of Aboriginal tertiary students' perceived experiences of racism and of cultural resilience on educational engagement*, The Australian Journal of Indigenous Education. 51(2)

[700] Australia National University Centre for Social Research and Methods (2019) *Findings from the 2017 Speak Out Against Racism (SOAR) student and staff surveys*, CSRM Working Paper No. 3/2019

[701] McGown M (2019) *Racism Study Finds One in Three School Students Are Victims of Discrimination*, The Guardian, https://www.theguardian.com/australianews/2019/aug/27/racism-study-finds-one-in-three-school-students-are-victims-ofdiscrimination

students to experience racism through micro-aggressions from teachers and peers, as well as systemic exclusions based on Eurocentric curricula that exclude non-white students' experiences and preferences[702].

More recently, Australian Human Rights Commission surveyed over 76,000 students and staff and found nearly 1 in 6 respondents experienced direct interpersonal racism at university and 7 in 10 experienced indirect racism. The report concluded that 'racism was reported at all universities at similar rates, indicating this is a systemic issue'[703].

Sport is another battleground for racism, as I found out with the 'beautiful game'.

After employing African-background public housing tenants in the eco-retrofit of their neighbourhood's social housing to raise awareness and reduce energy usage, they asked for help to establish a soccer team.

Confused, I asked why they didn't play at the nearby soccer club, before realising it had a Greek heritage and the coaches certainly didn't want the naturally gifted African boys to displace their sons. So, under the guise of *Harmony Day*, we got the club to agree to hold a family day with local MP and then Minister for Families, Housing, Community Services and Indigenous Affairs, Jenny Macklin. Amidst the sound of drums, the African kids had an amazing time displaying their athleticism and passion.

Visiting 3 months later, none had been invited back.

I don't blame the soccer club. After all, for past decades they had been referred to as 'wogs' and their sport as 'wog-ball'.

As the great unifier in Australian culture, it would seem that 'sport provides a unified sense of community with Aussies cheering on our cross-cultural representation, where respect and teamwork create an inclusive environment of camaraderie that rises above intolerance and exclusion'[704]. However, according to *Sport Integrity Australia*, racism exists in all levels of Australian sport – from juniors through to elite – from participants through to match officials, volunteers, fans, coaches and beyond.

---

702 Yared H, Grové C & Chapman D (2020) *How does race play out in schools? a scoping review and thematic analysis of racial issues in Australian schools*, Social Psychology of Education: An International Journal, 23(6), 1505–1538. https://doi.org/10.1007/s11218-020-09589-5

703 Australian Human Rights Commission (2026) *Respect at Uni: Study into antisemitism, Islamophobia, racism and the experience of First Nations people*, p.15 & 16

704 https://www.sportintegrity.gov.au/news/integrity-blog/2024-03/racism-sport

Racism starts early. A 2019 study found that 'racial vilification was a common occurrence among players in junior sports, as well as with spectators…with non-white children being the targets of most abuse'[705].

Even our governments have been found to be racist. A 2024 report by the *Australian Human Rights Commission* found governments and their departments at all levels across the country are failing to adequately identify and address racism – even avoiding the term 'racism' – and that approaches across the board are ad-hoc, disjointed, reactive, and lacking coordination between governments, agencies and sectors[706].

Racist reporting is rife in the Australian media. Over 3/4 of television news and current affairs presenters, commentators and reporters have an Anglo-Celtic background. Just 6 per cent were from an Indigenous or non-European background. Nearly 8 in 10 journalists with diverse backgrounds believe having a diverse cultural background is a barrier to career progression[707].

A 2021 media snapshot by charity *All Together Now* found that 89 per cent of the negatively racialised opinion pieces were authored by people of Anglo-Celtic and/or European backgrounds, while most of the opinion pieces authored by Aboriginal, Torres Strait Islander and people of colour were inclusive[708].

Even our national broadcaster has been found to have entrenched racism. In an independent review in October 2024, ABC staff reported being subjected to racial slurs, exclusion due to their cultural background, and being mistaken for a more junior person based on their racial appearance.

In the meantime, the growth in, and anonymity of, social media has resulted in an explosion of racism online. Australia's e-Safety Commissioner reported in 2025 that adults who identify as sexually diverse, Aboriginal and/or Torres Strait Islander, with disability, and/or as linguistically diverse are more likely both to see (41 per cent) and to personally experience (24 per cent) online hate. A minority of targeted adults surveyed who had encountered online hate said

---

[705] https://theconversation.com/racial-abuse-is-rife-in-junior-sports-and-little-is-being-done-to-address-it-118589

[706] Australian Human Rights Commission (2024) ***Mapping government anti-racism programs and policies*** at file:///C:/Users/paulb/Downloads/mapping_government_anti-racism_programs_and_policies_report_1.pdf

[707] Media Diversity Australia (2019) ***Who Gets to Tell Australian Stories?*** at https://www.mediadiversityaustralia.org/wp-content/uploads/2020/08/Who-Gets-To-Tell-Australian-Stories_LAUNCH-VERSION.pdf

[708] https://alltogethernow.org.au/our-work/media-monitoring/

they took action after seeing it (28–32 per cent) or personally experiencing it (38–44 per cent)[709].

WHY

Captain William Mynors of the East India Company vessel *Royal Mary* named Christmas Island when he sailed past it on Christmas Day in 1643. From 1899, the Phosphate Mining and Shipping Company mined the guano with indentured workers from Singapore, Malay and China under administration from United Kingdom Colonial Office and later the Crown Colony of Singapore.

After the island was occupied by the Japanese in the second World War, at Australia's request, the United Kingdom transferred sovereignty to Australia, with a $20 million payment from the Australian government to Singapore as compensation for the loss of earnings from the phosphate revenue. Being 5 times closer to Indonesia than Australia, Christmas Island has seen increasing arrivals of boats carrying asylum seekers.

At dawn on 24 August 2001, one of these boats, a 20-metre wooden fishing boat with 438 mainly Hazara asylum seekers, became stranded in international waters about 140 km north of Christmas Island. On 26 August, as the closest ship, the *MV Tampa*, en route from Fremantle to Singapore, responded to a request from Rescue Coordination Centre Australia to respond.

The Tampa captain, Arne Rinnan, later reported that ‘when we arrived it was obvious to us that it was coming apart. Several of the refugees were obviously in a bad state and collapsed when they came on deck to us. 10 to 12 of them were unconscious, several had dysentery and a pregnant woman suffered abdominal pains’. He requested the Australian government's permission to unload the asylum seekers at Christmas Island, arguing that the ship could not sail to Indonesia because it was unseaworthy.

The Australian government threatened to prosecute the captain as a people smuggler if he did so, denying any obligation under international law as Christmas Island lay within a zone designated as Indonesia's responsibility for rescue, Indonesia had accepted coordination of the rescue, and the closest suitable port was Merak in Indonesia.

---

[709] eSafety Commissioner (2025) *Fighting the tide: Encounters with online hate among targeted groups*, Australian Government, Canberra, p.9-10 at https://www.esafety.gov.au/sites/default/files/2025-02/Online-hate-report_Main-Feb25.pdf?v=1739318400031

On 29 August, Captain Rinnan felt he had no other option but to declare a state of emergency and proceeded to enter Australian territorial waters without permission. In response, the Australian SAS boarded the ship to prevent it from approaching any closer to Christmas Island and move the boat back to international waters. He refused, claiming the ship was unsafe to sail until the asylum seekers had been offloaded. The ship-owners said they agreed with his decision, and the Norwegian government warned the Australian government not to seek to force the ship to return to international waters against the captain's will.

The Australian government tried to persuade Indonesia to accept the asylum seekers. Indonesia refused. Norway also refused to accept the asylum seekers and reported Australia to the United Nations. After failing to pass legislation giving the government power to remove any ship in the territorial waters of Australia, the government subsequently acted to excise Christmas Island and a large number of other coastal islands from Australia's migration zone, effectively meaning that any asylum seekers who did not reach the Australian mainland would not be able to apply for refugee status.

The Tampa incident marked a turning point in Australia's treatment of asylum seekers. Henceforth, with John Howard's electioneering statement "we decide who comes into this country and the circumstances in which they come" and with popular support, they became 'queue jumpers' and 'illegal'. Apart from 150 taken by New Zealand, the Tampa refugees were transported to detention camps on Naura where they were subsequently joined by thousands of other asylum seekers under Australia's *Pacific Solution* which also included camps on Manus Island in Papua New Guinea, even if they applied for asylum immediately upon arrival in Australia or had characteristics warranting special consideration, such as being an unaccompanied minor, a survivor of torture and trauma, a victim of trafficking, having special health needs requiring treatment in Australia, or immediate family already living in Australia.

The fear of boat arrivals was successfully etched into the Australian psyche and then hammered home by Tony Abbott's 2013 election winning TWS (three word slogan) 'Stop the Boats'.

So began Operation Sovereign Borders, where boats entering Australian waters seeking asylum were intercepted and turned back at sea, or otherwise returned to their countries of origin or sent to Nauru. In the last decade, 23 boats have arrived in Australia with 1,309 people, 47 boats towed back with 1,121 people, and 25 boats with 1,205 people transferred to offshore processing.

Then Immigration Minister, Scott Morrison, instructed departmental and detention centre staff to publicly refer to asylum seekers as 'illegal' arrivals and as 'detainees'[710]. People smugglers became the arch enemy, and we were indebted to the government for keeping us safe from the marauders.

In the meantime, 170,015 people came by plane and applied for refugee status over the same period.

Despite Australia having obligations international treaties[711] not to return people who face a real risk of violation of certain human rights or send people to third countries where they would face a real risk of violation of their human rights, the fear that we could be overrun by people flocking to live here and threaten our safety and way of life is now deeply planted in our consciousness. As is our demonisation and punitive approach to asylum seekers and refugees.

Briefly in 2022, the plight of a group of 32 refugees and asylum seekers from war-torn countries including Afghanistan and Myanmar - many feeling forgotten and abandoned after up to nine years of indefinite detention - came into public view when Serbian tennis star Novak Djokovic was detained in the same hotel after the federal government cancelled his visa for failing to meet its entry requirement that all non-citizens be fully vaccinated against COVID-19. Locked away 24/7 with sealed windows and no outdoor facility, residents complained of disgusting conditions, including maggots and mouldy food, medical neglect, mistreatment and lack of hygiene[712].

Indefinite detention is inhumane. Carolyn Graydon, principal solicitor for the Asylum Seeker Resource Centre, stated that 'the problem is we don't have any human rights protection or any minimum standards of immigration detention that's enshrined in Australian law by which we can use legal means to have these men released'. And unlike prisons that house convicted criminals 'there is no statutory framework for minimum conditions' for people in immigration detention. Under Australian law, anyone who arrives by boat to seek asylum must be detained and there is no limit on how long that detention can last.

The fear resurfaced in 2024 when 153 asylum seekers were released from detention following the High Court decision that indefinite detention was unlawful, half of whom were convicted of assault and violent offending, kidnapping or armed robbery. Some went on to commit fresh crimes, including

---

710 https://www.smh.com.au/politics/federal/minister-wants-boat-people-called-illegals-20131019-2vtl0.html

711 *International Covenant on Civil and Political Rights*, the *Convention Against Torture* and the *Convention on the Rights of the Child*

712 https://www.abc.net.au/news/2022-01-09/park-hotel-detainee-speak-out/100745456

a violent home invasion. A year later, the Albanese Government made a secret deal costing up to $7 billion with Nauru for the transfer of this so-called NZYQ cohort. The deal was signed alongside new laws allowing deportations to occur without any consideration of the consequences people would face, such as whether a person might die without proper medical care, be permanently separated from their families, or face persecution in Nauru[713].

Then, in December 2025, the United Nations found that Australia's long-running mandatory detention regime for people who seek asylum in Australia by boat is a violation of international human rights[714].

Because of the marginalised economic circumstances and poor health of many asylum seekers and refugees on arrival in host countries, they are more likely to face financial hardship. Language, transport and discrimination also affect their work prospects, with only a quarter of refugees who arrive in Australia finding employment within 2 years of arriving in the country and 40 per cent experience mental health problems in the first 5 years of settlement[715].

With housing so important to new arrivals, refugees are put on the same long public housing waiting lists as all Australians, without receiving any specific or targeted help. Even when supported by service providers, many are unlikely to secure public housing in the short or medium term[716], and refugees are regularly discriminated against in the private rental market, including landlords viewing refugees as riskier tenants, conflating their escaping conflict-hit countries and their future behaviour as home occupants[717].

So, after risking their lives to flee persecution, being locked up in detention in inhumane conditions for years, eventually being granted a temporary protection visa and having to wait more years for a decision on a permanent visa whilst under the threat of deportation, and suffering ongoing racism and discrimination, it is no wonder that, in the words of Refugee Council Deputy

---

713 https://www.refugeecouncil.org.au/first-deportation-under-multi-billion-dollar-nauru-deal-a-dark-new-chapter-for-australia/

714 United Nations Working Group on Arbitrary Detention (2025) *Preliminary Findings from its visit to Australia (1 to 12 December 2025)* at https://www.ohchr.org/sites/default/files/statements/20251212-eom-stm-australia-wg-arbitrary-detention-en.pdf

715 Australian Institute of Family Studies, *Building a New Life in Australia,* Department of Social Services at https://bnla.aifs.gov.au/research-findings

716 Settlement Council of Australia (2019) *The effects of discrimination on refugee and migrant housing needs. Research Report* at https://scoa.org.au/wp-content/uploads/2019/08/The-Effects-of-Discrimination-of-Refugee-and-Migrant-Housing-Needs.pdf

717 https://www.sbs.com.au/news/article/refugees-are-finding-it-hard-to-rent-a-home-in-australia-for-this-pervasive-reason/g43llcod4

CEO Adama Kamara in November 2024, 'if they knew what it would have been like they may not have come'[718].

In Australia, racism remains historically and structurally entrenched, interpersonally pervasive, and has harmful consequences across various life spheres, including economic participation, justice and incarceration, and health and wellbeing[719].

Beginning with the British settlers in 1788, racism has 'derived from colonial extraction, dispossession, exploitation, expropriation, competition with and violence against Indigenous peoples into discrimination and exclusion of different immigrant populations'[720].

The post-WWII fears of Japanese expansionism (having nearly taken New Guinea and bombing the Northern Territory) and the need for labour led to the 'Populate or Perish' policy in 1945 with a goal of 2 per cent population growth each year, with half of the growth coming from immigration through schemes to encourage people from Britain and Europe to immigrate to Australia.

Under this White Australia policy, the country enacted racism as an institutionalised state policy restricting non-white immigration, facilitating an Anglo-European cultural privilege that to-date limits the inclusion of non-Anglo Australians across multiple sectors'[721]. In drafting the related act, Australia's first Prime Minister, Sir Edward Barton stated in Parliament that there 'is no racial equality… nothing we can do by cultivation, by refinement, or by anything else will make some races equal to others'. A 110 years later, Anne Barton, the great granddaughter of Sir Edmund argued that racial inequality cannot begin to be addressed until white Australia finally confronts its colonialist culture of racism[722].

Living in the grey, cold, industrial wasteland of post-war northern London, and with a commitment of only 2 years, with the prospect of sun, sea and sand in

---

[718] https://www.sbs.com.au/news/article/a-plan-for-australia-to-end-racism-has-been-delivered-but-some-refugees-wish-they-never-came/ytn3xz46h

[719] Ben J et al (2023) *Racism Data in Australia: A Review of Quantitative Studies and Directions for Future Research,* Journal of Intercultural Studies, 45(2), 228–257. https://doi.org/10.1080/07256868.2023.2254725

[720] Ben J et al (2023) *Racism Data in Australia: A Review of Quantitative Studies and Directions for Future Research, Journal of Intercultural Studies, 45*(2), 228–257. https://doi.org/10.1080/07256868.2023.2254725

[721] Ben J et al (2023) *Racism Data in Australia: A Review of Quantitative Studies and Directions for Future Research, Journal of Intercultural Studies, 45*(2), 228–257. https://doi.org/10.1080/07256868.2023.2254725

[722] Barton A (2011) *Going white: claiming a racialised identity through the white Australia policy,* Indigenous Law Bulletin, 7(23), 16–19.

the brochure, it is no wonder that my parents, and over a million fellow Brits, jumped at the 10 pound assisted passage offer.

The comfort and moral power of their white privilege was reinforced by the government, church, schools, sport, arts, and workplaces and continues today.

As a child, I remember the family watching UK sitcoms that made humour out of non-Anglo white characters, such as the black man humorously referred to as *Chalky* in *On the Buses* and Alf Garnet spouting vitriol about wogs on *Till Death Us Do Part*[723]. Australian TV programming continued this racist tradition. Everyone's staple, *Hey Hey It's Saturday*, had guest singer Kamahl being the butt of racist jokes, including that his album would 'go black' instead of gold or platinum, the singer getting hit in the face with white powder and told 'you're a real white man now', and a caricature of him sitting in a pot on a fire with a bone through his nose[724].

Then, when *Neighbours* introduced its first non-white family in 1993, the Lims from Hong Kong, their first major storyline was to be accused of eating another neighbour's dog.

The lack of multicultural representation continues today on our screens. More than 75 per cent of presenters, commentators and reporters have an Anglo-Celtic background, while only 6 per cent have either an Indigenous or non-European background[725].

In articulating 50 daily effects of white privilege in her invisible backpack, the seminal work of Peggy McIntosh 30 years ago recognised that her 'racial group was being made confident, comfortable, and oblivious, other groups were likely being made unconfident, uncomfortable, and alienated. Whiteness protected me from many kinds of hostility, distress, and violence, which I was being subtly trained to visit, in turn, upon people of color'[726].

Although Australia has accepted 8 million migrants from nearly 200 countries and over 300 ethnic ancestries since, the prevailing attitude to migrant settlement, based on the expectation of assimilation, means that we expect

---

[723] https://www.vice.com/en/article/all-your-favourite-old-british-sitcoms-are-racist-as-hell/

[724] https://www.theguardian.com/tv-and-radio/2021/apr/18/whitewashed-why-does-australian-tv-have-such-a-problem-with-race

[725] Media Diversity Australia (2020) *Who Gets to Tell Australian Stories? Putting the spotlight on cultural and linguistic diversity in television news and current affairs* at https://www.mediadiversityaustralia.org/wp-content/uploads/2020/08/Who-Gets-To-Tell-Australian-Stories_LAUNCH-VERSION.pdf

[726] McIntosh P (1988) *White Privilege and Male Privilege: A Personal Account of Coming To See Correspondences through Work in Women's Studies,* Working Paper 189, Wellesley Collage Center for Research on Women

migrants to become 'Australian' like us. As Pauline Hanson claims 'Asian immigrants have their own culture and religion, form ghettos and do not assimilate'.

Who is Australia's greatest cricketer? Is it Sir Donald Bradman, Sir Hubert Opperman or Walter Lindrum? The question, said to have been personally written by cricket fanatic and former Prime Minister John Howard, is part of the homework recommended for migrants and refugees taking the citizenship test. As Kristine Klugman, president of Civil Liberties Australia, stated 'the test is clearly skewed to disadvantage refugees and humanitarian immigrants not from Western nations. Cricket is not a high priority when just eating and surviving is all they have time for'[727].

This rhetoric was repeated by then Prime Minister, Tony Abbott, who stated 'everyone has got to be on team Australia', meaning that 'everyone has got to put this country, its interests, its values and its people first, and you don't migrate to this country unless you want to join our team'[728].

Aided by the Sydney shock jocks and the News Corporation press, One Nation, Advance Australia and the Liberal Party's politicising of refugees and migrants on 'safety grounds' is only rising.

As the head of ASIO has warned, this language emboldens white supremacism and Neo-Nazism, which can be traced back to the 1930s in Australia, but in recent years, with recruiting through the dark web and encrypted messaging services, it has re-emerged to become more visible and a growing threat, fuelled by Donald Trump's US presidency and his return in 2025.

Whilst it has been unlawful to discriminate against people based on race or ethnicity since 1975, it hasn't helped that, for the last 50 years, Australian governments have failed to pass legislation to make the incitement of racial hatred an offence. The latest attempt after the Bondi killings again fell short of passing a standalone offence of inciting racial hatred, instead legislating stronger criminal penalties for hate crimes motivated by race or ethnicity and powers to designate and ban hate groups.

Racism sells. In what the Race Discrimination Commissioner calls the calls 'the monetisation of racism: that is, using racism as a way to attract interest, increasing ratings and adding advertising value to a program'[729], Sky News

---

727 https://www.theguardian.com/world/2008/jan/30/australia.international

728 https://www.smh.com.au/politics/federal/you-dont-migrate-to-this-country-unless-you-want-to-join-our-team-tony-abbott-renews-push-on-national-security-laws-20140818-3dvbx.html

729 https://ethicaljournalismnetwork.org/australia-media-racism

Australia has become the country's first TV channel to reach 5 million YouTube subscribers and their viewing on Foxtel is up 6 per cent year-on-year, reaching more than one million monthly Australians on average in 2024.

Then there is targeted racism in Australia as a result of international conflicts, most notably the white Christian democratic peoples of the free world versus the axis of evil coloured Arabs, Muslims, ISIS and other undesirables after 9/11. As a result, the culture and religion of people from a Muslim background are seen as incompatible with a Western way of life and its values.

Australia's Special Envoy to Combat Islamophobia, Aftab Malik, notes that Islamophobia is a pervasive and at times terrifying reality that has devastating consequences for victims, eroding social cohesion. The normalisation of Islamophobia is so widespread that many incidents go unreported[730].

More recently, the conflict in Israel and Occupied Palestinian Territories has sparked protest and division in Australia with a skyrocketing of incidents of Islamophobia with girls and women bearing the brunt of hatred towards Muslims in Australia[731] and antisemitism with a spate of attacks on Jewish homes, synagogues, businesses and childcare centres. Then, on 14 December 2025, a father and son killed 15 people during a Hanukkah celebration at Bondi Beach. The Albanese government was accused of not doing enough to stem the rising antisemitism, including not officially responding to the Plan to Combat Antisemitism produced by his Special Envoy to Combat Antisemitism, Ms Jillian Segal AO, five months before. 4 weeks later, bowing to public pressure, the Prime Minister announced a royal commission into antisemitism and social cohesion, and new hate laws were passed to allow the Minister of Home Affairs to ban hate groups, increase penalties for so-called hate preachers who advocate or threaten violence and expand powers to revoke or refuse visas for people with extremist views coming to Australia.

Even if we are not consciously racist, we all have unconscious biases that influence our behaviour, whether we are aware of them or not.

Our brains are wired to form stereotypes. As assumptions made about individuals or things, based on their belonging in a particular group rather than their own individual characteristics, stereotyping helps our brains make

---

[730] The Special Envoy to Combat Islamophobia (2025) *A National Response to Islamophobia: A Strategic Framework for Inclusion, Safety and Prosperity*, The Office of the Special Envoy to Combat Islamophobia at https://www.oseci.gov.au/sites/default/files/2025-09/national-response-final-report.pdf

[731] Carland S, Alziyadat N, Vergani M & O'Brien K (2025) *Islamophobia in Australia Report V*, Islamophobia Register Australia, Sydney: at https://islamophobia.com.au/wp-content/uploads/2025/03/Islamophobia-in-Australia-Report-5.pdf

efficient shortcuts when processing the overwhelming volume of information it receives. Unconscious biases represent social stereotypes about certain groups of people that individuals form outside their own conscious awareness.

Racism, in particular, involves *perception bias* - the tendency to judge an individual based on a stereotype of a group of which they are a member. Given the pervasive racism in our workplaces, media, sports, governments and communities, we are all involved even if we do not realise it, which is why we all need to act.

In the face of rising racism, in June 2025, the Albanese Government re-established the Office of Multicultural Affairs and moved the ministry into cabinet. As Australia's first female federal parliamentarian of Islamic faith, Dr Anne Aly became the Minister for Multicultural Affairs. Her vision is: 'I want to make multiculturalism about all Australians. I want to make all Australians proud of our multicultural character, our multicultural nature. I want it to be more than about celebrating diversity. I want it to be about valuing diversity in all its forms'[732].

More than just celebrating different cultures, we need to consciously address racism and enable the rightful inclusion and representation of all cultures in all aspects and levels of our society in sport, business, politics and media.

ACT

In a sign of progress, in November 2024, the Australian Human Rights Commission launched the *National Anti-Racism Framework* which calls for a whole of society approach to eliminate racism, with 63 recommendations for reforms across Australia's legal, justice, health, education, media and arts sectors as well as workplaces and data collection. The Framework provides a roadmap for governments, businesses and community organisations to address all forms of racism[733].

Participate

Join more than 25,000 Australians and challenge your understanding of racism by downloading *Everyday Racism,* a world-first mobile phone game app which challenges players to live a week in the life of an Aboriginal man, a Muslim woman, an Indian student or just yourself. Over the course of one week, you'll receive texts, tweets, images and videos that will challenge you and your

[732] https://ministers.dfat.gov.au/minister/anne-aly/transcript/sbs-weekend-one-one-rania-yallop

[733] Australian Human Rights Commission (2024) *The National Anti-Racism Framework: A roadmap to eliminating racism in Australia* at

assumptions. It will help you understand the importance of speaking up when you witness racism[734].

Complaints of racism can be made in writing to the Australia Human Rights Commission[735]. In some cases, a racially discriminatory act will constitute a crime and can be reported to the police.

Campaign

Join the *Refugee Council of Australia* in advocating for better policies and systems for refugees with their *A platform for change: Reforming Australian refugee policy*[736] and *Raise Your Voice* to increase Australia's annual refugee intake[737].

Become an *Anti-Racism Ally* with Amnesty International Australia by signing up to get the guide[738].

With engineers driving Ubers, help make migrant and refugee skills and qualifications recognition faster, fairer and more affordable so they can fully use their skills and be paid accordingly by joining the *Activate Australia's Skills* campaign[739].

Workplace

Make Diversity, Equity, and Inclusion (DEI) a priority in your workplace by becoming a member of the *Diversity Council of Australia* and use their tools and resources to create and enact a D&I Plan to build inclusive teams [740].

The Australian Human Rights Commission's *Racism. It Stops With Me* campaign has a *Workplace Cultural Diversity Tool* to assess your workplace's relationship to cultural diversity and anti-racism is still on the website[741].

All Together Now offers bespoke anti-racism training tailored to the needs of your workplace and organisation[742].

---

734 https://alltogethernow.org.au/our-work/everyday-racism/

735 http://www.humanrights.gov.au/complaints/make-complaint

736 https://www.refugeecouncil.org.au/platform-change/

737 https://action.refugeecouncil.org.au/refugee_intake_email_your_mp

738 https://action.amnesty.org.au/ally-guide

739 https://activateaustralia.org.au/

740 https://www.dca.org.au/resources/di-planning

741 https://humanrights.gov.au/resource-hub/resources-for-organisations-businesses/workplace-cultural-diversity-tool-overview/workplace-cultural-diversity-tool-start-assessment

742 https://alltogethernow.org.au/training-and-workshops/bespoke-anti-racism-training/

A number of charities offer unconscious bias training for the workplace, including *Diversity Australia*[743].

Schools

The *RacismNoWay* website provides resources to support the delivery of anti-racism education in the classroom, assisting students to engage positively with other peoples and cultures and to understand Australia's cultural diversity and history better[744].

Sport clubs

Play by the Rules provides information, resources, tools and free online training to increase the capacity and capability of administrators, coaches, officials, players, parents and spectators to assist them in preventing and dealing with discrimination, harassment, child safety, inclusion and integrity issues in sport[745].

Buy

Many fantastic social enterprises across Australia enable refugees and migrants, especially women, to engage and build the skills needed to enter the workforce. *Humans like Us* has an online directory of refugee businesses around Australia[746], as does the *Welcome Merchant*[747].

For instance, if you need Hi-Vis jackets, award-winning social enterprise, *Assembled Threads*, pays ethical wages to refugee, asylum seeker and migrant women[748].

UNCHR Australia's *Flavours of Hope* cookbook features ten recipes and stories from refugees[749].

Employ

Issues with recognising overseas qualifications, poor English and discrimination mean that half of skilled migrants are working in occupations they are overqualified for, including 100,000 qualified engineers driving Ubers

[743] https://www.diversityaustralia.com.au/services/unconscious-bias/
[744] https://racismnoway.com.au/
[745] https://www.playbytherules.net.au/
[746] www.humanslikeus.org/support-refugee-businesses
[747] www.welcomemerchant.com
[748] https://assembledthreads.com/
[749] https://www.unrefugees.org.au/get-involved/flavours-of-hope/

or other non-engineering work according to *Engineers Australia*[750]. Furthermore, almost half of all refugees previously working as managers and professionals are, ten years later, still not working in those kinds of jobs in Australia[751].

Settlement Services International found there is potential for a $9 billion benefit in the employment of refugees and other migrants whose skills are thought to be chronically under-utilised[752].

Humans Like Us has a directory of employment services specialising in refugees. You can also join other businesses like ANZ, IKEA and Allianz and join the *Australian Employer Network for Refugee Inclusion*[753]. The *Refugee Council of Australia* also has a directory[754].

Run by *Talent Beyond Barriers*, the *Skilled Refugee Labour Agreement Pilot (SRLAP)* makes it easier for employers in Australia to hire from skilled professionals and tradespeople who have been displaced from their homes and are living in refugee-hosting countries[755].

Or you can hire an intern for 12 weeks with *CareerSeekers* which assists humanitarian entrants with tertiary qualifications to find work in the fields they trained for back in their home countries, as well as, support university students to complete internships in their study breaks each year[756].

Volunteer

You can help refugees improve their English, prepare resumes, provide career support, practice their interview skills, or get their driver's licence by volunteering your skills. *Humans Like Us* have a directory of organisations[757].

---

750 Australian Financial Review, *Migrants are 'driving Ubers' not working skilled jobs*, 27 May 2024 at https://www.afr.com/politics/federal/migrants-are-driving-ubers-not-working-skilled-jobs-20240523-p5jg1c

751 https://www.abc.net.au/news/2025-06-11/refugee-workers-occupational-downgrade-report/105398792

752 Settlement Services International (2024) *Billion Dollar Benefit. The economic impact of unlocking the skills potential of migrants in Australia* at https://www.ssi.org.au/wp-content/uploads/2024/06/DAE_SSI_Skills_Mismatch_Report_19062024_WEB.pdf

753 https://www.humanslikeus.org/refugee-employment-services-directory

754 https://www.refugeecouncil.org.au/employing-refugees/

755 https://www.talentbeyondboundaries.org/blog/introducing-the-australian-skilled-refugee-pilot

756 https://careerseekers.org.au/employers

757 https://www.humanslikeus.org/support-job-seekers

Become a settlement volunteer with your local settlement service with AMES in Victoria, SA or Tasmania[758]; SSI in Sydney and regional NSW[759]; Multicultural Australia in Queensland[760]; Red Cross in WA and ACT[761]; and Melaleuca in the NT[762].

Based on a highly successful Canadian program, the *Community Refugee Integration and Settlement Pilot (CRISP)* enables a Community Supporter Group of 5 or more Australian adults to support a refugee household referred by UNHCR to come to Australia and assist them in their settlement journey. The Group is expected to fundraise around $12,000 to augment the refugees' access to income support and government services. Facilitation and training are provided by the charity Community Refugee Sponsorship Australia [763].

Celebrate

Started by the Howard Government in 1999, wear orange and attend/host an event in *Harmony Week* in March[764] which celebrates Australia's multiculturalism, but don't forget to observe the real reason of this time as the United Nations International Day for the Elimination of Racial Discrimination on the 21st of March - the day the police in Sharpeville, South Africa, opened fire and killed 69 people at a peaceful demonstration against apartheid 'pass laws' in 1960[765]. It has been argued that Harmony Week obscures the reality and lack of action against racism[766].

Celebrate cultural diversity at work by hosting a morning tea or lunch for *A Taste of Harmony* in March-April[767]. It's a great opportunity for staff to bring in, share and tell the story of their culture's cuisine.

Get your family, school, community group or organisation involved in *Refugee Week* each June, including booking a Refugee Ambassador to talk[768].

---

758 https://www.ames.net.au/volunteering/settlement-volunteers

759 https://www.ssi.org.au/

760 https://www.multiculturalaustralia.org.au/volunteer/

761 https://www.redcross.org.au/volunteer/

762 https://melaleuca.org.au/volunteer/

763 https://refugeesponsorship.org.au/

764 https://www.harmony.gov.au/

765 https://www.un.org/en/observances/end-racism-day#:~:text=The%20International%20Day%20for%20the,%22pass%20laws%22%20in%201960.

766 https://www.sbs.com.au/language/english/en/article/is-harmony-day-muzzling-the-uncomfortable-discord-of-racism-in-australia/9ex6dom9t

767 https://www.tasteofharmony.org.au/

768 www.refugeeweek.org.au

Donate

Refugees come to Australia with little. If they are fortunate enough to get public housing, typically it is unfurnished and lacks bedding, appliances, crockery and cutlery. The *Refugee Council of Australia* has a directory of organisations taking donations, as well as being the leading authority on researching and campaigning for humane and lawful treatment of refugees and people seeking asylum.

FAMILY AND DOMESTIC VIOLENCE

'I want to tell people that family violence happens to anybody, no matter how nice your house is, no matter how intelligent you are'

ROSE BATTY AO

As I strode into the Toronto head office of The Body Shop Canada, a huge yellow flower with some petals missing faced me. I was there to meet owner Margot Franssen who, in 1980 as a 27-year-old philosophy graduate with no business experience, signed a franchise agreement to bring the retailer to Canada. Like founders Graeme Wise and Barry Thomas in Australia, she was a pioneer in spreading the company outside of the UK. Her first store in Toronto was just the 7 Body Shop outlet in the world[769].

Over dinner that night with Margot and her partner Quig Tingley, I asked what the flower meant. They told me that they had read a shocking headline in a newspaper that reported 51 per cent of Canadian women had experienced violence from the age of eighteen.

At that time, violence against women was a taboo subject. In the entrepreneurial spirit of The Body Shop founder Anita Roddick, with women making up 90 per cent of customers and staff (and the previous year's campaign against poverty falling flat and actually decreasing sales), they decided to take up violence against women as the campaign for the year.

Margot explained that the flower was a daisy, a symbol of resilience as the flower grows anywhere, even in cracks in the concrete, which had half its petals

[769]Family and domestic violence
https://www.canadianbusiness.com/innovation/bye-bye-body-shop/

remaining plus one, signifying the 51 per cent in the news story. The loss of the daisy's petals also showed the game 'love me, love me not', reflecting the cycle of violence then regretful behaviour from their partner.

They started by printing and handing out bookmarks with the daisy motif and campaign information, offering to donate $1 to the Canadian Women's Foundation for each bookmark returned to a shop in the month of December. There was a huge response and they decided on a full campaign with posters in shop windows the following year. Shop staff were trained in the issue and given information so they could answer questions in advance of victims coming into the shop looking for help.

Despite some threats, the staff felt they were trailblazers and change agents. Women started coming into the shop with posies of daisies to say thank you. With some of the funds raised the company partnered with Outward Bound to pay for additional places for victims on their *women of courage* program, including self-identified staff victims. Company staff were also given the opportunity of 17 paid hours per month to volunteer at local women's refuges.

With the success of the first campaign, the couple continued the cause, picking a different sub-theme each year, such as teen date violence and violence in the home. Customers and sales continued to grow.

Importantly, Margot and Quig were great marketers – they framed the issue in a way that resonated with the media, their customers and the wider Canadian public. For instance, the company's post-Christmas sales message read 'for some women Boxing Day has a very different meaning', with the company donating $1 from each purchase to support the charities working to fight domestic assault[770].

Over the years, Margot became the spokesperson for violence against women and ended up chairing the Canadian Women's Foundation, before being asked by the government to co-chair the National Task Force on Sex Trafficking of Women and Girls in Canada, a prelude to co-founding and co-chairing The Canadian Centre To End Human Trafficking.

In 2002, she was made an Officer of the Order of Canada. She received the Queen's Diamond and Golden Jubilee Award and the United Nations Grand Award for addressing an issue of vital concern to the UN.

Today in Canada, gender-based violence is widely recognised and responses are in place, including the Canadian Government's *It's Time: Canada's*

770 https://o.canada.com/business/the-body-shop-boxing-day

Strategy to Prevent and Address Gender-Based Violence, a whole-of-government approach that includes a range of actions to specifically address violence against Indigenous women and girls. A new Gender-Based Violence Knowledge Centre within Status of Women Canada is the focal point of the Strategy.

Margot ended up living out Anita's belief – 'if you think you're too small to make a difference, you've never been to bed with a mosquito'.

WHAT

Family and domestic violence (FDV) is a major national health and welfare issue that can have lifelong impacts for victim-survivors and perpetrators. It occurs across all ages and backgrounds, but mainly affects women and children. 'Violence' refers to behaviours that cause, or intend to cause, fear or harm. Violence can occur in the form of threat, assault, abuse, neglect or harassment and is often used by a person or people, to intimidate, harm or control others. Not all forms of violence are physical[771].

We now know that FDV is pervasive and rising across Australia with over 1 in 4, or 2.7 million, women having experienced FDV since the age of 15[772].

FDV-related sexual assault victimisation rates have increased by 78 per cent between 2014 and 2023 with more than 1 in 2 or 120,000, police-recorded assaults related to FDV nationally (excluding Victoria) in 2023[773]. However, it is estimated that this only represents 40 per cent of actual levels due to under reporting[774] given that fewer than 1 in 10 women who experience sexual assault in Australia contact police. Even when reported, the New South Wales justice department revealed in 2024 that just 7 per cent of sexual assaults reported to police resulted in a criminal conviction[775].

---

771 Australian Government Australian Institute of Health and Welfare (2024) *Family and Domestic Violence*

772 Australian Bureau of Statistics (2023) *Personal Safety Survey 2021-22* at https://www.abs.gov.au/statistics/people/crime-and-justice/personal-safety-australia/latest-release

773 Australian Government Australian Institute of Health and Welfare (2024) *Family, domestic and sexual violence. FDV reported to police* at https://www.aihw.gov.au/family-domestic-and-sexual-violence/responses-and-outcomes/police/fdv-reported-to-police

774 Equity Economics (2021) *Nowhere to Go. The Benefits Of Providing Long-Term Social Housing To Women That Have Experienced Domestic And Family Violence*, Everybody's Home. p.7

775 https://www.theguardian.com/australia-news/ng-interactive/2025/feb/07/without-punishment-can-a-different-kind-of-justice-offer-something-more-to-sexual-assault-survivors-ntwnfb?CMP=Share_iOSApp_Other

With over half of these women having children in their care, 2.2 million Australians have witnessed partner violence against their mothers when they were children[776]. The impact on these children - emotional and social issues, anxiety and depression, poor educational and employment outcomes, suicide ideation, contact with youth justice and homelessness - lasts a lifetime[777].

FDV has a dramatic effect on education and employment prospects. For young women, by the time they are 27, there is a nearly 15 per cent gap in the rates of university degree attainment between victim-survivors and other women[778]. Additionally, a 2019 study found that women aged 24–30 who had experienced sexual violence were 63 per cent more likely not to have completed Year 12 and 7 per cent less likely to be in full-time employment[779].

A subset of family and domestic violence, *Intimate Partner Violence (IPV)*, refers to any behaviour within an intimate relationship (current or previous) that causes physical, sexual or psychological harm. Intimate relationships involve varying levels of commitment, and include marriages, couples who live together, and dating relationships.

The proportion of Australian men reporting using intimate partner violence has risen to over one in three according to the longitudinal study from the Australian Institute of Family Studies which has been tracking more than 16,000 boys and men since 2013. The research estimates that 120,000 men nationally are starting to use violence for the first time each year [780].

There have been 1,733 female victims of IPV in Australia between July 1989 and December 2024, including 35 women who were murdered by their current

---

[776] Australian Government Australian Institute of Health and Welfare (2023) *Family and Domestic Violence* at https://www.aihw.gov.au/family-domestic-and-sexual-violence/types-of-violence/family-domestic-violence

[777] Equity Economics (2021) *Nowhere to Go. The Benefits Of Providing Long-Term Social Housing To Women That Have Experienced Domestic And Family Violence*, Everybody's Home. p.13

[778] Summers A; Shortridge T; Sobeck K (2025) *The Cost of Domestic Violence to Women's Employment and Education*, University of Technology Sydney, p.9&10 https://doi.org/10.71741/4pyxmbnjaq.28489736.v2

[779]Australian Government Australian Institute of Health and Welfare (2024) *Family, domestic and sexual violence. Economic and financial impacts* at https://www.aihw.gov.au/family-domestic-and-sexual-violence/responses-and-outcomes/economic-financial-impacts#economic

[780] O'Donnell K, Woldegiorgis M, Gasser C, Scurrah K, Andersson C, McKay H, Hegarty K, Seidler Z, & Martin S (2025) *The use of intimate partner violence among Australian men. Insights #3, Chapter 1. Melbourne: Australian Institute of Family Studies* at https://aifs.gov.au/sites/default/files/2025-06/TTM-Insights-3-IPV%20Chapter.pdf

or former partners in 2024. Despite legislative reforms and other measures, the system is failing these women and their children[781].

Tragically, 1 woman is killed every 11 days by an intimate partner on average and 1 in 6 homicides relate to IPV, with 89 per cent of those victims being women[782].

Such is the scale of the issue, male intimate partner violence contributes more to the disease burden for women aged 18 to 44 years than any other well-known risk factor like tobacco use, high cholesterol or use of illicit drugs[783].

Most women stay in violent relationships. About 70 per cent of women in 2021–22 who experienced violence by their current partner while living together had never separated and nearly 1 in 2 of these women did not want to leave their current partner[784].

According to the 2016 Personal Safety Survey, 30 per cent of women suffering physical and/or sexual violence had temporarily left the violent partner on at least one occasion but later returned. Mostly, they returned because they still loved their current partner, wanted to work things out, or the partner had promised to stop the threats and the violence. But for around 1 in 6 of these women, the reason for returning was that they had no money or nowhere else to go. Returning to their violent partner seemed a better choice than being homeless or trying to subsist in poverty[785].

When their relationship with a violent previous partner that they lived with has ended, it is estimated that about 2 in 3, or 867,000, women move away from their home. Of those that moved away, 7 in 10, or 597,000, left property or assets behind.

---

[781] Commonwealth of Australia (2025) *Inquiry into family violence orders*, House of Representatives Standing Committee on Social Policy and Legal Affairs, Canberra, February 2025, ISBN 978-1-76092-673-1

[782] Australian Government Australian Institute of Health and Welfare (2024) *Domestic homicide* at https://www.aihw.gov.au/family-domestic-and-sexual-violence/responses-and-outcomes/domestic-homicide#:~:text=One%20woman%20was%20killed%20every,(ADFVDRN%20and%20ANROWS%202022).

[783] Webster, K 2016, *A preventable burden: Measuring and addressing the prevalence and health impacts of intimate partner violence in Australian women*, ANROWS, Sydney

[784] Australian Bureau of Statistics (2023) *Partner Violence* at https://www.abs.gov.au/statistics/people/crime-and-justice/partner-violence/2021-22

[785] Summers A (2022) *The Choice: Violence or Poverty*, University of Technology Sydney https://doi.org/10.26195/3s1r-4977 at https://www.violenceorpoverty.com/the-choice

But the violence doesn't necessarily end when the woman leaves. For nearly 4 in 10 of the single mothers who had experienced violence more than once while living with their most recently violent previous partner, the violence increased after the final separation[786].

Although 60 per cent of the single mothers who had experienced partner violence were in employment, for many their earnings were insufficient to support themselves and their children and they experienced considerable financial stress. Those on benefits receive the Parenting Payment Single (PPS) until their youngest child turns eight, when they are forced to go onto the lower JobSeeker, the second-lowest unemployment benefit in the OECD.

So, despite government action on reducing IPV, government policy, through payments policy and other welfare measures, ensures that as many as half the women who choose to leave will end up in poverty[787].

Women are also most frequently the victims of Adolescent Family Violence (AFV) by their child or young person, including physical, emotional, financial, and sexual abuse. It includes a range of behaviours used to control, coerce and threaten family members. In a 2022 national online survey of 5,000 people aged 16–20, 1 in 5 reported that they had used a form of violence against a family member. About one in seven used verbal abuse, 1 in 10 physical violence and 1 in 2 emotional/psychological abuse[788].

WHY

Family and domestic violence (FDV) can affect any individual, family or community in Australia. The majority of people who experience these forms of violence are women, and another Theme of this book - gender inequality - is considered to be an underlying driver of FDV[789], along with other Themes in this book – child abuse, mental health, poverty and disadvantage, racism and discrimination, as well as violent pornography and drug and alcohol abuse. In

---

786 Summers A; Shortridge T; Sobeck K (2025) *The Cost of Domestic Violence to Women's Employment and Education*, University of Technology Sydney, p.11

787 Summers A (2022) *The Choice: Violence or Poverty*, University of Technology Sydney https://doi.org/10.26195/3s1r-4977 p.12

788 Fitz-Gibbon K, Meyer S, Boxall H, Maher J & Roberts S (2022) *Adolescent family violence in Australia: A national study of prevalence, history of childhood victimisation and impacts*, Research report, 15/2022, ANROWS at https://www.anrows.org.au/publication/adolescent-family-violence-in-australia-a-national-study-of-prevalence-history-of-childhood-victimisation-and-impacts/

789 Australian Government Australian Institute of Health and Welfare (2024) *Family, domestic and sexual violence. Factors associated with FDV* at https://www.aihw.gov.au/family-domestic-and-sexual-violence/understanding-fdsv/factors-associated-with-fdsv

turn, FDV directly impacts other Themes – homelessness, poverty and disadvantage, mental health and child abuse.

Furthermore, with so many children witnessing FDV, 'exposure to violence and abuse in childhood and adolescence is a risk-factor for developing anti-feminist attitudes and for perpetuating violence'[790]. In this way, FDV is normalised behaviour that is transmitted from one generation to the next.

Australia is a signatory to the 1993 UN *Declaration on the Elimination of Violence against Women* which covers physical, sexual and psychological violence, as well as violence both at home and elsewhere in society. It defines violence against women as 'any act of gender-based violence that results in, or is likely to result in, physical, sexual or psychological harm or suffering to women, including threats of such acts, coercion or arbitrary deprivation of liberty, whether occurring in public or in private life.'

According to the Declaration, violence against women is rooted in the historically unequal power relations between women and men, and emphasises that violence against women is 'one of the crucial social mechanisms by which women are forced into a subordinate position compared with men'.

Most female homicide victims have suffered a history of abuse. Between 1 July 2010 and 30 June 2018, over 3 in 4 cases involved a male killing a current or former female partner, with the vast majority of those male offenders identified as primary abusers of the woman they killed[791].

Australia's National Research Organisation for Women's Safety (ANROWS) lists 10 'lethality/high risk factors' in its national risk assessment principles: a history of family violence, actual or pending separation, sexual violence, non-lethal strangulation/choking, stalking, threats to kill, access to and use of weapons, escalation in frequency and/or severity, coercive control, and pregnancy and new birth.

Of the 212 male primary domestic violence abusers who killed their current or former female partner:

- 82 per cent exhibited emotionally and psychologically abusive behaviours against the female partners they killed – behaviours

---

[790] Hill J (2025) *Losing It. Can We Stop Violence Against Women and Children*, Quarterly Essay , Issue 97, p.32

[791] Australian Domestic and Family Violence Death Review Network (2022) *Australian Domestic And Family Violence Death Review Network Data Report. Intimate partner violence homicides 2010–2018*, Australia's National Research Organisation for Women's Safety Limited (ANROWS)

employed to frighten, belittle, humiliate, unsettle and undermine the victim's sense of self-worth.

- 63 per cent had perpetrated social abuse, which involves isolating the victim from support networks and controlling her movements.
- 42 per cent had stalked the woman they killed.
- 27 per cent used economically or financially abusive tactics to diminish the victim's ability to support themselves and force them to depend on the abuser financially.

With 40 per cent of cases involving persistent and disorderly offenders, whose violence was highly visible across police, child protection and health services, but police practices varying across States and Territories, there are calls for more consistent policing[792].

Historically, FDV was understood as physical and/or sexual violence, with a focus on single or episodic acts of violence. It is now seen to cover a wider range of behaviours and harms, including emotional abuse, harassment, stalking and controlling behaviours, with coercive control, used by a 3rd of perpetrators, now understood as a commonly occurring foundation for family and domestic violence[793].

Occurring repeatedly, subtly and sometimes over a long period of time, coercive control is a pattern of abusive and manipulative behaviours used by one person to dominate another and can involve: intimidation (frighten a person with threats); monitoring (watch, check in with, or keep a record of someone's movements and activities); regulating (control someone with rules or standards); isolating (keep someone apart from their family and friends); humiliating (make someone feel ashamed, embarrassed or small); manipulating (make a plan to control someone to get something the perpetrator wants); punishing (treat someone badly or cause them pain or suffering because they have acted a certain way, or broken a rule the perpetrator made); and frightening (stop someone from doing something by making them afraid)[794].

Analysis undertaken by the NSW Domestic Violence Death Review Team identified that, among 112 incidents of intimate partner homicide that occurred

---

[792] https://www.theguardian.com/law/2025/apr/26/domestic-violence-does-australia-need-a-national-police-strategy-ntwnfb?CMP=Share_iOSApp_Other

[793] ANROWS (Australia's National Research Organisation for Women's Safety) (2021) '*Defining and responding to coercive control: Policy brief- external site opens in new window*', *ANROWS Insights,* 01/2021

[794] Government of Western Australia (2022) *Legislative Responses to Coercive Control in Western Australia. Fact Sheet*

between June 2000 and July 2019, coercive controlling behaviour was a feature of the relationship between couples involved in all but one case.

In a 2021 study of 1,023 Australian women who had recently experienced coercive control by their current or former partner, the most frequently reported behaviours were jealousy and suspicion of friends, constant insults, monitoring of movements and financial abuse. Over half of the respondents also reported experiencing physical forms of abuse, including severe forms such as non-fatal strangulation. Nearly 1 in 3 of these women also reported experiencing sexual violence during the survey period[795].

Awareness of coercive control has increased significantly in Australia with regular harrowing media reports, such as the murder of Hannah Clarke and her 3 children in February 2020 by her former partner. Her former partner had attempted to regulate every aspect of her life, including what she wore and ate, her access to medical care and her social media accounts, and had been stalking her online[796].

In most Australian States and Territories, FDV has not been an offence in itself. Rather, FDV is recorded using existing criminal offences, such as assault, indecent assault, rape, sexual assault, attempted murder, stalking or intent to do grievous bodily harm.

Criminalising coercive control would involve moving from an incident-based approach to an approach that criminalises ongoing abusive behaviour[797]. Due to the considerable advocacy of victims, such as by Rosie Batty AO after tragic murder of her son, Luke, by her former partner, all State governments now have, or are planning to pass, legislation to create a new criminal offence for coercive control.

In October 2022, the Australian, State and Territory governments released the second *National Plan to End Violence against Women and Children 2022–2032* as the overarching national policy framework that addresses the social, cultural, political and economic factors that drive gendered violence to end

---

[795] Boxall H & Morgan A (2021) *Experiences of coercive control among Australian women*. Statistical Bulletin no. 30. Canberra: Australian Institute of Criminology. https://doi.org/10.52922/sb78108

[796] King M (2020) *Intimate terrorism: Why the murders of Hannah, Aaliyah, Laianah and Trey must spark change*, Sydney Morning Herald, 20 November. https://www.smh.com.au/lifestyle/life-andrelationships/intimate-terrorism-why-the-murders-of-hannah-aaliyah-laianah-and-trey-must-sparkchange-20200910-p55ubz.html

[797] ANROWS (Australia's National Research Organisation for Women's Safety) (2021) *Defining and responding to coercive control: Policy brief*- ***external site opens in new window' ANROWS*** *Insights,* 01/2021

violence against women and children, after the first Plan failed to achieve a significant and sustained reduction in violence by 2022.

Despite governmental commitment to this Plan, in August 2024, the first yearly report pointed out that 'frontline and crisis services need to be better and more sustainably resourced' and that the 'Department of Social Services should also design funding models that provide more certainty through longer funding periods.' The report also highlighted the need 'to offer more support options for men who are concerned about their behaviour and increase the capacity of related service sectors to respond to men's needs'[798].

There is a clear link between violence towards women and attitudes of disrespect and gender inequality. The United Nations has concluded that 'violence against women and girls is both a cause and a consequence of gender inequality'[799]. Similarly, *Our Watch* notes that 'gender inequality sets the underlying context for violence against women'[800] and 'research shows there are strong links between socially dominant forms and patterns of masculinity, men's sexist attitudes and behaviours, and men's perpetration of violence against women'[801].

Embodied in Sustainable Development Goal 5, gender equality is not only a fundamental human right, but a necessary foundation for a peaceful, prosperous and sustainable world[802].

With a driver of violence as unequal power between women and men, where there are inequalities of power and resources between women and men, violence is more likely to occur[803]. The Federal government's *2024 Working for Women: A Strategy for Gender Equality* outlines how harmful gender attitudes and stereotypes are the foundation of gender inequality[804].

---

[798] Commonwealth of Australia (2024) *Yearly Report to Parliament*, August 2024, Domestic, Family and Sexual Violence Commission at https://www.aph.gov.au/Parliamentary_Business/Tabled_Documents/7093

[799] https://www.undp.org/blog/violence-against-women-cause-and-consequence-inequality#:~:text=The%20lack%20of%20women's%20empowerment,a%20consequence%20of%20gender%20inequality.

[800] https://action.ourwatch.org.au/what-is-prevention/the-link-between-gender-inequality-and-violence-against-women/

[801] Our Watch (2021) *Change the Story. A shared framework for the primary prevention of violence against women in Australia (second edition)*, p.27

[802] https://www.un.org/sustainabledevelopment/gender-equality/

[803] https://www.vicsport.com.au/blog/1312/sports-clubs-and-organisations-can-battle-violence-against-women

[804] Commonwealth of Australia (2024) *Working for Women. A Strategy for Gender Equality*, Department of the Prime Minister and Cabinet, Canberra

These attitudes are unconscious, yet firmly entrenched, among many Australian adults and children. Gender inequality is present when unequal value is afforded to women and men and there is an unequal distribution of power, resources and opportunity between them[805].

The National Plan and Our Watch's *Change the Story*[806] recognise that the challenge is to tackle gender inequality, discrimination and entrenched social norms across the 4 levels of: 1) individual and relationship (individual knowledge, attitudes, behaviours, beliefs as well as the influences from a person's closest social circle – peers, partner and family members); 2) organisation and community; 3) systems, institutions; and 4) societal.

However, 45 prominent feminists criticised the second National Plan for its noble sentiments and platitudes, without learning the lessons of why the first Plan failed or a clear strategy with targets[807]. They made it clear that the effects of other Themes in this book - poverty and disadvantage, mental illness, child maltreatment and social isolation, along with violent pornography and drug and alcohol abuse – also contribute to FDV, but are ignored in the second National Plan, relying instead on long-term gender equality behaviour change.

Professor Michael Slater and Jess Hill's White Paper on 'Rethinking Primary Prevention' followed, calling for a fundamental reorientation of the approach from universal, population-level strategies that aim to improve gender equality over the long-term, to other strategies and interventions that could be incorporated into a multi-faceted, multi-level approach to primary prevention that increase women's and children's safety while the longer-term goal of gender equality is pursued[808].

After angry Australians demonstrated across the country over the ongoing killing of women by their partners, Prime Minister Albanese declared that Australia faced a 'national crisis' of violence against women. National Cabinet met and, after a Rapid Review of Prevention Approaches with an expert group, substantial reforms were announced, including a review of how alcohol laws

---

805 Australian Government Department of Social Services (2023) *Theory of Change 2022–2032 Under the National Plan to End Violence against Women and Children 2022–2032* at https://www.dss.gov.au/sites/default/files/documents/08_2023/np-theory-change.pdf

806 Our Watch (2021) *Change the Story. A shared framework for the primary prevention of violence against women in Australia (second edition)*

807 https://womensagenda.com.au/latest/grace-tame-brittany-higgins-anne-summers-among-prominent-women-concerned-about-the-draft-plan-to-end-violence-against-women-and-children/

808 Hill J & Slater M (2024) *Rethinking Primary Prevention* at https://jesshill.substack.com/p/rethinking-primary-prevention

affect FDV victims, with an additional $800m in Commonwealth government funding[809].

Despite recent improvements to Federal family law by the Albanese government to assist courts and parents to resolve parenting disputes safely and efficiently with a clear focus on the best interests of the children involved, including the removal of the presumption of equal shared parental responsibility that has allowed some parents to be coerced into agreeing to equal time arrangements that are unsafe, drawn-out family law proceedings expose victim-survivors and children to an extended period of elevated FDV risk, including threats of physical violence to women and children, and financial and systems abuse. Victim-survivors are told '...you will lose your child. I'm going to bankrupt you. I'll get every cent out of you.' Delays in finalising proceedings only extend the FDV victim-survivors' trauma. In addition, high legal costs can mean victim-survivors do not commence proceedings when they should, do not respond to proceedings brought by their perpetrators, or settle and agree to unsafe parenting arrangements simply because they cannot afford to continue proceedings[810].

A court can grant a family violence intervention order (FIVO) as a legally enforceable document that aims to provide a person, their children and their property with protection. The order served on the perpetrator is designed to stop the behaviour; not contact or communicate with the protected person, or get someone else to do it for them; not go to or stay near the protected person, or get someone else to do it for them.

A parliamentary inquiry into FIVOs in 2025 recommended that the Australian government must act swiftly to coordinate rules for protection orders across States and Territories, finding that the wide variation across the country is a barrier to justice for victim survivors. The inquiry also called for children and young people to be able to apply for their own FIVOs, rather than having to rely on a 3rd party like a parent or a police officer[811].

---

[809] https://www.pmc.gov.au/resources/unlocking-prevention-potential/national-emergency-and-ongoing-national-priority

[810] Standing Committee on Social Policy and Legal Affairs (2025) *Inquiry into family violence orders*, Chapter 3 - The family law system — barriers to safety and fairness for victim-survivors, Canberra at https://www.aph.gov.au/Parliamentary_Business/Committees/House/Social_Policy_and_Legal_Affairs/Familyviolenceorders/Inquiry_into_family_violence_orders/Chapter_3_-_The_family_law_system__barriers_to_safety_and_fairness_for_victim-survivors

[811] Commonwealth of Australia (2025) *Inquiry into family violence orders*, House of Representatives Standing Committee on Social Policy and Legal Affairs, Canberra, February 2025, ISBN 978-1-76092-673-1

Whilst perpetrators who breach an order can be charged with a criminal offence, just in Victoria, a total of 11,919, or 1 in 6, breach their order, an increase of 32 per cent in the last five years[812]. In order to address the breaches, Western Australia is the first government to impose electronic monitoring on repeat and high-risk family violence perpetrators who are on bail or supervised in the community.

In another Australian first, the NSW government's *DV Notify* alerts survivors of domestic and family violence when an alleged perpetrator is released from custody. Real-time text and email updates, from the time a violent offender is arrested through to their final sentencing, will also be available to users.

With community legal centres supporting victim survivors to escape violence, overwhelmed and having to turn people away, the recent Australian Government announcement of the $3.9 billion *National Access to Justice Partnership* funding has provided additional legal assistance[813].

In the meantime, some communities are taking control.

In April 2024, people in Ballarat flooded the streets in a powerful protest for change following the disappearance and alleged murder of 51-year-old Samantha Murphy, the death of mother Rebecca Young in a suspected murder-suicide by her partner, and the murder of Hannah McGuire by her ex-boyfriend. Their deaths sent shock waves through the whole community and galvanised the city to call for action on gendered violence. People of all ages marched together to express grief, outrage, and disbelief. Many held the grief of other historic tragedies and injustices as they marched, with ribbons tied to the fences of institutions close by.

In the weeks after, the principals of 3 of the regional Victorian city's high schools brought their students together for a joint forum. Young women said they avoided going for a run at night. Others spoke of fear becoming part of their daily life. Young men spoke about their desire to be more vulnerable and the constraints of traditional gender roles. All of them said they wanted things to change.

With a relative who experienced family violence, Stephan Fields, the principal of Ballarat High School, spent the next year co-designing a response. He found that although young people often receive the right messages in the classroom,

---

812 https://www.vic.gov.au/ending-family-violence-annual-report-2021/family-violence-outcomes-framework-measures/domain-3-perpetrators/perpetrators-stop-all-forms-of-family-violence-behaviour

813 https://www.pm.gov.au/media/national-access-justice-partnership

they were undermined by the attitudes and behaviours they encounter elsewhere – including at home, in sports clubs and among their peers. Sport, in particular, stood out as 'woven into the culture of Ballarat', with high participation among children under 14 and adults in their 30s. But despite efforts to promote inclusion, 'misogyny, homophobia and excusing of violence on and off the field' remains prevalent.

In September 2025, the co-design process led to the launch of the Victorian government backed Respect Ballarat – an Australian-first trial of a saturation model to prevent gender-based violence, involving flooding the community with multiple programs, campaigns, education and support services to shift the attitudes and behaviours that drive violence. In the initial stages, efforts will focus on workplaces, community sports clubs, schools, and early childhood, prenatal, and neonatal settings[814].

ACT

Our Watch notes that 'no single person or organisation can bring about an end to violence. A collective, national effort is needed to address the drivers of violence against women across all areas of society. Individuals, families, communities, organisations and systems (like the legal system) all play a role[815].

We can start by challenging the beliefs that justify, excuse, trivialise or downplay violence against women, or shift blame from perpetrators to victims.

Workplace

Employers have a responsibility to provide a safe and supportive workplace for employees experiencing FDV. This includes providing paid leave, flexible work arrangements, and confidentiality. All employees can access 10 days of paid family and domestic violence leave each year, including full-time, part-time and casual employees[816].

White Ribbon Australia provides training and workplace accreditation to ensure your workplace prevents violence against women[817]. Where a colleague has disclosed that they are experiencing FDV, *White Ribbon* has advice on

814 https://www.theguardian.com/society/2025/sep/18/deaths-three-women-ballarat-australian-first-trial-gender-based-violence-ntwnfb
815 https://www.ourwatch.org.au/how-to-prevent-violence-against-women
816 https://www.fairwork.gov.au/leave/family-and-domestic-violence-leave#family-domestic-violence
817 https://whiteribbon.org.au/services/

support[818], as well as resources for men to show up for women at work, actively help to promote gender equality and be an ally to colleagues who might be experiencing domestic violence[819].

Fair Work has a small business employer guide to family and domestic violence[820] and *Safe Work Australia* has an information sheet that provides guidance for businesses about duties under work health and safety laws and how to manage the risks of family and domestic violence at the workplace[821].

Donate

Each State and Territory has government funded, area-based family and child services provided by local not-for-profit organisations to respond to FDV. To find those in your area for donations or volunteering, type in 'FDV' into *askizzy.org.au*.

Nationally, *Women's Community Shelters* recognises that women need a range of support services, not just help finding appropriate housing, including access to counselling, health care, assistance to navigate government bureaucracy, legal help, further education, and employment to re-establish control over their lives. *Women's Community Shelters* offer a tripartite funding model in which government, philanthropy, business and community all work to provide funding to establish and operate shelters[822].

Nationally, *Australia's National Research Organisation for Women's Safety (ANROWS)* is a world-leading independent, not-for-profit research organisation established to produce evidence to support the reduction of violence against women and children.

The *Australian Childhood Foundation* is a leader in trauma-informed therapeutic services for children suffering abuse and neglect due to FDV[823].

Participate

November is *White Ribbon* month. Take part and buy a white ribbon[824].

---

818 https://whiteribbon.org.au/wp-content/uploads/2023/06/WR_WhatToDoWHenSomeone_FactSheet-v1.pdf

819 https://whiteribbon.org.au/education-hub/#support-guide

820 https://www.fairwork.gov.au/sites/default/files/migration/1414/employer-guide-to-family-and-domestic-violence.pdf

821 https://www.safeworkaustralia.gov.au/sites/default/files/2021-01/family_and_domestic_violence_information_sheet.pdf

822 https://www.womenscommunityshelters.org.au/what-we-do/

823 https://www.childhood.org.au/our-work/

824 https://whiteribbon.org.au/

Buy

Examples of certified social enterprises that specifically empower women victims of FDV are *Two Good Co*[825] (food and products), *Mettle Gifts*[826] (hampers, giftboxes & event goodie bags) and *Raven Collective* (gift boxes).

Participate

Take part in UN Women's *16 Days of Activism against Gender-Based Violence*, an annual international campaign that kicks off on 25 November, the International Day for the Elimination of Violence against Women, and runs until 10 December, Human Rights Day[827].

Helplines

For anyone who needs help, FDV help lines are:

1800 RESPECT	1800 737 732	24-hour national sexual assault, family and domestic violence counselling line for any Australian who has experienced, or is at risk of, family and domestic violence and/or sexual assault
Men's Line Australia	1300 789 978	24/7 telephone and online support for men and boys who are dealing with family and relationship difficulties
Men's Referral Service	1300 766 491	This service from *No to Violence* offers assistance, information and counselling to help men who use family violence
Rainbow Sexual, Domestic and Family Violence Helpline	1800 497 212	For anyone from the LGBTIQ+ community whose life has been impacted by sexual domestic and/or family violence
National Disability Abuse and Neglect Hotline	1800 880 053	A free and confidential service for reporting abuse and neglect of people with disability. Anyone can contact the Hotline, including family members, friends, service providers or a person with disability

825 https://twogood.com.au/

826 https://www.mettlegifts.com/

827 https://unwomen.org.au/our-work/focus-area/ending-violence/unite-to-end-violence-against-women/

YOUTH JUSTICE

'Tragically, by not addressing their human rights early on, and instead taking a punitive approach to their offending, we are essentially criminalising some of the most vulnerable children in Australia.'

ANNE HOLLONDS, NATIONAL CHILDREN'S COMMISSIONER

WHAT

As the *Justice Reform Initiative* points out, 'currently we are unnecessarily incarcerating thousands of children each year – often on remand, for short, harmful, disruptive periods of time. Children are being 'managed' in prisons, rather than receiving support, care, programs, education and opportunities in the community'[828].

Unfortunately, youth crime has long been a media and political football, irrespective of the actual rate of youth offending at the time. The fear of youth crime is stoked by the right-wing media and political parties compete to be seen as the toughest on crime with an arms race of new police numbers and criminal laws announced before an election.

The fact is, however, that youth crime is declining in Australia, with the rate of youth offenders is at its lowest in 15 years.

According to the Australian Institute of Health and Welfare (AIHW), over the 5 years from 2019-20 to 2023-24, the number of young people (aged 10-17)

---

[828] Youth justice
Justice Reform Initiative (2024) *Children, Youth Justice & Alternatives To Incarceration In Australia* at
https://assets.nationbuilder.com/justicereforminitiative/pages/441/attachments/original/1720409799/JRI_YOUTH_JUSTICE_JUNE_2024.pdf?1720409799

under supervision (community-based or detention) on an average day fell from 5,158 to 4,227, a drop of 18 per cent. The rate dropped from 16 to 12 per 10,000 young people.

But youth crime is changing.

Whilst fewer young people are offending, the number and seriousness of crimes by repeat youth offenders is increasing across the country. A relatively small group of repeat offenders is responsible for a large share of violent incidents with backgrounds in child protection, trauma, homelessness, family violence and school disengagement. With the other Themes in this book contributing, when this high-risk cohort grows even slightly, violent crime trends appear to spike, even while overall youth crime is stable or falling.

For instance, young people from the lowest socioeconomic areas are about 7 times as likely as those from the highest socioeconomic areas to be under supervision[829].

Of the 1,422 permanently funded beds in Australia's 17 youth detention centres, the average number of children in prison each night around Australia over the course of the year was 828 in 2023-23. Over 4 in 5 of these were unsentenced[830]. Meanwhile, the annual cost per child in detention has more than doubled in the last 10 years and averages at over $1 million. Across Australia, nearly a billion dollars is spent each year on locking up children.

More and more, youth detention is a revolving door with high rates of youth recidivism.

Of the young people aged 10–17 who were under youth justice supervision at some time between 2000–01 and 2021–22, over 4 in 10 returned to sentenced supervision before turning 18. Of young people aged 10–16 in 2020–21 released from sentenced community-based supervision, 40 per cent returned to sentenced supervision within 6 months, and 57 per cent within 12 months. Of those released from sentenced detention, 66 per cent returned within 6 months, and 85 per cent within 12 months[831].

---

829 Australian Institute of Health and Welfare (2024) *Youth Justice* at https://www.aihw.gov.au/reports/australias-welfare/youth-justice

830 Justice Reform Initiative (2023) *Children's Imprisonment in Australia 2023. An Overview of Youth Detention*, p.*9* at https://assets.nationbuilder.com/justicereforminitiative/pages/410/attachments/original/1713851456/JRI_Children_Imprisonment_Overview_April24.pdf?1713851456

831 Australian Institute of Health and Welfare (2023) *Young people returning to sentenced youth justice supervision 2021–22* at https://www.aihw.gov.au/reports/youth-justice/young-people-returning-to-sentenced-supervision/summary

In Victoria, young people aged 10 to 14 years have the highest reoffending rates of all ages in the criminal justice system, with more than 80 per cent reoffending at some time, and more than 60 per cent reoffending with an offence against the person[832].

Of young people aged between 10 to 17 years old in NSW in 2019, nearly 2 in 3 reoffended after 12 months and nearly half reoffended for convicted offenders who received a penalty order other than prison[833].

The percentage of young people who reoffended within twelve months of being released from Queensland youth detention centres was between 84 and 96 per cent in 2023[834].

Under the Crimes Act 1914, the minimum age of criminal responsibility for Commonwealth offences is 10 years of age. Section 4M of the Crimes Act provides that a child under 10 years old cannot be liable for an offence against a law of the Commonwealth. However, the principle of *doli incapax* operates throughout Australia, which assumes that children aged 10 to 14 are 'criminally incapable' unless proven otherwise.

Australia's minimum age of criminal responsibility is one of the lowest among OECD member countries. In 2019, the *United Nations Committee on the Rights of the Child* recommended that all countries increase the minimum age of criminal responsibility to at least 14 years of age. The Committee specifically urged the Australian Government to raise the minimum age of criminal responsibility to an internationally accepted level and make it conform with the upper age of 14 at which *doli incapax* applies[835].

The *Law Council of Australia* states that 'the current low minimum age of criminal responsibility is out of step with international human rights standards and the most recent medical evidence on child cognitive development. It also ignores the large body of social research highlighting the harmful effects of early contact with the criminal justice system, including entrenchment and

---

[832] State of Victoria (2016) *Reoffending by children and young people in Victoria*, Sentencing Advisory Council, Melbourne at https://www.sentencingcouncil.vic.gov.au/sites/default/files/2019-08/Reoffending_by_Children_and_Young_People_in_Victoria.pdf

[833] YMCA (2022) *An Investigation into NSW State Programs in Reducing Youth Crime*

[834] https://www.qfcc.qld.gov.au/news-and-media/young-people-reveal-solutions-reduce-reoffending#:~:text=The%20percentage%20of%20young%20people,about%20the%20rehabilitative%20prospects%20of

[835] Australian Human Rights Commission (2021) *The Minimum Age of Criminal Responsibility* at https://humanrights.gov.au/sites/default/files/2020-10/australias_minimum_age_of_criminal_responsibility_-_australias_third_upr_2021.pdf

recidivism, and a correlation with being less likely to complete education or find employment. Further, it ignores the social determinants that lead to certain cohorts, such as First Nations children, children in out-of-home care, and children with significant health issues, being disproportionately represented in the criminal justice system'[836].

In response, in 2019, the *Council of Attorneys-General* established the *Age of Criminal Responsibility Working Group* to examine raising the age. A draft report produced by the Group in 2020 found that 'most children under youth justice supervision come from backgrounds that are disadvantaged. These children have often experienced violence, abuse, disability, homelessness and drug or alcohol misuse. They may have witnessed family members who are part of the criminal justice system, thereby normalising their own potentially criminal behaviour'[837].

The evidence regarding the psychological, cognitive and neurological development of children indicates that a child under the age of 14 years is unlikely to understand the impact of their actions or to have the required maturity for criminal responsibility. Detention may not be an effective deterrent for a child because of their immature brain development and cognitive functions, as well as a lack of capacity to understand the consequences of their actions[838].

Indeed, early contact with the justice system is a key predictor of recidivism with 85 per cent of young people who were supervised between the ages of 10 and 14 years returned to, or continued under, supervision when they were aged 15 to 17 years.

The report recommended that the minimum age of criminal responsibility should be raised to 14 years of age, without exception. However, this report was not agreed by all jurisdictions at the officer level and so not formally considered by the Council.

Despite this, there has been some movement by governments. The ACT has raised the age to 14 and the Victorian Government to 12. The Tasmanian

---

[836] Law Council of Australia (2020) Submission to the Council of Attorneys General – Age of Criminal Responsibility Working Group Review at https://lawcouncil.au/publicassets/c74ddce5-375c-ea11-9404-005056be13b5/3772%20-%20CAG%20Review%20of%20age%20of%20criminal%20responsibility.pdf

[837] Council of Attorneys-General (2020) *DRAFT Final Report 2020,* Age of Criminal Responsibility Working Group

[838] Council of Attorneys-General Age of Criminal Responsibility Working Group (2020) *Draft Final Report 2020* at https://www.ag.gov.au/sites/default/files/2022-12/draft-report-2020-age-of-criminal-responsibility.DOCX

government has committed to raising the age to 14 with no exceptions, alongside raising the minimum age of detention to 16 by 2029.

Unfortunately, the Liberal governments in the Northern Territory and Queensland have returned the age for incarceration back to 10 years old, the latter on the back of their 'adult crime, adult time' policy and admitting that their policy violates human rights and directly discriminates against children by limiting their protection from cruel, inhumane and degrading treatment.

WHY

There is a direct correlation between criminality and entrenched social and economic disadvantage. The major risk factors for youth criminality include other Themes in this book - poverty and disadvantage, homelessness, child abuse, mental illness, disability inclusion (especially intellectual impairment) and having one or more parents with a criminal record.

As the *Australian and New Zealand Children's Commissioners, Guardians and Advocates* note 'children in the justice system have fragmented education experiences, marked by periods of exclusion and expulsion, resulting in poor educational outcomes. They have precarious living arrangements including homelessness and/or placements in out-of-home care. They have often experienced drug and alcohol related addiction, struggle with complex, unresolved trauma, and live with mental illness and/or disabilities. Children in the justice system have higher rates of speech, language and communication disorders, attention deficit hyperactivity disorder, autism spectrum disorders, foetal alcohol spectrum disorder and acquired/traumatic brain injury'[839].

Studies have shown that the younger the child is when first having contact with the justice system, the more likely they are to go on to reoffend. This suggests that criminalising the behaviour of young children results in their entrenchment in the justice system.

Led by regular headlines in the right-wing media, radio shows and social media sensationalising crimes committed by children and young people, in reality, both sides of government have passed policies to be 'tough on crime', including to limit bail for young offenders, causing the population of children in detention to soar.

---

[839] Commonwealth of Australia (2025) *Australia's youth justice and incarceration system*, The Senate, Legal and Constitutional Affairs References Committee, p.11 re Australian and New Zealand Children's Commissioners, Guardians and Advocates (ANZCCGA*), Submission 74*, p. 1

In 2023, the Queensland government announced 'even tougher' responses to youth offending, including longer sentences and the construction of two new youth detention centres, in response to the stabbing death of Brisbane woman Emma Lovell.

In response, the head of the *Queensland Family and Child Commission* said he is 'deeply concerned' at public sentiment calling for more punitive responses to youth crime in the face of clear evidence that 'tough' approaches don't work. Professor Ross Homel, a criminologist at Griffith University, echoed that the detention of young people 'makes the community less safe. Detention centres are the worst possible places for fixing our broken kids' [840].

In 2024, NSW Labor introduced trial reforms to make it harder for 14 to 18 year-olds charged with serious break-and-enter and motor vehicle theft offences while on bail to get bail again.

Then the Victorian government buckled to media pressure in 2025, with the Labor government revoking a clause in the Bail Act that remand be a last resort for children charged with a crime, and elevating community safety as the overriding principle for bail decision-making. With 'adult time for violent crime', the Premier introduced the 'toughest bail laws in Australia' with life sentences for children and removing detention as a last resort, admitting that the changes will lock up more children[841].

It's now the turn of the South Australian Labor government, which unveiled plans to 'treat teens like bikies', as termed by the Adelaide Advertiser's front page.

In the view of the *Human Rights Commission*, 'the treatment of children in the criminal justice system, some as young as 10 years old, is one of the most urgent human rights issues facing Australia today. Numerous inquiries and reviews, including Royal Commissions and UN Committees, have highlighted serious breaches of rights and systemic problems with our child justice and related systems over many years. However, Australia continually fails to implement evidence-based reforms to our child justice systems which would reduce offending behaviour and make our communities safer'[842].

---

840 https://www.theguardian.com/australia-news/2023/jan/25/australians-urged-to-ditch-tough-on-mindset-for-youth-justice-as-it-does-not-work

841 https://www.theage.com.au/politics/victoria/why-jacinta-allan-is-pushing-for-laws-that-will-lock-up-more-kids-20250313-p5ljgo.html

842 Australian Human Rights Commission (2024) *'Help way earlier!': How Australia can transform child justice to improve safety and wellbeing*, Sydney, p8

As the *Law Council of Australia* notes, 'these harsh policies do not make our communities safer—especially in the long run. The detention and institutionalisation of children in their formative years is a proven key factor in recidivism rates. It needs to be clearly understood and consistently communicated that policies of remanding and imprisoning children—popular as they may be during perceived youth crime waves—have been comprehensively debunked as effective community safety solutions'[843].

People who commit or are alleged to have committed a crime when aged 10–17 are dealt with under each State and Territory government's youth justice system. Young people may be supervised, such as in the community or in a corrections facility, when they are awaiting the outcome of their court matter or sentencing, or they may be sentenced to supervision in the community or a corrections facility after being proven guilty in court.

Each State and Territory government provides a range of services under their youth justice departments that endeavour to balance: holding young people accountable for their actions; encouraging young people to reintegrate into the community; giving young people skills to create a better future; and promoting community safety.

These services comprise:

Children's courts and other specialist courts, such as the drug and alcohol treatment court in Victoria. Sentencing includes community service, probation, and participation in diversion or rehabilitation programs, with detention used as a last resort.

Youth justice centres that accommodate young people who have been remanded in custody or sentenced for a criminal offence and include an education and training facility.

Youth conferences that include the offender and the victim to make decisions and agree on an outcome plan about how the offender can make up for their offence, for example, community service, attend a rehabilitation program or write an apology to the victim.

Rehabilitation and diversion programs run by the court or charities that reduce reoffending and support rehabilitation, which involve a holistic and therapeutic

---

[843] Law Council of Australia (2024) *Australia's youth justice and incarceration system*, Senate Legal and Constitutional Affairs References Committee at https://lawcouncil.au/publicassets/d2f05c83-b895-ef11-94ab-005056be13b5/4609%20-%20S%20-%20Australias%20youth%20justice%20and%20incarceration%20system.pdf

approach addressing mental and physical health, social activities, and education, training, and employment.

Offending young people are victims themselves, having been damaged by adults in their care and the inadequacy of social services, as we have seen in the child abuse, family and domestic violence, and homelessness Themes in this book. For instance, a snapshot of the characteristics of children and young people in Youth Justice in Victoria gives a typical overview:

- 53 per cent were a victim of abuse, trauma or neglect as a child
- 41 per cent either have a current child protection case or were previously subject to a child protection order
- 49 per cent present with mental health issues
- 42 per cent have been witness to family violence
- 52 per cent have a history of alcohol and drug use
- 21 per cent live in unsafe or unstable housing
- 31 per cent present with cognitive difficulties that impact on daily functioning[844].

A survey of 14–17-year-olds in contact with the justice system between 2016 and 2018 in Queensland and Western Australia, found that the 3/4 had experienced some form of non-sexual abuse, about 2/3rds had at least 1 mental health disorder, and nearly 1 in 4 had attempted suicide[845].

Drug and alcohol disorders are highly represented in the child justice population, with a Queensland report indicating that as many as 64 per cent of those in child justice systems have a drug and alcohol disorder[846].

Many children involved in child justice systems experience poverty and unstable or unsuitable accommodation. National data shows that almost 2 in 5

[844] Youth Parole Board (2021) *Victoria Government Annual Report 2020-21* at https://files.justice.vic.gov.au/2021-10/Youth%20Parole%20Board%20Annual%20Report%202020-21.pdf

[845] Carla Meurk et al (2020) *Changing Direction: mental health needs of justice-involved young people in Australia* at https://www.kirby.unsw.edu.au/research/reports/changing-direction-mental-health-needs-justice-involved-young-people-australia

[846] Atkinson B (2018) *Report on Youth Justice*, Version 2, 8 June 2018 at https://desbt.qld.gov.au/__data/assets/pdf_file/0016/17170/youth-justice-report.pdf

children under youth justice supervision on an average day in 2022–23 were from the lowest socioeconomic areas[847].

Research completed in South Australia shows that of 3,058 children who experienced child justice contact, 84 per cent had been notified to child protection, and a 3rd had experienced out-of-home care. Further, the *Queensland Youth Justice Census* survey in 2023 showed that 25 per cent of the young people surveyed had at least 1 parent who spent time in adult custody.

A 2018 study by the *Telethon Kids Institute* and the *University of Western Australia* showed 9 out of 10 children who were incarcerated in WA had some form of neuro-disability, ranging from dyslexia or similar learning disability, language disorder, attention deficit hyperactivity disorder, intellectual disability, executive function disorder, memory impairment or motor coordination disorder. More than 1 in 3 of these children had Foetal Alcohol Spectrum Disorder[848].

Furthermore, a 2024 report by the *NSW Bureau of Crime Statistics and Research* found more than half of all 10-13 year-olds facing criminal penalties in NSW courts had been the victim of violence and about a 3rd had accessed specialist homelessness services[849].

In addition, youth detention, in itself, is associated with an increased risk of suicide, psychiatric disorders, and drug and alcohol abuse. Locking young people up during their crucial years of development also has long-term impacts. These include poor emotional development, poor education outcomes, and worse mental health in adulthood[850].

I experienced this firsthand while providing health services to the 2 youth detention centres in Victoria. The level of violence, especially gang-related, meant long periods of lockdown which severely affected the time the young

---

[847] Australian Institute of Health and Welfare (2024),*Youth Justice in Australia 2022–23* at https://www.aihw.gov.au/reports/youth-justice/youth-justice-in-australia-annual-report-2022-23/contents/about

[848] Drum M and Buchanan R (2020) *Western Australia's prison population 2020: Challenges and reforms*, The University of Notre Dame Australia and the Catholic Archdiocese of Perth

[849] Freeman F and Donnelly N (2024) *The involvement of young people aged 10 to 13 years in the NSW criminal justice system*, Crime And Justice Statistics Bureau Brief, Number 171, NSW Bureau Of Crime Statistics and Research, August 2024 at https://bocsar.nsw.gov.au/documents/publications/bb/bb151-200/bb171-report-involvement-of-young-people-nsw.pdf

[850] https://www.uow.edu.au/media/2022/locking-up-kids-has-serious-mental-health-impacts-and-contributes-to-further-reoffending.php#:~:text=Youth%20detention%20is%20also%20associated,worse%20mental%20health%20in%20adulthood.

people could attend education, health services, and recreation activities, leading to a vicious circle of frustration, anger, and bad behaviour.

In 2024, it was reported that gang conflict has emerged in recent years as one of the biggest issues within the youth justice system with high-level incidents including assaults linked to vicious disputes between the gangs[851].

Over the years, we have seen repeated reports of the death and serious harm to young people in youth detention from the authorities.

In 2016, the Royal Commission into the treatment of children in detention centres in the Northern Territory found that these facilities were unfit to accommodate or rehabilitate children and that children were verbally and physically abused, as well as subjected to inappropriate, punitive and degrading treatment in places of detention such as forced restraint.

Nine years later, an investigation by the Northern Territory's Office of the Children's Commissioner found that a young Aboriginal person detained at the Don Dale detention centre was kept in isolation for 84 hours, unable to leave their cell or make contact with any support person, and was denied food for some of that time as a coercion tactic by officers[852].

Four Corners in 2022 reported prolonged lockdowns, solitary confinement and self-harm and suicide attempts at Perth's Banksia Hill detention centre[853]; in 2023 the South Australian Children's Guardian observed that children in the Kurlana Tapa children's prison were being locked in their cells for up to 23 consecutive hours, partly due to staffing shortages, resulting in increased incidents of self-harm, reduced hours of school attendance for children in prison and difficulties for children to be able to meet with their lawyers[854]; and in 2024 in Queensland ongoing media reports of indefinite detention of children as young as 10 in police watchhouses[855] and the Cleveland youth detention centre's use of solitary confinement in youth detention where 2 First Nations

---

[851] https://www.heraldsun.com.au/truecrimeaustralia/police-courts-victoria/claims-teens-are-running-riot-at-states-newest-youth-justice-facility-cherry-creek/news-story/9c24c73d63b50926c86c700b70e9dc20

[852] https://www.theguardian.com/australia-news/2025/sep/05/don-dale-detention-centre-84-hours-isolation-denied-food-coercion-technique-ntwnfb

[853] https://www.theguardian.com/australia-news/2022/nov/15/lives-placed-at-serious-risk-four-corners-report-sparks-new-calls-for-youth-justice-overhaul

[854] https://www.theguardian.com/society/2023/jun/29/children-locked-in-cells-for-up-to-23-hours-at-south-australias-youth-detention-centre

[855] https://www.sbs.com.au/news/article/locked-in-a-cell-for-20-hours-a-day-queensland-youth-prisons-accused-of-torture/vb55ku4ux

children with disabilities died after spending extensive time in isolation at overcrowded and understaffed youth detention centres[856].

In 2025, an Australian Human Rights Commission review found that solitary confinement and similar practices remain widespread across Australian youth detention settings with children routinely subjected to isolation for extended periods, often under conditions that fail to meet basic standards of care. These practices cause profound harm to children's mental health, physical wellbeing and development, and disproportionately impact First Peoples children and children with disability. They also undermine rehabilitation, increase the risk of self-harm and suicide, and perpetuate cycles of trauma and disadvantage[857].

Our treatment of children in custody has also raised the ire of the United Nations. In 2017, Australia ratified the *Optional Protocol to the Convention Against Torture*, which requires Australia to introduce a system that allows all places of detention to be inspected and monitored by certain independent international and domestic bodies. In January 2023, Australia missed the extended deadline to establish the required National Mechanism for the Prevention of Torture and a month later, the *United Nations Subcommittee on Prevention of Torture and other Cruel, Inhuman or Degrading Treatment or Punishment* terminated its visit to Australia because two state governments refused to guarantee unrestricted access to its detention facilities. A spokesperson for the NSW Attorney-General stated that the State Government required greater federal funding to implement its obligation[858].

The 2025 inspection by the United Nations Working Group on Arbitrary Detention, which was denied entry to a number of detention facilities, including the site of the death of First Nations teenager Cleveland Dodd, concluded that the treatment of children and teenagers in the justice system was a 'stain on Australia's reputation' and called for Australia to urgently adopt a nationally consistent and enforceable prohibition on the solitary confinement of children[859].

---

[856] https://www.theguardian.com/australia-news/2024/mar/15/queensland-youth-detention-solitary-confinement-first-nations

[857] Australian Human Rights Commission (2025*) 'Left Alone': A Review of Solitary Confinement and Similar Practices in Australia's Youth Justice Systems* at https://humanrights.gov.au/about-us/media-centre/search-listing-media-releases/left-alone-a-review-of-solitary-confinement-and-similar-practices-in-australias-youth-justice-systems

[858] https://www.humanrights.unsw.edu.au/students/blogs/regulating-torture-australia-obligations-convention

[859] United Nations Working Group on Arbitrary Detention (2025) *Preliminary Findings from its visit to Australia (1 to 12 December 2025)* and https://www.abc.net.au/news/2025-12-13/united-nations-warn-australia-prison-detention-human-

Meanwhile, the Australian Government is yet to ratify the *Optional Protocol to the Convention on the Rights of the Child on a Communications Procedure*, which would allow children to make complaints to the United Nations Committee on the Rights of the Child for breaches of their rights.

Given the embedded, complex, interrelated issues these young people face, any diversion program needs substantial resources and time, but can save governments much more, given that it costs over $1 million to house one youth offender[860].

It is not surprising then that youth recidivism became the basis of the first Social Impact Bond (SIB) in the UK in 2010, where 60 per cent of incarcerated young people were convicted of at least 1 offence in the year after release. The outcome was a 9 per cent reduction, exceeding the target of 7.5 per cent. SIBs are explained further in the Ways to make an Impact chapter.

Under the indefatigable former NSW Minister, Pru Goward, in July 2016, the NSW Government entered into Australia's first SIB designed to reduce recidivism. The *On TRACC* SIB provided 3,900 parolees with a medium to high risk of reoffending with intensive support in the first 16 weeks of parole and after-care for an additional eight months from charities *Australian Community Support Organisation* and *Arbias*, supported by a joint investment from National Australia Bank. Unfortunately, 2 years later, the SIB ended after its review found no statistically significant difference in the rate of re-incarceration between On TRACC participants and those supported through Corrective Services NSW's existing services.

Not to be deterred, in 2023, Social Ventures Australia, Vacro, the Victorian Government and housing providers launched the *Arc Social Impact Bond*, to better support people leaving prison and reduce reoffending and homelessness.

What we do know works for young people in recidivism programs is a combination of decreasing known crime-related risk factors and increasing protective factors; linking them to sustained employment, training and education opportunities; and increasing their connectedness with the community[861]. This takes a person-centred, integrated, place-based approach

---

rights/106136950?utm_source=abc_news_app&utm_medium=content_shared&utm_campaign=abc_news_app&utm_content=other

860 https://nit.com.au/25-01-2024/9449/new-data-shows-youth-incarceration-costing-public-over-1-million-per-child

861 State of Victoria (2022) *Youth Crime Prevention Grants Program Evaluation Final Report Evidence and Insight* at https://files.crimeprevention.vic.gov.au/2022-05/Youth%20Crime%20Prevention%20Grants%20Program%20Evaluation%20Final%20Report%20March%202022_.pdf

across a range of health, housing, training, employment and human services, by police and charities that already work effectively with this cohort on one or more of these services.

One successful evaluated recidivism program is Victoria's *Embedded Youth Outreach Program* (EYOP) which pairs a police officer with a youth outreach worker 'to support the complex needs of young people at high risk of antisocial or criminal behaviour, and/or victimisation'. The youth workers, who are experienced in high-risk young people, identify the criminogenic needs, vulnerability factors, and protective factors of the young people; make referrals to local support services, and support them to attend. The EYOP achieved a 9 per cent reduction in the annual rate of offending in the young people with a history of offending following intervention, compared to a 38 per cent increase in the annual rate of offending in a matched cohort over the same period[862].

For young people who have contact with or have demonstrated risk of being involved with the criminal justice system, the Victorian government's *Youth Crime Prevention Program* funds local youth charities to provide more than 1,800 young people with intensive case management support, including family-based interventions, and engages more than 3,000 young people in pro-social activities in areas with higher rates of youth offending, with the evaluation showing a 29 per cent reduction in offending, and a 24 per cent reduction in severity of offending for participants[863]. Sadly, as evidence of the fleeting nature of these programs, funding was cut in 2025.

Youth on Track is a NSW government program that supports 10-17 year-olds who are not yet entrenched in the criminal justice system but who have been assessed as having a medium to high likelihood of re-offending. The program works with the young person, their family, local charities, caseworkers, and government youth justice workers to reduce their risk of re-offending or committing more serious offences. The program achieved a 100 per cent reduction in risk, especially with the young people's participation in school and work, as well as an improvement in family relationships[864].

Transition 2 Success is the Queensland government's program to lower the risk of offending by young people aged 15-17 years who are involved in the youth

---

[862] Luebbers. S., Pichler. A.S., Fullam. R. & Ogloff. J. R. P. (2019) *Embedded Youth Outreach Program Evaluation, Final Report*, Centre for Forensic Behavioural Science

[863] State of Victoria (2022) *Youth Crime Prevention Grants Program Evaluation Final Report Evidence and Insights* at https://files.crimeprevention.vic.gov.au/2022-05/Youth%20Crime%20Prevention%20Grants%20Program%20Evaluation%20Final%20Report%20March%202022_.pdf

[864] https://www.nsw.gov.au/legal-and-justice/youth-justice/youth-on-track/reporting-and-evaluation

justice system or are assessed as being at-risk of entering by engaging with education, training and employment through a vocational training and therapeutic service model. 2 in 3 of all participants who completed a course did not offend or reoffend within 12 months of completing their course. Over four in ten participants with a prior offending history who completed a course did not reoffend within 12 months of completing their course, whilst a similar proportion of participants with a prior offending history who completed the program saw a substantial decrease in their offending magnitude[865].

In Logan, Queensland, *Resolve* is an early intervention program for young people aged 12 to 16 years old who are at risk of justice system involvement delivered through a partnership between the Youth and Family Service, Griffith University, Overflow Foundation, and the Queensland Police Service. The program includes community outreach as well as intensive case management that uses a flexible, relational, and strengths-based approach. In 2023, a Griffith University evaluation of the program found that participation in the program resulted in a significant reduction in risk levels evident in relation to housing, schooling, family relationships, social connections, physical health, drug and alcohol use, mental health and safety and the law, and considerable increases in young people's hopefulness both in relation to their sense of agency and confidence in goal achievement.

Western Australia's *Youth Partnership Project (YPP)* brings together state government, local government, and the community sector in a place-based, collective impact approach to youth justice. The project focuses on early identification of young people aged 8 to 12 years old with complex needs, and the delivery of targeted community services to prevent their involvement with the justice system. The *Armadale Youth Intervention Partnership,* as part of the YPP, achieved a 50 per cent reduction in reoffending for those who completed the program. Evaluation of the Project found that the participants' future reliance on government fell by 10 per cent, which means that the program almost pays for itself[866].

[865] Deloitte Touche Tohmatsu (2019) *Additional Analysis of Transition to Success Program Evaluation,* Final Report, Department of Child Safety, Youth and Women, February 2019 at https://desbt.qld.gov.au/ data/assets/pdf file/0019/17434/t2s-supplementary-report.pdf

[866] Youth Partnership Project (2021) *Youth justice model: 2021 practice framework & evaluation summary* at https://www.youthpartnershipproject.org.au/ files/ugd/d180ab 64766464fe62447c9d3c536354e18b4b.pdf

We know that these programs work, but they are transient. We need the political will that commits to long-term, consistent and adequate resourcing to make them mainstream.

As the Paul Ramsey Foundation concludes, 'the promise of justice reinvestment is that community-led prevention approaches can reduce demand for the criminal justice system and create cost savings that fund a cycle of place-based investments. However, despite much community-based work and the expansion of justice reinvestment grant programs, a mechanism for reinvestment has not been fully developed or implemented at either the State or Federal level'[867].

ACT

Campaign

Sign the petition to raise the minimum age of criminal responsibility across Australia to 14 at *Raise The Age*[868].

Volunteer

Become a mentor with *Women and Mentoring* through their early intervention program, which supports women and non-binary individuals in contact with the legal system in Victoria[869], the *Youth Frontiers Program* with YWCA Australia[870], *Stand as One* program with Shine for Kids in NSW[871], *Lived Experience Mentoring Project* with the Centre for Multicultural Youth (CMY) in Victoria[872] and *Transitions to Success* in Queensland[873].

Employ

There is no better intervention than to provide a job for a young person. Work enables self-esteem, purpose, belonging, financial empowerment and a future. The government employment services (now called Workforce Australia) have providers in your area whose role is to find you suitable candidates.

---

867 Paul Ramsey Foundation (2025) *Justice Reinvestment Portfolio Review*, July 2025 p.9

868 https://raisetheage.org.au/take-action

869 https://www.womenandmentoring.org.au/

870 https://www.ywca.org.au/support/youth-frontiers-mentoring-program/

871 https://shineforkids.org.au/programs/stand-as-one/

872 https://www.cmy.net.au/youth-justice/lived-experience-mentoring-project/

873 https://www.youthjustice.qld.gov.au/partnerships/partnerships/t2s-involvement#:~:text=Transition%20to%20Success%20(T2S)%20gives,by%20sharing%20your%20career%20choices

Reboot Australia can provide you with skilled and unskilled candidates to many industries throughout WA, QLD and VIC through their mentoring, industry-relevant education and employer tailored training pre and post-release program to increase the likelihood of successful reintegration[874].

Success Works Partners in NSW is the only recruitment agency specialising in supporting and placing women with a criminal record into meaningful employment[875].

Buy

A number of social enterprises provide training employment for young ex-offenders, such as *Green Fox Studio*, an award-winning, full service national Graphic Design and Creative Agency[876]; YMCA's *ReBuild* in Victoria delivers commercial construction services[877]; *Mates on the Move* provides office/IT equipment relocation services to companies who need to get staff set-up to work from home in NSW[878]; and *Fruit2Work* provides office fruit and other supplies in Vic and Qld[879]. For more, go to the Social Traders directory of social enterprises[880].

Donate

There is a desperate need to further develop and invest in evidence-based early intervention services, such as those outlined above, instead of incarceration, to break entrenched cycles of engagement with the criminal justice system and recidivism.

The *Justice Reform Initiative* is backed by an impressive list of Patrons, including a former Governor General, former Police Commissioner, former Chief Justice, former Attorney General and many leading figures in health, economic development and child rights. With the tag line 'jailing is failing', they work in partnership with other organisations seeking justice reform[881].

Nationally, significant contributions to advocacy and policy in youth justice have been made by *Save the Children* calling for a rights-based approach to

---

874 https://www.rebootaustralia.com/ourservices

875 https://successworks.org.au/

876 https://greenfoxstudio.com.au/

877 https://vicyouth.ymca.org.au/social-impact/rebuild

878 https://matesonthemove.org/

879 https://fruit2work.com.au/

880 https://www.socialtraders.com.au/find-a-social-enterprise

881 https://www.justicereforminitiative.org.au/

youth justice[882]; *Jesuit Social Services* who have been committed to long-standing policy, research and advocacy work and have produced multiple publications on this topic of youth justice[883]; and *Amnesty International*, who have been campaigning on a range of youth justice issues, including their work outlined in their *National Plan for Youth Justice*[884].

---

[882] Save the Children (2023) *"Don't judge a book by its cover": A rights-respecting approach to youth justice in Queensland*, Submission to Youth Justice Reform Select Committee at https://www.savethechildren.org.au/getmedia/0da6a34f-cd4f-49af-b8c9-852b7edff678/submission-to-youth-justice-reform-select-committee.pdf.aspx#:~:text=Rather%20than%20punishing%20and%20incarcerating,strengths%20rather%20than%20reinforcing%20deficit.

[883] https://jss.org.au/what-we-do/justice-reconciliation/our-work/

[884] https://action.amnesty.org.au/act-now/cie-national-plan-of-action-kids-in-detention

SOCIAL COHESION

'Being a citizen means much more than having a vote or holding a passport. It means being able to share in the life of the community. It means enjoying a certain level of security. It means belonging. If we accept this broader definition of citizenship, we will be well on the way to building a stronger democracy and fair, more secure and more cohesive society'

HON JENNY MACKLIN AC[885]

Standing in my garden on Saturday 7 February 2009 felt apocalyptic. We were used to hot days in summer, but at 46 degrees and blustery, the spate of fire warnings over the radio created a sense of threat and fear.

That day, 400 fires were recorded across Victoria, affecting 78 communities. A total of 173 people died in the fires and over 2,000 houses were lost.

In the office a few days later, I heard over the radio that the welfare agencies needed suits for people attending funerals. I sent an internal email to staff to see if we could assist. 2 hours later, there was a queue from our office entrance running down the street, of people bringing donated suits. The queue continued for days.

Our social enterprise would later see unemployed young people help farmers to re-fence their properties, as *Blaze Aid* took off after Kevin Bulter put an advert in the local paper requesting assistance to re-fence his property to keep his sheep in. What would have taken 3-4 months took just a week with 25 volunteers.

---

[885] Social cohesion
Macklin J & Deane J (2025) *Making Progress. How Good Policy Happens*, Melbourne University Press, Carlton, Victoria, p.65

Volunteers came from all around Australia and the world and worked for the next 11 months to clear and rebuild 500 kilometres of burnt fences[886].

Not only was there an unprecedented outpouring of compassion, goodwill and community connectedness with $379 million raised[887] and over 26,000 people registering to volunteer, *Australian Unity* found that personal wellbeing also rose significantly as a result[888].

10 years later, with over 17 million hectares of land destroyed, a billion animals killed, over 3,000 homes lost and 35 deaths, the Australian bushfires saw over half of all Australians donating $240 million[889].

Another 10 years later, the pandemic showed us the same spirit of community when, street by street, neighbours created groups to help with shopping, walking dogs and calling single and aged people. Overnight, we saw the creation of hundreds of new volunteer-run grassroots mutual aid organisations, such as the Canberra Region Coronavirus Mutual Aid Group, and the sudden mobilisation of thousands of existing charities in order to respond.

However, today, in a world of rising conflict, misinformation, extremism, protests, inequality and divisive politics, our social cohesion is under attack.

WHAT

In what we call developing countries, I've found a deep and abiding community spirit based on the unquestioned support for others. The Zulu name for this in South Africa is *ubuntu*, *unhu* in Zimbabwe, *Ujamaa* in Tanzania and *uMunthu* in Malawi. It means *I am because we are*. Then President Bill Clinton summed it up at Nelson Mandela's memorial to mean 'we are all bound together in ways that are invisible to the eye; that there is a oneness to humanity; that we achieve ourselves by sharing ourselves with others, and caring for those around us'[890]. In Melanesia and Papua New Guinea, it is *wontok*, or literally 'one talk'. In the Philippines it is *kapwa*.

In poverty stricken sub-Saharan West Africa, in tsunami devastated Aceh, in war-torn Bosnia, in earthquake destroyed north Pakistan, or conflict-ravaged Eastern Congo - communities torn apart by poverty, disaster, war and disease -

886 https://blazeaid.com.au/about-us

887 http://www.bus.qut.edu.au/news/news/news-event.jsp?news-event-id=36171

888 Cummins R, Woerner & Chester M, 2009, Australian Unity Wellbeing Index, Survey 20.1, Australian Centre on Quality of Life, Melbourne

889 https://good2give.ngo/2021/11/11/2019-2020-australian-bushfires-12-months-on/

890 https://www.businessinsider.com/obama-nelson-mandela-memorial-service-speech-full-text-2013-12?r=AU&IR=T

I've experienced these communities to be resilient and cohesive. They survive and rebuild because they work together, as they have done for millennia.

When we think about what really matters to us and makes life worth living, it isn't the things that we acquire in our lives, although they make life easier and more pleasurable (or increasingly don't provide the life-changing benefits that are advertised as the 2024 word of the year 'Enshittification' encapsulates). As herd animals and a social species, it is the benefits we get from relationships that nature and sustain us from families, friends, work, leisure, sports, clubs and community groups.

As Hugh Mackay notes, 'here's the beautiful symmetry of the human condition: we need communities and communities need us. We need them to nurture us and preserve our sense of belonging; they need our engagement and participation if they are to survive'[891].

All these relationships create social cohesion which enables belonging, participation, connectedness, cooperation and belief that we all yearn and need. To take a Canadian definition, it is an ongoing process of developing a community of shared values, shared challenges and equal opportunity, based on a sense of trust, hope and reciprocity[892].

Social cohesion, in turn, creates social capital, the networks of trust and reciprocity that are now recognised as making an enormous difference in our lives and critical in achieving sustained economic and social development[893]. It is the glue that holds us all together and makes life meaningful. It's the sense of common purpose, shared values, and belonging[894].

Social cohesion is an essential condition for democratic security, with divided and unequal societies not only unjust, but also unable to guarantee stability in the long term[895].

Young Australians understand the importance of social cohesion. A 2025 survey of young Australians reported they see social cohesion as community and social belonging (30 per cent), followed by harmony and cohesiveness (27

---

891 Mackay H (2024) *The Way We are. Lessons from a lifetime of listening*, Allen & Unwin, NSW, p.10

892 Social Cohesion Research Workplan, March 1997 at www.socialsciences.uottawa.ca/governance/eng/documents/social_cohesion_research_workplan.pdf

893 The Benevolent Society, 2008, *Bridging the Gap: A literature review of social cohesion*

894 MacKay H, 2010, *What Makes Us Tick?: The Ten Desires that Drive Us*, Hachette Australia, Sydney

895 Council of Europe, 2000, *Strategy for Social Cohesion and Quality of Life*, at http://www.coe.int/t/dg3/socialpolicies/socialcohesiondev/source/RevisedStrategy_en.pdf

per cent), collaboration and cooperation (22 per cent), social interaction (12 per cent) and mutual support and shared values (9 per cent). The shared values that young people raised in consultations were respect for First Nations peoples, multiculturalism, inclusiveness, fairness, equality and equity. When asked about the values our community should aspire to, young people reported community and social cohesion (39 per cent), respect and understanding (33 per cent), fairness and equality (22 per cent), faith and beliefs (16 per cent), and health and wellbeing (13 per cent)[896].

The building block of social cohesion is social capital, defined by the OECD as 'networks, norms, values and understandings that facilitate co-operation within or among groups'[897]. Areas with higher levels of social capital have been shown to have improved health, greater wellbeing, better care for children, lower crime and improved governance[898].

Both bonding (amongst similar people) and bridging (amongst people of different race, area, income) social capital are crucial. Whilst the former is often needed to get a job or to socialise in our groups, it becomes easier to develop misplaced stereotypes of those who are unlike ourselves. The latter, which can be widely found in diverse organisations and groups, fosters tolerance and breaks down the stereotypes that can develop if we mix with only those similar to us[899].

According to the Department of Home Affairs, the key values that underpin our society and social cohesion are summarised in the *Australian Values Statement*, which visa applicants must sign to 'acknowledge those Australian values and undertake to conduct yourself in accordance with these values'. They include: equality of opportunity for all people, regardless of their gender, sexual orientation, age, disability, race, or national or ethnic origin; and a 'fair go' for all that embraces mutual respect, tolerance, compassion for those in need, and equality of opportunity for all[900].

In *Measuring What Matters*, Australia's first national wellbeing framework, the Australian government has included 'cohesive' as one of the 5 themes as 'a

---

[896] Johnson A (2025) *Redreaming and reimagining Australian communities Social Cohesion and young people 2025*, thrive international

[897] http://www.oecd.org/dataoecd/36/6/37966934.pdf

[898] OCED, 2001, *The wellbeing of nations: The role of human and social capital*, Organisation for Economic and Social Capital at http://www.oecd.org/dataoecd/24/51/2671078.pdf

[899] Leigh A, 2010, *Disconnected*, University of New South Wales Press Ltd, Sydney

[900] https://immi.homeaffairs.gov.au/help-support/meeting-our-requirements/australian-values

society that supports connections with family, friends and the community, values diversity and promotes belonging and culture'[901].

The Scanlon Foundation Research Institute's *Australian Cohesion Index* measures trust in society, belonging and engagement, economics and material wellbeing, and Australia's health and personal wellbeing.

Trust is a basis for our involvement and engagement in society and our social wellbeing and connectedness, whilst belonging is the sense to which we feel connected to other people, places and collective experiences. To belong is to have a place in the world, to feel a part of the communities and societies around us and is critical to our identity and self-perception. To feel we belong is often regarded as a fundamental human need, rooted in our biology as social beings.

In essence, social cohesion is 'the peace, harmony, and connectedness of society' which is 'most commonly indicated by the degree of trust people have in one another and in government, their sense of belonging and their participation in their communities'.

Internationally, Australia scores reasonably highly on the degree to which people trust others and the pride felt in their nationality[902].

But we can't take social cohesion for granted. Indeed, it may be unravelling.

Concerningly, the *2025 Australian Cohesion Index* found that our sense of belonging, sense of worth and social justice are at their lowest levels since the research began in 2007. The report also found that our sense of community continues to decline with Australians less trusting and more pessimistic, whilst Australians' sense of belonging and pride in their national culture continues to decline. Young adults, those who have immigrated to Australia and those who are struggling financially have the weakest levels of belonging[903].

Australians with a weaker sense of Australia's social fabric are more likely to feel socially isolated and less likely to feel a sense of belonging in Australia. Almost 1 in 7 Australians experience social isolation as 'having objectively few social relationships or roles and infrequent social contact'[904], whilst social

---

901 Commonwealth of Australia (2023) *Measuring What Matters. Australia's First Wellbeing Framework,* July 2023

902 https://www.ipsos.com/en-au/geography-interpersonal-trust-australia-ranks-7th-trust-other-people-among-30-countries?utm_source=chatgpt.com

903 Scanlon Foundation Research Institute (2025) *Mapping Social Cohesion 2025* p.6

904 Australian Institute of Health and Welfare, *Social isolation and loneliness* at https://www.aihw.gov.au/mental-health/topic-areas/social-isolation-and-loneliness

exclusion affects 6.7 million Australians and costs the Australian economy $45 billion each year[905].

A 2022 survey reported that 1 in 4 Australians is lonely, including 37 per cent of young people. This rate worsened to nearly 1 in 3 Australians in a 2023 survey, with 69 per cent of Australians recognising loneliness is a serious issue for our community[906], whilst the *2024 Australian Unity Wellbeing Index* reports that Australians aged 18-24 experience double the loneliness as those over 75.

Loneliness and social isolation were concerns before the onset of COVID, but have been exacerbated with the pandemic. Loneliness, defined as a subjective experience of social disconnectedness and isolation, has been identified as the next public health epidemic of the 21st century[907] given that it is associated with a 26 per cent increased likelihood of mortality[908].

The 2025 Household, Income and Labour Dynamics in Australia (HILDA) Survey, which has been following the same 17,000 people every year since 2001, reported that those in agreement with the statement 'I seem to have a lot of friends' have fallen noticeably from 2010 to 2023. The report shows that a low perceived number of friends is associated with fewer social activities, greater feelings of loneliness and poorer mental health[909].

Loneliness increases our risk of experiencing poorer health outcomes from decreased immunity, increased inflammatory response, elevated blood pressure, decreases in cognitive health, and faster progression of Alzheimer's disease.

It is no surprise that higher levels of loneliness are related to more severe mental health symptoms. While loneliness is most commonly associated with

---

905 Soutphommasane, T, Whitwell, G, Jordan, K & Ivanov, P (2018) *Leading for change: A blueprint for cultural diversity and inclusive leadership revisited*, Australian Human Rights Commission

906 Ending Loneliness Together (2023) *State of the Nation Report. Social connectedness in Australia 2023* at https://endingloneliness.com.au/wp-content/uploads/2023/10/ELT_LNA_Report_Digital.pdf

907 https://psychology.org.au/for-members/publications/inpsych/2018/august-issue-4/is-loneliness-australia-next-public-health-epide

908 Holt-Lunstad, J., Smith, T. B., Baker, M., Harris, T., & Stephenson, D. (2015). Loneliness and Social isolation as risk factors for mortality: A meta-analytic review. *Perspectives on Psychological Science, 10*(2), 227-237. doi:10.1177/1745691614568352

909 Laß I, Botha F, Peyton K and Wilkins R (2025) *The Household, Income and Labour Dynamics in Australia Survey: Selected Findings from Waves 1 to 23*, Melbourne Institute of Applied Economic and Social Research, The University of Melbourne.

depression, anxiety has been found to also play a role, with evidence from large population studies indicating that anxiety increases the odds of feeling lonely[910].

The healthcare costs associated with loneliness are estimated at $2.7 billion per annum. It has a social impact too, with those affected more predisposed to poor diet, physical inactivity and smoking, problem gambling, and even aggressive behaviour and bullying[911].

WHY

Social cohesion is being eroded by many of the issues outlined in other Themes of this book, most notably racism and discrimination, and poverty and disadvantage. Its decline leads to worsening mental health, family and domestic violence, child abuse, youth justice, disability inclusion, gender equality and homelessness.

Household finances, in particular, are the single most important predictor of how people perceive cohesion in Australia. People who are struggling to pay bills or who describe themselves as poor or 'just getting along' are much less likely to say they have a great sense of belonging in Australia, have a much lower sense of happiness and self-worth, perceive substantially weaker social inclusion and justice in Australia, are less likely to trust other people or the government, and are more likely to disagree that multiculturalism has been good for Australia[912].

Cost-of-living pressures mean that households are unable to afford the cost of going to events and clubs, or even putting fuel in the car to travel to friends and community activities. Additionally, whilst entertainment, social connection, and understanding other perspectives and cultures continue to be the most common motivations to attend arts and cultural events, Australians are attending arts events and festivals less frequently due to the cost[913].

With our sense of social cohesion reaching its lowest level since the Scanlon-Monash Index of Social Cohesion began in 2007, this research shows that the

---

[910] https://psychology.org.au/for-members/publications/inpsych/2018/august-issue-4/is-loneliness-australia-next-public-health-epide

[911] Groundswell Foundation (2022) *Connections Matter. A Report on the impacts of loneliness in Australia* at https://www.groundswellfoundation.com.au/post/connectionsmatter-a-report-on-the-impacts-of-loneliness-in-australia

[912] https://www.abc.net.au/religion/social-cohesion-australia-diversity-inequality-threats/103133458

[913] Creative Australia (2023) *Creating Value. Results of the National Arts Participation Survey* at https://creative.gov.au/wp-content/uploads/2023/09/National-Arts-Participation-Survey-results-2022-1.pdf

profound concern over personal finances, economic prospects and housing affordability has driven this fall. Those who do not believe that Australia is still a place of economic equality, fairness or opportunity (which has declined by 16 percentage points over the last decade) are unlikely to register high levels of national pride and belonging[914].

Almost half of Australians say our nation is more divided today than in the past. The rich and powerful are identified as the major dividing force (72 per cent), followed by hostile foreign governments (69 per cent), journalists (51 per cent), and government leaders (49 per cent).

Worryingly, the majority of Australians think the nation's social fabric has become too weak to serve as a foundation for unity and common purpose. More than 6 in 10 think the lack of civility and mutual respect today is the worst they have ever seen. Reflecting the increasing racism and discrimination, only a quarter of Australians would help a person in need who strongly disagreed with their own strong view on a societal issue, only 1 in 5 would be willing to live in the same neighbourhood as them and would be willing to work alongside them[915].

The decline is compounded by an ongoing fall in trust in our institutions with establishment leaders not trusted to tell us the truth. Nearly 6 out of 10 Australians report that government, business leaders and journalists are purposely trying to mislead people by saying things they know are false or gross exaggerations[916].

Given its rich and eclectic migration history, Australia has always had to grapple with how to create a unified national identity among a population that has, increasingly, come from elsewhere.

What unites us as a country usually combines people fighting against adversity with skill and fairness, as exemplified by the Anzac spirit. For instance, we are the only country to require 'fairness' for the award of the best player for our major sports codes.

---

914 O'Donnell J (2023) *Mapping Social Cohesion 2023*, Scanlon Foundation Research Institute at https://scanloninstitute.org.au/sites/default/files/2023-11/2023%20Mapping%20Social%20Cohesion%20Report.pdf

915 Edelman Trust Institute (2023) *2023 Edelman Trust Barometer. Australia Report* at https://www.edelman.com.au/sites/g/files/aatuss381/files/2023-02/2023%20Edelman%20Trust%20Barometer%20Report%20-%20AUS%2002-2023.pdf

916 Edelman Trust Institute (2024) *2024 Edelman Trust Barometer. Australia Report* at https://www.edelman.com.au/sites/g/files/aatuss381/files/2024-03/2024%20Edelman%20Trust%20Barometer_Australia%20Report_1.pdf

The word Anzac has been a part of Australian thought, language, and life since 25 April 1915 when a signaller in Egypt coined the acronym for *Australian and New Zealand Army Corps*. The term became popular largely due to the work of the official correspondent and historian Charles Bean. While still at Gallipoli, Bean edited *The Anzac Book*, which sold tens of thousands of copies. In describing the evacuation of the Anzac Cove area, Bean wrote 'by dawn on December 20th Anzac had faded into a dim blue line lost amid other hills on the horizon as the ships took their human freight to Imbros, Lemnos and Egypt. But Anzac stood, and still stands, for reckless valour in a good cause, for enterprise, resourcefulness, fidelity, comradeship, and endurance that will never own defeat'[917].

Is it then any coincidence that the first question of the Australian citizenship practice test is 'what do we commemorate on Anzac Day?'.

In the spirit of battling adversity with skill and fairness, we saw the nation rise as one when Australia II took the America's Cup off the United States for the first time with its innovative design and skilful tactics, and then forty years later when the Matildas fought and beat teams ranked above them to reach the semi-finals of the 2023 FIFA Women's World Cup, followed by the final of the 2026 Asian Cup. It was not only their success, we loved their grit and fair play, avoiding the theatrical diving associated with men's soccer.

We were riveted to the TV pictures of Anaesthetist Richard Harris and his dive partner Craig Challen rescuing 12 young boys and their soccer coach from a flooded cave system in Thailand. 5 years later, we were all proud to see Arnold Dix lead the dramatic rescue of 41 Indian workers who had been trapped in a collapsed tunnel for 17 days.

Notwithstanding the occasional outpouring of national pride for great feats, sport is the great unifier with 9 out of 10 adults participating in sport at least once a year, together with 3.8 million children. More than 70 per cent of us believe that Australia's elite athletes are some of the best role models for ourselves, for children and young people to aspire to. Nearly 9 out of 10 Australians believe that sport is good for bringing their communities together[918]. However, the serious racism and discrimination at all levels of sport described in this Theme seriously undermine sport-related social cohesion.

Ray Oldenburg's 1989 *The Good Place* introduced the concept of 'third places' as social settings that are separate from home (first place) and work (second place). A third place is a public gathering spot that facilitates community

---

[917] Bean C E W (2014) *Anzac to Amiens*, Penguin, ISBN: 9780143571674

[918] https://www.clearinghouseforsport.gov.au/

interaction, like a coffee shop, library, or pub, where people can socialise, run into acquaintances, or meet new people[919].

As a social species that needs to be around people, third places encapsulate the core of community life, promoting informal interactions vital for fostering individual identity and collective cohesion[920].

Australia faces growing pressure on third places with rising rents and operating costs, commercialisation favouring chain stores over local independent venues that historically functioned as third places, closure of live music venues, our car-centric urban design, limited public transport and less walkable neighbourhoods limiting access.

With over 3 million Australians giving their time and talent annually, volunteering is at the heart of our communities and critical to social cohesion. Volunteering is a social outlet that enables a way to engage with people who share common interests and values, and leads to building both bonding and bridging social capital.

Our sports clubs, charities and community groups rely on the expertise and labour of Australians to operate, but volunteering has been on a steady decline from 34 per cent in 2006 to less than 1 in 4 Australians in 2020. COVID then decimated volunteering, with 2/3rds of volunteers estimated to have stopped volunteering between February and April 2020[921]. Volunteering numbers since have not returned to pre-pandemic levels[922] despite 83 per cent of charities needing more volunteers.

Charities report a disconnect between the need for regular, ongoing roles and the preference of volunteers for more episodic or project-based opportunities[923],

---

919 Oldenburg R (1989) *The Great Good Place*, Da Capo Press, Philadelphia, USA

920 Finlay J, Esposito M, Kim M H, Gomez-Lopez I & Clarke P (2019). *Closure of "Third Places"? Exploring Potential Consequences for Collective Health and Wellbeing*, Health & Place, 60(102225). https://doi.org/10.1016/j.healthplace.2019.102225

921 Volunteering Australia (2021) *Volunteering and the ongoing impact of COVID-19* at https://www.volunteeringaustralia.org/wp-content/uploads/VA-Volunteering-and-the-Ongoing-Impact-of-COVID19-14-May-2021.pdf

922 ANU Centre for Social Research and Methods (2023) *Ongoing trends in volunteering in Australia* at https://csrm.cass.anu.edu.au/sites/default/files/docs/2023/10/Ongoing_trends_in_volunteering_in_Australia.pdf

923 Volunteering Australia (2023) *National Strategy for Volunteering 2023–2033*, p.68 at https://volunteeringstrategy.org.au/wp-content/uploads/2024/01/National-Strategy-for-Volunteering-2023-2033.pdf

with work and family commitments preventing Australians from regularly volunteering, alongside increasing work hours and cost-of-living pressures.

The *Inquiry into Volunteering in Queensland* in 2025 found that while volunteering contributes immense civic, social, and economic value—estimated at over $117 billion annually—participation rates have declined significantly, falling from 76 per cent in 2020 to 64 per cent in 2023, equating to a loss of around 200,000 volunteers. Those who remain are increasingly burdened by rising expectations, financial costs, and regulatory hurdles[924].

Research increasingly shows a clear connection between heavy social media use and feelings of social isolation and loneliness. People who spend the most time on social media (over 2 hours each day) have twice the odds of perceived social isolation than those who spend half an hour or less a day on those sites[925].

Furthermore, the rise in one-person households, to more than 1 in 4, up from 24 per cent in 2016 and 18 per cent in 1981[926], correlates with the rise in the rate of loneliness to 40 per cent of those who live alone, compared to 30 per cent of people who do not live alone.

In 2018, the UK created the first *Minister for Loneliness* after a *Commission on Loneliness* reported more than 9 million people in Britain— 1 in 7 of the population—often or always feel lonely. The government launched a *Loneliness Engagement Fund* dedicated to reducing loneliness with 126 projects to transform the lives of thousands of lonely people across England and the inaugural *#LetsTalkLoneliness* campaign to help raise awareness and tackle stigma. In addition, the UK's universal personal care now includes 'social prescribing', which links those who are lonely or isolated to community activities and groups[927].

In response to the growing public incidents of racism, especially by far-right groups, the importance of social cohesion has been recognised by the Albanese government, appointing MP, Peter Khalil, the son of Egyptian migrant parents, as the country's first Special Envoy for social cohesion, alongside a government Office for Social Cohesion under the Department of Home Affairs.

---

[924]Local Government, Small Business and Customer Service Committee (2025) *Report No. 4, 58th Parliament – Inquiry into volunteering in Queensland*, Queensland Parliament at https://www.parliament.qld.gov.au/Work-of-Committees/Committees/Committee-Details?cid=267&id=4456

[925] https://www.npr.org/sections/health-shots/2017/03/06/518362255/feeling-lonely-too-much-time-on-social-media-may-be-why

[926] https://aifs.gov.au/sites/default/files/2023-08/Media-release-FF-Households-shrinking.pdf

[927] https://www.england.nhs.uk/personalisedcare/social-prescribing/

All levels of government provide grants for community building initiatives, such as the National Community Hubs Program, which comprises 92 hubs in 19 local government areas across 4 states where migrant families, particularly mothers with young children, come to connect, share and learn.

However, we have yet to see a nationally coordinated and resourced approach to reverse our decline in social cohesion. So, it is time for you to act.

ACT

Participate

Get more involved in your community by hosting or taking part in an event on *Neighbour Day* on the last Sunday in March[928].

In order to gain awareness, understanding and tolerance of other cultures, and build bridging capital, there are a plethora of cultural activities and events to get involved in, such as the Indian festival of light, *Diwali*, with music, Bollywood dancing, henna painting, and traditional cuisine in October or November each year.

A list of cultural dates can be found at

https://www.homeaffairs.gov.au/about-us/our-portfolios/multicultural-affairs/about-multicultural-affairs/calendar-of-cultural-and-religious-dates.

Markets in multicultural areas are a great way to experience the food and music of other cultures and join over 400,000 Australians and 170 cultures in February in Canberra for Australia's largest celebration of cultural diversity at the National Multicultural Festival[929].

With religious understanding and tolerance critical to social cohesion, visit a mosque on National Mosque Open Day[930] or take part in Vesak Day, also known as Buddha Day, which is celebrated in May[931], and experience the *Islamic Museum of Australia* in person or online[932].

Post COVID, there has been a surge in the popularity of running clubs to connect, exercise and have fun, growing to 77,000 Australians in almost 500

928 https://neighbourseveryday.org/day-of-action/
929 https://www.multiculturalfestival.com.au/
930 https://www.vic.gov.au/victorian-mosque-open-day-2024
931 https://buddhaday.org.au/
932 https://education.islamicmuseum.org.au/Website

locations in 2024, a 22 per cent increase on the previous year. *Park Run*, which now numbers over 500 across the country, celebrated its millionth runner in 2024.

Or how about Monday night board games, the tough guy book club, Toastmasters, salsa class, journaling for wellbeing, night badminton, tavern trivia, walk and shoot[933], paint and sip, whale watching, film night, Thoughtstorm, cheese tasting, MathsJam, speak Japanese, beach clean-up, or performing in the Pope John Paul II musical. These and much more can be found at *MeetUp.com.*

Workplace

Of the 8 employees in my first workplace coming back to Australia 25 years ago, only I was born in Australia. The others originated from Turkey, Greece, South Africa, Ireland, New Zealand and the UK. They all regarded themselves as Australian first, compared to 'African Americans' in the US who after generations see themselves as African first (when I lived in The Gambia, as descendants of slaves, they would visit Jufureh, the home of Kunta Kinte in Alex Halley's *Roots* hoping to connect to their homeland, only to be appalled by the begging children and lack of amenities).

Your workplace provides an excellent opportunity to build bridging capital through work and social activities, such as sharing a meal at the annual *Taste of Harmony* in March[934].

Volunteer

There is no shortage of volunteering opportunities near you with GoVolunteer and Seek Volunteer (both run by SEEK), listing over 10,000 volunteer roles. For those who want to volunteer from home, *Vollie*[935] specialises in online volunteering and *Communiteer* for skills-based opportunities[936]. Volunteer at home with the *Australian Red Cross* telephone Telecross and Telechat services[937] or with our helplines, like Lifeline[938]. Your State/Territory

[933] Photography, that is

[934] https://www.tasteofharmony.org.au/

[935] https://www.vollie.com.au/

[936] https://communiteer.org/volunteers

[937] https://www.redcross.org.au/act/action-catalogue/volunteer/connect-with-people-over-the-phone/

[938] https://melbourne.lifeline.org.au/volunteer/

welcomes volunteers for its emergency services and firefighting or join 140 years of volunteers with *St John's Ambulance*[939].

Even easier is *Do Something Near You*, which shows the volunteering opportunities in your suburb[940].

The Australian government funded *Aged Care Volunteer Visitors Scheme* recruits volunteers to visit older people who live in residential aged care or receive Home Care packages to build connections and reduce isolation through social activities[941].

Become a *citizen scientist* and help collect and analyse scientific data. The *Australian Citizen Science Association* has a project finder with over 500 projects[942] and the *CSIRO* is requesting your help, including 'Chart your Fart', a fun and informative way to delve into the fascinating world at the bottom end of the diet'[943], counting flying foxes in NSW[944], finding Bogong moths in Victoria[945], spotting sea lions in South Australia[946], monitoring of WA's bats[947].

Birdlife Australia invites you to participate in the *Big Aussie Bird Count* in October[948], or you can spot, log and map marine species that are uncommon along our coast with *RedMap*[949], count frogs in November[950] or go on a fungi hunt[951].

But why stop with the Earth? Help search for extraterrestrial intelligence with *UC Berkeley*[952] or help to classify galaxies with *Galaxy Zoo*[953].

---

939 https://stjohnnsw.com.au/volunteering

940 https://dosomethingnearyou.com.au/

941 https://www.health.gov.au/our-work/aged-care-volunteer-visitors-scheme-acvvs/volunteer

942 https://citizenscience.org.au/ala-project-finder/

943 https://www.csiro.au/en/work-with-us/citizen-science/Projects

944 https://www2.environment.nsw.gov.au/research-and-publications/your-research/citizen-science/get-involved/count-flying-foxes

945 https://mothtracker.swifft.net.au/

946 https://www.environment.sa.gov.au/topics/science/citizen-science

947 https://www.ccwa.org.au/bat_monitoring_program

948 https://aussiebirdcount.org.au/

949 https://www.redmap.org.au/

950 https://www.frogid.net.au/frog-id-week

951 https://fungimap.org.au/6265-2/

952 https://setiathome.berkeley.edu/

953 https://www.zooniverse.org/projects/zookeeper/galaxy-zoo/

DISABILITY INCLUSION

'It is time for all of you to challenge your unconscious biases, leave your preconceptions at the door and lift your expectations of what we think people with disability can do, because it is always more than you think'

DYLAN ALCOTT AO

After 30 years of supporting children with brain illnesses and injuries, *Brainwave* has seen these children grow up to become wonderful young people with the love and care of their families and support from health and social service systems, including the National Disability Insurance Scheme (NDIS).

The debate about the cost of the NDIS (which, in brief, is due to the broadening of the scope of those included and the range services included than first designed) masks the fact that the Scheme has been life-changing for hundreds of thousands of people with disabilities and their families.

Yes, it has design flaws and governance failures[954] and is overly bureaucratic, adversarial, inconsistent and inflexible, with low-quality support services from a lack of accredited providers, but the NDIS has supported each participant's growth as a person, kept them thriving in life, and significantly improved their

[954]Disability inclusion
Bennett S, Jessurun J and Orban H (2025) *Saving the NDIS. How to rebalance disability services to get better results*, Grattan Institute, p.3

wellbeing[955]. In the words of *People with Disabilities*, the NDIS 'stands as a beacon of hope and progress for disabled individuals across Australia'[956].

The NDIS was always intended for disabled people with the highest support needs. It was designed to sit within a broader support system so that disabled Australians who were not eligible for the NDIS could still get their needs met. But for those who do not qualify for the NDIS, support can be scarce, as the State and Territory governments largely took their funding of community disability services to pay for their share of the NDIS.

So, as a recommendation of the *Independent Review of the NDIS*, the Australian government is endeavouring to get State and Territory governments to establish 'Foundation Supports' for those not eligible for NDIS, including information and advice, individual and family capacity building, peer support, self-advocacy, and disability employment supports[957].

One downside of the NDIS, however, is welfare dependency. These young people have, since they can remember, been identified as disabled first. Disability has defined their development, relationships, health, education and support services. They have been told what to do their whole life.

Disability is their life – all day, every day. In reality, they, and we, do not see and nurture their considerable abilities to play an equal role in our society.

Like so many, I was inspired by Dylan Alcott AO's speech when he was awarded the Australian of the Year in 2022. Having had a tumour wrapped around his spinal cord when he was born, 'he has known nothing but having a disability'. He hated being disabled and being different. He never saw anyone like him in the media, other than a road safety advert when someone has an accident and ends up 'someone like me in tears because their life was over'. He believed that was going to his life. With the motivation of disability sport heroes such as Kurt Fernley, through sport, he got to love his disability, saying, 'it is the best thing that ever happened to me'.

Dylan challenges the unconscious bias of employers who presume disabled people 'can't do the role' and advocates for a future where workplaces are

---

955 https://pwd.org.au/what-you-told-us-during-the-ndis-review/

956 https://pwd.org.au/why-we-need-the-ndis/

957 Commonwealth of Australia (2023) ***Working together to deliver the NDIS Independent Review into the National Disability Insurance Scheme, Final Report,*** October 2023 at https://www.ndisreview.gov.au/sites/default/files/resource/download/working-together-ndis-review-final-report.pdf

accessible, provide reasonable supports, and employ people with disability not because they're disabled, but 'because they're good'.

Before Brainwave, I established 5 social enterprises that enabled unemployed young people with mental health issues, drug and alcohol dependence, offending and other disadvantages, who would otherwise be considered unemployable, to develop the life, employability and technical skills needed to enter and sustain mainstream employment.

The change happens at 9 am on day one. Instead of being told to attend yet another program, they are treated as a worker alongside a professional team that role modelled the behaviours and expectations they needed in a workplace.

For the first time in their lives (and often the lives of their family) they go from a stigmatised welfare recipient to a valuable worker, with a newfound confidence that they can actually do this 'work thing'. In fact, they do pretty well.

The 10 year partnership with Mercedes-Benz provided the opportunity to pitch a new social enterprise for the young people supported by Brainwave who were unemployed after leaving school.

It had to fit with Mercedes' mobility and sustainability values, and I knew from running the donated goods business at the Brotherhood of St Laurence and being on the Board of Good Cycles, that no organisation was collecting, refurbishing and reselling used bikes at scale.

Having found out that Emil Jellinek, the automobile entrepreneur responsible in 1900 for commissioning the first modern automobile, the Mercedes 35hp and establishing the Mercedes trademark in 1902 in honour of his daughter, Mercédès, originally purchased and sold bicycles, we were off.

With millions of used bikes, half of which ending up in landfill, a $120m market for used bikes in Australia and the hands-on nature of working with bikes, *Brainwave Bikes*[958] was established in partnership with Mercedes-Benz, 99 Bikes, Cleanaway (bikes from hard rubbish collections), local governments (bikes at transfer centres) and WISE Employment (for referrals). In its first 4 years, the social enterprise has collected over 10,000 bikes, refurbished and sold nearly half at its superstore and pop-up stores, and recycled the rest, saving over 100 tonnes of waste and 700 tonnes of carbon emissions, whilst providing affordable and quality bicycles for all ages, including donations to local refugee children.

[958] https://brainwavebikes.org.au/

Such is the quality of the bikes and the business, many customers have come into the store not realising they are used bikes. Brainwave is on a journey to change the attitude of Australians to used bikes – from sitting in their backyards as waste to deserving a second life – and the disabled people who serve them, as well as employers, to employing very abled people living with a disability.

WHAT

Disability is an umbrella term for impairments of body function or structure, activity limitations or participation restrictions. Disability can be related to genetic disorders, illnesses, accidents, ageing, injuries or a combination of these factors. Importantly, how people experience disability is affected by environmental factors – including community attitudes and the opportunities, services and assistance they can access – as well as by personal factors[959].

The *United Nations Convention on the Rights of Persons with Disabilities* calls on member States to ensure and promote the full realisation of all human rights and fundamental freedoms for all persons with disabilities without discrimination of any kind on the basis of disability[960].

In Australia, to uphold the rights of people with disabilities, the *Disability Discrimination Act 1992* requires that people with disabilities be given equal opportunity to participate in and contribute to the full range of economic, social, cultural and political activities. The Act protects people with a disability by setting standards for education, employment, accommodation, services (such as banking, the internet and public transport), and access to public places.

A critical element of inclusion is the opportunity and entitlement of people with disability to live, learn, work, play, create and engage alongside people without disability - a future where people with disability live free from violence, abuse, neglect and exploitation; human rights are protected; and individuals live with dignity, equality and respect, can take risks, and develop and fulfil their potential.

As Ashleigh, an artist with a brain injury, testified to the *2023 Disability Royal Commission*, Australians need to recognise disability as 'just another part of being human. I would love to be recognised as an artist and member of the community first, and a person with disability second. I would also like the

---

959 Australian Institute of Health and Welfare (2007) *People with disability in Australia* at https://www.aihw.gov.au/reports/disability/people-with-disability-in-australia/contents/about-this-report/defining-disability

960 https://social.desa.un.org/issues/disability/crpd/article-4-general-obligations

meaningful, significant contributions that all people with disability make to society to be better recognised'[961].

A person is considered to have a disability if they have any limitation, restriction, or impairment that restricts everyday activities and has lasted, or is likely to last, for 6 months or more. 15 per cent of Australians aged 0-64 years have disability, compared to over half of people aged 65 years and over[962].

The latest statistics from the Australian Bureau of Statistics show that nearly a million children and young people have a disability with half having a profound or severe disability, a nearly 50 per cent increase from 2018. Over two thirds need some support with everyday activities[963].

At 6.6 per cent, or over 500,000 children and young people, the largest group are those with learning and understanding disability, such as differences with learning new things, solving problems, focusing or remembering things.

Nearly half, or 445,000 have a psychosocial disability, which includes nervous or emotional conditions, mental illness, memory problems or periods of confusion, and social or behavioural difficulties. At 1 in 27 children, the prevalence of intellectual disability in this age group is due principally to autism, a persistent developmental disorder characterised by symptoms evident from early childhood, including difficulty in social interaction, restricted or repetitive patterns of behaviour and impaired communication skills. Australia has one of the highest prevalence rates in the world, around double that of Canada, 1.6 times the US and around 2.5 times higher than the UK[964].

A Third, or 310,000, have a physical disability, which includes breathing difficulties, blackouts, seizures or loss of consciousness, chronic or recurring pain or discomfort, incomplete use of arms or fingers, difficulty gripping or holding things, incomplete use of feet or legs, restriction in physical activities or work, and disfigurement or deformity

---

[961] Disability Royal Commission (2023) *Final Report. Executive summary. Our vision for an inclusive Australia and Recommendations*, Commonwealth of Australia, Canberra at https://disability.royalcommission.gov.au/publications/final-report-executive-summary-our-vision-inclusive-australia-and-recommendations

[962] Australian Bureau of Statistics (2024) *Disability, Ageing and Carers, Australia: Summary of Findings* at https://www.abs.gov.au/statistics/health/disability/disability-ageing-and-carers-australia-summary-findings/2022

[963] Australian Bureau of Statistics (2025) *Children and young people with disability, 2022* at https://www.abs.gov.au/articles/children-and-young-people-disability-2022

[964] https://www.afr.com/politics/federal/australia-s-record-high-autism-rates-plausibly-linked-to-ndis-20231108-p5eilg

Over 1 in 4, or 280,000, of these children and young people had a sensory disability, which includes loss of sight, loss of hearing and speech difficulties.

Over half of these children and young people are in 2 or more disability groups.

As the most common physical disability in Australian children, about 35,000 Australians live with the disability. 'Cerebral' meaning 'of the brain' and 'palsy' referring to 'a lack of muscle control' affects body movement, muscle control, muscle coordination, muscle tone, reflex, posture and balance. People who have cerebral palsy may also have visual, learning, hearing, speech, epilepsy and intellectual impairments. The good news is that, at one in 700 children, the rate of Cerebral Palsy has fallen to 1.5 in 1,000 live births, one of the lowest rates in the world and a sustained decrease of around 40 per cent from twenty years ago[965].

Additionally, about 1 in 200 children, or 25,000, have epilepsy, a neurological condition where children have a predisposition to recurrent, unprovoked seizures, which can be life-threatening[966].

Up to 120 babies and 400 children have a stroke in Australia each year, including in utero. Stroke is more common in newborns and young babies than older children, affecting 1 in 2,300 to 5,000 newborns[967].

An acquired brain injury (ABI) refers to any type of brain damage that happens after birth from trauma or injury to the head, brain tumour, stroke, degenerative brain conditions, drugs, alcohol or poisons, or not getting enough oxygen to the brain for an extended time (for example, a near-drowning). About 20,000 children aged under 15 years have an ABI[968].

Sadly, the challenge of their disability is compounded by other Themes in this book, particularly poverty and disadvantage, homelessness, family and domestic violence, child abuse, youth justice and social cohesion.

Almost 1 in 2 people with a disability in Australia live in or near poverty, with nearly a 3rd of children with disability (or 475,000) living in a household with

---

965 https://cerebralpalsy.org.au/our-research/research-projects-priorities/cp-register/#:~:text=The%20report%20includes%20data%20from,severity%20of%20CP%20is%20declining.

966 https://www.rch.org.au/neurology/patient_information/about_epilepsy/

967 https://strokefoundation.org.au/about-stroke/learn/childhood-stroke/about-childhood-stroke

968 Australian Institute of Health and Welfare (2023) *Disability in Australia: acquired brain injury* at https://www.aihw.gov.au/reports/disability/disability-australia-acquired-brain-injury/summary

a low level of household weekly income[969]. This is more than double the rate of poverty experienced in the general population and more than double the OECD average[970].

Disabled Australians are more likely than those without disability to have experienced violence, abuse or sexual harassment at some point in their lives. Nearly 2 in 3 of disabled adults have experienced violence after the age of 15, compared to 45 per cent without disability; over half of adults with disability have experienced physical violence after the age of 15, compared to a 1 in 3 without disability; and over 1 in 5 adults with disability have experienced at least one incident of sexual violence after the age of 15, compared to 1 in 10 without disability[971].

Disabled people, particularly those with cognitive disabilities, are significantly overrepresented at all stages of the criminal justice system, from police contact and arrest, through to court processes and correctional settings. People with disability have also come into contact with the justice system at high rates as victims of crime.

In response to the widespread community concerns about violence, neglect, abuse and exploitation faced by disabled people over many years, the Australian Government launched the *Royal Commission into Violence, Abuse, Neglect and Exploitation of People with Disability,* commonly known as the *Disability Royal Commission.* Their report in 2023 made 222 recommendations on how to improve laws, policies, structures and practices to ensure a more inclusive and just society that supports the independence of people with disability and their right to live free from violence, abuse, neglect and exploitation[972].

The *Disability Discrimination Bill 1992* was described in parliament as 'the vision [for] a fairer Australia where people with disabilities are regarded as equals, with the same rights as all other citizens, with recourse to systems that redress any infringements of their rights'. The Commission noted that 'these expectations have not been realised and recommended amendments to make

---

[969] Australian Institute of Health and Welfare (2024) *People with disability in Australia* at https://www.aihw.gov.au/reports/disability/people-with-disability-in-australia/contents/income-and-finance/income

[970] OECD (2009) *Sickness, disability and work: Keeping on track in the economic downturn – background paper* at http://www.oecd.org/dataoecd/42/15/42699911.pdf

[971] Centre of Research Excellence in Disability and Health (2021) *Nature and extent of violence, abuse, neglect and exploitation against people with disability in Australia* at https://credh.org.au/nature-and-extent-of-violence/

[972] Royal Commission into Violence, Abuse, Neglect and Exploitation of People with Disability (2023) *Final Report*, Commonwealth of Australia, Canberra

the Disability Discrimination Act more effective in promoting equality and enhancing the right of people with disability to live free from discrimination'[973].

The Commission also found that Australia is party to the 7 'core' international human rights treaties, including the *Convention on the Rights of Persons with Disabilities (CRPD)*, but existing measures do not give sufficient effect to Australia's obligations under the CRPD and people with disability are not adequately protected against violence, abuse, neglect and exploitation. They recommended that, to translate the international human rights of people with disability into Australian domestic law, the Australian Government should commit to the enactment of an Australian Disability Rights Act[974].

In terms of services for disabled people, the Commission's report concluded that 'mainstream systems must be significantly reformed to remove barriers to people with disability accessing education, employment and housing to improve outcomes and to enable meaningful inclusion'[975].

Despite businesses that employ disabled people benefiting from the diverse range of skills, talents and qualifications that they have to offer, as well as higher rates of retention, better attendance and fewer occupational health and safety incidents than those without a disability[976], the unemployment rate for disabled people is more than twice the rate for people without disability[977].

Even when they have gained employment, increasing discrimination means that many workers with disability across Australia are still working in environments that undermine their safety, wellbeing and ability to contribute fully. A 2025-26 survey reported that nearly half of workers with disability reported discrimination and/or harassment at work in the last 12 months, compared with a quarter of workers without disability, meaning workers with disability were almost twice as likely to face these behaviours[978].

---

[973] ibid, p.61

[974] Ibid, p.53

[975] Ibid, p.89

[976] K Hindle, J Noble, and B Phillips (1999) *Are workers with a disability less productive? An empirical challenge to a suspect axiom* Paper submitted to the refereed stream of the ANZAM 99 Conference, University of Tasmania), p 5; J Graffam, A Shinkfield, K Smith, and U Polzin (2002) *Employer benefits and costs of employing a person with a disability* 17 Journal of Vocational Rehabilitation, pp 251-263.

[977] Australian Bureau of Statistics (2024) *Disability, Ageing and Carers, Australia: Summary of Findings* at https://www.abs.gov.au/statistics/health/disability/disability-ageing-and-carers-australia-summary-findings/latest-release

[978] Disability Council of Australia (2025) *The Case for Inclusion @Work. Inclusion@Work Index 2025–2026* at https://www.dca.org.au/wp-content/uploads/2025/11/DCA-Inclusion-Index-2025-The-Case-for-Inclusion-FINAL-V2.pdf

Disability discrimination is when a person with a disability is treated less favourably than a person without the disability in the same or similar circumstances. It is also disability discrimination when there is a rule or policy that is the same for everyone but has an unfair effect on people with a particular disability[979].

Discrimination directly affects a person's participation and inclusion in everyday activities. It can also lead to people avoiding everyday activities, such as going to school or work, attending events or seeking medical help. This, in turn, increases the risk that disabled people will experience social isolation, which can affect their overall health and wellbeing. More than 4 in 5 (or 216,000) people aged 15–64 who have experienced disability discrimination in the previous year also avoided situations because of their disability in that time, such as using public transport, school or work, going to the shops and social occasions.

People with disability may also experience discrimination in terms of environmental or structural elements that limit their access to, and ability to participate in, the community.

About 663,000 disabled people aged 15–64 had challenges with mobility or communication when they left their homes. Of these, 3 in 10 (or 198,000) found it difficult to access buildings or facilities, including around 2 in 3 (or 126,000 people) faced difficulty getting around the building (including with stairs, internal doors, corridor widths or obstructed walkways), 4 in 9 (or 90,000) had difficulty with car parking facilities, and 4 in 10 (82,000 people) faced difficulty with approach areas, including ramps, handrails and lighting[980].

About 1 in 6, or 326,000, disabled people have difficulty using some or all forms of public transport, including using steps, facing fear or anxiety, getting to stops or stations and finding a seat or standing. A further 1 in 9, or 221,000, people are unable to use public transport at all.

Inaccessible services can limit a person's ability to receive the support they need. An estimated 1 in 7 (or 105,000) disabled people aged 15–64 avoided medical facilities in the previous year.

The unpaid carers of people with disability are Australia's unsung heroes, providing practical and emotional support to help them live their best lives. In

---

979 https://humanrights.gov.au/our-work/disability-rights/know-your-rights-about-disability-discrimination-and-harassment

980 Australian Institute of Health and Welfare (2024) *People with Disability Australia* at https://www.aihw.gov.au/reports/disability/people-with-disability-in-australia/contents/justice-and-safety/disability-discrimination?gh_jid=5590456003

2022, of the 3 million carers, 1 in 20 of all Australians, or 1.2 million people, were primary carers (providing the most assistance with the core activities of mobility, self-care, and communication), a 39 per cent increase from 2018. In addition, there were 383,600 secondary carers and almost 1.5 million other carers[981].

Nearly 1 in 7 of all carers (391,300 people) were under the age of 25, a 2/3rds increase from 2018, and almost 2 in 5 had a disability themselves.

As a cause and effect of the Gender Equality Theme, 7 in 10 primary carers are women. Becoming a carer increases their financial vulnerability as they sacrifice income, future income potential and superannuation to look after someone they love.

WHY

In the 1970s and 1980s, disability theorists rejected the medical model of disability, which saw disability as an individual defect to be eliminated, cured, or hidden away, in favour of the social model, which focuses on the environment in which a person with disability lives. However, this history of exclusion has shaped the settings, systems, and daily lives of disabled people to this day.

The social model sees people being disabled by social barriers, including discriminatory attitudes, inaccessible physical environments and forms of communication, and failures to provide adjustments needed to enable disabled people to participate in education, workplaces and the wider community[982].

The harsh truth is posed by Associate Professor Lorna Hallahan – 'people with disability and their close allies can rightly ask of their fellow Australians: do you truly value us as members of this society? The record of exclusion, discrimination and maltreatment, evident across time and into the present, suggests that this question cannot receive an unequivocal 'yes''[983].

---

[981]Australian Bureau of Statistics (2024) *Disability, Ageing and Carers, Australia: Summary of Findings* at https://www.abs.gov.au/statistics/health/disability/disability-ageing-and-carers-australia-summary-findings/latest-release

[982] Disability Royal Commission (2023) *Final Report. Executive summary. Our vision for an inclusive Australia and Recommendations*, Commonwealth of Australia, Canberra at https://disability.royalcommission.gov.au/publications/final-report-executive-summary-our-vision-inclusive-australia-and-recommendations

[983] Hallahan L and Flinders University *(2021) Disability in Australia: Shadows, struggles and successes,* Report prepared for the Royal Commission into Violence, Abuse, Neglect and Exploitation of People with Disability, November 2021, p.105 at

As a result, disabled people often confront dehumanising attitudes and are treated as 'different', 'other' and 'less than'[984]. Low expectations about what people with disability can do and achieve also shape their experiences in schools, workplaces, the community and other settings.

Ableism describes attitudes that motivate harmful or discriminatory behaviour toward people with disability and their experience of segregation, isolation, discrimination, prejudice, systemic bias and oppression[985]. Ableism is more than just negative and prejudiced attitudes about disabled people, it occurs when prejudice is accompanied by the power to discriminate against, repress or limit the rights of others.

Ableism identifies attitudes and behaviours that classify disabled people as different, less than, or inferior to people without disability, incapable of exercising choice and control, and a burden on society[986]. While there are multiple complex causes behind the violence, abuse, neglect and exploitation experienced by people with disability, ableism is a fundamental driver[987].

Ableism influences how individuals, communities and society view, value and treat people with disability, including the internalised beliefs a person holds about themselves or others; in interpersonal relationships and the treatment of people with disability with whom we live, socialise and engage; the social and cultural norms that implicitly or explicitly condone ableism; institutional or

---

https://disability.royalcommission.gov.au/system/files/2023-05/Research%20Report%20-%20Disability%20in%20Australia%20-%20Shadows%2C%20struggles%20and%20successes.pdf

984 Clifton S (2020) *Hierarchies of power: theories and models of disability and their implications for violence, abuse, neglect, and exploitation of people with disability*, Report prepared for the Royal Commission into Violence, Abuse, Neglect and Exploitation of People with Disability, October 2020, pp 15–16.

985 Transcript, Ronald Sackville (Chair), Public Hearing 28, 10 October 2022, P-4 [30–40]; Transcript, Natalie Wade, Public Hearing 18, 8 November 2021, P-45 [16–18]; Shane Clifton, *Hierarchies of power: theories and models of disability and their implications for violence, abuse, neglect, and exploitation of people with disability*, Report prepared for the Royal Commission into Violence, Abuse, Neglect and Exploitation of People with Disability, October 2020, pp 15–16.

986 Shane Clifton, *Hierarchies of power: theories and models of disability and their implications for violence, abuse, neglect, and exploitation of people with disability*, Report prepared for the Royal Commission into Violence, Abuse, Neglect and Exploitation of People with Disability, October 2020, pp 15–16; Transcript, Natalie Wade, Public Hearing 18, 8 November 2021, P-45 [16–18]; People with Disability Australia (PWDA), We Belong Here: Our Nation Must End Exclusionary Systems that Harm People with Disability, Submission in response to *Promoting Inclusion Issues Paper*, 27 July 2021, ISS.001.00700, pp 7–8, 16; Children and Young People with Disability Australia, *Education of children and young people with disability: Submission No 1*, Submission, 28 October 2019, SUB.100.00115, pp 8, 17–18, 35–36.

987 Submissions of Counsel Assisting the Royal Commission following Public hearing 31, 3 February 2023, p 7 [4].

organisational policies and practices that exclude people with disability from particular settings, such as schools or workplaces; political and legal structures, the delivery of government services, laws and regulation, design of buildings, products, transport and public infrastructure; and access to public places and technology[988].

As well as lower labour force participation rates, the level of income support for disabled people leads to high rates of poverty. Disabled people rely on the Disability Support Pension (DSP), which, even at the maximum rate, is less than the poverty line. A 2022 Senate inquiry found that the DSP was not enough and its application process was too hard. Its 30 recommendations have largely been ignored by successive governments[989].

As the government's *Disability Strategy 2021-31* notes, building positive community attitudes towards disabled people with disability is central to achieving an inclusive society and improving all outcomes for people with disability' and 'will lead to better education outcomes, job opportunities, increased feelings of safety, and improved mental health and wellbeing for many people with disability'[990].

US research has shown that companies that have improved their disability inclusion over time were four times more likely to have total shareholder returns that outperform their peers, compared to non-improvers. On average, the improvers' total shareholders' returns outperform industry peers by 53 per cent, while other companies outperform their peers by only 4 percent[991].

However, the *Disability Royal Commission* identified 26 barriers to open employment for people with disability in Australia, including: discriminatory attitudes and behaviours during recruitment and in the workplace; employers incorrectly assuming hiring people with disability will be costly, burdensome, less productive, and risky which may result in overlooking a person's unique skills; employers lacking knowledge, skills, leadership, and resources to

988 Submissions of Counsel Assisting the Royal Commission following Public hearing 31, 3 February 2023, p 7 [4].

989 https://www.abovethelaw.com.au/calls-for-government-to-revamp-disability-support-pension-dsp/

990 Commonwealth of Australia (2021) *Australia's Disability Strategy 2021-2031*, Department of Social Services, Canberra at https://www.disabilitygateway.gov.au/document/3106

991 Accenture (2020) *Getting To Equal: The Disability Inclusion Advantage* at https://www.accenture.com/content/dam/accenture/final/a-com-migration/pdf/pdf-89/accenture-disability-inclusion-research-report.pdf

support people with disability; employers refusing to provide flexible work arrangements or workplace adjustments, including during recruitment[992].

A 2023 survey of employers found that 1 in 5 report the fear of saying or doing the wrong thing would prevent them from employing a person with disability[993].

Former Disability Discrimination Commissioner, Graeme Innes AM, advocates for targets as the only way to get people with disabilities into employment. Disability employment quotas are used in over 100 countries, including Germany, Japan, France, China, India, Russia and Indonesia, to promote work opportunities for persons with disabilities. Employers who do not meet their quota obligation are required to pay a levy or fine. In China, for example, a disability employment fee is payable into a fund for promoting the employment of people with disabilities[994]. In Australia, we only have quotas for the public service.

In 2017, the UK government set a goal to see 1 million more disabled people in work by 2027. In the first 2 years, the number of people with disability in work increased by 404,000. The target was exceeded by May 2022, with 1.3 million more disabled people in employment, 5 years ahead of schedule. The whole-of-government initiative included the *Disability Confident Scheme* which helped employers think differently about disability, and improve how they attract, recruit and retain disabled workers.

In the meantime, Australia only has the government's $1.2 billion *Disability Employment Service (DES)*. The mid-term review in 2020 found that 'providers lack specialist skills and professionalism; individual needs are neglected; program processes, information, and incentive structures are not transparent; and the number of employment outcomes achieved through the program has not shown a substantial increase since the 2018 reforms'[995]. As a result, the Australian Government in 2025 established the *Centre for Inclusive*

---

992 Disability Royal Commission (2023) *Final Report: Volume 7: Inclusive education, employment and housing—Part B*, p. 416.

993 Australian Government (2023) *Understanding workplace attitudes toward disability. Results from national research commissioned by JobAccess* at https://www.jobaccess.gov.au/sites/default/files/documents/12_2023/understanding-workplace-attitudes-toward-people-disability.pdf

994 International Labour Organization (2019) *Promoting Employment Opportunities for People with Disabilities, Quota Schemes, Volume 1* at https://www.ilo.org/publications/promoting-employment-opportunities-people-disabilities-quota-schemes-vol-1-1

995 Department of Social Services (2020) *Mid-term Review of the Disability Employment Services (DES) Program*, August 2020 at https://www.dss.gov.au/system/files/resources/des-mid-term-review-august-2020-v2.pdf

Employment and rebadged the program to Inclusive Employment Australia with improved accessibility and flexible, tailored support.

As 'what you can't see, you can't be', we marvel at the feats of the Paralympians every 4 years, but the lack of positive day-to-day role models in media, business, and our communities hinders the needed change in our attitudes towards people with disabilities. Despite 1 in 5 Australians having a disability, how many are visible?

With only 1 per cent of adverts and 30 per cent of television programmes including disabled people, Dylan Alcott's *Shift 20 Initiative* is a coalition of the nation's top brands working towards increased disability representation, inclusion, and accessibility in marketing and communications[996].

ACT

Attitudinal change is critical in shifting towards a more inclusive society. All Australians need to understand that disabled people are not a problem to be fixed, managed, or hidden away. Disabled people are no less than people without disability, incapable or a burden.

On the contrary, disabled people are strong, creative, talented and determined. They have fought long and hard to make Australia a more inclusive society where everyone can flourish. People with disability are a vital part of our diverse society. When that society is shaped to include them, they will thrive[997].

To promote a more inclusive society, we all have a role to play in addressing Ableism and enabling people with disability to play their rightful part in our communities and workplaces.

---

996 https://shift20.org/

997 Disability Royal Commission (2023) *Final Report. Executive summary. Our vision for an inclusive Australia and Recommendations*, Commonwealth of Australia, Canberra at https://disability.royalcommission.gov.au/publications/final-report-executive-summary-our-vision-inclusive-australia-and-recommendations

Participate

Go and watch the amazing skills of disability sports, such as the world champion ParaMatildas[998]. There are 22 blind sports[999], deaf sports[1000], wheelchair sports[1001], and many more para-sports[1002].

Attend an event for International Day of Persons with Disabilities[1003] on 3 December or World Autism Awareness Day on 2 April[1004].

Visit one of Dylan Alcott's initiatives, Ability Fest, Australia's first inclusive and accessible music festival, designed for everyone to experience the magic of live music.

Join *STEPtember* and step up to the challenge with your friends, colleagues, students or run club mates, and move 10,000 steps a day this September whilst fundraising to make a positive impact for people with cerebral palsy[1005].

In a plug for my agency, set and ride your cycling goal this October with *Ride for the Kids* and support children and young people with brain illnesses and injuries and their families to live their best lives.

Campaign

With a primary carer losing $392,500 in lifetime earnings to age 67 and $175,000 in superannuation at age 67, sign the *Cost of Caring* petition that asks the government to pay superannuation to unpaid carers[1006].

Join

Sign up as a member of *Children and Young People with Disability Australia (CYDA)* which promotes equal opportunity and full inclusion for children and young people with disability across Australia[1007]. And I encourage you to join *People with a Disability Australia*, the country's peak rights and advocacy organisation by and for people with disability in promoting the human rights, equality and dignity of all people with disability as a member[1008].

---

998 https://www.paramatildas.com.au/
999 https://blindsportsaustralia.com.au/sports/
1000 https://deafsports.org.au/sports/
1001 https://www.sports.org.au/
1002 https://www.paralympic.org.au/play-para-sport/
1003 https://www.idpwd.com.au/events/calendar/
1004 https://www.autismawareness.com.au/
1005 https://www.steptember.org.au/
1006 https://www.costofcaring.com.au/p/1
1007 https://cyda.org.au/get-involved/become-a-member/
1008 https://pwd.org.au/

Employ

National Disability Services has estimated that there could be as many as 200,000 Australians with disability who are not working now but want to work and could do so if they had the right assistance.

Employ people with disabilities through your local *Disability Employment Services (DES)* provider[1009], register as an employer and post jobs to attract job hunters with disabilities at *The Field*[1010] and engage job-ready job seekers with disability with *Jigsaw*[1011].

Employers can also sign up to *Children and Young People with Disability Australia's DREAM Employment Network* to connect with young people with disability, learn about reasonable adjustments, find out how to access funding and support to make your workplace accessible and get tips on how to support young people with disability to thrive in the workforce[1012].

Workplace

In the words of Leisa Hart, CEO of *Disability Services Australia*, 'diversity is about having a wide mix of people in the room. Inclusion is about ensuring that everyone there receives treatment that is beneficial to them, regardless of their specific needs. Belonging is the feeling that arises if a place actually has a culture that creates genuine space and care for differences'.

As the peak body for disability inclusion in the workplace, with 450 employers, the *Australian Disability Network* provides expert guidance, services and programs to employers, including an Access and Inclusion Index tool to give organisations insights into their strengths and opportunities on their journey to be accessible and inclusive of disabled people. The tool provides a roadmap for year-on-year progress and supports key business functions to achieve greater disability confidence and maturity[1013].

Dylan Alcott challenges the unconscious bias of employers who presume people with disability 'can't do the role' and advocates for a future where workplaces are accessible, provide reasonable supports, and employ people with disability not because they're disabled, but 'because they're good'. His

1009 https://www.dss.gov.au/our-responsibilities/disability-and-carers/programmes-services/disability-employment-services

1010 https://www.thefield.jobs/Job/Home

1011 https://jigsawaustralia.com.au/jigsawbusiness/

1012 https://cyda.org.au/youth-hub/dream-employment-network/

1013 https://australiandisabilitynetwork.org.au/resources/access-and-inclusion-index/

Get Skilled Access can assist your organisation to enhance disability accessibility and inclusion through a Disability Inclusion Action Plan[1014].

The Australian Human Rights Commission has created *IncludeAbility* to increase meaningful employment opportunities for disabled people, and to close the gap between people in the workforce with and without disability. The program includes resources for employers[1015] for an inclusive workplace and the *IncludeAbility Employer Network.*

JobAccess is a free Australian Government service that offers expert advice, practical resources and good practice strategies on matters ranging from workplace adjustments to building employer confidence in order to drive disability employment[1016].

Buy

Buy from disability social enterprises listed on *Buyability*[1017], an initiative of National Disability Services. This directory includes *Australian Disability Enterprises (ADEs)* which provide worthwhile employment for people with severe disability in areas such as manufacturing, light engineering, horticulture and landscaping, printing, packaging and distribution, agriculture, timber and furniture manufacture, recycling, hospitality, commercial laundries, car detailing, and commercial and domestic cleaning.

Given the criticism of unfair low wages, segregated employment and lack of transition to open employment at ADEs[1018], the Australian government is currently assisting ADEs to transform into award wage employers.

Certified social enterprises that support people with disabilities into employment include Wise Employment's *Clean Force*[1019] which operates in Sydney, Melbourne and Bendigo and provides quality commercial cleaning services for offices, apartment complexes, entertainment venues and vacated residences, as well as roads and grounds maintenance[1020]; *OC Connections* which sells 100 per cent recycled bollards[1021]; *Auticon's* data services, software

---

1014 https://getskilledaccess.com.au/

1015 https://humanrights.gov.au/our-work/disability-rights/disability-resources-employers

1016 https://www.jobaccess.gov.au/

1017 https://buyability.org.au/

1018 Inclusion Australia (2022) *Wage equity and more choices in employment for people with an intellectual disability Research review* at https://www.inclusionaustralia.org.au/wp-content/uploads/2022/04/ADE-research-brief-April-2022.pdf

1019 https://cleanforce.com.au/

1020 https://wiseemployment.com.au/social-enterprises/clean-force-property-services/

1021 https://occonnections.org/commercial-services/eco-bollards/

development, quality assurance testing and penetration testing[1022]; graphic design from *Blend Creative*[1023]; *GG's Flowers and Hampers*[1024]; *Aussie Biscuits*[1025] and chocolate from the *Mildura Chocolate Company*[1026].

A recent success story is *Australian Spatial Analytics*, which, since 2020, has provided careers in the geospatial and engineering professions for over 150 young neurodivergent adults who may otherwise be unemployed. Neurodiverse people often have the natural skills for technology jobs. They are natural systems thinkers and problem solvers, yet they are under-employed due to biases against them[1027]. Their founder and CEO, Geoffrey Smith, became Queensland Australia of the Year in 2025.

As Geoffrey notes, Australia will need over 6.5 million big-data jobs by 2030 to keep up with technological developments. At the same time, people with Autism Spectrum Disorder are at least 6 times more likely to be unemployed than neurotypical people, despite them having the skills to drive Australia's technological transformation. We know neurodiverse people are the rock stars of the big-data economy. That's why we are passionate about matching a group of under-employed people who have excellent skills, with careers in the Digital Engineering and Geospatial industries'[1028].

Volunteer

The *Disability Australia Hub* by the Australian Federation of Disability Organisations lists the disability agencies in your State or Territory[1029]. Reach out to see how your time and skills can assist them.

Little Dreamers supports young people who provide care for a family member affected by disability, chronic or mental illness, addiction or frail age. Volunteer to become a Team leader or Group Facilitator[1030].

For 55 years, *Riding for the Disabled* has enabled people with disabilities to experience enjoyment, challenge and a sense of achievement through participation in equestrian activities to improve their quality of life, attain

1022 https://auticon.com/au/
1023 https://www.blendcreative.com.au/
1024 https://www.ggsflowers.com.au/
1025 https://www.aussiebiscuits.com.au/
1026 https://mildurachocolatecompany.com.au/
1027 https://www.asanalytics.com.au/
1028 https://www.bennelongfoundation.com/story/driving-inclusivity-in-tech
1029 https://www.disabilityaustraliahub.com.au/organisations/
1030 https://www.littledreamers.org.au/get-involved/volunteer/

personal goals and develop life skills. Join over 3,000 volunteers at a centre near you[1031].

Donate

Led by an elected Board of its members, *People With Disability* is Australia's peak disability rights and advocacy organisation which has been advancing and protecting the rights, health and wellbeing of disabled people for over forty years[1032]. *Children and Young People with Disability Australia* is the peak organisation representing the rights and interests of children and young people with disability[1033].

To help grow disability sport, *Disability Sports Australia* connects Australians with disabilities to local active and adaptive opportunities through programs like the Abilities Unleashed Program, the Sports Incubator Program, and the Accessibility Champion Certification[1034].

Help our para-athletes compete in the next Paralympics by buying a lottery ticket[1035].

1031 https://www.rda.org.au/volunteering/

1032 https://pwd.org.au/

1033 https://cyda.org.au/

1034 https://www.sports.org.au/who-we-are

1035 https://fundraise.paralympic.org.au/

GENDER EQUALITY

'Until there is true gender equality, we cannot reach our full potential and be the Australia we want to be'

SAM MOSTYN AO, GOVERNOR GENERAL

In February 2025, a prime-time radio show shone a searchlight on Australia's misogynistic underbelly.

18 months after an estimated 7 million Australians got up early in the morning to watch Australia play Italy in the second round of the FIFA World Cup in the most-watched TV event in Australian history, Triple M's Marty Sheargold likened the national women's team to year 10 girls, saying that he 'would rather hammer a nail through the head of [his] penis' than watch them play in next year's Asian Cup held in Australia. Of the SheBelieves Cup, Sheargold said 'she believes in what? It better be men'.

His comments were met with laughter from the men in the studio.

The next day, Sheargold said live on air that endometriosis was 'fake' in comparing his ability to cope with a back injury with that of women who suffer from the painful condition.

His comments were set to join the unchallenged, powerful misogynistic undercurrent that flows through Australian society, until former Hockeyroo Rosie Malone posted an edited clip of Sheargold's comments on Instagram. Matildas Alex Chidiac and Clare Wheeler responded to Malone's post, with Chidiac saying 'so sick of this shit' and Wheeler 'sport is for everyone and these views are for no one'.

The subsequent media storm drew responses from Diamonds netballers Gretel Bueta and Bianca Chatfield, while Olympian Libby Trickett said she was "livid".

A statement from Football Australia said Sheargold's remarks "not only diminish the extraordinary achievements and contributions of our women's national football team but also fail to recognise the profound impact they have had on Australian sport and society".

The next day, Sheargold issued an apology saying "any comedy including mine can miss the mark sometimes, and I can see why people may have taken offence at my comments regarding the Matildas". Triple M also apologised 'for any offence or distress caused'.

After the story went viral around the world and Prime Minister Anthony Albanese called the comments "shocking," "completely unacceptable," and "offensive", that night Triple M reported that they and Sheargold had "mutually agreed to part ways".

WHAT

Women's rights

In many ways recently, women have been at the forefront of our collective consciousness. As well as the Matildas, Barbie became one of the highest grossing films of all time with feminism and the patriarchy being talked about by millions of people; our female Olympic athletes winning nearly 3 in 4 of Australia's gold medals, 6 of the 7 gold in the pool and coming 3rd on the female medal table; Sam Mostyn AC becoming the 28th Governor General; and women become CEOs of our largest companies, such as Shemara Wikramanayake at the millionaires factory, Macquarie, Amanda Bardwell at Woolworths, Leah Weckert at Coles and Vanessa Hudson at Qantas.

However, despite some progress over recent years, Australian women still face deep and widespread gender inequality and continue to shoulder a disproportionate burden of unpaid labour across all spheres of life. From being caregivers, nurturers, and educators to taking on professional roles and community leadership, women's contributions are often undervalued and unpaid, perpetuating economic inequality[1036].

This progress may be stalling with Australians who view gender equality as 'very important' falling from 85 per cent in 2022 to 70 per cent in 2025, while

[1036]Gender equality
Commonwealth of Australia (2023) *Women's Economic Equality Final Report*, Department of the Prime Minister and Cabinet, Canberra at https://www.pmc.gov.au/sites/default/files/resource/download/womens-economic-equality-taskforce-final-report.pdf

those who believe Australia has gone 'too far' in promoting equality have doubled to 19 per cent[1037].

Our gender equality is poor compared to other countries. The *2024 Global Gender Gap Index* shows that Australia is 42nd with economic participation and opportunity, just ahead of Mongolia and behind China; 84th for educational attainment, behind Kyrgyzstan and Armenia; and 88th for health and survival, equal with Ecuador and The Gambia[1038].

Gender inequality occurs when men are valued more than women, and have more power, resources and opportunities, whilst gender equality means that women, men, girls and boys enjoy equal rights, resources, opportunities and protection. The *Sex Discrimination Act 1984* protects women from unfair treatment based on their sex, marital or relationship status, pregnancy, family responsibilities and breastfeeding. It also makes sexual harassment against the law.

Gender equality is a human right. It gives all people more choices and opportunities to reach their potential and live happy and fulfilled lives. Gender equality is also good for the community and for the economy. More equal societies are more cohesive and gender equality boosts economic growth[1039].

Australian women are among the most highly educated in the world. Girls are more likely than boys to complete Year 12 education and women aged 25 to 44 are far more likely than men to have tertiary qualifications. However, this has not translated into better economic outcomes for women[1040].

The lack of gender equity in STEM (science, technology, engineering and maths) has been highlighted by all governments. Girls and women are underrepresented at all stages of the STEM pathway, from schooling through to tertiary education and employment. For instance, women make up only 37 per cent of enrolments in university STEM courses and just 17 per cent of VET

[1037] Biddle N, Ryan M, Sheppard J (2025) *The Gender Gap Revisited: Polarisation, Progress, and Party Politics in Contemporary Australia*, Australian National University at https://politicsir.cass.anu.edu.au/files/docs/2025/4/The-gender-gap-revisited---For-web.pdf

[1038] World Economic Forum (2024) *Global Gender Gap 2024*, Insight Report, June 2024 at https://www3.weforum.org/docs/WEF_GGGR_2024.pdf

[1039] https://genderequality.gov.au/working-for-women/working-women-strategy-overview/gender-equality-australia

[1040] Australian Government (2023) *National Strategy to Achieve Gender Equality. Discussion Paper* at https://www.pmc.gov.au/sites/default/files/resource/download/national-strategy-gender-equality-discussion-paper_0.pdf

STEM enrolments. Only 15 per cent of STEM-qualified jobs are held by women[1041].

In 2025, *AirTrunk* founder Robin Khuda announced a gift of $100 million to the University of Sydney to fund a 2-decade program addressing the under representation of women studying and working in STEM with a particular focus on western Sydney.

With his view that 'talent is equally distributed in the community but opportunity is not', starting at 6 partner high schools from 2027, the program will offer tutoring and mentoring in maths, physics and engineering across years seven to 10, before 1,200 girls will be offered a place in the 'Khuda Academy' in years 11 and 12. Those who graduate from the academy will receive a guaranteed scholarship and place at the university, including funds for university accommodation and mentoring throughout their degree[1042].

The Australian Government's *Workplace Gender Equality Agency (WGEA)* notes that 'workplace gender equality is achieved when people are able to access and enjoy the same rewards, resources and opportunities regardless of gender'[1043]. But, 55 years after the landmark equal pay decision that first saw Australian women win the right to be paid the same as men for doing the same work, Australia's full-time total remuneration gender pay gap remains at 22 per cent, meaning men working full-time earn $28,425 on average a year more than women working full-time. This is not isolated to women-dominated industries - 100 per cent of occupations have a gender pay gap in favour of men[1044], with the worst sector being financial and insurance services[1045].

For instance, it is inexcusable that in Australia the accountancy profession has a 'stubborn' 18 per cent gender pay gap with men earning an extra $29,445 in

---

[1041] Australian Government (2023) *The state of STEM gender equity in 2023*, Department of Industry, Science and Resources at https://www.industry.gov.au/news/state-stem-gender-equity-2023#:~:text=Women%20make%20up%2037%25%20of,slightly%20larger%20than%20in%202021.

[1042] https://www.theguardian.com/australia-news/2025/feb/05/billionaire-robin-khuda-100m-donation-university-of-sydney-diversity-stem-sector?CMP=Share_iOSApp_Other

[1043] https://www.wgea.gov.au/topics/workplace-gender-equality/the-business-case

[1044] Workplace Gender Equality Authority (2025) *Employer gender pay gaps report* at https://www.wgea.gov.au/sites/default/files/documents/WGEA-Employer-gender-pay-gaps-report-FINAL.pdf

[1045] Workplace Gender Equality Authority (2026) *Employer gender pay gaps report 2024-25*, p.7

total remuneration annually due to women holding less than 1 in 4 equity partnerships in public practice, in addition to systematic bias[1046].

The *Workplace Gender Equality Act 2012* mandates that employers with 100 or more employees report annually on their progress towards gender equality using specific indicators like gender composition of the workforce and equal remuneration. This has enabled the WGEA to publish the gender pay gaps of nearly 5,000 Australian employers annually. These employers are now being held to account on their gender equality performance by employees, investors and the community. For the first time, employers are being challenged to articulate the drivers of their gap and their plans to address it.

The pay gap starts early with university-educated women earning less than men from the very start of their careers. For instance, dental graduates earn $10,700 more in their first full-time job if they are male, and female law graduates earn $4,700 less than men. Male architects receive a $2,400 pay premium for their first full-time job, whereas female scientists earn $3,000 less than their male counterparts with a degree in mathematics or science[1047].

Superannuation balances for men at retirement are, on average, a 3rd more than those of women. In practice, this means that women, particularly single women, are at greater risk of experiencing poverty, housing stress, and homelessness in retirement. 1 in 3 Australian women does not have any superannuation at all, including 60 per cent of women aged 65 to 69.

Despite heightened awareness and public discourse about gender equality in Australian workplaces, *Chief Executive Women's* analysis of the companies in the ASX300 showed only 25 women CEOs with 91 per cent of CEO positions held by men. With 82 per cent of CEO pipeline roles filled by men, an increasing number of companies have no women leaders in pipeline roles. Furthermore, only 27 per cent have gender balanced executive leadership teams and 7 in 10 executive leadership roles are still held by men[1048].

The underrepresentation of women in the workforce has an adverse impact on the Australian economy. If women's participation matched men's, Australia's GDP would increase by $30.7 billion annually, or 8.7 per cent, to $353 billion

---

[1046] Chartered Accountants Australian and New Zealand (2025) *Remuneration Survey Report 2024*

[1047] Herald Sun, Graduate job salaries reveal massive 'unfair' gender pay gap, Natasha Bita, National Education and Social Affairs Editor, News Corp Australia Network, 15 November 2020 accessed at https://www.heraldsun.com.au/education/schools-hub/graduate-job-salaries-reveal-massive-unfair-gender-pay-gap/news-story/ff09c0acdc6d38d258bfa2a51edf6b7a

[1048] Chief Executive Women (2024) *Senior Executive Census 2024. Keeping Score of a Losing Game* at https://cew.org.au/research-resources/research

by 2050 and create an additional 1 million full-time equivalent workers with post-school qualifications[1049]. Another analysis adds $128 billion to the value of the Australian economy that can be realised by purposefully removing the persistent and pervasive barriers to women's full and equal participation in economic activity[1050].

Unsurprisingly, gender equality has been shown to increase organisational performance and enhance the attraction and retention of employees. A study of over a thousand leading firms across 35 countries and 24 industries found that gender diversity relates to more productive companies, as measured by market value and revenue, but only where there is the widespread cultural belief that gender diversity is important[1051].

Research by *McKinsey & Company* found that companies in the top quartile for gender diversity on their executive teams were 21 per cent more likely to experience above average profitability whilst companies with low representation of women and other diverse groups were 29 per cent more likely to underperform on profitability[1052].

Women entrepreneurs are also under represented. A 2022 *Deloitte Access Economics* report found that only 22 per cent of Australian start-ups are founded by women, with only 0.7 per cent of private start-up funding in 2021/22 received by solely women-founded businesses[1053]. *Boston Consulting Group*, in partnership with the *Cherie Blair Foundation*, found that boosting the number of female entrepreneurs to parity with men would boost the Australian economy by between $71 billion and $135 billion[1054].

[1049] Equity Economics (2021) *Back of the pack – How Australia's parenting policies are failing women and our economy*, December 2021, p 9 and Chief Executive Women (2002) *Addressing Australia's critical skill shortages: Unlocking women's economic participation*, Sydney

[1050] Deloitte Access Economics and Australians Investing in Women (2022) *Breaking the Norm: Unleashing Australia's Economic Potential'*, Deloitte Access Economics, November 2022, p. vii

[1051] Zhang, Letian. "An Institutional Approach to Gender Diversity and Firm Performance." *Organization Science* 31, no. 2 (March–April 2020): 439–457

[1052] McKinsey & Company (2018) *Delivering Through Diversity*, accessed at https://www.mckinsey.com/business-functions/organization/our-insights/delivering-through-diversity

[1053] Deloitte Access Economics (2022) *Accelerating women founders: The untapped investment opportunity*, page 6 at https://www.deloitte.com/au/en/services/economics/analysis/accelerating-women-founders.html

[1054] Boston Consulting Group (2019) *Want to Boost the Global Economy by $5 Trillion? Support Women as Entrepreneurs* at https://www.bcg.com/publications/2019/boost-global-economy-5-trillion-dollar-support-women-entrepreneurs

As well as being disadvantaged in education and employment, women bear the burden of care at home. While there have been changes in traditional caring roles, with increasing numbers of women entering the workforce and more gender balance in care, particularly parenting roles, women are still overwhelmingly responsible for care. On average, women spend 64 per cent of their 'working hours' with no remuneration, compared to 36 per cent for men[1055].

Australia's entrenched gender inequality has serious implications for the health, safety, and wellbeing of women and girls in Australia.

2 in 3 of Australian women report experiencing gender bias in health care, especially in sexual and reproductive health and chronic pain. Common themes included women's sense of dismissal and not being believed, disrespectful treatment, significant financial burdens and poorer health outcomes due to delayed diagnoses and treatments[1056]. Furthermore, a 2025 Victorian report found the health care system was built around 'Caucasian male biology', making it difficult for women and girls to access care and support for pain[1057].

Because of a lifetime of gendered inequality, income poverty, family violence and caring responsibilities, tragically, single older women are the fastest growing group of those presenting to homelessness services[1058]. Half of women who choose to leave a violent relationship will end up in poverty or homelessness[1059].

[1055] Workplace Gender Equality Agency (2016) *Unpaid care work and the labour market* at https://www.wgea.gov.au/sites/default/files/documents/australian-unpaid-care-work-and-the-labour-market.pdf

[1056] Australian Government, Department of Health and Aged Care (2024) #EndGenderBias Survey Summary Report, National Women's Health Advisory Council, p.4 at https://www.health.gov.au/sites/default/files/2024-03/endgenderbias-survey-results-summary-report_0.pdf

[1057] Victorian Government Department of Health (2025) *Bridging the Gender Pain Gap. The Inquiry into Women's Pain Report 2025*, Women's Health and Wellbeing Program at https://www.health.vic.gov.au/inquiry-into-womens-pain#the-inquiry-into-womens-pain-report

[1058] https://www.rpsgroup.com/about-us/news/rps-and-haa-throw-spotlight-on-women-s-homelessness-for-iwd-2024/#:~:text=In%20recent%20years%2C%20there's%20been,income%20poverty%2C%20and%20caring%20responsibilities.

[1059] Summers A (2022) *The choice: Violence or poverty*, University of Technology Sydney, Impact Economics

With less time in the paid workforce than men, the gender pay gap, separation, unpaid caregiving for older family members and family violence, women have less savings and up to $94,700 lower income during retirement than men[1060].

Gender inequality feeds into family and domestic violence through the entrenched power and influence held by men, whether in our political systems, workplaces, sport, arts, home and the community, with violence against women through excusing male behaviour, sense of ownership of female partners and gender stereotyping[1061].

This also means that sexual harassment is still common in Australian workplaces. In a 5 year period to 2022, more than 2 in 5 women reported having been sexually harassed at work. In male-dominated sectors, that's even higher. 3 out of 5 women working in telecommunications, over half of all women working in construction[1062] and more than half of migrant women (including 82 per cent in construction)[1063] reported sexual harassment. It is estimated that workplace sexual harassment costs the Australian economy $2.6 billion annually in lost productivity[1064].

Other genders

Gender equality applies to all genders, including those that identify as lesbian, gay, bisexual, transgender, gender diverse, intersex, queer, asexual and questioning (LGBTQIA+) and means that people have equal rights, responsibilities and opportunities, regardless of gender.

However, the 1 in 20, or 900,000, Australians who identify, express, and/or experience gender outside the traditional gender binary suffer varied forms of discrimination, stigma, and exclusion[1065]. Indeed, several Australian studies

---

[1060] Ruting B & Blane N (2025) *Economic security in retirement. How life events affect older Australian women*, Super Members Council, Impact Economics and Policy, p.9

[1061] https://www.ourwatch.org.au/link-between-gender-inequality-and-violence

[1062] Australian Human Rights Commission (2022) *Time for respect: Fifth national survey on sexual harassment in Australian workplaces* at https://humanrights.gov.au/sites/default/files/document/publication/2022.11.25_time_for_respect_2022_final_digital.pdf

[1063] Unions NSW (2024) *Disrespected, Disregarded, and Discarded: Workplace exploitation, sexual harassment, and the experience of migrant women living in Australia on temporary visas* at https://www.unionsnsw.org.au/wp-content/uploads/2024/11/REPORT-NICSHR.pdf

[1064] Deloitte Access Economics (2020) *The economic costs of sexual harassment in the workplace* at https://www.deloitte.com/au/en/services/economics/perspectives/economic-costs-sexual-harassment-workplace.html

[1065] https://theconversation.com/almost-1-million-australians-are-lgbtqia-and-for-the-first-time-theres-a-new-national-health-plan-for-them-246143#:~:text=New%20data%20released%20by%20the,the%20Australian%20Capital%20Territory%20combined.

have found that LGBTQI+ people report high levels of verbal and physical abuse, harassment and sexual assault, including within their homes[1066].

Abuse starts early. A 2021 study found more than 90 per cent of LGBTQ+ students hear homophobic language at school with teachers within earshot not intervening, with more than 1 in 3 confronted with slurs on a daily basis[1067].

Similarly, a *La Trobe University* survey found that, in the past year, 6 in 10 LGBTQIA+ young people reported having felt unsafe or uncomfortable at secondary school due to their sexuality or gender identity, as well as one in three at TAFE and university. 1 in 4 had experienced verbal harassment; 23 per cent sexual harassment or assault; and 1 in 10 physical harassment or assault. Over 8 in 10 reported high or very high levels of psychological distress. Due to family rejection, nearly 1 in 4 had experienced homelessness[1068].

A 3rd of 3,000 LGBTQIA+ young people interviewed nationally in a *Minus 18* study had experienced physical harm for their identity in their lifetime, with 1 in 10 physically assaulted in the last year[1069].

Research indicates that most LGBTIQA+ people experience some form of violence in intimate partner or family relationships in their lifetime. The impacts of these experiences are profound, far-reaching and compounded by stigma, prejudice and discrimination towards LGBTIQA+ people. The drivers of violence are often the same as those identified for violence against women[1070].

The *eSafety Commissioner* has identified that LGBTQI+ people are an at-risk group for serious online abuse. LGBTQI+ people in Australia experience online harassment and abuse at higher rates than the national average with the research

---

1066 Carman M, Fairchild J, Parsons M, Farrugia C, Power J and Bourne A (2020) *Pride in Prevention. A guide to primary prevention of family violence experienced by LGBTIQ communities*, Rainbow Health Victoria, p.6

1067 https://www.westernsydney.edu.au/newscentre/news_centre/story_archive/2021/opinion_9_in_10_lgbtq_students_say_they_hear_homophobic_language_at_school,_and_1_in_3_hear_it_almost_every_day

1068 https://www.latrobe.edu.au/news/articles/2021/release/lgbtqa-youth-national-survey-published

1069 Minus18 (2025) *Queer Youth Now. The National Survey of LGBTQIA+ Youth Voice in Australia* at https://res.cloudinary.com/minus18/image/upload/v1749769528/Queer%20Youth%20Now/Queer_Youth_Now_Report_2025_fnz7rx.pdf

1070 Australian Institute of Health and Welfare (2024) *LGBTIQ+ People* https://www.aihw.gov.au/family-domestic-and-sexual-violence/population-groups/lgbtiqa-people

showing that the LGBTIQ+ community experiences online hate at more than double the national average[1071]. Nearly 1 in 4 lesbian, gay and bisexual people experience image-based abuse compared with 1 in 5 heterosexual people in Australia[1072].

Abuse of LGBTQI+ Australians is not confined to education, home or online. Nearly half of people who are gay or lesbian have experienced workplace sexual harassment in the last 5 years[1073] and 80 per cent have witnessed or experienced homophobia in sport[1074]. A 2024 study reported that over half of LGBTIQA+ young people have witnessed discrimination and 4 in 10 have experienced discrimination in sport, mostly through verbal vilification. With sport unwelcoming and hostile to LGBTIQA+ communities, the impact of this discrimination in sport and movement settings, most common in youth environments, has significant short- and long-term impacts on young LGBTIQA+ people's health and wellbeing[1075].

This was brought home in August 2025 when Adelaide star Izak Rankine became the 6th reported homophobic slur in the AFL in the previous 18 months, followed by former West Coast Eagles defender Mitch Brown coming out as the first current or former openly bisexual male player in the AFL's nearly 130-year history. He said there were times in his life and career in the AFL when he stayed silent due to the 'fear of people thinking that I was gay or bisexual'[1076].

As a result, LGBTIQ+ communities experience higher levels of mental ill health, suicidality and self-harm, compared with the general population. 3 in 4 experience a mental disorder at some time in their life, compared with 1 in 4 heterosexual people, and nearly 3 in 5 had a 12-month mental disorder,

---

[1071] https://www.esafety.gov.au/lgbtiq/learning-lounge/dealing-with-online-abuse/online-hate-discrimination#online-hate-targeting-lgbtiq-people

[1072] https://www.esafety.gov.au/communities/protecting-voices-risk-online

[1073] https://www.genderequalitycommission.vic.gov.au/intersectionality-work/chapter-5-gender-and-LGBTIQ-employees

[1074] https://outonthefields.com/wp-content/uploads/2020/11/Summary-of-Australian-Results-Out-on-the-Fields.pdf

[1075] Storr R, Yeomans C, Albury K, Ridgers N and Sherry E (2024) *Free to Exist. Documenting participation data on LGBTIQA+ young people in sport and physical activity*, Swinburne Sport Innovation Research Group at https://www.vichealth.vic.gov.au/sites/default/files/2024-05/Free_to_Exist_Report_2024.pdf

[1076] https://www.abc.net.au/news/2025-08-31/afl-culture-issues-homophobia/105709128?utm_source=abc_news_app&utm_medium=content_shared&utm_campaign=abc_news_app&utm_content=other

compared with 1 in 5 of heterosexual people[1077]. 9 in 10 display lifetime prevalence of suicidal thoughts[1078].

It is no wonder then that over 1 in 4 LGBTQI+ people still hide their sexuality or gender identity at social and community events[1079].

WHY

Patriarchy

When Millicent Fawcett's purse was stolen at Waterloo station in London, the pickpocket was caught and charged with 'stealing from the person of Millicent Fawcett a purse containing £1. 18s 6d, *the property of Henry Fawcett*'[1080]. Millicent became the prime mover in the fight for women's suffrage in England leading to the Womanhood Suffrage League being formed in Australia in 1891. 3 years later, South Australia became the first electorate in the world to grant women the right to vote and to stand for parliament.

Women have been fighting for their rights ever since in the face of ongoing male dominance of business, politics, law and the media. As the recent South Australia Royal Commission noted 'the ongoing and systematic social conditions that enable domestic, family and sexual violence across generations are rooted in harmful patriarchal norms embedded within society'[1081].

Gender stereotypes see girls and boys treated differently from when they are babies. They shape the vocational aspirations of school-aged children, relationship dynamics for young people and adults, and can lead to women and men taking on roles at home and at work that flow through to economic security at retirement. These attitudes can be produced and reinforced in households, workplaces, clubs and institutions and are experienced differently across communities and cultures.

Powerful and outdated gender norms on current policy settings that rely on assumptions that women will (or should) do the bulk of unpaid care and

---

[1077] Australian Bureau of Statistics (2024) *Mental health findings for LGBTQ+ Australians* at https://www.abs.gov.au/articles/mental-health-findings-lgbtq-australians

[1078] Australian Institute of Health and Welfare (2024) *LGBTIQ+ Australians: suicidal thoughts and behaviours and self-harm* at https://www.aihw.gov.au/suicide-self-harm-monitoring/data/populations-age-groups/suicidal-and-self-harming-thoughts-and-behaviours

[1079] https://www.theequalityproject.org.au/key-stats

[1080] Brenda Hale, 'On Courage', Millicent Fawcett Memorial Lecture 2018, 13 December 2018, 1–2.

[1081] Government of South Australia (2025) *Royal Commission into Domestic, Family and Sexual Violence. Report*, August 2025

domestic work, result in a disrupted career trajectory, earning less and accumulating fewer assets across their lifetimes.

Male authority is entrenched from birth, literally, with researchers finding that a cultural preference for sons among some ethnic groups has led to more boys than girls being born in Victoria in recent years[1082].

By the early years of primary school, gender stereotypes have already influenced children to aspire to traditionally male and female designated vocations. These patterns of care are generally driven by social and economic structures that reflect and reinforce gendered care norms that frame women as primary caregivers. Think of traditional girls' toys – dolls, tea sets – compared to Tonka toys and army figures for boys.

The recent agreement by State and Territory Education Ministers with $77 million from the Australian Government will roll out *Consent and Respectful Relationships Education* in schools for 2204-2028, providing: evidence-based professional learning for staff; whole-school approaches to preventing gender-based violence; partnering with high-quality external providers to support delivery; and delivering targeted support for vulnerable and marginalised groups[1083].

Women face multi-faceted, complex and deeply embedded barriers to participation, retention and progression at all stages of the STEM pathway. These barriers are compounded for women from underrepresented groups. Barriers negatively affect girls' and women's perceptions of their STEM abilities, reduce their interest, confidence and motivation to pursue STEM study and careers, and hinder long-term STEM engagement[1084].

Over the past decade, Australia has had hundreds of disconnected STEM activities that have been ineffective in addressing gender equity issues. For instance, even though university enrolments for women in STEM courses have increased, their completion rates are much lower than men, especially in engineering (18 per cent of completions) and technology (23 per cent of completions)[1085]. The government's 2023 *Women in STEM Evaluation report*

1082 https://www.latrobe.edu.au/news/articles/2018/release/gender-bias-leads-to-more-male-births

1083 https://www.education.gov.au/newsroom/articles/funding-consent-and-respectful-relationships-education-australian-schools

1084 ACIL Allen (2023) *Women in STEM Evaluation Final Report*. Report for the Department of Industry, Science and Resources at https://www.industry.gov.au/sites/default/files/2023-08/women-in-stem-evaluation-final-report-2023.pdf

1085 https://theconversation.com/australias-key-program-for-gender-equity-in-stem-was-scrapped-last-week-this-could-actually-be-good-news-231321

emphasised the importance of greater coordination across programs to avoid duplication, lack of connection, and missed opportunities, as well as monitoring and evaluation with clear indicators of success or failure. The government's recommendations included that 'urgent action is needed to create safe and inclusive workplaces that value diverse skills and experiences. This is critical to attract and retain diverse people in STEM jobs'[1086].

It is no wonder that women are turned off from working in male dominated industries and are underrepresented with 75 per cent of women in the construction industry in Australia report having experienced gender-based adversity within their careers and 43 per cent feeling that they don't have the same opportunities and career advancements as their male counterparts.

In male dominated careers, such as surgery and the veterinary profession, women (compared to men) report less career engagement because of their more frequent experiences of gender discrimination and lower perceived fit with those higher up the career ladder. In turn, these barriers predicted reduced expectations of success in their field and expected success of their sacrifices, which in turn predicted lower willingness to make sacrifices[1087].

Women and men can experience work very differently. Women are more likely to work in lower paid roles and lower paid fields, are more likely to work part-time or casually, and are more likely to take breaks from paid employment to provide unpaid care for others. As a consequence, over their lifetimes, they will earn significantly less than men.

Australia's retirement income system does not adequately accommodate this difference. It structurally favours higher income earners who work full-time, without breaks, for the entirety of their working life. The women who do not fit this pattern of work face a significant handicap when saving for their retirement. For instance, many women prefer to return to work part-time to accommodate caring for children and are frequently forced to 'dumb down' their careers — taking roles with less skill, responsibility and pay — in order to get the flexibility they need.

In Australia, health and personal care workforces are highly feminised. The predominance of women in these workforces is strongly driven by gender norms and further contributes to a gender pay gap in Australia, resulting from

---

[1086] Australia Government (2024) *Pathway to Diversity in STEM Review. Final Recommendations* at https://www.industry.gov.au/sites/default/files/2024-02/pathway-to-diversity-in-stem-review-final-report.pdf

[1087] Ryan MK (2023) *Addressing workplace gender inequality: Using the evidence to avoid common pitfalls.* Br J Soc Psychol. 2023 Jan;62(1):1-11. doi: 10.1111/bjso.12606. Epub 2022 Nov 22. PMID: 36415906; PMCID: PMC10100361.

casual, part-time work arrangements and the low pay within the sectors. These factors continue to support the stereotype that care is 'women's work' or work that can be done in the home and not paid. Stereotypes also hold that care work is something women do for the love of it rather than for money or recognition. These stereotypes can also mean that men who do care work face discrimination about their ability to do their job.

Gendered attitudes also drive violence against women by reinforcing rigid gender roles that normalise men's control and condone their disrespect against women, while undermining women's independence and autonomy[1088]. As part of *the National Plan to Reduce Violence against Women and their Children*, the *Stop it at the Start* campaign has raised awareness of the need to change norms and behaviours relating to violence, with recent evaluation research suggesting that '68 per cent of influencers recalled the campaign, with 73 per cent of those people taking action as a result'[1089].

With sport playing such an important role in Australian society, in 2024, the Australian Government, Australian Sports Commission and the State and Territory Agencies for Sport and Recreation launched the *National Gender Equity in Sport Governance Policy* to address the under representation of women in sports leadership with Gender Equity Targets set for the governance of government funded national and state level sport bodies. This will require the Australian sport sector to reach the following standards by 1 July 2027: 50 per cent of all board directors are women and/or gender diverse; 50 per cent of board chairs are women and/or gender diverse; and 50 per cent of specified board sub-committee members are women and/or gender diverse[1090].

In sport, it has been refreshing to see the success of women's teams in male-dominated sports, such as the women's leagues in Australian Rules Football and the National Rugby League, equal prize money for women players in the Australian Open and the world champion women's sevens rugby team, the Wallaroos.

However, there is still considerable resistance to change that would elevate women's social and economic position with Australian men being more

[1088] Our Watch (2021) *Change the Story*, Second Edition at https://assets.ourwatch.org.au/assets/Key-frameworks/Change-the-story-summary-AA.pdf

[1089] https://plan4womenssafety.dss.gov.au/initiative/stop-it-at-the-start-campaign/

[1090] https://ministers.pmc.gov.au/gallagher/2024/mandated-gender-equity-targets-sport#:~:text=For%20the%20first%20time%20in,women%20and/or%20gender%20diverse.

traditional in their gender attitudes than the global average, with 30 per cent of Australian men believing gender inequality doesn't really exist[1091].

A similar result was reported by *Plan International's 2023* survey, which found that 17 per cent of people believe gender equality is no longer an issue in Australia and that the change for equality for women had gone too far. Nearly a 1 in 3 agreed that equality doesn't make sense when there are basic biological differences between males and females, and a quarter agreed that families function well and children are best supported when mothers do the caring and fathers earn the income[1092].

Then there is the intensifying global backlash against progressive 'woke' policies by anti-rights political leaders (including Trump), influencers and groups that are 'well organised, well funded and highly effective' who 'exploit the growing social isolation of some young men to pull them into the misogynistic space and use them as foot soldiers'[1093]. Consequently, 'across the world, the belief that gender equality policies harm boys and men is fast gaining traction'[1094].

As the United Nations warns, this growing online 'manosphere' of websites, blogs, and online forums promoting masculinity, misogyny, and opposition to feminism is moving misogyny to the mainstream[1095].

So, it is up to all of us to continue to challenge male power and privilege in all the settings in which we live and work. And with most vast majority of Australian boys believing that girls should be treated as equals across all areas of life despite the pressures to be 'masculine', we need to encourage our sons, grandsons, nephews and cousins to challenge the peer pressure. After all, 'despite the growing influence of online spaces, boys continue to rely on 'real-life' relationships — especially parents — for guidance on personal issues and their understanding of masculinity[1096]'.

[1091] Ipsos and Global Institute for Women's Leadership (2022) *One in five Australians thinks women who say they were abused often make up or exaggerate claims of abuse or rape – the highest of any western nation* at https://www.ipsos.com/en-au/one-five-australians-thinks-women-who-say-they-were-abused-often-make-or-exaggerate-claims-abuse-or

[1092] Plan International Australia (2023) *Gender Compass. A segmentation of Australia's views on gender equality* at https://www.plan.org.au/wp-content/uploads/2023/09/GenderCompass_Report.pdf

[1093] Ibid, p.22

[1094] Ibid p.23

[1095] https://news.un.org/en/story/2025/03/1160876

[1096] Jesuit Social Services (2025) *The Adolescent Man Box Findings from a survey with Australian adolescents aged 14–18 years*, p.5

Other genders

It seems incredible now that, in my lifetime, homosexual acts between consenting adults in private were a criminal offence and that homosexuality was included in the list of the Australian Medical Association's illnesses and disorders, as well as a psychiatric disorder.

Police harassment was commonplace with the first Sydney Mardi Gras in 1978, resulting in dozens of people being beaten and arrested by local officers.

In Australia, gay rights organisations were established during the late 1960s and early 1970s. The *ACT Homosexual Law Reform Society* was formed in 1969 and the *Daughters of Bilitis* in Melbourne in 1970. Sydney-based *Campaign Against Moral Persecution* galvanised the movement and branches were soon set up in Australia's other capital cities and on university campuses.

The 1972 drowning murder in Adelaide's Torrens River of a homosexual academic, Dr George Duncan, raised public awareness of the widespread harassment of homosexuals and led to the first decriminalisation with South Australia's *Criminal Law (Sexual Offences) Amendment Act 1975* which abolished offences of buggery, gross indecency and soliciting, and also created an equal age of consent for homo- and hetero-sexual acts. The Australian Capital Territory followed in 1976.

In 1978, a small group of gay people formed the *Gay Solidarity Group* and created a day of events in Sydney to raise awareness and promote political activism with their march an act of protest against the visit of homophobic National Festival of Light campaigner Mary Whitehouse, and to promote the Fourth National Homosexual Conference. At 10pm, the activists marched down Oxford Street and towards the city but were greeted by police officers who blocked their access to Hyde Park. As the activists changed their path to Kings Cross, the police moved in. 53 people were arrested. The names and occupations of the arrestees were subsequently published in the Sydney Morning Herald.

This event shook Australia, with supporters becoming more vocal. The charges were subsequently dropped, and laws concerning street marches and parades were liberalised.

Today, the march - the Sydney Gay and Lesbian Mardi Gras - draws hundreds of thousands of people and is one of the largest LGBTQI+ festivals in the world.

Over the next decade, other States and Territories gradually reformed their laws, starting with Victoria in 1980, the Northern Territory in 1983, New South Wales in 1984, Western Australia in 1989, and Queensland in 1990.

But it wasn't until 1994, when, to implement Australia's international treaty obligations under the *International Covenant on Civil and Political Rights*, a federal law, the *Human Rights (Sexual Conduct) Act 1994*, legalised sexual activity between consenting adults in private throughout Australia. It took another 3 years for the law in Tasmania prohibiting gay male sexual conduct to be repealed.

However, conservative attitudes prevailed with Prime Minister John Howard in 1997 refusing to offer a message of support to *Sydney Gay & Lesbian Mardi Gras*, saying on the TV program *A Current Affair* that he would be 'disappointed' if one of his children were to tell him they were gay or lesbian[1097].

In 2003, Prime Minister John Howard was again in the news when the *UN Human Rights Commission* declared his government in violation of equality and privacy rights under *the International Covenant of Civil and Political Rights* after it had denied a man a de facto spouse veteran's pension based on his 38 year same-sex relationship. The request from the UN that Australia take steps to treat same sex couples equally was ignored.

Then, in 2004, in response to a proposed ACT *Bill of Rights* that would allow gay couples to adopt children, the Howard government quickly enacted the *Marriage Legislation Amendment Bill* to prevent any possible court rulings allowing same-sex marriages or civil unions, with marriage legally defined as 'the union of a man and a woman to the exclusion of all others, voluntarily entered into for life'.

At the same time, State governments were removing legislative discrimination against same-sex couples, but national same-sex marriage legislation would fail 22 times in the Federal Parliament in the next thirteen years.

However, since 2007, Australian public opinion polls have indicated that most Australian citizens support same-sex marriage. The ABC's *Vote Compass* survey during the 2013 election campaign, as well data from the Australian Bureau of Statistics, commercial opinion polls and other sources, found that just one electorate – Maranoa, a vast conservative seat in south-western Queensland, opposed same-sex marriage[1098].

[1097] https://www.smh.com.au/opinion/john-howards-love-and-disappointment-20040722-gdjea1.html

[1098] https://www.theguardian.com/australia-news/2017/sep/08/australias-politicians-are-late-to-the-marriage-equality-party-but-they-are-finally-arriving

With conservative MPs dominating the Coalition, then Prime Minister Tony Abbott hoped that proposing a plebiscite on same-sex marriage would electorally wedge Labor and that same-sex marriage could be either defeated, in a 1999 republic-like turnaround, or at least substantially delayed. Unlike a referendum, which needs a majority of votes to pass, a plebiscite does not oblige the government to enact its result.

With the government's attempts to hold a plebiscite voted down in parliament, Coalition leader and supporter, Malcolm Turnbull, decided on a postal survey to gauge support for legalising same-sex marriage.

Over 1,300 companies joined the *Equality Campaign* and millions of posters appeared in local shop windows, workplaces and homes. Australian celebrities, including Chris Hemsworth, Margot Robbie and Kylie Minogue, came out en masse urging people to vote yes.

As we stood in front of the TV in our *Equality* T-shirts, we cheered as the 80 per cent turnout resulted in a 61.6 per cent "Yes" vote in favour of legalisation, including overwhelming support from voters in some of the most conservative seats. Subsequently, the Federal Parliament passed a law amending the *Marriage Act 1961* to allow same-sex couples to marry in December 2017.

Whilst we have made progress in LGBTQI+ rights, including openly trans and gender diverse people allowed to serve in the Australian Defence Force and governments apologising to people convicted under unjust laws that previously criminalised homosexual acts, we still have a way to go in Australia to change attitudes and behaviours towards LGBTQI+ people.

With sport so important to our national identity, our two largest codes that attract over 12 million fans have come up wanting. Whilst the Australian Football League has had Pride games for ten years, and now a Pride round, in 2024, Gold Coast's Wil Powell was banned for five games for a homophobic insult, just a month after Port Adelaide's Jeremy Finlayson was suspended for a similar slur. A year later, the same occurred with Adelaide's Izak Rankine.

In 2022, the National Rugby League cancelled its plans for a Pride round after 7 Manly players boycotted a key match over the team's decision to wear a Pride jersey. Other codes are doing better with Netball Australia having several initiatives to celebrate Pride, including Pride Ally programs, Pride in Sport, and Pride Rounds, the A-League's annual Pride round and Tennis Australia's *Glam Slam* held during the Australian Open.

Recognising that LGBTIQA+ people experience significant health disparities in a broad range of areas, very often shaped by experiences of stigma, discrimination or hostility that are directed towards these communities, in December 2024, the Australian Government launched the *National Action Plan for the Health and Wellbeing of LGBTIQA+ People 2025-2035* to: build capacity and scale of health and wellbeing services for LGBTIQA+ people; support LGBTIQA+ people navigating through the health system; support LGBTIQA+ people to access appropriate domestic, family and sexual violence support; minimise barriers to accessing LGBTIQA+ inclusive care; and ensure mental health and suicide prevention services are culturally safe and responsive to the needs of LGBTIQA+ people[1099].

Currently, LGBTQI+ people are not explicitly counted in the census. This means that health policy and funding, which is determined by census data, routinely leave out this population, perpetuating a cycle of invisibility in service planning and delivery.

The recent public uproar following the Australian Government's decision to renege on a commitment to have LGBTIQA+-related questions and topics in the 2026 Census and the government's backdown shows that we still want progress. Below are ways you can take action.

ACT

Gender attitudes and stereotypes can and do shift over time. To achieve gender equality in Australia, rigid attitudes and behaviours around gender need to keep changing. This means challenging stereotypes that limit how people behave, are perceived and are treated at work, at school, in relationships, in their homes, online and by their communities.

We all have a role to play, especially men, in challenging patriarchal notions of masculinity and harmful narratives that promote dominance and control over women. In particular, men and boys need to call out sexist and misogynistic behaviours anywhere they encounter them, and be encouraged, supported and recognised to do so.

Workplace

Research shows that gender equity is not simply a matter of fairness. Organisations that achieve balanced leadership are more likely to outperform their peers in company value, profitability and resilience. Gender balance delivers better decision making, stronger innovation, and enhanced capacity to

---

[1099] Commonwealth of Australia (2024) *National Action Plan for the Health and Wellbeing of LGBTIQA+ People 202 –2035*, Department of Health and Aged Care, Canberra at https://www.health.gov.au/sites/default/files/2024-12/national-action-plan-for-the-health-and-wellbeing-of-lgbtiqa-people-2025-2035.pdf

navigate shocks[1100]. Your organisation can lead the way in ensuring gender equality, especially in Board and management composition, enterprise agreements (such as domestic violence being included in personal leave), flexible work arrangements, leadership behaviours and staff training, including unconscious bias.

There is a compelling business case for more women in organisations, including:

- Companies with more women in senior management score more highly on organisational criteria than companies with no women at the top
- Companies with more women on their boards have been shown to financially outperform companies that have no women on their boards
- Companies with women in key board committee roles (such as risk and audit) perform better
- Women bring different leadership skills and behaviours to the table with teams smarter, more effective and creative[1101].

As the government agency charged with promoting and improving gender equality in Australian workplaces, the Australian Government's *Workplace Gender Equality Agency (WGEA)*[1102] provides a one-stop-shop organisations to put in place gender equality with the Gender Equality Strategy Guide and the Gender Equality Diagnostic Tool[1103].

With the WGEA Guide, join the 5,000 organisations that analyse their gender pay gap and take action[1104] and apply to WGEA to become an *Employer of Choice for Gender Equality*[1105].

1100 Bankwest Curtin Economics Centre (2025) *Gender Equity Insights 2025: The Power Of Balance* at https://www.wgea.gov.au/sites/default/files/documents/BCEC-WGEA-2025-Gender-Equity-Insights-Report.pdf

1101 Robert W (2013) Centre for Ethical Leadership, University of Melbourne at https://sage-pilot.uq.edu.au/files/127/building_a_business_case_for_gender_diversity_per cent28april_2013_per cent29.pdf

1102 https://www.wgea.gov.au/sites/default/files/documents/WGEA-EOCGE-2019-20-Guide-to-Citation-v3.0.pdf

1103 https://www.wgea.gov.au/topics/gender-strategy

1104 https://www.wgea.gov.au/take-action/gender-pay-gap/employer-gender-pay-gap-analysis-guide

1105 https://www.wgea.gov.au/leading-practice/employer-of-choice-for-gender-equality

As well as the WGEA, *Our Watch* provides free tools to help you identify key actions to ensure that gender equality and respect are at the centre of your organisation, including training[1106].

The *Champions of Change Coalition* has developed an Organisational Gender Equality Dashboard as an internal measurement framework for tracking progress towards inclusive gender equality across workplaces, target setting and reporting to the WGEA[1107].

Work180 is an employment platform that pre-screens employers to see how well they support women's careers by considering policies like paid parental leave, pay equity, flexible working arrangements, employee engagement scores, and more[1108].

LGBTIQ+ inclusion is about building a safe and productive workplace for all staff, regardless of their sexuality, gender identity, or bodily diversity. A number of organisations can guide you in creating a LGBTQI+ inclusive workplace, including *SBS*, *Minus18*,[1109] and *ACON*[1110].

Become a member of *Welcome Here* to receive the Welcome Here rainbow stickers and charter to display in a prominent place to let everyone know that LGBTQI+ diversity is welcomed and celebrated within your business[1111].

In addition, the *Rainbow Tick* Accreditation Program is for all organisations seeking to provide a safe and inclusive workplace and services for the LGBTQI+ community[1112].

Sports club

A *VicHealth* survey reported that one in three Victorians have witnessed sexism in their sports club, workplace or among family and friends – including sexist attitudes, jokes and discrimination towards women. However, less than half of those people had taken action at the time, while almost 9 in 10 believe local

---

1106 https://www.ourwatch.org.au/workplace

1107 https://championsofchangecoalition.org/wp-content/uploads/2025/08/ChampionsofChangeCoalition_Organisational_Gender_Equality_Dashboard.pdf

1108 https://work180.com/en-au

1109 https://www.minus18.org.au/workshops/workplace/

1110 https://www.pridetraining.org.au/

1111 https://www.welcomehere.org.au/

1112 https://rainbowhealthaustralia.org.au/rainbow-tick

sports clubs should take a leadership role in promoting respectful relationships between men and women within the community[1113].

Creating a Place for Women in Sport has created a pre-tool survey, gender equity self-assessment guide, gender equity action plan guide & template for sport and recreation clubs[1114].

To implement a code for your club, Our Watch has *Equality and Respect in Sport Standards*[1115] and *Club Respect* helps sports clubs build and maintain a deep culture of respect against abuse, violent attitudes and behaviours[1116]. *Our Watch* has developed a range of tools and resources to support sporting organisations address gendered drivers and prevent violence against women[1117]. *Pride in Sport* is a national charity that assists sporting organisations of all levels with the inclusion of employees, athletes, coaches, volunteers and spectators with diverse sexualities and genders[1118].

The standard you walk past …………

Whenever and wherever we are, everyone one of us, especially men, has a responsibility to challenge gender stereotypes that limit how people behave, are perceived and are treated at work, at school, in relationships, in their homes, online and by their communities.

Every man has been in situations where women have been demeaned. It could have been a joke, passing comment, gesture or opinion.

As the 2016 Australian of the Year, David Morrison, said as part of his campaign to champion gender equality in the army, 'the standard you walk past is the standard you accept'. Today, we must challenge the behaviours and actions detrimental to gender equality and stand up to the right of women and girls to be treated equally.

With children becoming aware of gender stereotypes from around 18 months old and typically, before the age of 2, are conscious of the social relevance of

---

[1113] VicHealth (2012) *More than ready: Bystander action to prevent violence against women in the Victorian community*, Victorian Health Promotion Foundation, Melbourne

[1114] https://thewellresource.org.au/topics/gender-equality-and-preventing-family-violence/share/creating-a-place-for-women-in-sport-1

[1115] https://sport.ourwatch.org.au/taking-action/the-standards/

[1116] https://clubrespect.org.au/

[1117] https://www.ourwatch.org.au/sport

[1118] https://www.prideinsport.com.au/

gender[1119], as parents, aunts, uncles and grandparents to our family, friends, colleagues and teammates, we can shift how children understand stereotypes from an early age which can have long-term impacts by changing how boys and girls view themselves and opening up more choices later in life.

When you and your family are watching TV, see how many gender stereotypes you can spot – from the pop-pom girls at a sporting event, to women (or the hapless Dad) cooking and doing household tasks in adverts, to the lack of women hero figures in action movies.

Buy

Female Owned is a social enterprise that has a directory of registered female-owned businesses in Australia[1120].

Over fifty certified social enterprises support marginalised women on the *Social Traders* directory[1121], including *WomenCAN Australia* which helps women who have been out of the paid workforce for years to get skills and jobs. Their *WomenCAN Build* division offers various facilities maintenance services delivered by female tradespeople[1122].

Other social enterprises supporting women include sauces from the *Kimchi Club*[1123], vegan-friendly, gluten-free desserts from *Chris' Kitchen*[1124], certified organic cotton period products from *TABOO*[1125], and gifts from *Global Sisters*[1126] and *Two Good Co.*[1127]

For your home and workplace, buy 100 per cent organic, plastic-free and carbon-negative pads and tampons with *Pixii*[1128].

Order your catering from *Queer Food*, a sustainable social enterprise catering company and food retailer run by Trans and Queer people[1129].

1119 Kane E. (2006) *No Way My Boys are Going to be like That! Parents' Responses to Children's Gender Nonconformity* in Gender and Society, vol. 20: 2, pp. 149- 176.

1120 https://femaleowned.com.au/directory

1121 https://www.socialtraders.com.au/find-a-social-enterprise

1122 https://www.womencanaustralia.org/social-enterprise

1123 https://kimchiclub.com.au/

1124 https://www.chriskitchen.com.au/

1125 https://tabooau.co/

1126 https://marketplace.globalsisters.org/

1127 https://twogood.com.au/

1128 https://www.pixii.com.au/

1129 https://www.queerfood.com.au/

Donate

With more than 3,000 scholarships available to Australian students across both the higher education and vocational sectors, we have a proud tradition of providing scholarships to enable disadvantaged students the opportunity to reach their potential in higher education. State governments offered merit-based scholarships for university entry before Federation. You can donate to add another place for a woman to a university scholarship program by searching for scholarships at the *Open Universities Guide*[1130].

Each State and Territory has a women's legal service which provides free and confidential advice, information, referral, community legal education and law reform, which can be found at *Women's Legal Service Australia*[1131].

Charities that focus on developing programming skills and related employment prospects for girls include *She Codes*[1132], *Code Like a Girl*[1133], *Girls Programming Network*[1134] and the *Geek Girl Academy*[1135].

In2science places STEM university students into high schools as peer mentors to help engage students and inspire them to pursue STEM studies at school and beyond[1136].

As well as providing grants to LGBTQI+ organisations, the *Pride Foundation* commissions and supports research and publications that contribute to the increased health and wellbeing of LGBTQIA+ Australians[1137].

Mentor

In Queensland, New South Wales and Victoria you can mentor women and gender diverse people with the *YWCA*[1138]. If you are in Sydney, mentor a young woman with *Warrior Women* on a structured 6 month program to enable under represented, vulnerable young Australian women aged 17- 25+ years who lack the necessary familial or community support to become resilient and independent[1139]. In the ACT, mentor with *Fearless Women*[1140].

1130 https://www.gooduniversitiesguide.com.au/scholarships
1131 https://www.wlsa.org.au/members/
1132 https://shecodes.com.au/
1133 https://www.codelikeagirl.com/
1134 https://www.girlsprogramming.network/
1135 https://girlgeekacademy.com/
1136 https://in2science.org.au/
1137 https://pridefoundation.org.au/publications/
1138 https://www.ywca.org.au/mentoring-leadership/youth-mentoring/
1139 https://warriorwoman.org.au/what-we-do/become-a-wise-warrior-mentor/
1140 https://fearlesswomen.org.au/how-we-help/mentoring/

Women 4 Stem runs the *mentor(SHE:)* program to connect women with industry-leading professionals[1141]. *Curious Minds* invites female professionals working in the STEM industry to coach high-performing girls in years 8, 9 and 10 to explore their potential in STEM studies and careers[1142]. *STEM Professionals in Schools* is a national volunteer program that creates flexible partnerships between Australian teachers and STEM professionals to provide engaging and relevant STEM learning experiences for students[1143]. The *Australian Academy of Science* also has mentor programs[1144].

Volunteer

There are plenty of women and LGBTQI+-focused charities that need your time and talents. Search on *GoVolunteer* or *SEEK Volunteer* (both run by SEEK).

Donate goods

Help end period poverty by donating women's sanitary products to *Share The Dignity* who distribute period products to those in need and work to achieve menstrual equity here in Australia.

Donate your business clothes to help women and gender-diverse jobseekers to become work-ready and find meaningful employment with *Dress for Success*[1145] and *Fitted for Work*[1146].

Participate

Host or attend an event on *International Women's Day* on or around 8 March.

To raise awareness of discrimination against the LGBTIQA+ community while also celebrating progress, take part in the *International Day Against Homophobia, Biphobia and Transphobia (IDAHOBIT)* on 17 May[1147]. Trans Awareness Week is in November[1148]. Pride events held across the country are listed on the *Australian Pride Network* website[1149].

1141 https://women4stem.com.au/mentorshe/

1142 https://curiousminds.edu.au/coaches/

1143 https://www.csiro.au/en/education/programs/stem-professionals-in-schools-program

1144 https://www.stemwomen.org.au/resources/mentoring?category=All&tagged&nid=&page=1

1145 https://dressforsuccess.org/

1146 https://fittedforwork.org/

1147 https://www.idahobit.org.au/

1148 https://www.minus18.org.au/campaigns/trans-awareness-week/

1149 https://australianpridenetwork.com.au/lgbtiq-festivals/

Campaign

With LGBTQI+ attacks on the rise, especially against the trans community and gay men, sign up to Equality Australia's *Stand Up Against Hate* for stronger laws[1150].

Pledge

In August, for *Wear It Purple Day*, make a promise to *Show Up for Queer Young People* with Minus18[1151].

[1150] https://equalityaustralia.org.au/our-work/areas-of-work/stand-up-against-hate/
[1151] https://www.minus18.org.au/campaigns/wear-it-purple-day/

INTERNATIONAL DEVELOPMENT

'Development consists of the removal of various types of unfreedoms that leave people with little choice and little opportunity of exercising their reasoned agency'

AMARTYA SEN, *DEVELOPMENT AS FREEDOM*[1152]

G'day.
I jumped.

Leaning on a new, white, gleaming four wheel drive, he looked like an Aussie tradie in shorts, singlet and boots. The vehicle was standard international aid issue, but, in a small expat community, hearing another Australian accent took me by surprise.

It was day one for Paul, starting an 18 month, US$4 million contract to build 6 machines across this dry sub-Sahal land in West Africa to take the husk off millet seed, a staple crop alongside rice, groundnuts, and corn, that is highly nutritious and can be added to soups, bread, porridge and stews.

The inedible husk must be removed before it is ready to cook. This process is known as dehulling. For generations, the women in the village have laboriously pounded the millet in a log with a bowl-shaped top, before transferring to a mat that is held on each corner and thrown up in the air for the wind to take the husks. These new machines would end their drudgery and enable large quantities of millet to be dehulled in just minutes. The women would be relieved of this burdensome daily chore and free up time for other duties.

[1152] International development
Sen A (1999) *Development as Freedom*, Knopf and Oxford University Press, New York

The size, colour, weight and shape of an anvil and bolted into concrete, the dehulling machine was protected from the elements with a corrugated iron roof atop a wooden framed hut.

To ensure future financial sustainability, the villagers paid a small amount to have their millet dehulled to fund the three mechanics on motorbikes that Paul trained up to maintain and repair the machines.

With an election coming (even though the country was a 'one-party democracy'), the President was keen to get a photo with his thankful constituents into the newspaper. The project's funder was even keener to get a photo with the President.

The trials of the machines went well. The village men turned up to get their millet dehulled and notionally paid their contribution. They stood and stared in awe at the technology.

With the 6 dehullers and their huts in place, 3 smiling trained mechanics on their motorbikes and the thankful communities, the day came for Paul to go onto another aid project. Wearing the same shorts, boots and singlet, we helped carry his luggage across the tarmac.

As his plane trundled down the runway, the mechanics drove off, never to be seen again. The villagers took the wood and iron from the huts to recycle for their own use, leaving the black anvils in their concrete bases to enjoy the baking sun and sandstorms. Monuments to the white saviour complex.

The regional head of the country's agriculture department commandeered the vehicle for a more comfortable drive.

What we see as a problem, as Westerners - the burdensome, laborious, manual dehulling of the millet - is not so to the villagers. The women value the time they get to come together and talk, away from the men. Sometimes they sing along with the beat of the pounding. It didn't make sense to the men either. With their free female labour, why would they pay? In any case, any change to the intergenerational traditions that have seen the villagers through the harsh environment will always be seen as threatening to their future.

Like so many aid projects, the locals will never question, let alone turn down, the offer of resources. They are enterprising and resilient enough to find a way to get some benefit.

The country will always go along, fearing that a lack of cooperation will jeopardise its chances of overseas assistance and international loans.

I've told this story to thousands of Australians at their last training session before they head out to one of 26 countries to illustrate the perils of the 'white saviour' complex, where we, as more knowledgeable, educated, and skilled people, think we have the solution, as well as the right to intervene.

However, I tell them that, to effect lasting change, it is each of them who has to change first. They have to take the time to first understand the context, culture and community in which we wish to achieve change, adapt to the environment and develop the mutual trust and respect needed to work closely and equitably with the community to really appreciate the challenge, before working alongside to respond.

Or as my former colleague, the 'Forest Maker', Tony Rinaudo, says 'achieving sustainable and enduring transformation requires friendship, empathy, trust, humility and a willingness to be a co-learner in the adventure of change'[1153].

It is the same for anyone who wants to create lasting positive change, especially in international development.

WHAT

The Sustainable Development Goals (SDGs) were born at the United Nations Conference on Sustainable Development in Rio de Janeiro in 2012, replacing the Millennium Development Goals, which started a global effort in 2000 to tackle the indignity of poverty.

The 17 SDGs with 169 targets are a set of universal goals to 2030 that meet the urgent environmental, political and economic challenges facing our world:

1. No poverty
2. Zero hunger
3. Good health and well-being
4. Quality Education
5. Gender equality
6. Clean water and sanitation
7. Affordable and clean energy
8. Decent work and economic growth
9. Industry, innovation and infrastructure

[1153] Rinaudo T (2021) The Forest Underground. Hope or a planet in crisis, ISCAST, Australia, p.77

10. Reduced inequalities
11. Sustainable cities and economies
12. Responsible consumption and production
13. Climate action
14. Life below water
15. Life on land
16. Peace, justice and strong institutions
17. Partnership for the goals

Like the Themes in this book, the SDGs are inter-related and affect each other.

The SDGs apply to all the 193 United Nations member countries, who periodically report on their progress, including Australia.

Overall, 10 years in, and with 5 years to go, 18 per cent of the SDGs are on track or the target met; 17 per cent have moderate progress; 31 per cent report marginal progress; 17 per cent have stagnated; and 18 per cent are in regression.

In brief, the first 6 SDGs are[1154]:

SDG 1 No poverty - End poverty in all its forms everywhere

Extreme poverty persists, affecting 1 in 10 people worldwide.

Whilst economic development over the last 35 years, particularly in East and Southeast Asia, has reduced those living in extreme poverty (less than $3 a day) from 2.3 billion to 831 million today[1155], over 400 million are children and nearly 1 in 3, or 240 million, are working.

But with global poverty reduction slowing substantially over the last decade, due to sluggish economic growth, high levels of debt, the effects of the COVID-19 pandemic, conflict and fragility, and severe weather-related shocks, only 1 in 5 countries are projected to have halved its national poverty by 2030.

Nearly three-quarters of people living in extreme poverty reside in Sub-Saharan Africa. Here, economic growth is not enough to break the cycle of poverty. Sub-

[1154] At https://unstats.un.org/sdgs/report/2025/The-Sustainable-Development-Goals-Report-2025.pdf

[1155] World Bank Group (2025) Poverty & Inequality Update, October 2025 at https://thedocs.worldbank.org/en/doc/229ff18129687a785f08af7cfb28e5e1-0350012025/original/WBG-Poverty-and-Inequality-Update-Fall-2025.pdf

Saharan Africa comprises the 48 countries below the Sahara Desert with a total population of $1.3 billion.

The UN also defines 44 'least developed countries' (LDCs) as nations with the lowest socioeconomic development indicators, including low-income, weak human resources, and high economic and environmental vulnerability[1156]. In our region, they are Timor-Leste, Tuvalu, Solomon Islands and Kiribati.

More than 1 billion people currently live in countries classified as fragile or conflict-affected situations. This figure has more than doubled since 2005, with nearly half living in extreme poverty.

For the first time on record, over half of the world's population now receives at least one form of social protection benefit. Despite this milestone, 3.8 billion people remain uncovered.

SDG 2 Zero hunger - End hunger, achieve food security and improved nutrition and promote sustainable agriculture

Global hunger and food insecurity have declined in recent years but remain above pre-pandemic levels. 1 in 12 of the global population, or 700 million, faces hunger, with nearly 1 in 4 in Sub-Saharan Africa. Nearly 1 in 3, or 2.3 billion people, were moderately or severely food insecure, up 44 per cent from 2015. Sub-Saharan Africa saw the sharpest rise, with over 2 in 3 of its population affected, compared to nearly 50 per cent in 2015.

Tragically, more than 3 million children die from hunger every year, nearly half are under 5. Between conflict, climate change and the COVID-19 pandemic, the number of hungry children is on the rise.

By 2030, a projected 582 million people will be chronically undernourished, more than half of them in Africa.

SDG 3 Good health and well-being - Ensure healthy lives and promote well-being for all at all ages

With significant improvements in this SDG, the good news is that, over the last 15 years, the number of childhood deaths has been cut in half. Effective HIV treatment has cut global AIDS-related deaths by half since 2010.

However, insufficient progress has been made on reducing maternal mortality and expanding universal health coverage. Globally, an estimated 260,000

1156 https://policy.desa.un.org/least-developed-countries

women died during pregnancy and childbirth in 2023, with some 17 million births still occurring without skilled assistance. And 344 million people were pushed or further pushed into extreme poverty in 2019 due to out-of-pocket payments for health.

Furthermore, malaria cases are rising (more than 40 per cent of children under 5 and pregnant women in sub-Saharan Africa were not protected by insecticide-treated nets), tuberculosis returned to being probably the world's leading cause of death from a single infectious agent in 2023, and non-communicable diseases killed 18 million people under age 70 in 2021.

SDG 4 Quality education - Ensure inclusive and equitable quality education and promote lifelong learning opportunities for all.

Education is vital for sustainable development, yet progress remains off track. While enrolment and completion rates have improved, nearly 300 million children and young people remain out of school, up 3 per cent since 2015.

Between 2015 and 2024, over 100 million more children entered school. The primary school completion rate increased from 85 to 88 per cent, the lower secondary completion rate from 74 to 78 per cent, and the upper secondary completion rate from 53 to 60 per cent. However, only 2 in 3 children in sub-Saharan Africa complete primary school on time.

This reflects the challenges that the least developed countries face in providing schools with basic resources. A 3rd of primary schools lack basic sanitation, more than half lack electricity and over 2 in 3 lack digital tools.

SDG 5 Gender equality - Achieve gender equality and empower all women and girls

Three decades after the landmark Beijing Declaration and Platform for Action, gender equality remains elusive.

Despite some progress, discriminatory laws and gender-based norms continue to hinder gender equality. Women remain underrepresented in decision-making and leadership roles and often lack autonomy over sexual and reproductive health, land rights and technology access. Women's disproportionate share of unpaid domestic and care work continues to limit their access to education, career opportunities and political engagement.

Harmful practices, such as child marriage and female genital mutilation (FMG), persist globally. Each year, 4 million girls undergo FGM, with over 2 million before the age of 5. Meantime, nearly 1 in 5 young women are first married or in a union before age 18, rising to nearly 1 in 3 in sub-Saharan Africa.

Secure land rights are vital for empowering rural women and strengthening agrifood systems. Women with secure tenure are more likely to invest, innovate, boost productivity and lift their families out of poverty. A global review of 84 countries shows that 58 per cent lack adequate legal protections for women's land rights across family, inheritance and land laws. Many laws remain outdated, fragmented and misaligned with constitutional and international standards.

As nearly 80 per cent of human trafficking, the International Labour Organisation estimates there were 4.8 million sex victims trafficked for commercial sexual exploitation around the world in 2016, including 1 million children. Globally, 99 per cent of victims were women and girls[1157]. Working in north Luzon in the Philippines, I experienced this first-hand. With 3,000 year-old rice terraces cascading down the mountains, it was a picturesque, but extremely poor region with undernutrition co-existing with micronutrient deficiencies.

Men would come up from Manila to offer the farmer 'a loan' in return for their daughter working in factories to pay off the loan. A US$5,000 loan represented more than they would earn in a year. With added interest and accommodation costs, the money would never be able to be repaid. It was the last time the family saw their daughter, who spent her youth in a brothel. Escape would mean death for her or her family. No longer useful, she would be out on the streets, too ashamed to return home.

SDG 6 Clean water and sanitation - Ensure access to clean water and sanitation for all

Between 2015 and 2024, global access to essential water, sanitation and hygiene (WASH) services steadily improved. The share of the population using safely managed drinking water rose from 68 to 74 per cent, safely managed sanitation coverage increased from 48 to 58 per cent, and basic hygiene services coverage grew from 66 to 80 per cent. Despite these gains, major challenges persist. In 2024, 2.2 billion people still lacked safely managed drinking water, 3.4 billion were without safely managed sanitation, and 1.7 billion lacked basic hygiene services at home.

1157 https://traffickinginstitute.org/breaking-down-global-estimates-of-human-trafficking-human-trafficking-awareness-month-2022/

WASH access in schools remains insufficient for ensuring safe and inclusive learning environments with 447 million children lacking basic drinking water services and 447 million without basic sanitation.

WHY

The lower rate of social and economic development, as compared to the 'developed' countries, is due to a range of historical, cultural, geographical and political reasons.

Wealth inequality

Extreme wealth inequality is persistent and increasing, deny billions of people the opportunity to escape poverty. Incredibly, about 56,000 people, or 0.001 per cent of the world's population, control 3 times as much wealth as the bottom half of humanity combined. The richest 10 per cent of the world's population own 3/4 of global wealth and the bottom half just 2 per cent[1158].

With wealth inequality increasing rapidly around the world, in almost every region, the top 1 per cent is wealthier than the bottom 90 per cent combined.

In comparison, developing countries face a $4.3 trillion annual financing gap to meet the SDGs, including $1.8 trillion for climate needs, or 0.7 per cent of the estimated US$600 trillion of global wealth[1159].

Colonisation

The European invasion and exploitation of the physical, human, and economic resources of countries, especially in Africa, changed their future forever.

The Atlantic slave trade of the 18th century saw over 10 million Africans shipped to the New World, devastating Africa by causing massive depopulation, particularly of young, able-bodied individuals, which led to social, economic, and political instability.

Economic incentives for warlords and tribes to engage in the slave trade promoted an atmosphere of lawlessness and violence. With a large percentage of the people taken captive in Africa being women in their childbearing years and young men who normally would have been starting families, and a continuing fear of captivity, economic and agricultural development is almost impossible throughout much of western Africa.

1158 https://wir2026.wid.world/insight/executive-summary/

1159 https://unctad.org/news/financing-development-reforming-global-systems-drive-progress

The Congo Free State fared particularly badly under King Leopold II of Belgium in the late 19th/early 20th century with 1 researcher estimating 'many millions, possibly 10 million or more' died from forced labour, killings and related causes[1160].

The introduction of colonial rule, and the subsequent division into countries, drew arbitrary boundaries where none had existed before, dividing ethnic and linguistic groups and natural features, and laying the foundation for the creation of numerous states lacking geographic, linguistic, ethnic, or political affinity.

For instance, The Gambia began with early Arab traders in the 9th and 10th centuries, followed by rule under the Mali and Songhai empires. The Portuguese claimed the country in the mid-15th century, followed by the French and the British in the 17th century, the latter establishing it as a protectorate in 1894 and set its modern boundaries with France in 1889, before gaining its independence from Britain in 1965. The Gambia's 765 km land border represents its colonial trading licences, following lines of latitude and longitude and a 10-kilometre buffer on either side of the Gambia River. As the smallest mainland country in Africa and is almost entirely surrounded by Senegal, it survives through Scandinavian tourism (it is cheaper to come to The Gambian summer than heat their homes in their winter). It did. However, make it the ideal country to establish the world's first relay run across a nation by an enterprising young accountant.

Resources curse

Also called the 'paradox of plenty', this is where countries with an abundance of natural resources suffer lower economic growth along with higher rates of authoritarianism, corruption and political instability than countries with fewer resources.

For instance, Nigeria's reliance on oil has led to economic instability and debt with over half the population living below the poverty line; the Democratic Republic of Congo possesses over $24 trillion in untapped mineral deposits but has 3/4 of the population in extreme poverty; and Sierra Leone's abundant diamond wealth fuelled a brutal civil war from 1991 to 1999.

Patriarchy

Male-centred norms hinder development when they limit women's participation in economic, social, and political life, as well as reinforce power imbalances.

1160 https://www.hawaii.edu/powerkills/COMM.7.1.03.HTM?utm_source=chatgpt.com

In working across West and East Africa, my experience is that men control the family and community in rural settings. Men own the assets and politics. Women do all the manual work of the household, village and fields. Polygamy is practised in numerous African countries, with the highest rates in West and Central Africa.

Women continue to work more and earn less than men, capturing just over a quarter of total labour income, a share that has barely shifted since 1990. In the Middle East & North Africa, women's share is only 16 per cent; in South & Southeast Asia it is 20 per cent and in Sub-Saharan Africa it is 28 per cent[1161].

Practised in 30 countries in Africa, the Middle East and Asia and recognised internationally as a violation of the human rights of girls and women, Female Genital Mutilation (FGM) removes part or all of the clitoral glans and/or the labia minora. FGM is often linked to beliefs that women must be sexually controlled, reducing sexual desire prevents "promiscuity" and virginity before marriage ensures family honour. The practice has no health benefits for girls and women and can result in severe bleeding and problems urinating, and later cysts, menstrual difficulties, infections, as well as complications in childbirth and increased risk of newborn deaths.

Girls in developing countries face multiple disadvantages, such as limited access to education, higher rates of poverty, and increased vulnerability to violence, forced marriage, and trafficking.

Education

For individuals, education promotes employment, earnings, health, and poverty reduction. For communities, it drives long-term economic growth, spurs innovation, strengthens institutions, and fosters social cohesion.

Under the Millennium Development Goals, the world failed on its promise for all children to go to primary school by 2015. The new education goal, SDG 4, set the level of ambition a step higher, calling for all young people to complete secondary school by the 2030 deadline. To achieve this, all children of school starting age should have begun school in 2018. In reality, only 70 per cent did so in low-income countries.

COVID has not helped. In low and middle-income countries, the share of children living in *Learning Poverty* (the proportion of ten year-old children that are unable to read and understand a short age-appropriate text) increased from 57 per cent before the pandemic to an estimated 70 per cent in 2022.

1161 https://wir2026.wid.world/insight/executive-summary/

With an additional $97 billion annually needed by developing countries to meet SDG 4 by 2030, the funding of education remains inadequate. In 2025, average education spending per child in Sub-Saharan Africa stood at just $400, compared with €13,000 in Europe and $16,000 in North America.

Corruption

Developing countries are synonymous with the abuse of public office for massive private gain. Corruption costs developing countries $1.26 trillion every year (enough money to lift 1.4 billion people in extreme poverty above the poverty threshold and keep them there for at least six years)[1162], hindering economic growth, accumulating debt, eroding public and international trust, and perpetuating poverty. According to the Presidential Commission on Good Government, the Marcos family stole US$5 billion–$10 billion from the Central Bank of the Philippines. Mobutu was famous for corruption and nepotism while the people of Zaire suffered from poverty and human rights abuses. He embezzled an estimated $4-15 billion during his time in office.

Unsurprisingly, developing countries feature at the lower end of Transparency International's Corruption Perceptions Index[1163].

Conflict

Tribal territorial disputes, poverty, food and water shortages, land tenure, political power grabs, resources and religious ideologies, corruption and foreign interventions by Western powers all contribute to ongoing conflict and destabilisation in developing countries.

Today, roughly 2 billion people – 1 in 4 of humanity – live in conflict-affected countries. Over 122 million people have been forcibly displaced by conflict, violence, and persecution worldwide, 6 in 10 of whom are internally displaced people[1164].

Africa hosts more than 35 domestic armed conflicts taking place in Burkina Faso, Cameroon, Central African Republic, Congo, Mali, Egypt, Ethiopia, Democratic Republic of the Congo, Libya, Morocco, Mozambique, Nigeria, Senegal, Somalia, Sudan, South Sudan and Western Sahara. Several armed groups – fighting against government forces and/or against each other – are involved in these conflicts. Western powers and/or neighbouring countries are

---

1162 https://www.weforum.org/stories/2019/12/corruption-global-problem-statistics-cost/

1163 https://www.transparency.org/en/cpi/2024

1164 https://www.unrefugees.org/refugee-facts/statistics/#:~:text=Global%20Trends%20At%2Da%2DGlance,protection%2C%20a%20majority%20from%20Venezuela

intervening in these conflicts in Burkina Faso, Mali, Mozambique, Nigeria, and Somalia.

Debt burden

Many lower-income countries rely on a few commodity exports (such as oil, copper, coffee, cocoa and peanuts). Prices are volatile and when they fall, governments borrow to fill budget gaps. Governments also borrow to fund essential services when they don't raise sufficient revenue through taxes.

Add to this, corruption and capital flight, inefficient public spending, weak financial institutions, borrowing for consumption rather than productive investment and vanity infrastructure projects.

Tripling in 15 years, public debt in sub-Saharan Africa reached an estimated $1.15 trillion in 2023. At the same time, African currencies have depreciated sharply against the debt-denominated US dollar or Euro, while global borrowing costs have surged. Together, these dynamics mean African governments now spend unprecedented amounts and servicing their debt. In 2024, 34 African countries spent more on external debt payments than on their healthcare and/or education budgets. Meanwhile, debt servicing costs have tripled and interest payments have quadrupled over the past decade[1165].

Land

With land the most important asset for households and individuals in the developing world, the majority of whom rely on agriculture for their nutrition and livelihoods, most of the world's population lacks secure rights to the land on which they live. Nearly half of the world's economies limit the ability of women to own property. For instance, in Africa, women account for 70 per cent of all food production, yet few women have rights to the land on which they depend[1166].

Land tenure issues in developing countries include poorly defined property rights, insecure tenure for the poor, and conflicts between formal and customary systems. These problems lead to a lack of investment, food insecurity, and displacement, and are often exacerbated by pressures from population growth, market forces, and climate change.

Small-scale food producers are essential for resilient agriculture, food security and the fight against hunger. But with land bequeathed to sons, the size of land ownership becomes ever smaller and less productive. Add to this land

---

[1165] https://www.undp.org/publications/dfs-undp-debt-update-development-gives-way-debt

[1166] https://studentbriefs.law.gwu.edu/ilpb/2022/10/12/womens-land-rights-a-powerful-tool-for-development/

degradation from over-cultivation, water shortages and climate change and households remain highly vulnerable.

Climate change

Developing countries contribute the least to global emissions but suffer the most from extreme weather, rising temperatures and drought, with income losses in low-income countries attributed to climate impacts about 5 times larger than those in high-income countries[1167]. Of the 124 million people worldwide who face crisis levels of acute food insecurity, over 3/4 have been affected by climate shocks and extremes.

The impacts of climate change are both many and compounding on developing countries. More cases of diseases such as malaria, increasing water shortages and worsening water quality, rising prevalence of crop failures and higher food prices. With rising sea levels, almost 90 per cent of the world's flood-exposed population is based in developing countries.

The World Economic Forum predicts that by 2050, over 200 million climate refugees will have been displaced in 6 world regions, with the top 3 being in sub-Saharan Africa (86 million), East Asia and the Pacific (49 million) and South Asia (40 million)[1168].

International aid

The level of Official Development Assistance (ODA) provided by governments to developing countries has been declining. ODA dropped 9 per cent in 2024 with France, Germany, United Kingdom and the United States all cutting their ODA. A further 9-17 per cent reduction is expected for 2025, with least developed countries projected to see a 13-25 per cent fall and countries in sub-Saharan Africa facing a 16-28 per cent decline[1169].

With the SDG 17 target of 0.7 per cent of donors' gross national income, the aid actually provided is now less than half. Australia's ODA has also been declining and is currently around 0.19 per cent, compared to 0.34 per cent 30 years ago, or only 1.56 per cent of total ODA. At $172 per person, behind New Zealand, we are among the lower-ranked donor countries[1170].

1167 https://www.cgdev.org/blog/climate-and-development-three-charts-update
1168 https://www.weforum.org/stories/2023/01/climate-crisis-poor-davos2023/
1169 OCED (2025) Policy Brief. Cuts in official development assistance: OECD projections for 2025
and the near term at https://www.oecd.org/en/publications/cuts-in-official-development-assistance_8c530629-en/full-report.html
1170 https://aidtracker.devpolicy.org/comparisons/

Over the years, the international aid sector and its funders have been criticised for their top-down development approach that neglects the understanding, wishes and skills of the communities. The White Saviour complex treats those in developing countries as helpless victims who need to be saved. It risks a lack of understanding of the challenges and solutions, local skills and resources available and acceptance by the community, and, accordingly, can lead to harm, unsustainability and waste.

Under the 2016 UN-led Grand Bargain, the INGOs and donors agreed to reach more people in need and spend less money on administration and overheads, whilst also improving the design and delivery of humanitarian action. The Grand Bargain 2.0 in 2021 focused on *localisation* (supporting local responders), quality funding (more flexible and predictable funding for aid agencies), and the participation of affected communities in decision-making.

Localisation involves a fundamental shift in power, decision-making, and equitable partnerships. Meeting the target of 25 per cent of international humanitarian funding channelled as directly as possible to local and national actors has been challenging with only 7 per cent recorded in 2023.

ACT

It is easy to be overwhelmed by the scale of the challenge in developing countries with millions of people in need. At the same time, the ability to change many lives and their environment is so much greater.

There are 430 registered Australian charities that work overseas. Of these, 130 are members of the *Australian Council for International Development (ACFID)*[1171] which audits compliance to a world-leading code of conduct and standards. The Australian government allocates $143 million to fund accredited charities to undertake approved projects primarily in the Indo-Pacific region[1172]. These charities are known as International Non-Governmental Organisations (INGOs).

From Christian church missionaries, the Universal Declaration of Human Rights saw INGOs founded on rights-based international development, led by Oxfam. This approach recognises that imbalances in power relations contribute to marginalisation and prevent poor people from exercising their rights; is participatory, recognising that all people, including those living in poverty, have a right to be involved in processes that impact on their lives; recognises

[1171] http://acfid.asn.au/

[1172] https://www.dfat.gov.au/development/who-we-work-with/ngos/list-of-australian-accredited-non-government-organisations

that all development actors and all stakeholders are accountable to one another; promotes equality and non-discrimination, with a particular focus on vulnerable or marginalised people(s); is holistic - recognising that economic poverty has deeply felt social, cultural and political causes and effects, and that the spectrum of human rights must be understood together to constitute the basic necessities for a life of dignity and freedom; recognises that rights also involve corresponding responsibilities – the fact that we all have human rights means we are also all duty bearers; makes use of existing legal systems, and, depending on the context, develop links between development goals and international human rights laws[1173].

Although you won't receive a tax deduction, there is nothing to stop you sending money to an overseas organisation, such as a school, charity, clinic or community.

Apart from responding to humanitarian crises from natural disasters and conflict, my advice is to either select a theme (health, women's empowerment, education, climate change) or a community or region.

The *Australian International Development Network* publishes a useful guide and runs events for donors[1174].

Emergencies

An enterprising merchant had set up a fridge selling cold drinks from an electric wire connected to the PLTD Apung 1, a large, 2,600-ton floating power plant that lay in the middle of a wasteland - what was a city home to 260,000 Indonesians. The decimation was apocalyptic. Debris and bodies extended as far as I could see, before a calm sea that lay in the distance. At that moment, an aftershock filled the air with screams.

I will never forget the hour and half long helicopter ride from Banda Aceh down to Meulaboh. Looking down, apart from the odd concrete slab, there was nothing left of the villages along the 238 km coastline. We sat in silence for the whole time, unable to relay the horror of what we saw.

The 9.3 earthquake struck with an epicenter off the west coast of Aceh in northern Sumatra on 26 December 2004, causing a massive tsunami with waves up to 30 metres which killed 170,000 Indonesians, and another 50,000 in 13 countries, including 26 Australians.

[1173] https://policy-practice.oxfam.org/resources/quick-guide-to-rights-based-approaches-to-development-312421/

[1174] https://aidnetwork.org.au/wp-content/uploads/2025/11/FINAL-Better-Giving-Framework-Edition-2-2025-1.pdf

The outpouring of humanity saw Australians donate a record $330 million to INGOs in addition to the Australian government's $60 million in emergency relief and $1 billion for reconstruction.

The INGOs also realised the opportunity that emergencies presented for increased donation income, government grants and the acquisition of new donors, leading to intense competition to be first on the scene. As well as the rapid response team to assess the needs, my next assignment to the Pakistan earthquake emergency saw the communications team with their satellite dish and the tender writers ensconced.

Thankfully, 15 Australian INGOs with expertise in different areas of disaster response have formed the Emergency Action Alliance to act as one point for your donations and information[1175].

Place

Most INGOs focus on an area to carry out coordinated, place-based development across health, agriculture, education, livelihoods, climate change, water and sanitation. The agreement of these areas avoids duplication and competition between INGOs, although it can create a sense of ownership and a colonial culture.

INGOs have traditionally set up country offices to fund and coordinate their programs. With the localisation agenda, they should be moving to working with and the building the capacity of local organisations.

A leader is *Live and Learn*, an environmental INGO which acts as a network of autonomous local organisations in the Pacific and south-east Asia to build their capacity to create more equitable, sustainable and climate resilient communities[1176].

Other INGOs focus on a specific country or region, such as the *Australian Himalayan Foundation*, *Palmera* which works in Sri Lanka, *Water for a Village* in Ethiopia, and *This Life* and *See Beyond Borders* in Cambodia.

Health

I am standing in the middle of a village on a tropically hot and steamy day talking to a distraught man sat slumped and forlorn on a chair outside his house. Life carries out around him. Excited children run around women sat cross-

1175 https://emergencyaction.org.au/who-are-we
1176 https://livelearn.org/

legged on a mat talking and preparing the evening meal. The sadness runs deep on his face, his eyes glazed and hollow.

His left leg from the knee down is hideously swollen and disfigured, five times the size of his other leg. In constant pain, he had been the proud head of the family and active elder of the community. Unable to work, now he is ostracised as useless and needy.

As a child, and in common with millions of other children around the world, he had been bitten by a mosquito, the world's most deadly animal. It had injected a roundworm parasite carried in the blood of another infected human. Living for 6-9 years, the worm nests in the lymphatic vessels and disrupts the normal function of the lymphatic system, producing millions of immature larvae that circulate in the blood during their lifetime.

Called Lymphatic Filariasis, or elephantiasis, 893 million people living in tropical areas are in need of treatment for this disease. The good news is that this is one disease that can be easily eliminated from the face of the Earth with 3 cheap and widely available drugs given once a year for up to 6 years. Alternatively, to break the cycle, the fruit flavoured tablets can be given to children by teachers annually at school.

I was in the country to meet members of the Global Programme to *Eliminate Lymphatic Filariasis, which* was set up in 2000 to coordinate efforts to eradicate the disease by 2020. I came with commitments from companies to donate the drugs required. But, like so many basic health priorities in developing countries, progress has been painfully slow. Currently, of the 72 endemic countries, only 14 have been validated by the World Health Organization (WHO) to have succeeded.

At a cost of a billion US dollars to wipe this disease off the face of the planet[1177], I came home from my visit to the news that the cost of the redevelopment of a railway station in my city had cost more.

Médecins Sans Frontières (Doctors Without Borders) is the most well-known INGO in health with a reputation for providing medical services in the most challenging of places.

With diarrhoeal disease a leading cause of child mortality and morbidity in the world, killing over 400,000 children under five, *Water Aid* is a leader in water, sanitation and hygiene.

1177 https://www.ncbi.nlm.nih.gov/pmc/articles/PMC5630187/

From its roots as a virology laboratory in Fairfield Hospital in Melbourne, the *Burnet Institute* is a globally recognised medical research institute and has strengthened the health systems in Myanmar and PNG.

Women's empowerment

I was petrified one Tuesday morning at World Vision. It was the first time a business had presented at the weekly devotions, let alone a Jewish family business.

Three months earlier in a cramped small room in a village in North Uganda stood 6 sweating Australians and a translator around a young local women who was sitting at a table sewing a dress.

We learnt that she was 20 years old and had been a child bride in the Lord's Resistance Army (LRA). Joseph Kony (of the viral video fame) formed the LRA in northern Uganda in 1987 to overthrow the government of President Yoweri Museveni. An estimated 30,000 children were abducted from their homes, drugged and forced to fight, along with thousands of young girls who were trafficked and forced into sexual slavery[1178].

She told the harrowing story of being raped, falling pregnant and having a baby. Returning to her village, she had been ostracised by her family and the community. I asked the age of the baby. 'Ten', she replied. Silence. Tears started to flow as we did the maths in our minds. She was raped at 10 years old.

My relationship with the Spotlight Group had started some 2 years earlier after I had earlier visited a large refugee camp in Northern Uganda and noticed a women's sewing enterprise. The camp was home to some 20,000 refugees and had turned into a town with a main street and shops. In the middle sat 8 immaculately dressed women at tables with donated sewing machines making beautiful clothes to sell in the camp.

World Vision had programs in the area to support the refugees escape the camp and transition back to their villages or start their own businesses in urban areas. When I visited, the training consisted of bicycle and vehicle repair courses for men. Sending sewing machines would be an opportunity to train the women and start their own businesses.

Spotlight is Australia's biggest retailer of sewing machines through over 100 stores across the country, but sales struggle because sewers come to cherish their machines and the level of technical change is low.

[1178] Allen T (2010) The Lord's Resistance Army : Myth and Reality, London, UK

I pitched a program which I called *Stitch in Time* for Spotlight's customers to donate their working sewing machines to World Vision in return for a discount voucher to buy a new machine together with Spotlight staff volunteering to test the machines before being shipped to Uganda.

It worked. Over 2,000 sewing machines were donated, checked and shipped to women in North Uganda and other World Vision programs, whilst Spotlight's sewing machine sales increased.

Spotlight went further with staff visiting the program to train the women before coming back to tell their story to the staff at their annual conference. Whilst there, they worked together on a design for a tote bag to be made for Spotlight to purchase and sell in their stores. They even successfully lobbied for the local electricity supply to be extended to the new sewing business hub.

Women's empowerment in international development is not just a human right, it leads to highly effective development outcomes. The *International Women's Development Agency* has been a leader for over 40 years[1179]. *Plan International, CARE Australia* and *The Hunger Project* also take an active gender lens.

The 'bank for the poor', Grameen Bank, demonstrated the outstanding development outcomes of micro-finance and financial literacy at scale to build micro and small businesses, especially with women, to escape poverty.

In Australia, *Opportunity International* and *Good Return* provide responsible finance to local entrepreneurs, as well as education and business training to women and other excluded groups to build confidence and financial capability. *Palmera* has a similar approach in Sri Lanka and the *Pollinate Group* empowers marginalised women as entrepreneurs so they can earn an income, learn valuable skills, and step into leadership roles.

Despite long hours away from their families, working full time plus many hours of overtime, big Australian clothing brands do not pay garment workers enough money to cover the basics of life – food, medicine, decent shelter and an education for their children. Demand big brands pay the women who make our clothes a living wage with *Oxfam Australia*[1180].

With nearly 2 in 3 of women in PNG experiencing intimate partner violence in 2025, *FemiliPNG Australia* works in partnership with local and international organisations to prevent and respond to family and sexual violence in Papua

---

[1179] https://iwda.org.au/

[1180] https://www.oxfam.org.au/what-we-do/advocacy-and-campaigns/

New Guinea, as well as hold the government to account on its newly enacted National Strategy to Prevent and Respond to Gender-Based Violence.

Marie Stopes International (MSI) has a long history of providing access to sexual and reproductive healthcare and rights.

Following the discovery of the world's first cervical cancer vaccine at the University of Queensland, the *Australian Centre for the Prevention of Cervical Cancer* is a world-leader in the prevention and control of cervical cancer.

To respond to sex trafficking, *Hagar International*[1181] and *Destiny Rescue Australia*[1182] are NGOs accredited by ACFID.

Environment

I connected with Tony Rinaudo - the 'Forest Maker' - at World Vision over our love of Niger. He had a deep understanding and passion for the West African country, consistently one of the poorest on Earth. With over 80 per cent of its land area lying in the Sahara, Niger has a proud cultural heritage as a strategic position on the Trans-Saharan trade routes.

Tony worked in Niger for 18 years overseeing long-term rural development and periodic, large-scale relief programs. He witnessed firsthand the devastating impact of deforestation and land degradation on the world's most vulnerable people – children, women and poor farm families. It didn't help that the trees were regarded as weeds competing with food crops for nutrition and ripped up for peanut planting, the chosen crop of the colonists.

The traditional reforestation – the raising of seedlings in nurseries before being transported and planted – was not working with less than 20 per cent of the 60 million trees planted in Niger in a 12 year period surviving. The trees died neglected in the harsh Sahel environment of drought, sandstorms and termites. Disillusioned and pulling that day's trailer loaded with tree seedlings, he stopped to let air out of the tyres to cushion the ride. A bush on the side of the road caught his attention. Thinking that the bushes strewn across the landscape were just weeds or shrubs, he found that the bush was shoots sprouting from a tree stump. He realised that he was standing on a subterranean forest whose root systems remained alive underground, even in the harshest, desert-like landscapes, especially in cleared land from tree stumps. They just needed

1181 https://www.hagar.org.au/

1182 https://www.destinyrescue.org.au/

protection from animals and selective pruning so the best shoots could grow into trees[1183].

He demonstrated his low-cost, sustainable *Farmer Managed Natural Regeneration* across Niger over 20 years, resulting in the reforestation of 5 million hectares of previously barren farmland with 200 million trees, an extra 500,000 tons of grain produced annually, benefiting 2.5 million people, storing 5-10 million tons of CO_2 annually, and generating an additional gross income of $900 million annually, benefiting 4.5 million people[1184]. Crucially, as an experienced community development practitioner, he understood that the innovation needed community engagement and ownership, a legal framework for the management and ownership of the trees, and the demonstration of greater crop yields through improved soil protection and fertility. With trees seen as an obstacle to farming and a ready source of firewood, most importantly, over time, he built trust and a movement by being authentic, ardent and hands-on. The technique has been replicated by World Vision in Uganda, Kenya, Ethiopia and Zambia as part of the *Bonn Challenge*, a global goal to bring 350 million hectares of degraded and deforested landscapes into restoration by 2030[1185]. You can read more and support the project at the *FMNR Hub*[1186].

For environmental community development in our Pacific region, *Live and Learn* is a highly effective network of local agencies and communities.

For advocacy, as well as *Greenpeace Australia Pacific*, join the global movement *350.org*[1187] (named after the safe limit of 350 parts per million of carbon dioxide in the atmosphere to avoid the worst impacts of the climate crisis) and *350 Pacific*[1188], a youth-led grassroots network working with communities to fight climate change from the Pacific Islands and diaspora.

Disability

In order to destroy the forest cover and crops for the North Vietnamese, the US military dropped Agent Orange on 4.5 million acres of land and 4.8 million

---

1183 Rinaudo T (2021) The Forest Underground. Hope for a planet in crisis, ISCAST, Australia, p.107

1184 https://www.genevapolicyoutlook.ch/regreening-the-global-safety-net-accelerating-fmnr-through-faith-driven-movement-building/#:~:text=FMNR%20has%20demonstrated%20remarkable%20success,roughly%20with%20Cambodia's%20surface%20area.

1185 https://www.bonnchallenge.org/

1186 https://fmnrhub.com.au/

1187 https://350.org/

1188 https://350pacific.org/get-involved/

Vietnamese from 1961 to 1971. The highly toxic dioxin has created health impacts that have lasted for last generations, with children, grandchildren, and even great-grandchildren of people exposed to the chemicals suffering from health complications ranging from cancer to birth defects that affect the spine and nervous system.

Those I saw crippled with Spina bifida in rural Vietnam from Agent Orange had absolutely nothing. They were left to shuffle around in their huts as burdens. No mobility, no use.

I was there to develop a local wheelchair building project that could cope with the terrain, initially with imported materials that could be easily assembled, before looking for local products.

With developing countries lacking the resources to even measure those living with disability, let alone respond, and funding for disability representing a paltry 0.5 per cent of total international aid, the estimated 800 million people with disabilities in developing countries get little support.

cbm (previously the Christian Blind Mission) has over 100 years of working alongside people with disabilities living in the world's poorest places to fight poverty and exclusion.

Founded by eye surgeon Professor Fred Hollows thirty years ago, the *Fred Hollows Foundation* has restored sight or prevented blindness to over 150 million people worldwide.

Volunteer

Australians of all genders, abilities, and identities between the ages of 16 and 24 can volunteer for a year to be part of PLAN International's *Youth Activist Series*, a platform for young people to learn more about global issues surrounding climate and gender justice[1189] or their *Youth Impact Academy*[1190]. UNICEF Australia has an 18-month *Young Ambassador program*[1191] and Pollinate has a *Student Fellowship Program*[1192].

The world's oldest and best international volunteering for development organisation is here. Australian Volunteers International has recruited, sent and supported thousands of skilled Australians to meet the local capacity building needs of governments, businesses and charities across the globe. Funded by the

[1189] https://www.plan.org.au/you-can-help/youth-activist-series-yas/

[1190] https://www.plan.org.au/news/stories/youth-impact-academy/

[1191] https://www.unicef.org.au/our-people/young-ambassadors

[1192] https://pollinategroup.org/student-fellowship-program/

Australian government, volunteers receive travel, insurance, local living allowance and accommodation, and are supported by a local in-country team[1193]. Assignments are up to two years.

Australian professionals can volunteer in developing countries with *Engineers Without Borders*[1194], *Accounting for International Development*[1195], *Australian Pro-Bono Centre*[1196] *and Australian Doctors International*[1197].

Beware of organisations offering unskilled volunteering in developing countries, called 'voluntourism'. These can be money-making ventures that exploit local communities and environments, and offer no real development outcomes.

And please avoid orphanages. Over 5 million children live in these institutions and, on average, 80 per cent of children have at least one living parent. Many orphanages are run for profit rather than for children's wellbeing, with harm to children's physical and cognitive development and exposure to a higher risk of abuse and neglect[1198].

Campaign

Join *PLAN International's* movement fighting for girls' rights[1199].

Despite long hours away from their families, working full time plus many hours of overtime, big Australian clothing brands do not pay garment workers enough money to cover the basics of life – food, medicine, decent shelter and an education for their children. Demand big brands pay the women who make our clothes a living wage with *Oxfam Australia*[1200].

Save the Children reported that 2024 saw a 30 per cent jump in children being killed, maimed, sexually assaulted and abducted in record numbers in conflict zone. Sign up to their *Stop the War on Children* campaign[1201].

1193 https://www.australianvolunteers.com/

1194 https://ewb.org.au/volunteer/professionals/

1195 https://www.afid.org.uk/intro/

1196 https://www.probonocentre.org.au/

1197 https://adi.org.au/

1198 https://www.wearelumos.org/why-were-here/the-problem/

1199 https://www.plan.org.au/you-can-help/join-the-movement-for-girls-rights/

1200 https://www.oxfam.org.au/what-we-do/advocacy-and-campaigns/

1201 https://www.savethechildren.org.au/petitions/stop-war-on-children-pledge

Buy

Purchase (as a tax-deductible donation) a chicken, goat, fish, duck, cow or seeds for a family in poverty with *Oxfam Unwrapped*[1202] or buy Oxfam's Fair range of coffee[1203]. Water Aid has similar gifts for water and sanitation[1204].

Save The Children op shops are a great way to find a bargain[1205].

1202 https://unwrapped.oxfam.org.au/

1203 https://faircoffee.com.au/

1204 https://www.wateraidgifts.org.au/

1205 https://www.savethechildren.org.au/get-involved/op-shops?currentSort=

ANIMAL CRUELTY

'I've spent my life speaking out on behalf of animals. And there is one issue that stands out uniquely as one of the worst threats to their survival. The illegal wildlife trade... Without doing something today, we could face a world in which thousands and thousands of species go silent'

DR JANE GOODALL

'Elephants sell' was the mantra at Intrepid Travel. Everybody wanted to ride elephants on their popular Chiang Mai trip and the front cover of their Thailand brochure had a joyful traveller atop an adorned elephant.

Dating back to the 1500s, as warm-blooded armoured tanks, Indian elephants in Thailand were captured to fight in battles against the Burmese, Malays and the Khmer to protect the Kingdom, earning their place as the national symbol and playing a starring role in cultural festivals to this day. In lieu of machinery, elephants have been used extensively in farming and commercial logging.

An elephant requires an area of at least 100 km^2 to ensure sufficient food, so with Thailand's forest cover shrinking from 90 per cent to 32 per cent, numbers have declined from over 100,000 domesticated elephants at the start of the 20th century to between 3,000-5,000 now, with all but a thousand in captivity. As a result, the elephant became an endangered species in Thailand in 1986.

Elephants are not built to carry weight on their backs. In order to be ridden, elephants must first go through a process known as *Phajaan* (the crush), in which they are bound with ropes, confined in tight wooden structures, starved, and beaten repeatedly with bull hooks, nails, and hammers until their will is crushed[1206].

The banning of elephants for logging in 1989 led to jobless elephants and their mahouts ending up on the streets, wandering across farmlands or taking shelter in dangerous spots like highway underpasses. To survive, the mahouts took their elephants to tourist spots, roaming the streets with baskets of fruits for the tourists to buy and feed the animal in return for performing tricks. On 17 June 2010, elephant protection laws were passed making these acts illegal.

However, a doubling of tourism to Thailand from 15.9 million to 32.6 million visitors between 2010 and 2016, led to a 30 per cent rise (1,688 to 2,198) in elephants poached from the wild and held in captivity for tourist activities[1207], replicating the money-making human orphanage business model.

It started with a query from a traveller in 2010, who expressed their discomfort to their Intrepid Starting Guide about the treatment of the elephant on their ride. With responsible travel at its heart, the word got up to management which partnered with *World Animal Protection* to commission a study into captive elephant venues. Of the 220 sites offering rides by 2,923 elephants at tourist venues in Thailand, Sri Lanka, Nepal, India, Laos and Cambodia investigated, 77 per cent were found to be treated appallingly, including being taken young from the wild, separated from their familial groups, broken again and again using sharp hooks and other tools, chained up at night and denied good nutrition[1208]. The study's author noted that any elephant tourism, no matter how well-intentioned, drives a market where abuse is inevitable.

As a result, in a world first, Intrepid Travel, from January 2014, no longer offered elephant rides on any of its trips[1209]. Since then, some 160 travel companies have committed to stop selling tickets to, or promoting venues offering, elephant rides and shows. In 2016, TripAdvisor announced that it

---

1206 Animal cruelty https://www.nationalgeographic.com/magazine/2019/06/global-wildlife-tourism-social-media-causes-animal-suffering/#:~:text=Phajaan per cent20is per cent20the per cent20traditional per centE2 per cent80 per cent94and,many per cent20of per cent20the per cent20country's per cent20captives.

1207 https://www.worldanimalprotection.org/news/taken-ride-thousands-elephants-exploited-tourism-are-held-cruel-conditions

1208 Schmidt-Burbach J (2017) *Taken for a Ride. The conditions for elephants used in tourism in Asia*, World Animal Protection, accessed at https://www.worldanimalprotection.org.au/sites/default/files/media/au_files/taken_for_a_ride_report.pdf

1209 https://www.intrepidtravel.com/adventures/why-not-ride-elephants/

would end the sale of tickets for wildlife experiences where tourists come into direct contact with wild animals, including elephant riding[1210].

WHAT

Poaching and illegal trafficking

On the banks of Lake Kivu in eastern Democratic Republic of the Congo (DRC), just across the Rwandan border, Goma sits uncomfortably on the lava flows from the active Nyiragongo Volcano that lies just north in the beautiful Virunga National Park, home to the endangered mountain gorillas that Dian Fossey studied and made famous by the 1988 film *Gorillas in the Mist.*

The size of Western Europe, the country is rich in diamonds, gold, copper, coltan, cobalt and zinc. This so called 'resource curse' has led to mass exploitation and enslavement by European colonialists, most notably King Leopold's Belgium made famous in Joseph Conrad's *Heart of Darkness*, and then Mobutu Sese Seko's harsh 32 year totalitarian regime, which included the hanging of the Prime Minister and 3 cabinet ministers in front of 50,000 spectators and the embezzlement of up to $15 billion.

In 1994, Rwandan Hutu militia forces fled Rwanda into eastern DRC during the genocide following the ascension of the Tutsi-led government and then used the Hutu refugee camps as bases to attack ethnic Tutsis in the area and into Rwanda. The Rwandan forces attacked the camps in 1996, before the Hutu militia forces joined forces with the DRC army to fight against the Tutsis militia who were now joined by Ugandan troops, in what would become known as the First African War. A year later, the Tutsis coalition marched into Kinshasa, ousting Mobutu and its leader, Laurent Kabila, declared as President.

A year later, however, Kabila's former allies in Uganda and Rwanda had turned against him and backed a new rebellion in the same eastern region which led to another 5 years of war, this time with Angola, Namibia, and Zimbabwe joining Kabila, along with a variety of local Congolese warlords. In total, over 5 million have died in the conflict, mostly from disease and starvation, and countless millions displaced.

I arrived 4 years after Kabila's son had taken over following the assassination of his father and two attempted coups. Not only were the Rwandan and Ugandan backed militia still launching raids on villages, raping women and children and burning their huts, Congolese army militias were doing the same.

[1210] https://www.bbc.com/news/science-environment-40501667

We were greeted by a band of green bereted, machine gun toting young rangers as we drove up to the ranger station in the Virunga National Park. The day before one of their colleagues had been shot and killed by one of the militia groups that lived in the forest, logging and poaching illegally, especially for elephants, to fund their activities. Understandably, there were a bit jittery.

Despite being outnumbered and out gunned, I've never met more dedicated, positive and passionate people who have an unshakeable belief in conserving the park and its animals. Since then, another 150 rangers have lost their lives at Virunga.

But 1 Australian believed that he could prevent these deaths.

In 2003, park ranger, Sean Willmore sat around the fire at an international conference one evening, hearing the stories of his fellow ranger delegates. To his surprise, a Zimbabwean ranger revealed his head scar from a machete when he had been attacked by poachers. One by one, others followed suit, showing their wounds. Sean decided there and then to sell his car and mortgage his house to travel around world to film the stories.

Coming back broke, Bryce Courtney saw his story on the ABC's *7.30 Report* and sent a cheque, followed by other donors. Sean wanted to donate the money to the ranger's families, but couldn't find a dedicated charity. Sitting next to him on a plane was a specialist in setting up charities and *The Thin Green Line* was born[1211], which 'Protects Nature's Protectors' by bringing equipment and training to rangers, together with support to the families of those killed, including paying for their kids to go through school[1212]. Sean had become the ranger for rangers.

As one of the world's most trafficked mammals with their scales prized in traditional medicine and folk remedies, we all know what pangolins look like now as suspect number 1 in the transference of COVID19 from bats and onto humans.

Because their scales are sought after for traditional Chinese medicine, over 100,000 pangolins are estimated to be trafficked annually to China and Vietnam, making them the world's most trafficked mammal globally[1213].

As well as pangolin scales, the trafficking and unsustainable trade in wildlife commodities such as elephant ivory, rhino horn, tiger bone, bear bile, and

---

[1211] The Hawke Centre, An evening with Sean Willmore - Founder and Director of The Thin Green Line Foundation, Youtube, 21 March 2016

[1212] https://thingreenline.org.au/story/

[1213] https://animalsurvival.org/chinas-illegal-trade-in-wildlife/

rosewood are causing unprecedented declines in some of the world's most charismatic, as well as some lesser-known, wildlife species.

African Elephants are arguably the most well-known species to be heavily impacted by illegal trade and wildlife crime, given that approximately 90 per cent have been decimated within the last century. Incredibly, each year, at least 20,000 African elephants are illegally killed for their tusks. Singapore and China do not allow a domestic ivory trade, but other Asian countries do[1214].

With 95 per cent of rhino horns sourced from Africa for trafficking to Southeast Asia coming from black rhinos, their population has dropped by a drastic 96 per cent, leaving a mere 2,400 individuals. In 2022, an estimated 561 black and white rhinos were killed in Africa.

Despite 185 countries and regional bodies ratifying the Convention on International Trade in Endangered Species of Wild Fauna and Flora[1215], with a value of between $7 billion and $23 billion each year, illegal wildlife trafficking is the 3rd most lucrative global organised crime after drugs and arms[1216].

Under Australia's national environmental law, the *Environment Protection and Biodiversity Conservation Act 1999*, it is illegal to trade Australian native animals to overseas markets. However, as 87 per cent of Australia's mammals, 93 per cent of reptiles, and 45 per cent of birds are found nowhere else on Earth[1217], they are highly sought after on the international market.

Australia is no stranger to animal trafficking. Australian Border Force intercept around 4,000 illegal shipments in a single year[1218]. Despite the export ban, 2 recent research studies have revealed the scale of the international trade in threatened Australian animals with over 580 invertebrate[1219] and 170 reptile and amphibian species sold internationally, including 33 that had not been recorded on the international market before[1220].

1214 https://www.worldwildlife.org/our-work/wildlife/wildlife-crime/stopping-elephant-ivory-demand/
1215 https://www.cites.org/eng/disc/what.php
1216 https://www.ifaw.org/au/journal/what-is-wildlife-trafficking
1217 https://nit.com.au/24-03-2025/16978/australias-black-market-wildlife-trade-a-crime-against-culture-and-conservation
1218 https://www.sbs.com.au/news/article/wildlife-black-market-in-australia/r4p7qz2m7
1219 De Smedt P et al (2023) *Rise of terrestrial isopods in the pet trade and the need for their inclusion in trade regulation*, Conservation Biology, 10.1111/cobi.70166
1220 Zhong Chen Z, Cao Y-S, Dong M-S & Li W-B (2024) *Human activities and climate change are the main factors of amphibian extinction*, Global Ecology and Conservation, 10.1016/j.gecco.2025.e03747, **62**, (e03747)

According to international charity, *TRAFFIC*, Australian blue-tongue lizards and shingleback skinks can be sold for $1,000-$20,000 per animal, while rare black cockatoos have been priced at up to $15,000 overseas.

Industrial farming

I suppose it should be no surprise that animals are treated as commodities in a food manufacturing system that uses factory farming to produce quantity of food over quality of lives. Nonetheless, it is distressing to actually see the conditions. I will never forget seeing and smelling a massive feedlot strewn over hillsides as far as eye could see with thousands of cattle being fattened up in the last few weeks of their life. Some animals, unable to support their own weight, just sat in their own excrement.

Tasmania supplies over 90 per cent of Australian Atlantic salmon, valued at over $1 billion. The colonists of the 'Britain of Australia' wanted to be able to fish for salmon in their new home. At first, it seemed impossible when the transportation of live fertilised eggs across the ocean failed. In 1857, the Tasmanian Parliament announced an impressive reward of 5 hundred pounds for 'the introduction of live salmon', and a Salmon Commission was formed.

Enter settler, James Youl and his decades-long obsession with bringing the iconic salmon of his homeland to the Southern Hemisphere, a mad endeavour that stretched the limits of science and technology, and defied the accepted laws of nature. After many years of trial and error, he took French advice and put the eggs inside moss with cool running water in a special icehouse built on board the *Norfolk* square-rigged wooden ship to transport them.

Today, dominated by foreign-owned companies like Tassal, Huon, and Petuna, Tasmania's Atlantic salmon farming industry in sea cages, including in World Heritage listed Macquarie Harbour and the D'Entrecasteaux Channel is worth over $1 billion annally. The relatively warmer water temperatures mean that Tasmanian Atlantic salmon can grow to a harvestable size within 16-18 months, but led to bacterial outbreaks causing millions of dead fish in 2024 and 2025 dumped in landfill. The disease is now considered endemic in Tasmania's southern and eastern waters. Increasing water temperatures caused by climate change will only increase stress, disease and mortality, no matter the overuse of antibiotics and fresh water to bathe the fish.

At the same time, industrial salmon farming is having serious impacts on Tasmania's sensitive marine habitats and threatened species. The build-up of excess nutrients, such as nitrogen and phosphorus, from fish faeces and uneaten feed falling to the seabed from the cages in surrounding waters can result in eutrophication — the concentration of nutrients in a body of water — which can cause harmful algal blooms. These blooms can reduce oxygen levels in the water, leading to fish kills and other negative impacts on the local ecosystem[1221]. Tasmanian salmon farms produce 6 times more pollution each year than Tasmania's entire sewage[1222].

In Australia, animal farming on an industrial scale causes pain and suffering to billions of animals.

As by far the most popular animal protein consumed in Australia, 700 million chickens are raised in factory farms across Australia, tightly packed with up to 60,000 birds being housed in a single shed and unable to express natural behaviours such as roaming around and flapping their wings. Fast-growing breeds are used so that chickens grow to their full size in an average of just 6 weeks. This accelerated growth rate, combined with low light levels and insufficient space to move, can lead to serious health problems, including heart and lung failure, muscle weakness and lameness[1223].

We have known for over 2 decades that battery cages cause physical pain, injury and death. The extreme confinement denies natural behaviours that cause physical and psychological suffering for the hens. Hens in battery cages suffer from brittle bones and bone fractures, as well as feather loss and foot problems due to the restrictive environment and wire floors. Hens in battery cages can also experience high rates of a condition that leads to liver rupture and death, largely due to stress and lack of exercise. Despite the European Union banning battery cages from 2012, the move towards cage-free eggs since The Body Shop asked customers to sign postcards 20 years ago has been slow. More than 11 million hens, or 70 per cent of Australia's hens, are still confined to a battery cage[1224].

In 2023, Australian agriculture ministers agreed to phase out the production of battery eggs by 2036, in accordance with the new national animal welfare standards and guidelines for poultry. In the meantime, McDonald's, which uses more than 91 million eggs a year in Australia, phased out caged eggs at the end of 2017[1225]. Coles and Woolworths own-brand shell eggs are cage-free, but both

---

[1221] https://www.edo.org.au/why-salmon-farming-needs-new-rules/#:~:text=Salmon%20farms%20let%20faeces%20and,waters%20can%20destroy%20marine%20ecosystems.

[1222] https://australiainstitute.org.au/post/the-big-stink-of-tasmanian-salmon-farms-six-times-more-pollution-than-tasmanian-sewage/

[1223] https://www.worldanimalprotection.org.au/chickens-deserve-better-and-kfc-can-do-better

[1224] https://www.rspca.org.au/latest-news/blog/why-battery-cages-are-cruel/

[1225] https://www.smh.com.au/environment/mcdonalds-to-phase-out-caged-eggs-20140915-10h6ze.html

still sell caged eggs, despite their promised deadline of 2025 for a full phase-out.

The RSPCA reports that, despite 7 in 10 Australians supporting a phase out of farrowing crates, 90 per cent of Australian pigs are still farmed in confined, barren environments and suffer painful husbandry procedures[1226]. Pigs are kept in barren, small steel cages on factory farms with uncomfortable flooring, where there's no opportunity for these intelligent animals to explore, forage and engage in natural behaviours and which causes them to suffer painful skin lesions and diseases. Mother pigs have it especially bad as they are inseminated in a cage no bigger than an average household refrigerator, with barely enough room to move. While most are then moved into group housing, about 1 in 5 of mother pigs in Australia are still confined to sow stalls for most of their pregnancy. In the first week of a baby pig's life, his or her teeth are clipped or ground, the tail is cut, and males can be castrated, often without pain relief[1227].

As well as the cruelty of the feedlots, an estimated 40 per cent of cattle in Australia are treated with hormone growth promotants to boost weight gain in the animals. They are banned in Europe since 1989 due to concerns about the possible link with cancer, although this has not been scientifically proven.

Valued at over $10 billion annually, the Australian dairy industry, markets itself as natural, locally-sourced, nutrient-rich food for all ages. But, like all mammals, cows must give birth in order to produce milk, and so a mother cow is kept on an almost continuous cycle of pregnancy, birth and lactation throughout her adult life to ensure she continues to produce a high volume of milk. This cycle will eventually take a toll on her body and when her physical health, fertility or milk yield declines, she will generally be sent to slaughter, usually at around the age of 4–8 years. Annually, Dairy Australia reports that around 310,000 male 'bobby calves' are slaughtered, an unwanted by-product of producing the milk[1228].

Live exports

In 2018, Channel 9's *60 Minutes* broadcast footage taken by young trainee navigator Faisal Ullah who secretly recorded video on board 5 live export voyages on the giant livestock carrier, Awassi Express, from Fremantle to several ports in the Middle East. The sheep were stacked 10 storeys high and forced to stay standing for three weeks – that's if they survived the trip. On one

---

1226 https://www.rspca.org.au/key-issues/pig-farming/

1227 https://www.worldanimalprotection.org.au/our-work/factory-farming/animal-cruelty/#pigs

1228 https://www.dairy.com.au/you-ask-we-answer/how-many-bobby-calves-are-killed-each-year

voyage, the heat of the Persian Gulf caused 880 sheep to die in 1 day from heat stress, or one death every 2 minutes. The next day, 517 died with the 'death zone' heatwave continuing for 5 days. Export regulations require that any sick or injured livestock be given immediate treatment and be killed humanely where euthanasia is necessary. However, as Ullah's vision revealed, the vet on board simply couldn't keep up.

Subsequent shocking videos of death and suffering of sheep resulted in nearly 8 in 10 Australians supporting a phase out of live sheep export if affected farmers were provided with assistance to transition[1229], and led the Australian government to legislate an end to live sheep exports by sea, with a final phase-out date set for 1 May 2028.

Palm oil

Palm oil, which is squeezed from the fruits of the oil palm trees that grow in regions around the equator, represents 40 per cent of all vegetable oils consumed globally. Indonesia and Malaysia supply 85 per cent of the palm oil used globally. With 80 million tonnes produced annually, palm oil is an incredibly efficient crop, producing more oil per land area than any other equivalent vegetable oil crop.

Palm oil is ubiquitous, found in nearly half of the packaged products in your supermarket, including pizza, doughnuts, chocolate, deodorant, shampoo, toothpaste and lipstick.

With an estimated 3.5 million hectares of tropical rainforests cleared for palm oil plantations between 2010 and 2023[1230], its production is a major driver of deforestation of some of the world's most biodiverse forests, destroying the habitat of already endangered species like the orangutan, pygmy elephant and Sumatran rhino. This forest loss, coupled with the conversion of carbon-rich peat soils, releases millions of tonnes of greenhouse gases into the atmosphere and contributes to climate change.

In 2012, the UK government committed to achieving 100 per cent sourcing of credibly certified sustainable palm oil by the end of 2015. As a result, the proportion of UK imports of certified sustainable palm oil increased from 16 per cent to 68 per cent[1231].

1229 https://www.rspca.org.au/key-issues/live-sheep-export/

1230 https://farmonaut.com/blogs/deforestation-free-palm-oil-key-facts-statistics-2025

1231 Department for Environment, Food and Rural Affairs (2015) *UK Consumption of Sustainable Palm Oil*, Annual Review, October 2015

Sport

Originating in coursing, the pursuit of live hares, 2 thousand years ago, greyhound racing in Australia is big business. As the world's largest commercial greyhound racing industry, we have 60 tracks in operation, 4,228 race meetings and over 47,500 races. The sport attracted more than 611,000 attendees and offered $209 million in prize money[1232]. Wagering on Australian greyhound racing was over $8 billion in turnover in 2023[1233] and makes up to a Third of a State's overall racing turnover[1234].

With around 10,000 greyhound pups bred each year in Australia in the hope of finding a fast runner, it has been estimated that 40 per cent will never race[1235]. When they do, their racing career for a greyhound is very short, starting at one-and-a-half years of age and generally retired by 2 to 5 years of age. Injuries, especially fractures, are very common, with up to 200 dogs injured during official races each week, with, on average, around 5 dogs killed[1236]. Off the track, they can be kept in tiny, barren pens or kennels for the majority of their lives, only released to train or race.

In 2015, following a horrific exposé of live baiting by an ABC *Four Corners* program, a special commission of inquiry was set up in NSW to investigate the industry. The findings from the inquiry were extremely disturbing, including that at least 50 per cent of greyhounds who were of no value to the industry were killed – an estimate of at least 48,000 dogs (but could be as high as 68,000) would have been killed between 2003-2015[1237].

10 years later, the former chief vet of Greyhound Racing NSW, Alex Brittan, reported widespread animal abuse and persistent reporting and oversight failures. He found that 1 in 5 greyhounds in the industry died when they were less than 5 and 1/2 years old and, although the industry runs adoption programs, concluded that half of the racing dogs that retired each year were not rehomed, leaving at least 8,000 and up to 13,000 greyhounds to be 'shuffled through the industry to paid commercial kennels' to die. Brittan ultimately alleged nothing

---

1232 Greyhounds Australasia (2025) *Study of Taxation Generated and Governments Funding Received*, p.3 at https://www.grv.org.au/wp-content/uploads/2025/09/GA_FY23_Taxation-Report_FINAL-002.pdf

1233 https://www.bbc.com/news/articles/c8vdrzr9mq1o

1234 https://thestraight.com.au/seven-days-in-wagering-gone-to-the-dogs/

1235 https://kb.rspca.org.au/categories/sport-entertainment-and-work/greyhound-racing/what-are-the-animal-welfare-issues-with-greyhound-racing

1236 https://animalsaustralia.org/our-work/greyhound-racing/background/

1237 https://kb.rspca.org.au/categories/sport-entertainment-and-work/greyhound-racing/what-are-the-animal-welfare-issues-with-greyhound-racing

had changed in the 8 years since the industry was briefly shut down in 2016 over the scale of animal abuse.

The ACT is the only jurisdiction where greyhound racing is currently banned. Tasmania is phasing out the industry, with a full ban expected by mid-2029. In comparison, the United States, which once had a robust industry, has seen racing eliminated in all but 2 active tracks, with 42 states outlawing the practice. New Zealand announced a ban in December 2024, with racing to cease by 1 August 2026.

Similar overbreeding, injury and death issues exist in Australia's horse racing industry. Only 300 out of every 1,000 foals produced ever start in a race[1238]. Of the horses that do race, one Australian Study found that approximately 40 per cent earned no money at all and only 13 per cent earned enough money to cover costs[1239]. As a result, over 10,000 racehorses are killed each year in knackeries for pet and human food, simply because they didn't earn enough[1240].

Last year, 175 horses were confirmed killed on Australian racetracks, nearly half from a front limb injury - the highest recorded[1241]. Over a 1 in 3 had started racing as 2-year-olds, whilst horses don't reach skeletal maturity until they are 5-6 years old. One of Australia's richest races worth $3 million, the Queensland Magic Millions Classic, is for 2-year-old horses.

Jumps racing is 20 times more dangerous than flat racing, and the injuries sustained on jumps racing tracks can be horrific. At least 165 horses have died in jumps racing in the last 20 years. Every other state in Australia has acknowledged the cruelty of jumps racing and banned it - except Victoria.

Whipping has been a contentious issue for decades, with a Senate Select committee recommending banning the practice in 1991. Whipping causes significant pain to horses, but there is no evidence that whips are needed for safety or to control the horse. Padded whips were introduced in 2009, but a Tasmanian court in 2025 ruled that whipping a horse with a padded whip does indeed cause pain and suffering to the horse[1242].

1238 https://horseracingkills.com/campaigns/wastage/

1239 https://horseracingkills.com/campaigns/wastage/

1240 https://greens.org.au/vic/campaigns/protect-horses

1241 Coalition for the Protection of Racehorses (2025) *Deathwatch Report 2025* at https://horseracingkills.com/wp-content/uploads/2025/10/DeathWatch_2025_28_Oct_2025.pdf

1242 https://horseracingkills.com/2025/05/29/whipping-horses-with-a-padded-racing-whip-is-an-act-of-cruelty/

Cats and dogs

Over 1 in 3 Australian households includes a dog, and one in four is home to a cat. But, unrestricted breeding of cats and dogs simply means that there are more animals than the number of responsible, loving homes available at any one time. In *puppy factories* around Australia, dogs are kept in terrible conditions and bred continuously for profit. Victoria, NSW and WA have regulations, but Tasmania, Queensland and South Australia have no cap on how many dogs a puppy farmer can have as 'breeders' and how many litters they can be forced to have.

The COVID-19 pandemic has led to a significant increase in pet relinquishments and abandonments in Australia, driven by a combination of the initial impulse buying of pets during lockdowns, subsequent lifestyle changes and cost-of-living pressures[1243]. In 2023-24, RSPCA received 44,172 abandoned cats and dogs, with 7,990 euthanised. They also investigated 56,969 reports of animal cruelty. Pet Rescue estimates that 44,000 dogs and 50,000 cats are killed annually in the care of councils, shelters, and rescue groups[1244].

Cats are believed to have first arrived in Australia in 1788 on the First Fleet. Within 70 years, they had covered the continent and are now spread across more than 99 per cent of Australia's land area. The 1.4–5.6 million feral cats in the bush (depending on rainfall conditions) kill over 1.5 billion native mammals, birds, reptiles and frogs, and 1.1 billion invertebrates each year. Predation by cats is a recognised threat to over 200 nationally threatened species, and 37 listed migratory species. Feral cats have contributed to the extinction of more than 20 Australian mammal species, including the pig-footed bandicoot, lesser bilby and broad-faced potoroo. They are a major cause of decline for many land-based threatened animals such as the bettong and numbat.

WHY

A 2025 study found that illegal wildlife trade is converging with a multitude of organised crime activities, including drug trafficking, sex trafficking, child abuse, trafficking in human body parts, migrant smuggling, forced and bonded

---

[1243] Carroll GA, Reeve C and Torjussen A (2024) *Companion animal adoption and relinquishment during the COVID-19 pandemic: The experiences of animal rescue staff and volunteers.* Anim Welf. 2024 Mar 4;33:e12. doi: 10.1017/awf.2024.15. PMID: 38510425; PMCID: PMC10951665

[1244] https://www.petrescue.com.au/library/articles/petrescue-stats-on-pets-killed-in-pounds

labour, illegal alcohol trade, arms trafficking, vehicle theft, illegal trade in counterfeit and pirated goods, and illegal trade in mined resources[1245].

The fact is, given the value of the animals involved, Illegal wildlife trade is among the most lucrative illegal industries in the world. It is also a significant driver of biodiversity decline[1246].

China is the largest consumer of illegal wildlife products due to their use in traditional Chinese medicine and as status symbols and investments, as well as high profitability for supplying parties, complex and corrupt trafficking structures, and ineffective government policies and enforcement.

The traditional Chinese medicine market, worth an estimated $60 billion annually, is considered the primary driver behind wildlife trafficking. For instance, the demand for *ejiao*, a gelatin derived from donkey hides used in traditional Chinese medicine, has led to the slaughter of between 2.3 million and 4.8 million donkeys annually. This has caused significant declines in donkey populations, particularly in Africa, where some countries report population declines of up to 70 per cent.

The use of bear bile has led to the establishment of numerous bear farms in China, with between 9,000 and 20,000 bears kept in captivity. This bitterly cruel practice sees bears kept caged in abhorrent conditions so that bile may be extracted directly from their gall bladders. The bears languish in coffin-sized cages, are starved and stressed, and regularly endure severe suffering as their captors extract the bile from their bodies[1247].

Accordingly, authorities, including Australia's *Operation Ramsey* multi-agency Australian investigation into a criminal syndicate involved in the large-scale illegal export of native reptiles to China, focus on the money trail to determine the key players that are operating at the top level internationally and profiting the most from the exploitation of wildlife.

Now the dominant form of animal production globally and led by the rising demand for low-cost food, factory farms, as the systems of large-scale

---

[1245] Anagnostou M, Doberstein B, Armitage D, Stoett P, Glasson A (2025) *Disentangling and demystifying converging crimes and illegal wildlife trade in South Africa, Hong Kong, and Canada*, Journal of Economic Criminology, Volume 10, 2025, 100196, ISSN 2949-7914, https://doi.org/10.1016/j.jeconc.2025.100196

[1246] Mozer A and Prost S (2023) *An introduction to illegal wildlife trade and its effects on biodiversity and society,* Forensic Science International: Animals and Environments, Volume 3, 2023, 100064, ISSN 2666-9374, https://doi.org/10.1016/j.fsiae.2023.100064

[1247] https://animalsurvival.org/chinas-illegal-trade-in-wildlife/

confinement we know today, began in the United States with the industrial raising of chickens in the 1950s, aided by the discovery of antibiotics and vaccines which facilitated raising livestock in larger numbers by reducing disease. Over 90 per cent of all farmed animals around the world spend their lives on factory farms. This includes virtually all farmed fish and 3/4ths of farmed land animals such as chicken, cattle, and pigs[1248].

The Farm Transparency Project maps factory farms across the globe, including the 5,000 in Australia[1249]. Animal production in Australia continues to be more concentrated with fewer corporations and larger factories. For instance, the largest facilities can house more than a million chickens. There are approximately 400 accredited beef cattle feedlots across Australia, predominantly in Queensland and New South Wales. Some of these are 'mega-feedlots' confine tens of thousands of cattle at a time, with some expanding to hold 75,000 or more. There are around 4,300 pig production sites across Australia, with approximately 2.4 million pigs in factory farming at any one time.

ACT

Campaign

As well as a ban on live exports and cage-produced eggs, campaigning against animal cruelty has achieved a number of other wins.

In the first years of The Body Shop, Anita Roddick collected millions of signatures to protest against animal testing for cosmetics, resulting in the UK government introducing a ban in 1998[1250]. 22 years later, Australia introduced a ban on cosmetic testing on animals so that any new cosmetic ingredients manufactured in, or imported into, Australia are not able to use information from animal testing to prove safety[1251].

Join 4,000 others and tell McDonald's to go feedlot-free for their beef patties with World Animal Protection[1252].

1248 https://www.newrootsinstitute.org/articles/when-did-factory-farming-start-and-why-does-it-still-exist

1249 https://www.farmtransparency.org/map

1250 Roddick A (2000) *Business as Unusual*, HarperCollins, London, p.174

1251 https://www1.health.gov.au/internet/main/publishing.nsf/Content/ban-cosmetic-testing-animals#:~:text=Australia per cent20is per cent20implementing per cent20a per cent20ban,animal per cent20testing per cent20to per cent20prove per cent20safety.

1252 https://www.worldanimalprotection.org.au/take-action/mcdonalds-go-feedlot-free/

You can campaign to stop greyhound racing with *Humane World For Animals Australia*[1253]; ban jumps racing in Victoria with *Animals Australia*[1254]; stop overbreeding in the horse racing industry with the *Coalition for the Protection of Racehorses*[1255]; urge state leaders to free hens from cages sooner than 2036 with Animals Australia[1256]; end puppy farms with *Four Paws*[1257]; and ban the whip with *Animal Liberation*[1258].

Since 2009, *Zoos Victoria* has been campaigning to get labelling laws changed in Australia so that palm oil is no longer hidden as 'vegetable oil' on the products you buy. Join more than 470,000 Australians who have spoken up for palm oil labelling through their *Don't Palm Us Off* campaign[1259].

Pledge

Go vegan and pledge to end your consumption of animal-based food and products with the Farm Transparency Project[1260]. Join over 17,000 who have taken the pledge to never bet on or attend a horse race[1261].

Participate

The Coalition for the Protection of Racehorses invites you to join or hold a *Nup to the Cup* event on Melbourne Cup day[1262].

To get your young people involved, the Steve Irwin-founded *Wildlife Warriors* runs a youth ambassador program for 4-17 year-olds[1263].

Buy

Growing awareness of farmed animal welfare has led many caring Australians to actively seek more conscious choices with the products they buy.

A number of animal products on sale in supermarkets and restaurants have *RSPCA Approved* certification that ensures animal welfare[1264]. For chicken, this includes lower stocking density when inside the shed, access to perches and

---

1253 https://hsi.org.au/animal-welfare/stop-greyhound-racing/
1254 https://animalsaustralia.org/our-work/horse-racing/jumps-racing-tragedy/
1255 https://horseracingkills.com/campaigns/sign-to-give-mares-a-fair-go/
1256 https://animalsaustralia.org/our-work/factory-farming/battery-cage-phase-out-commitment/
1257 https://www.four-paws.org.au/campaigns-topics/campaigns/end-puppy-farming
1258 https://www.al.org.au/ban-the-whip
1259 https://www.zoo.org.au/dont-palm-us-off/
1260 https://www.farmtransparency.org/actions/leave-animal-products-off-my-plate
1261 https://horseracingkills.com/take-action-for-racehorses-killed-for-human-consumption/
1262 https://nuptothecup.org/
1263 https://wildlifewarriors.org.au/get-involved/visionary-wildlife-warriors/
1264 https://rspcaapproved.org.au/become-certified/standards/

quality bedding covering the entire shed floor. McDonald's, Grill'd, Nando's, Oporto, 7-Eleven and Zambrero use RSPCA Approved chicken[1265]. ALDI, Coles and Woolworths sell RSPCA Approved chicken products, as well as free-range options.

Australian Pork Certified Free Range and RSPCA Approved pork is available at butchers and supermarkets, including at Coles and Woolworths (Macro).

Whilst Australian free-range egg standards legally allow up to 10,000 hens/hectare (1 per sq metre), the actual number by the farm is displayed on the egg cartons to give you the choice for more space for the hens.

There are a number of cruelty-free dairies, such as *How Now Dairy*[1266] and *Mother Cow Dairy*[1267] in Victoria, *Bannister Downs Dairy* in WA[1268] and *The Little Big Dairy Company* in NSW[1269].

Look for certified organic lamb and beef, and certified grass-fed beef under the Pasture-fed Cattle Assurance Scheme[1270]. Marbled Wagyu beef production generally incorporates feed lotting.

Other accreditations are *PROOF* (Pasture Raised On Open Fields)[1271] and *Humane Choice*[1272].

Meat Free Mondays[1273] can help you eat less animal products, with many plant-based meat alternatives now available. Even KFC has seen the light, selling *Beyond Chicken* products in the US and the Original Recipe Vegan Burger in the UK.

Or join the over 1 in 20 Australian adults who are vegetarian or vegan.

One of the simplest and most direct actions you can take to end puppy factory cruelty is to choose not to buy a dog from a breeder. Instead adopt from a registered rescue group or shelter, including using RSPCA's *Adopt a Pet* website[1274].

1265 https://rspcaapproved.org.au/brands/

1266 https://hownowdairy.com.au/

1267 https://www.mothercowdairy.com.au/

1268 https://bannisterdowns.com.au/

1269 https://www.littlebigdairy.co/

1270 https://www.ausmeat.com.au/services/list/livestock/pcas/pcas-information/

1271 https://www.proof.net.au/

1272 https://www.auscertifiedhumane.com/

1273 https://meatfreemondays.com/

1274 https://www.adoptapet.com.au/

Social enterprises, *The Karma Collective*[1275] (gifts and homewares) and *SavourLife*[1276] (locally-made food and treats for dogs) donate 50 per cent of their profits to animal welfare organisations.

WWF recommends that we support sustainable palm oil and avoid boycotts, since substitutions with other vegetable oils can lead to even further environmental and social harm[1277]. To buy sustainable palm oil products, look for the globally recognised RSPO (Roundtable on Sustainable Palm Oil) certification. *Zoos Victoria* has an Easter chocolate guide[1278] and *WWF* has a palm oil scorecard for brands[1279].

Volunteer

Volunteer at your local animal shelter, including your State/Territory RSPCA[1280]. *The Gift Project* has a directory of wildlife shelters across the country[1281]. *Wildlife Heroes* has a directory of wildlife groups, specialists and carers[1282]. A list of wildlife rescue organisations can be found at the *Tiewelt Wildlife Foundation*[1283].

Alternatively, be a *Puppy Volunteer* and help train assistance dogs[1284] or foster a future detection dog with the Australian Border Force[1285]. You can also become a foster carer to provide temporary loving care for animals in need at your local animal shelter.

Report

State and territory governments are responsible for animal production and welfare laws and their enforcement. Animal cruelty can be reported to your State/Territory *RSPCA*[1286]. Suspected puppy farms can be reported to *Oscar's Law*[1287].

1275 https://thekarmacollective.com.au/

1276 https://www.savour-life.com.au/

1277 https://www.wwf.org.uk/updates/8-things-know-about-palm-oil

1278 https://zoos-prod-cdn.azureedge.net/media/av2i0pgr/zoos-victoria-easter-chocolate-guide-2025.pdf

1279 https://palmoilscorecard.panda.org/scores

1280 https://www.rspca.org.au/support-us/volunteer/

1281 https://thegiftproject.com.au/

1282 https://wildlifeheroes.org.au/groups/

1283 https://auswildlife.org/find-a-rescue/

1284 https://www.assistancedogs.org.au/volunteer/

1285 https://www.abf.gov.au/about-us/what-we-do/border-protection/detector-dogs/foster-a-detector-dog

1286 https://www.rspca.org.au/report-animal-cruelty/

1287 https://www.oscarslaw.org/submit-a-tip-off.htm

Donate

If you would like to financially support education and advocacy through donating or becoming a member, *Animals Australia* is the leader in consistently running high-profile campaigns to show the reality of factory farms and animal cruelty[1288].

The *Australian Wildlife Conservancy* has built the largest network of feral predator-free, fenced havens in the country. The large-scale safe havens enable the reintroduction of locally extinct wildlife into secure environments[1289].

Donate goods

Your local animal shelter would appreciate donations of clean blankets, towels, unopened pet food and pet toys.

1288 https://animalsaustralia.org/our-work/factory-farming/our-tvcs-for-farmed-animals/
1289 https://www.australianwildlife.org/what-we-do/fighting-weeds-and-feral-animals

ACKNOWLEDGEMENTS

I am indebted to the many amazing people in the charity world who have inspired me over the years, and continue to do so. I am constantly in awe of their passion, expertise and dedication.

The same goes for the quiet achievers in government and business who believe in a better Australia and strive to make a difference within their organisations.

My heartfelt appreciation goes to Justine Martin and the team at Morpheus Publishing. Justine is a very special person who has now devoted her life to support authors who have important stories to tell.

And a big thanks to Darrell Wade, Neil Salisbury, Michael Perusco, Stephen Bird, James Toomey, Andrew Bruun, and Michael Klim OAM who have brought me down to Earth and helped shape this book.

As a vocation, not just a job, working for a charity can be all consuming. To Tracey, India, Stephen, Georgie – thank you always for your understanding, love and support.

ABOUT THE AUTHOR

After getting lost in London's sewers, managing The Gambia's airline, chasing embezzlers in Niger, being shelled in Bosnia, starting farmer cooperatives in northern Philippines, confronting child soldiers in Eastern DRC and negotiating with warlords in earthquake-ravaged Pakistan, Paul returned to Australia to continue fighting for social and environmental justice with a range of charities. He published his first book in 2021, *PurposeFull. How businesses and not-for-profits do better as purpose-driven organisations* as a call to action for companies to embrace their purpose for greater customer loyalty, staff retention, product innovation and profitability, and for charities to rediscover their purpose and act to create the resourcing, policies and systems that would actually enable long-term change.

In a compassionate, fair-go and wealthy country, Paul can't accept that we are failing to make headway in our social and environmental challenges, causing unnecessary suffering and loss of opportunity for millions of Australians. His quest is to invite you to learn, act, find your purpose and make (or make more of) a lasting impact to achieve real change.

www.ingramcontent.com/pod-product-compliance
Lightning Source LLC
LaVergne TN
LVHW041102080826
845145LV00007B/1667